THE SWORD OF THE UNION

Federal Objectives and Strategies During the American Civil War

Howard M. Hensel

Military History Series 87–1

1989

**Air Command and Staff College
Montgomery, Alabama**

THE MILITARY HISTORY SERIES:

The United States Air Force Air Command and Staff College, in cooperation with the ACSC Foundation, publishes the Military History Series. The purpose of the series is to help professional military officers gain a greater appreciation for the lessons which may be derived from the military past. The contents of this study may be cited consistent with conventional research methods, but reprinting this work in part or in its entirety is prohibited without the express permission of the Commandant of the Air Command and Staff College.

DISCLAIMER:

The opinions, recommendations, and/or conclusions implied or specifically expressed within this series are solely those of the author or authors and should not be construed as representing the views of the Air Command and Staff College, the Air University, the U.S. Air Force, or any other agency of the United States government. This publication is cleared for unlimited public release.

Library of Congress Cataloging-in-Publication Data

Hensel, Howard M.
    The sword of the Union : Federal objectives and strategies during the American Civil War / Howard M. Hensel.
        p. cm. — (Military history series ; 87-1)
    1. United States—History—Civil War, 1861-1865—Campaigns. 2. United States—History—Civil War, 1861-1865—Causes. 3. United States—Politics and government—Civil War, 1861-1865. I. Title. II. Series.
E740.H58   1989
973'.7'3—dc19   89-6488
                                                                    CIP

For sale by the Superintendent of Documents
US Government Printing Office
Washington, DC 20402

iii

to
S.F.K.H.
and
N.D.H.

FOREWORD

I am pleased to introduce the *Sword of the Union* in commemoration of the one hundred and twenty-fifth anniversary of the American Civil War. As we reflect back over the century and a quarter since America's tragic internal upheaval, scholars have analyzed virtually every aspect of that conflict. Yet today, scholarly discussion continues and, in a number of significant areas, the debate has even intensified. In this work, Dr. Howard Hensel has analyzed the national objectives, grand and national military strategies, and theater operations of the United States government and the Union army during the four year conflict. In addition to contributing to a better understanding of these aspects of Federal war policy, Dr. Hensel has drawn generalizable conclusions from the actions of the Washington politico-military leadership. Of particular interest is the typology of offensively oriented, generic military strategies constructed from the experience of the Federal high command and its armies during this traumatic war. This typology may, in turn, provide the basis for continued research in delineating various generic types of both offensively and defensively oriented military strategies. The Air Command and Staff College is proud of its tradition of commitment to the study of military history and is pleased to present this work, the fourth in its Military History Series.

Frank E. Willis
Brigadier General, USAF
Commandant

CONTENTS

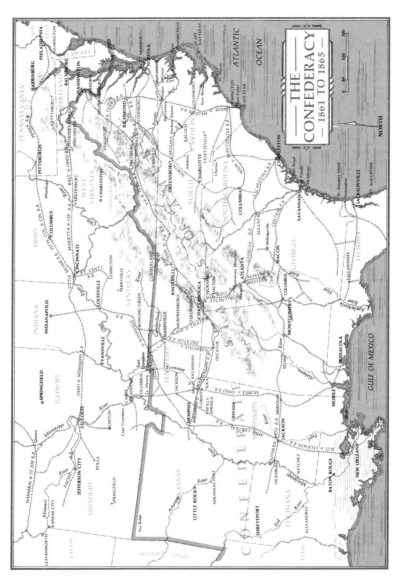

THE CONFEDERACY 1861 TO 1865

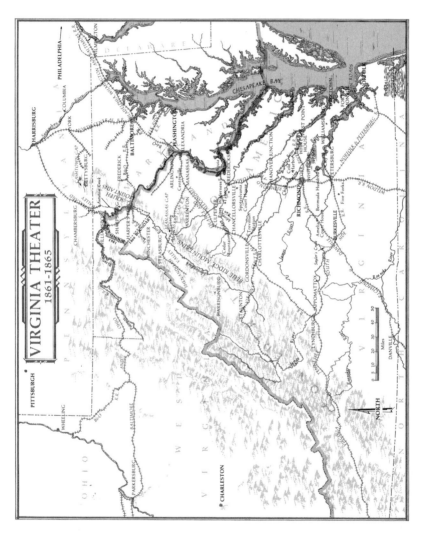

VIRGINIA THEATER
1861-1865

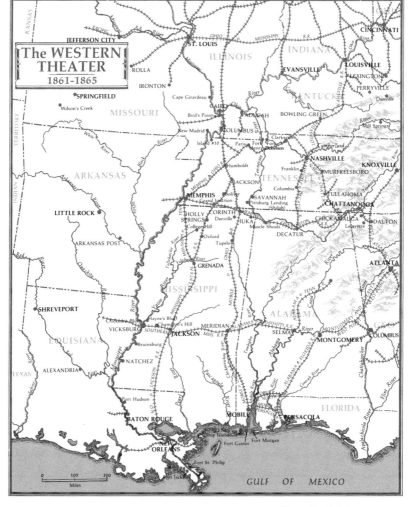

The WESTERN THEATER 1861-1865

Prepared by Air University Graphics

CHAPTER I

Spring 1861—Autumn 1861

On November 6, 1860, Abraham Lincoln was elected President of the United States, thereby beginning a succession of events which would directly lead to hostilities between the Northern and Southern states. A month and a half after the election, on December 20, 1860, South Carolina seceded from the Union. The "Palmetto State" was successively followed by six other Southern states: Mississippi, Florida, Alabama, Georgia, Louisiana, and Texas. In early February, 1861, representatives from these states met in Montgomery, Alabama and formed a new political entity, the Confederate States of America. Meanwhile, notwithstanding U.S. President James Buchanan's rejection of the principle of secession, Mr. Buchanan felt that the Federal government could not force the seceded states to remain in the Union. Hence, during the final weeks of his Administration, the President attempted to maintain symbolic Federal authority over U.S. government property in the South, while, simultaneously, attempting to avoid a military clash with the secessionists. In addition, he recommended that Congress take steps to hold the Union together by compromise. Efforts at achieving a compromise, however, proved unsuccessful as the leaders of the recently established Confederacy stood firm in the commitment to independence. As Allen Nevins observed,

> The successful conspiracy had been a drive, . . . to give the people of the Deep South full power to settle their own problems in their own way. Retreat would mean a sacrifice of their constitutional principles, a humiliating blow to their pride, and a definite subordination to the North and Northwest. The heads of the Confederacy were not bluffing, but in deadly earnest. They were determined to maintain their new nation at all hazards and whatever cost.[1]

Conversely, however,

> Because of the tremendous sentimental and moral values attached to the Union, because of the impossibility of dividing its assets and dis-

1

> severing a land where the greatest river systems and mountain valleys
> ran athwart sections, because secession meant a chain process of suicide,
> because the integrity of the republic was the life of world liberalism,
> and because to most observers it seemed that a squalid conspiracy had
> turned natural Southern aspirations and apprehensions to unnatural
> ends, the North could never give way.[2]

Hence, by March 4, 1861, when Abraham Lincoln was inaugurated the sixteenth President of the United States, the crisis remained unresolved. In his inaugural address, Mr. Lincoln held that "the Union was older than the Constitution, no State could of its own volition leave the Union, the ordinances of secession were illegal, and acts of violence to support secession were insurrectionary or revolutionary." In addition, Mr. Lincoln announced that he intended to uphold the law and protect Federal property throughout the South. Soon thereafter, however, on April 12, the crisis came to a head when Confederate authorities bombarded Federal Fort Sumter in the harbor of Charleston, South Carolina. The fort surrendered on April 14, thus beginning the greatest war in the history of the United States.[3]

Throughout his tenure in office, President Lincoln attempted to aggregate a wide coalition of diverse opinion in support of his Administration's policies. Consequently, in his initial formulation of Federal war objectives, he exclusively emphasized the preservation of the Union, the dissolution of the newly formed Confederate States of America, the restoration of " 'the national laws over the seceded States,' " and the protection of " 'the lives and property of all loyal men.' " For the moment, however, the President preferred to retain freedom of action with respect to the issue of slavery's future within the restored Union. As Allen Nevins wrote,

> Lincoln detested slavery for moral, economic, and democratic reasons
> alike; he had hated it ever since he told the Illinois legislature in 1837
> that it represented both social injustice and bad policy. He regarded it
> as the principal root of the war. It had divided the national house. While
> at home it had negated and crippled the American ideals of freedom
> and equality, abroad it had sullied the principles which, as he said in
> his Independence Hall speech, gave hope to the world for all future
> time. The South must be made to join in laying plans for its extirpation.
> But his hostility to the institution never carried him beyond a deep-
> seated belief that so disruptive a change should be effected gradually

in order to minimize its hardships, and that the results of extirpation would be more wholesome if it were coupled with at least a partial removal of the colored people to another land. Like most other white men of the time in Europe and America, he at first believed that inherent racial differences made it undesirable for Negro and Caucasian to dwell together. The stronger race would oppress the weaker group, and thus retarded, the colored man would pull down the white competitor to his own level. Some system for colonizing the freedmen abroad should therefore be attempted. But Lincoln had no fixed prejudices. As the war progressed, and as Negroes proved themselves brave fighters, industrious workers, and people of character, he began to discard the idea of inherent racial inequalities; while he simultaneously realized that large-scale colonization was impracticable. [4]

At the outset of the war, however, the President still subscribed to his preconceptions. In any case, by refusing to incorporate a specific policy position regarding the slavery issue into the definition of Federal war objectives, Mr. Lincoln reasoned that, notwithstanding the total nature of the political objective of the destruction of the Confederacy, the preservation of the Union, and the repudiation of the right of secession, these war aims could be endorsed by most Northerners, as well as many elements of Border state and Southern opinion, irrespective of political affiliation. In taking this position, however, the President especially sought the support of the Moderate Republicans and War Democrats. The former group, led by Mr. Lincoln himself, was prepared to preserve the Union at almost any cost, even if that meant continued toleration of slavery for the time being. Certainly, the Moderate Republicans were anti-slavery, but they felt that an orderly program of gradual, compensated emancipation was the best approach in abolishing slavery with a minimum of social and economic upheaval. Similarly, the War Democrats were prepared to support a war to preserve the Union, but not a violent crusade to forcibly bring about the immediate, uncompensated abolition of slavery. Hence, the President concluded that the incorporation of the abolition of slavery into the definition of Federal war objectives in 1861 would only serve to undermine his own political position, divide the North, alienate those Border states which had remained loyal to the Union, and unite the Southern people behind the banner of secession. Moreover, the President wanted to maximize the prospects of post-war harmony between the Northern and Southern states within a restored Union.[5]

During the initial months of the war, the position taken by the President coincided with the prevailing view of Congress. On July 22 and July 25, 1861, the U.S. House of Representatives and the U.S. Senate, respectively, overwhelming passed the resolution offered by John J. Crittenden of Kentucky which stated,

> ... that this war is not waged, upon our part, in any spirit of oppression, not for any purpose of conquest or subjugation, nor purpose of overthrowing or interfering with the rights or established institutions of these States, but to defend and maintain the supremacy of the Constitution and to preserve the Union, with all the dignity, equality, and rights of the several States unimpaired; that as soon as these objects are accomplished, the war ought to cease.[6]

The Lincoln Administration's refusal to go beyond this total political objective and supplement it with the radical social and economic objective of the immediate, uncompensated abolition of slavery, however, soon earned the President the hostility of the Radical Republicans. While supporting the Lincoln Administration's total political objective of preserving the Union, these Northerners were extremely hostile to both the institution of slavery, as well as those who endorsed or even tolerated it. Consequently, they soon wanted the Administration to go beyond the preservation of the Union and make the immediate, uncompensated abolition of slavery and, implicitly the destruction of the slave-based Southern economy, a co-equal national war objective. Even without the incorporation of these total socio-economic goals into the definition of national objectives, however, the total political goals being sought by the Federal government alone demanded nothing less than total victory over the Confederacy. The spirit of secession would have to be completely neutralized, optimally with a minimum of coercion. Indeed, eventually, the Southern people would have to voluntarily consent to rejoining the Union, since the Federal authorities could not maintain the Union by coercion in perpetuity. Moreover, it was important for the Federal authorities to achieve their goals as quickly as possible, since, the longer the war lasted, the greater the likelihood that the objectives sought by the Federal government would escalate from the total political objectives

4

presently sought to a total socio-economic-political revolution. Moreover, the rules of engagement were likely to liberalize as the war lengthened, thus transforming a ''soft war'' into a ''harsh war.'' Prosecution of the latter, in turn, would make a post-war reconciliation proportionately difficult. Conversely, the formula for a Southern victory was considerably less demanding. The Confederacy had merely to continue resistance until the Northern people tired of the sacrifices inherent in defeating the Southern rebellion and acquiesced to the independence of the Confederacy. In short, implicitly, a Federal victory required a sustained Northern commitment to pursue the war until total victory was attained.[7]

Initially, many Northerners, including President Lincoln, believed that extremist elements in the South had revolted in an emotional response to the election and felt that an effective counter-response by the Northerners would defuse the rebellion. They felt that the peoples of the Deep South did not have any uncompromisable differences with the North and, further, the Deep Southern and mid-Atlantic states would not constitute a viable political entity. Moreover, the Border states would draw them back into the Union. Finally, many argued that the Confederacy would be required to protect a long continental border against northward fleeing slaves. Hence, many felt that the crisis could and would be resolved peacefully, as had all the earlier sectional crises in the history of the Republic. Clearly, in retrospect, the President, joined by most Northerners, overestimated the political strength of Unionist sentiment in the Southern states, while underestimating both the resolve of the secessionists and the gravity of the present crisis.[8]

Notwithstanding the Northern hope that the crisis would pass peacefully, in the days following the fall of Fort Sumter, the crisis became more, rather than less serious. Virginia, Arkansas, Tennessee, and North Carolina threatened to join the Confederacy and it appeared possible that they could take the Border states of Missouri, Kentucky, and Maryland with them. If this occurred, the position of the Federal government within the District of Columbia would have become geographically untenable. Indeed, key Federal leaders feared for the safety of the city.[9]

President Lincoln's advisors quickly divided into three loose opinion groups concerning how to respond to the rapidly deteriorating situation. First, the Secretary of State, William H. Seward continued to hold the opinion which he had maintained since the Administration took office in March; that it was still possible to reconcile the sectional differences by compromise and, hence, the Federal government should refrain from provocative measures. Second, at the opposite extreme stood Montgomery Blair of the politically powerful Blair family of Missouri. Based upon the assumption that the Southern people were not really behind the secessionists and, hence, could easily be induced to abandon the new Confederate government, Mr. Blair emphasized from the outset of the crisis that an immediate, resolute show of Federal force would, in turn, yield a sufficiently large expression of pro-Union support throughout the South as to rout the forces of secession.[10]

Finally, the United States' foremost living soldier, Brevet Lieutenant General Winfield Scott, the hero of the War with Mexico a decade and a half earlier and, for nearly two decades, the General-in-Chief of the United States Army, argued against an immediate attempt to engage and destroy the Confederate field armies or the total military conquest of the rebellious states. He observed that,

> No doubt this might be done in two or three years by a young and able general . . . with 300,000 disciplined men, estimating a third for garrisons, and the loss of a yet greater number by skirmishes, sieges, battles and Southern fevers. The destruction of life and property on the other side would be frightful, however perfect the moral discipline of the invaders.[11]

General Scott further observed that not only would such a strategy of conquest involve an " 'enormous waste of human life to the North and Northwest,' " it would be extremely costly in treasure to the Federal government. Finally, even after the successful conquest of the South, the Federal government would have to administer " 'fifteen devastated provinces not to be brought into harmony with their conquerors, but to be held for generations, by heavy garrisons, at an expense quadruple the net duties of taxes which it would be possible to extort from them. . . .' "[12]

Instead, General Scott proposed his celebrated "anaconda plan," which, in turn, was predicated upon a more limited strategy designed to strangle the Confederacy into submission by forcing the South to exhaust its war-making resources. General Scott felt that, as the South's war-making potential progressively declined, pro-Union sentiment throughout the South would become increasingly powerful and ultimately force the secessionists to abandon their struggle for independence and rejoin the Union. To accomplish this, the aged warrior recommended " 'the complete blockade of the Atlantic and Gulf ports' " of the states in rebellion, thereby sealing the South off from all access to maritime commerce and possible overseas support. This, in turn, would force the South to rely exclusively upon its own domestically derived war-making resources. In addition, he proposed the limited territorial dismemberment of the Confederacy and the severance of the South's internal communications by isolating the three trans-Mississippi states in rebellion from those east of the great river, thereby accelerating the exhaustion of Confederate war-making resources. Along these lines, he proposed " 'a powerful movement down the Mississippi to the ocean, with a cordon of posts at proper points . . . the object being to clear out and keep open this great line of communications in connection with the strict blockade of the seaboard, so as to envelop the insurgent states and bring them to terms with less bloodshed than by any other plan.' " Discussing the move to permanently occupy the Mississippi Valley in more detail, General Scott stated,

> I propose to organize an army of regulars and volunteers on the Ohio River, of say, 80,000 men, to be divided into two unequal columns, the smaller to proceed by water on the first autumnal swell in the river, headed and flanked by gunboats (propellers of great speed and strength), and the other column to proceed as nearly abreast as practicable by land—of course without the benefit of rail transportation—and receiving at certain points on the river its heavier articles of consumption from the freight boats of the first column.[13]

The General also recommended a cordon of posts along the Confederacy's northern border. Finally, the General-in-Chief recognized the need for a Federal force to occupy the Confederate forces in the eastern theater, but he did not seem to feel that this force should be anything more than an army of observation. Even after this limited strategy produced the collapse of the Confederacy, however, General Scott predicted that it would still be necessary for the Federal government " 'to restrain the fury of the noncombatants.' " Yet, on balance, the General-in-Chief felt that, in view of the available and mobilizable resources at the disposal of the Lincoln Administration, this limited military/naval strategy, predicated upon the assumption that pro-Union elements in the South would eventually be able to assert themselves, displace the secessionists, and bring the Southern states back into the Union, was the only appropriate course of action open to the Federal authorities.[14]

General Scott, however, recognized that " 'the greatest obstacle in the way of the plan' " was " 'the impatience of our patriotic and loyal Union friends. They will urge instant and vigorous action, regardless, I fear of consequences. . . .' " Indeed, the General-in-Chief's strategy for strangling the Confederacy into exhausted submission by forcing the South to deplete its war-making resources through the Federal naval enforcement of Southern maritime isolation, combined with the severance of internal Confederate communications by Federal occupation of the Mississippi Valley, was open to criticism for being too slow to take effect against a relatively self-sufficient South populated by a people resolved to secure their independence from the United States. First, time consuming preparations would have to be made to establish a naval blockade and to occupy the Mississippi Valley. Second, additional time would be required to effectively isolate the South from access to overseas trade and possible support via the naval blockade. In addition, time would be required to successfully sever the Confederacy's internal communications by occupying the Mississippi Valley. Third, even after the Confederacy had been externally isolated and the Deep South severed from the trans-Mississippi portion of the Confederate States, it would require even more time for the Confederate government to exhaust the South's wealth of war-making resources, for centrally organized resistance to collapse, and for pro-Unionist elements to assert themselves and make peace. In addition to these considerations, General Scott's plan did not adequately take into account the activities of the Confederate field armies, particularly if these forces assumed the offensive. Notwithstanding these weaknesses, however, the aged General-in-Chief's strategy possessed a number of strengths. First, it stressed the importance of economic considerations in sustaining a war effort. Second, the General, at least implicitly recognized that, even after the Confederate government had ceased to be capable of sustaining the war effort and pro-Union moderates had displaced the secessionists and driven them "underground" or abroad, effective Southern resistance could continue as long as the people of the South remained committed to their goal of independence. Consequently, for a period of time following the war, the Federal authorities would have to be prepared to garrison an extensive hostile area. Beyond this, however, General Scott recognized that eventually the Southern people would have to voluntarily abandon their goal of independence and commit themselves to full participation within the restored Union.[15]

Finally, the Mississippi component of General Scott's plan had the great political merit of coinciding with the perceptions and interests of the people residing in the Ohio, upper Mississippi, and Missouri River Valleys. As Bruce Catton wrote,

> The Mississippi was basic in Western thinking. What happened in the East might or might not matter, but this river was the road to the world and the future, the inescapable geographic symbol of the fact that if the West would live and grow it must lie at the heart of a single undivided nation. The railway network was already replacing the river as a traffic artery, but that did not destroy the symbol. The river could be seen and felt, traditions had been built around it, men would fight for it and weave legends about their fighting, and they would make any sacrifice to keep this valley open.[16]

William Tecumseh Sherman, an officer who was to emerge as one of the principal architects of the eventual Union victory, articulately reflected the perspective of many Westerners. General Sherman almost mystically viewed the Mississippi Valley as " 'the spinal column of America,' " a "heartland binding together the Union in an indivisible whole, . . . (the) great center that made America unique and great and worth preserving." Hence, noting that " 'the valley of the Mississippi is America,' " the

General observed, " 'the inhabitants of the country on the Mon-
ongahela, the Illinois, the Minnesota, the Yellowstone, and Os-
age, are as directly concerned in the security of the Lower
Mississippi as are those who dwell on its very banks in Louisiana. . . .' " In 1861, as the Republic teetered on the edge of
political disintegration, General Sherman maintained that,
" 'were it not for the physical geography of the country it might
be that people would consent to divide and separate in peace.
But the Mississippi is too grand an element to be divided and
all its extent must of necessity be under one government.' "
Hence, for Sherman, peace between two political entities, "one
which owned the source and the other the mouth of the Mississippi River," was unthinkable. Moving from the mystical to the
practical, the General argued,

> How could it be otherwise with the agricultural South insisting upon
> free trade and the industrial North holding to its protective tariff? Im-
> porters at New Orleans, having no duty to pay, could send their com-
> modities by boat to the upper border and undersell the Eastern
> merchants who shipped their merchandise by rail. To enforce custom
> duties along the whole length of the Ohio River would be a terrific task.
> Instead, the Northern confederacy would blockade the Southern ports.
> Would Europe permit that?[17]

Thus, Sherman felt that, if Louisiana, Mississippi, and Arkansas
followed their sister states from the Deep South and mid-Atlantic
region out of the Union, the states of the Ohio, upper Mississippi, and Missouri Valleys would be compelled to resist with
force. Moreover, Sherman predicted that if Missouri left the
Union, Kentucky, southern Illinois, and southern Indiana would
possibly follow. Indeed, he would later write, " 'to secure the
safety of navigation of the Mississippi, I would slay millions.' "[18]
    In addition to emphasizing the geopolitical and economic im-
portance of the Mississippi Valley, General Sherman argued that,
while victory would not be quick or cheap, control of the Mississippi was "the key to ultimate victory." Just as he held that
he would " 'regard the loss of St. Louis as more fatal to our
future success than the capture . . . of Harrisburg and Philadelphia,' " or even Washington, the Federal seizure of the lower
Mississippi was more important to ultimate success than the
capture of any Eastern city, including the Confederate capital.

Simply put, he stressed " 'whatever nation gets control of the Ohio, Mississippi, and Missouri Rivers will control the continent,' " because the " 'Atlantic slope and the Pacific shores will follow' " the destiny of the Mississippi Valley " 'as sure as the limbs of a tree live or die with the main trunk.' "[19]

Initially, the entire cabinet, except the more aggressive Montgomery Blair, agreed with General Scott's hypothesis that by tightening pressure around the perimeter of the South, pro-Union moderates in the South would eventually displace the secessionists and return the Southern states to the Union. In supporting Scott's strategy, however, Mr. Seward continued to maintain that it was still not too late to resolve the dispute by compromise. In any case, with the support of his advisors, Mr. Lincoln took the first steps toward gradually pressuring the South to abandon the rebellion. On April 15, 1861, in an attempt to separate what the members of the Administration still felt was a strong pro-Union sentiment throughout the Southern states from the secessionists, the President stated that Federal forces would be used to " '. . . repossess the forts, places, and property which have been seized from the Union; and in any event, the utmost care will be observed, consistently with the objects aforesaid, to avoid any devastation, any destruction of, or interference with, property, or any disturbance of peaceful citizens in any part of the country.' " Thus, the President attempted to tell the Southern people, especially the pro-Union elements in the South, that he intended to "wage a limited war, engaging in no unnecessary punishment and destruction" and, thus, "suppress the insurrection with the least possible annoyance to well-disposed people everywhere."[20]

Four days later, on April 19, 1861, President Lincoln proclaimed a naval blockade of the Confederate States. Thus, from the outset of the war, the mission of the Federal Navy became,

1. The closing of all the insurgent ports along a coast of nearly three thousand miles, in the form and under the exacting regulations of an international blockade, including the naval occupation and defense of the Potomac river. . . .
2. The organization of combined naval and military expeditions to operate in force against various points on the southern coast, rendering efficient naval cooperations with the position and movements of such

expeditions when landed, and including also all needful naval aid to the army in cutting intercommunications with the rebels and in its operations on the Mississippi and its tributaries; and

3. The active pursuit of the piratical cruisers which might escape the vigilance of the blockading force.[21]

Initially, however, the United States Navy lacked sufficient power to assert complete command over the entire Southern coastline. With forty-two ships in commission and another forty-eight out of commission or laid up, the United States Navy was primarily a blue-water maritime force, inappropriately configured for coastal and inland operations. Quickly, the Navy Department moved to expand the size of its naval forces by building and purchasing appropriate vessels. Hence, by July, the Navy had increased in size to eighty-two ships and, by the end of 1861, it had grown to two hundred and sixty-four vessels. By the end of the war, the Navy had grown to approximately seven hundred ships.[22]

Simultaneously, the Federal Navy began to lay the groundwork for performing its blockading mission by establishing a network of forward bases for ship maintenance and refueling.

> The adoption of steam propulsion made a close blockade somewhat more realistic than it would have been in the age of sail, but it created prodigious logistical problems. Guarding some three thousand miles of coastline with dozens of ports, inlets, and rivers required a huge armada. These vessels needed support facilities within a short cruising distance of their blockade station. Maintaining a close blockade proved much more difficult when the vessels had to leave their station periodically for fuel or repairs, particularly for steamers stationed along the South Atlantic coast and in the Gulf of Mexico. . . . At the beginning of the war the navy created two blockading squadrons, one in the Atlantic and one in the Gulf. The board (of strategy established by Secretary Welles in May, 1861) recommended dividing each into two squadrons, making a total of four. Thus, the Atlantic Squadron became the North Atlantic Blockading Squadron and the South Atlantic Blockading Squadron, the border between North and South Carolina determining their areas of operation. Meanwhile, the Gulf Squadron became the East Gulf Blockading Squadron and the West Gulf Blockading Squadron. The east squadron received the responsibility for all of Florida east of Pensacola, including the Atlantic coast and the Bahamas and Cuba. The western squadron blockaded the Gulf ports west of Pensacola.[23]

Thus, throughout the first year of the war, Federal forces successfully established bases at: Hatteras Inlet on the North Carolina coast in late August, 1861; Ship Island just off the Mississippi coast in September; and Port Royal, South Carolina in early November. These acquisitions were supplemented by the Florida Forts Taylor at Key West, Jefferson at the Dry Tortugas off Key West, and Pickens at Pensacola, as well as Fort Monroe at Hampton Roads, Virginia, which had remained in Federal hands. In addition to providing the Federal government with tangible gains at which to point, the capture or retention of Federal control over these sites constituted important preliminary steps in implementing the maritime component of General Scott's "anaconda plan."[24]

While the Federal naval blockade of the Southern coastline would remain an important element of Federal military strategy throughout the entire war, its announcement in April, 1861 significantly complicated another important element of the Administration's effort to frustrate the Southern independence movement — preventing European intervention into the conflict. Great Britain, the most powerful of the European states, was interested in the outcome of the conflict in North America for a series of reasons. First, the power configuration in North America, as well as the international maritime power balance would be significantly influenced by the outcome of the struggle in the United States. The United States' transcontinental expansion during the first half of the nineteenth century, as well as the growth of American maritime power had increasingly challenged the position of Great Britain, both at sea and in the Western hemisphere. Hence, from this perspective, the political disintegration of the United States would significantly reduce its capacity to enforce the Monroe Doctrine and challenge British dominance at sea. Second, many Britons were interested in the implications of the struggle in the United States for the future of liberty and democracy. On the one hand, Great Britain's conservative, aristocratic elements had long regarded the experiment in democracy in the United States as a threat to their own socio-economic-political position. Hence, these elements hoped that the political disintegration of the United States would retard the spread of democracy. Moreover, Britain's upper classes identified more closely with what they perceived as the aristocratic South than with the commercial North. Conversely, however, many other Britons, individuals active in the British liberal movement, as well as significant portions of the middle and laboring classes were hostile to the institution of slavery and identified with the principles of democracy and liberty. Hence, these elements identified closely with the North and hoped that the Union might be preserved and continue to shine as a beacon of democracy throughout the world. Similarly, many Britons viewed the struggle in America only in terms of its impact upon the future of slavery. Third, while many Britons questioned the resolve of the North to translate its enormous potential into sufficient power to forcibly politically reintegrate the Union, they felt sympathetic to the South as the underdog in the struggle. Finally, the British textile industry used raw cotton from the Deep South in its manufacturing process. But while the interruption in the flow of cotton from America would cause suffering among the textile workers in Britain, they remained supporters of the Union cause. Moreover, offsetting its economic ties to the South, British commercial interests also had important ties to the Northern states.[25]

In addition to Great Britain, other European powers were also interested in the struggle in America. France was already considering the possibility of establishing a French presence in Mexico and, hence, the duration and outcome of the conflict within the United States would influence both the timing and the nature of Paris' plans. The conflict itself would distract Washington's attention from French activities in the Western Hemisphere, as well as dilute the American ability to resist French initiatives. Moreover, if the United States politically disintegrated, not only would this permanently weaken the U.S. and reduce its capacity to project power within the hemisphere, a friendly Confederacy could serve as a buffer between the remnants of the United States and the new French empire centered in Mexico and the Caribbean. From another perspective, French economic interests suffered as a result of the conflict in America. Indeed, of the major European powers, only Russia was wholeheartedly committed to the Union cause. From St. Petersburg' perspective, the political disintegration and resultant weakening of the United States meant a proportionate strengthening of Russia's main international rival, Great Britain.[26]

The principal objective of United States diplomacy throughout the war was to prevent the European powers from intervening in the conflict. Virtually from the outset, the French Emperor, Napoleon III, favored recognition of the Confederate states and some sort of political or military intervention. France, however, lacked the power to intervene alone. Consequently, Paris regarded London's cooperation in any interventionist scheme as essential. Indeed, had London and Paris been closely allied, the likelihood of Anglo-French intervention would have increased significantly. But traditional British enmity toward France, combined with the poor regard which British officials held for Napoleon III and their reservations concerning Paris' policy toward Mexico, considerably reduced the prospects for coordinated action. Within Britain itself, while there were powerful voices favoring British intervention in the American Civil War, these elements were counterbalanced by the working and middle classes who favored non-intervention. It should be noted, however, that, at the outset of the war, as the Lincoln Administration refused to incorporate the abolition of slavery into the definition of Federal war objectives and, further, while the prospect for Federal success in crushing the Southern rebellion remained questionable, the power of the middle and the working class opinion remained somewhat diluted. Finally, fortunately for the Union cause, Anglo-American relations were particularly cordial at the outset of the war.[27]

In an effort to reduce the chances of European intervention, the Lincoln Administration maintained from the outset of the war that the conflict should not be seen as a war between the Northern and Southern states. Instead, Secretary of State Seward emphasized, " 'there is here, as there always has been, . . . one political power, namely, the United States of America, competent to make war and peace, and conduct commerce and alliances with all foreign nations.' " Consequently, Secretary Seward argued that "what existed . . . was an armed sedition seeking to overthrow the government. Its suppression did not constitute a war or in any manner modify the character, rights, and responsibilities of either the United States or foreign nations in their diplomatic relationships." The Secretary acknowledged that international legal norms provided for recognition of a de-facto government, but he "denied that one existed in the South." The announcement of a Federal naval blockade, however, undermined the Administration's interpretation since, by doing so, the United States was implicitly "declaring itself a belligerent and claiming rights over foreign vessels admitted only in time of war." For Europe, the choice was one of recognizing the Confederate States of America as the de-facto government of the South or allowing its commercial relations with the South to be interrupted. Fearful of both a war with the United States at sea and the severance of her commercial ties with the South, on May 13, 1861, Great Britain "issued a declaration of neutrality which called upon British subjects to avoid hostilities between the North and South. . . . This recognition of Southern belligerency granted to Southern ships the privileges in neutral ports accorded the ships of the Federal government." From Washington's perspective, however, this appeared to be the prelude to recognition of the Confederacy. Consequently, in the strongest possible terms, the United States warned the European powers that recognition of the Confederate government would lead directly to war with the United States. In addition to consistently reaffirming this stance, the United States went further and repeatedly told the Europeans that even unofficial receipt of agents of the Confederacy by representatives of their governments would be interpreted by Washington as an act of hostility toward the U.S. Finally, the United States made it clear from the outset that any move by the European governments toward arbitration of the conflict was unacceptable to Washington. By the late spring and early summer, 1861, the British had decided to avoid entanglement in the conflict, at least until the situation clarified. Moreover, again, at least for the moment, the British decided not to challenge the Federal naval blockade. As Norman Graebner wrote,

> . . . the British resolve not to break the blockade resulted from a far more fundamental motive than a willingness to dispense with cotton,

for the blockade defied America's own precedents and doctrines of neutral maritime rights. In undermining the principle of the Declaration of Paris that blockades to be binding must be effective, the United States was releasing England in a future conflict from this burdensome feature of the past. American action weakened the stand of the smaller maritime powers in their perennial effort to force Great Britain to recognize neutral rights in time of war.[28]

In the largest sense, however, as Professor Graebner noted,

Europe's diplomatic tradition cautioned against any recognition of the Confederacy until the South had demonstrated the power required to establish and maintain its independence. Without the assurance of ultimate Southern success, European involvement would assume the risk of either an eventual ignominious retreat from a declared diplomatic objective or an unlimited military commitment to guarantee the achievement of Southern independence. Confronted with Europe's traditional realism, the Southern diplomatic cause in London and Paris could be no more successful than the Southern military cause.[29]

Thus, for the present, the European role in the conflict in the United States awaited developments on the battlefield.[30]

Meanwhile, as the Lincoln Administration took the first steps to erect a maritime blockade of the South, on land, the President and his politico-military advisors immediately recognized the imperative of holding the Border states and rendering the Federal capital secure. In the east, at minimum, this required securing Maryland, the southern bank of the Potomac, and the mountainous portion of western Virginia. In a partial effort to achieve this, on April 15, immediately after the fall of Fort Sumter, Mr. Lincoln moved to expand the size of the army. By mid-May, pro-Union elements, reinforced by the presence of Union troops, had defeated secessionist and neutralist forces in Maryland and had, thereby, secured that state for the Union cause. As the fate of Maryland was being decided, to the south, on April 17, three days after the Confederates seized Fort Sumter, the Virginia Convention had, by an 88 to 55 vote, passed an Ordinance of Secession, subject, in turn, to ratification by the people of Virginia on May 23. The Lincoln Administration felt that it was important not to take any provocative measures in Virginia before the voice of the people of the "Old Dominion" had been heard. Immediately following the popular ratification of the ordinance and Virginia's entry into the Confederacy, however, the Federal high command moved swiftly to secure the south bank of the Potomac. On May 24, 10,000 Union soldiers, under the leadership of the well-educated, newly promoted Brigadier General Irvin McDowell, occupied Arlington and Alexandria. Within a month, the Federals had secured a twenty mile long and at certain locations ten mile deep foothold on the south bank of the Potomac opposite Washington. Simultaneously, a large contingent of Union reinforcements was sent to Fort Monroe at the mouth of the James River, while another force occupied Harper's Ferry, Virginia.[31]

As the Administration attempted to secure Washington, while, simultaneously, gaining some maneuver room against the Confederate forces located at Manassas Junction, about twenty-five miles southwest of Alexandria, the President and his advisors also recognized the importance of securing western Virginia. Discussing this, Allen Nevins observed.

> Its strategic value was altogether too vital to the nation. This mountainous district offered a buffer zone protecting eastern Ohio, western Pennsylvania (including Pittsburgh), and the flank of any Federal army which marched into the Shenandoah Valley. It covered a long stretch of the Ohio River. It fairly secured the Baltimore and Ohio Railroad, the one line which with its direct links joined Washington with Louisville, Indianapolis, and St. Louis; a line enabling the United States to transfer troops between the eastern and western theaters much more readily than the South could move them. The protection which West Virginia gave eastern Kentucky would presently make the invasion of eastern Tennessee, toward Knoxville, much easier; while it was not actually valuable as a base for striking into the Confederacy, it did help protect some of the points of debouchment for energetic invasion of the South. Finally, retention of the western counties, with more than 350,000 population, kept fully 30,000 men out of the Confederate army, and at times tied up sizable Confederate forces.[32]

He went on to note, however, that, fortunately for the Union cause,

> The people beyond the Alleghenies, bound by natural economic ties more closely to their northern neighbors than to eastern Virginia, had cared little about the so-called wrongs of the South, but very keenly about the maltreatment they suffered from the Tidewater and Piedmont. They complained that they were grossly underrepresented in the legislature, that the three-fifths rule in counting slaves deprived them of their share of seats in Congress, that they were outrageously overtaxed, and

that while very poor in communications they got nothing like their share of public improvements. By no means least, they felt aggrieved by the disdainful attitude of proud eastern planters and merchants toward the "mountaineers."[33]

Finally, the people of western Virginia recognized their vulnerability to attack from the north. Hence, when the Virginians in Richmond adopted the Ordinance of Secession, because of their loyalty to the Union, combined with popular resentment over state-wide grievances, the Unionists of the trans-Alleghany portion of Virginia had already opted to create their own state. The western Virginians called for a special convention to meet on May 13, in Wheeling, to discuss the role of Virginia in the present crisis. Twenty-five counties from the mountainous portion of the state sent representatives and they, in turn, agreed not to secede from the Union and that, if the Ordinance of Secession were ratified, they would hold a special election for another convention to formulate a response. Meanwhile, the trans-Alleghany Virginia leaders appealed to the Governors of Pennsylvania and Ohio for help. In response, the Governor of Ohio directed George B. McClellan, recently appointed the Commander of the Ohio forces and soon to be commissioned a Major General in the Regular Army by the Federal government and named Commander of the Union forces assembling in the upper Ohio Valley, to prepare to cross the Ohio River if the Virginians withdrew from the Union. Therefore, immediately after the referendum in Virginia ratifying the Ordinance of Secession, General McClellan's forces undertook military operations to secure western Virginia, successfully completing the campaign by mid-July. Meanwhile, the second Wheeling convention convened with thirty-four western counties represented and this body moved to establish a loyal government for the entire state. "Under this plan, Union men were to be elected to all state offices and Washington was to treat their regime as constitutionally sovereign all the way from Norfolk to Wheeling." The Administration, in turn, recognized the new government of Virginia. Eventually, the trans-Alleghany Virginians moved to establish their own state and the "creation of the 'restored' government thus became a roundabout, awkward, perplexing mode of effecting the inevitable partition." Ultimately, on June 19, 1863, West Virginia entered the Union as the thirty-fifth state.

> What was important was the fact that as early as June, 1861, this important area was detached from Virginia; detached to make an effective shield for southeastern Ohio, southwestern Pennsylvania, the Baltimore and Ohio, and the armies west of Washington; and detached to be also an effective corridor for threatening the Confederacy.[34]

Meanwhile, on May 20, just over a month following the passage of the Ordinance of Secession in Virginia, North Carolina seceded from the United States and joined her sister states in the newly formed Confederate States of America.[35]

Concurrently, in the West, Arkansas withdrew from the Union on May 6, with Tennessee seceding on May 7. Of course, Union leaders recognized the importance of keeping Missouri, the wealthiest and most powerful trans-Mississippi state, within the Union. The loss of Missouri could, in turn, not only make trans-Mississippi Union communications more difficult, it would endanger southern Illinois, as well as loyalist elements in Kentucky. Unfortunately, however, the situation in Missouri rapidly deteriorated, as pro-secessionist and pro-Union elements first polarized and then, by mid-June, opened hostilities with each other. Feverishly, loyalists worked to retain control over the Missouri River, the Missouri bank of the Mississippi, at least as far as its confluence with the Ohio, the state's rail system, as well as St. Louis and Jefferson City. Simultaneously, pro-Union forces in Illinois worked to maintain the Union hold over the southern part of the state, especially Cairo, where the upper Mississippi joined the Ohio. Meanwhile, notwithstanding the Federal high command's anxiety concerning the situation in Missouri and southern Illinois and, further, despite the importance of the conquest of the Mississippi Valley in the strategy advocated by General Scott, the Washington leadership was slow in taking the initiative to coordinate Federal activities in the Mississippi River theater. Instead, the Administration continued to devote much of its attention to the eastern theater and to a lesser extent to the problem of Kentucky.[36] But, as Allen Nevins observed,

> Had Washington created its Western Department as soon as hostilities opened, by June 20; ... had it paid closer attention to the West, the

lowering storm might have been met. Yates, Morton, and other governors had been quite as strenuous as their Eastern compeers in getting men enlisted and brought into State camps; but . . . too little had been done to assemble, arm, and drill them.[37]

Finally, in contrast to his relative neglect of affairs in Missouri, Mr. Lincoln displayed what has been characterized as a "masterly comprehension and alertness" in Kentucky. He clearly recognized that "to lose Kentucky with her 1,200,000 people and her strategic position on the Ohio and the Mississippi would almost be losing 'the whole game.' " In mid-May, as her neighbors to the south and east were severing their links with the Union and joining the Confederacy, Kentucky formally assumed a neutral posture. Simultaneously, merchants in Kentucky maintained lucrative commercial relations with the Confederate states, as well as with those north of the Ohio River. Thus, despite the Union blockade of the Mississippi at its confluence with the Ohio River, Louisville and Nashville railway trains continued to carry supplies useful in sustaining the Confederate war effort southward. Indeed, "Louisville remained such a great collecting center for goods shipped into the Confederacy that she aroused the jealous wrath of Cincinnati." Moreover, the Kentucky Guard was assigned the mission of defending the state's neutrality and, if necessary, resisting either a Northern or a Southern invasion of Kentucky with force. While many Union men north of the Ohio River found Kentucky's neutrality intolerable, the President, "certain that Kentucky was the very pivot of the war, remained willing for the time being to accept her 'conditional Unionism.' " Mr. Lincoln believed that Kentucky's neutrality would keep the state intact as opinion coalesced favoring participation in the Federal effort to crush the Southern rebellion. Hence, while the Federal authorities authorized troop concentrations at strategic centers along the Ohio River, especially at Cairo, Illinois, Union troop movements onto Kentucky soil were forbidden. Of course, Mr. Lincoln's stance was ridiculed by his critics as a " 'Little Bo-Beep policy,' " not only " 'impolitic,' " but also " 'irresolute.' " Ultimately, however, the wisdom of the Administration's stance was certified. In contrast to Missouri which remained a problem region throughout the war, President Lincoln's initial stance "prevented angry factions from flying at each other's throats," thus allowing pro-Union sentiment to gather strength and consolidate its hold over the state. In the end, although Kentucky occupied a geographically vulnerable position, the "Bluegrass State" served as a bastion of Union strength in the United States' great internal confrontation.[38]

In short, notwithstanding its "partial failure" in Missouri, the Administration's policy toward the critical Border states was fairly successful. As Allen Nevins wrote,

> Strategically, the North held the entrances to the Shenandoah Valley, the Cumberland and Tennessee Rivers, and the Lower Mississippi. In population it had much the greater part of some thirty-four million people; in resources, it had grain, meat, minerals, factories, and shipping in abundance. Many vital parts of the Confederacy lay in a comparatively narrow strip along the Atlantic and Gulf, from Norfolk at one extremity to the Rio Grande at the other—exposed everywhere to attack by sea. Of the remainder, the interior states of Tennessee and Arkansas were vulnerable by river invasion. Far difficult would have been the situation had the Confederacy rounded out its domains by seizing Kentucky, Missouri, and western Virginia. The balance then would have swayed against the Union.[39]

But conversely, the Lincoln Administration's focus on retaining the Border states, combined with Confederate military preparations in southeastern Missouri and Tennessee, implied that, while Federal planning and preparations could proceed, General Scott's planned campaign to capture the Mississippi Valley would have to be postponed.[40]

As General-in-Chief Scott predicted, however, the Northern people and politicians were extremely eager for the Lincoln Administration to undertake an immediate offensive to suppress the rebellion. This popular pressure was especially focused upon the Virginia theater of operations where the Southern forces were deployed at Manassas, Virginia, provocatively close to the Federal capital and the forward deployed Union forces around Alexandria and Arlington. Undoubtedly, the concentration of military forces by both armies in Virginia, combined with the proximity of the two rival capitals, contributed significantly to the Northern public's sustained Virginia fixation. President Lincoln, of course, was also quite sensitive to popular Northern

22

pressure for an early overland advance by the newly raised Union forces against the Southern army in northern Virginia and the Confederate capital at Richmond. Any offensive land operations against the enemy in any region other than the Mississippi Valley, however, was alien to General Scott's strategy embodied in the "anaconda plan." But, given the impact of public opinion, symbolic victories, such as a successful, visible battle or the capture of the enemy's political capital are often popularly perceived as important military objectives, irrespective of their actual military significance. Consequently, they assume disproportionate importance in military strategic planning and, in fact, become important military objectives.[41]

Therefore, in the early days of summer, 1861, over the initial protests of General Scott, the President ordered the newly raised, but poorly prepared Union forces around Washington to advance and engage the equally unprepared Confederates located in northern Virginia. Mr. Lincoln obviously hoped that a highly visible, timely, successful military campaign in Virginia would yield several immediate, dramatic, and possibly decisive dividends. First, the President apparently hoped that the Union forces would optimally be successful in destroying the Southern army in northern Virginia in a single battle or series of battles and then move quickly to capture the newly established Confederate capital at Richmond. But even if the Union forces fell short of this highly ambitious goal and merely defeated, but did not destroy the Confederate field forces, Mr. Lincoln apparently believed that this, reinforced by the threat posed by the victorious Union army to Richmond, combined with the threat to the South's long-term capacity to materially sustain the war effort posed by General Scott's "anaconda plan" and the consolidation of Union control over the Border states, would be decisive in strengthening Southern moderates and discouraging secessionist elements, thereby causing the immediate collapse of the Confederacy and the termination of the rebellion. Certainly, the President was not alone in holding these optimistic hopes. Second, President Lincoln clearly felt that an early advance against the enemy army in Virginia would both accommodate public opinion and boost popular morale, especially in the

Northeast. Third, it would undermine Confederate efforts to secure European diplomatic recognition and material support. Both of the latter two considerations would be particularly important in sustaining the war effort should the hoped for battlefield victory fail to trigger the collapse of the rebellion or worse, the Union army be defeated, in either case making a longer war necessary. Finally, the ninety day enlistments of the initial body of volunteers which had answered the President's April 15 call for troops were about to expire and the Administration hoped to use these men in combat before they were mustered out.[42]

The Union forces in Virginia could move southward from a base of operations anywhere along an approximate southeast-northwest axis extending roughly along the Potomac River and the Baltimore and Ohio Railroad. In addition, the Union forces could utilize their naval superiority to advance inland, northwestward, up the James, York, Rappahannock, or Potomac Rivers from the north-south axis provided by the Chesapeake Bay. In short, it was possible for the Union armies to turn any Southern force located in northern Virginia close to the Federal capital. Conversely, the Confederates could advance northward from any point along the Virginia Central Railroad which provided an east-west axis linking Richmond with the Shenandoah Valley. Moreover, they could also use the northeast-southwest axis provided by the Shenandoah Valley as a base for an eastward operation designed to turn the Federal right in northern Virginia. Therefore, "with each contender having a two-sided base, the campaigns in Virginia consisted of three years of inconclusive seesaws of turning movements in which each side tried, but neither decisively reached the rear of the other." Moreover, as Warren Hassler observed,

> The terrain over which military operations were to be waged in the East was far from being ideal from the Union (offensive) point of view. Practically the whole countryside was covered with heavy forests. Roads were few and poor, thereby making the waterways, and especially the railroads, important as avenues of supply and communications. With Washington as the Union capital, and with Richmond ... the Confederate capital, an offensive southward from the former toward the latter could be reasonably expected. Here, however, the Southerners had a

defensive advantage; for, besides the narrow forest-lined roads, most of the important rivers ran in a west-to-east direction, perpendicular to the Federal line of advance. West of the Blue Ridge Mountains, the Shenandoah River flowed almost due northward and watered a fabulously rich valley which was to be used by one side or the other to outflank the main contending armies to the east. The Potomac River, of course, formed the chief west-to-east Federal defensive barrier. And at the point where the Shenandoah joined the Potomac stood Harper's Ferry, gateway to the Confederacy's wealthy Shenandoah Valley and to Pennsylvania's lush Cumberland Valley.[43]

Finally, the Confederate forces in Virginia, as well as the new Confederate capital at Richmond, were supplied from a variety of sources, but the principal source was "the rich granary of the Shenandoah Valley and the enormous supply depot at Lynchburg, a hundred miles west of Richmond" on the east side of the Blue Ridge. A series of arteries connected these consumers with the Shenandoah granary, as well as with points south and west.

There was the Virginia Central Railroad which ran northwest from Richmond, touched the Orange and Alexandria at Gordonsville, and went on to Staunton in the valley; and from Gordonsville a branch ran southwest through Charlottesville to Lynchburg. There was also the Southside Railroad, which met the Virginia and Tennessee at Lynchburg and, as its name implied, ran east from Lynchburg south of the James; it cut the Richmond and Danville line at Burkeville and then went on to the bigger junction point at Petersburg. Finally, there was the James River canal, coming down from Lynchburg to Richmond in the James River valley.[44]

In addition to the Richmond and Danville Railway, Richmond was linked to the Carolinas by the Weldon Railroad. Lastly, the Norfolk and Petersburg Railway connected the Southern capital with the tidewater area.[45]

With these geostrategic considerations as background, in July, 1861, Union forces were ordered to advance from Washington and engage the Confederates located at Manassas, Virginia. Simultaneously, another force was ordered to move southward from the Potomac at Harper's Ferry against the Southerners located in the Shenandoah Valley. General McDowell, commander of the force advancing from Washington, hoped to defeat the Confederates at Manassas by means of a successfully executed series of feints and a tactical turning movement. Strategically, however, the two Confederate forces occupied a central position between the two Federal armies advancing on exterior lines of communications. Indeed, the presence of a rail link connecting the two Confederate forces gave the Southerners a significant advantage over their Union counterparts. It could allow the Southern forces to concentrate against each of the advancing Union armies successively. Recognizing the threat that the Confederates might concentrate against General McDowell's army, General-in-Chief Scott directed the Union force advancing up the Shenandoah Valley to synchronize the timing of its advance to coincide with the advance of the Washington based force. Unfortunately for the Federal cause, however, perhaps due, in part, to somewhat confusing directives from the General-in-Chief, the Union force moving up the Shenandoah Valley failed to perform as expected. Hence, the Confederates were able to successfully detach the main body of their forces in the Valley, concentrate them with their troops at Manassas, and, on July 21, 1861, defeat General McDowell's army at the First Battle of Bull Run. Following their defeat, the Union forces hastily retreated to the Potomac River, leaving the victorious Confederates in possession of the field.[46]

The First Battle of Bull Run proved to be a typical Civil War engagement from a variety of perspectives, First, as with most Civil War battles, the victors failed to effectively pursue the vanquished. Indeed, as Professors Beringer, Hattaway, Jones, and Still observed,

> Even after the armies later became impressive organizations of well-led veterans, they still fought battles with essentially parallel fronts, and the victors usually lacked adequate cavalry or significant numerical superiority to pursue. Rarely did more than a fraction of the losing army suffer the heavy losses and the demoralization and disorganization of tactical defeat. Clausewitz noted difficult terrain as one more factor that would help prevent a decisive victory and hamper an effective pursuit. Since in the American Civil War the terrain was often rough or wooded, practically no battle ever met any of the conditions Clausewitz deemed essential for a formidable pursuit.[47]

Clearly, the First Battle of Bull Run suggested the difficulty of destroying, not merely defeating a mid-nineteenth century army. The battle proved typical in another respect: "throughout the war the tactical advantage of the defensive almost invariably resulted in heavier casualties for the attacker than the attacked." Moreover, the battle demonstrated the significance of railroads and the telegraph to facilitate communications and troop concentrations. Finally, it illustrated the firepower and the capacity of the mid-nineteenth century army to rapidly maneuver and redeploy its units on the battlefield. In the largest sense, however, President Lincoln's apparent hope that the Southern rebellion might collapse as a result of a Confederate battlefield defeat in northern Virginia, even a militarily indecisive defeat, reinforced by the threat to the Confederacy's long range war-making resource capabilities posed by the "anaconda plan," appears in retrospect to have been overly optimistic. Indeed, even a field victory, followed by the capture of the new Confederate capital at Richmond, would probably not have been decisive in causing the collapse of the rebellion. The Confederacy still had ample capability to field replacement armies and Richmond had not yet acquired the moral significance which it would later assume.[48] As B. H. Liddell-Hart noted,

> Even if Richmond had been attained, it is highly questionable whether at this stage of the war, or at a later, the effect would have been decisive. For although, on Virginia joining the Confederacy, the seat of Government had been transferred from Alabama to Richmond, rather as a general moves to an advanced headquarters for battle, Virginia was not the real seat of the Confederacy's hostile will and power. To reach and strike at the real seat was not a practicable possibility in 1861 . . .[49]

In short, given the South's capabilities, the comparative weakness of pro-Union moderates in the South, the popularity of the secessionists, and the Southern will to resist in 1861, if the war was to be won, it would take time. But, as the North renewed its resolve to crush the rebellion, few, if any, Northerners imagined the enormous scope of time, effort, blood, and treasure which would be required to preserve the Union.

Immediately following the catastrophe at Bull Run, panic gripped the Federal capital as fear spread that the Confederates would assault the city. For his part, however, the President remained calm and tightly gripped the reins of government. Resolving to redouble the pressure on the secessionists, Mr. Lincoln called for the strengthening of the Federal naval blockade, reinforcement of the Union forces at Fort Monroe, and sent more troops to the Shenandoah Valley. He further called for the reinforcement and reorganization of the defeated Union forces around Washington and the early capture of Manassas and the surrounding region. Finally, he called for an early Union advance down the Mississippi Valley. It was in this context that, on July 22, 1861, President Lincoln summoned thirty-four year old Major General George B. McClellan, the rising star of the Federal army, to Washington to assume command of the troops in the Washington area. Commander of the recently successful Union operations in western Virginia, the dashing, magnetic, and apparently energetic General appeared to be the personification of promise and was immediately welcomed throughout the city as the man of the hour. As Russell Weigley has observed, "no general of Lincoln's army more clearly recognized . . . that the way in which the war was fought would certainly shape its ends, or more thoroughly sympathized with Lincoln's wish to prevent 'remorseless revolutionary struggle,' than did Major General George B. McClellan." General McClellan felt that in order for the Federals to emerge victorious, it would be imperative "to accomplish the difficult balancing act of combining military victories, to convince the South that it must return to its old allegiance, with restraints upon destruction and an attitude of conciliation, to persuade the South that it ought to do so." Indeed, the General declared that "the North must avoid harshness and give the South as little offense as possible." Moreover he and Mr. Lincoln agreed concerning the slavery question; they both favored the gradual, compensated emancipation of the slaves and opposed the sudden, uncompensated wartime abolition of slavery advocated by the Radical elements of the Republican Party. Hence, the General repeatedly made it clear that he felt that "hostilities should not be waged against the civilian population of the South, but only against the enemy armed forces." As he later told a large Virginia landowner, " 'I have not come here to wage war upon the defenseless, upon non-combatants, upon private property, nor upon the domestic institutions of the land. I and the army I command are fighting to secure the Union and maintain its Constitution and laws, and for no other purpose.' " Similarly, the General told the President, " 'It should not be a war looking to the subjugation of the people of any state in any event.' " He emphasized, " 'neither confiscation of property, political executions of persons, territorial organizations of states, or forcible abolition of slavery, should be contemplated for a moment.' " Indeed, rather than be viewed as a war against the Southern people, the young General maintained that the war effort must be directed against the " 'armed forces and political organization' " of the Confederacy, in accord with the " 'highest principles known to Christian civilization.' " As such, he hoped to minimize the bitterness of both sides, while, simultaneously, convincing the Southerners that secession was doomed to fail. Since General McClellan shared Mr. Lincoln's moderate definition of Federal war objectives and methods for its prosecution, however, he would soon, like the President himself, become the target of Radical hostility and this would ultimately contribute to his dismissal.[50]

Operationally, the young General was quite sensitive to the significance of recent technological developments, especially railroads. He recognized that not only did railroads create new lines of operations and strategically important points, they also facilitated the speedy concentration of forces, as the Confederates had defensively demonstrated at Bull Run. In addition, General McClellan recognized the importance of sea power and seaborne lines of communications to both sustain and contribute to land operations. Moreover, while extremely sensitive to the tremendous potential of defensive firepower, especially when augmented by field and permanent fortifications, providing, in turn, a persuasive argument against frontal assaults, General McClellan felt confident that turning movements and methodical siegecraft techniques, if properly applied, would inevitably prevail with minimal loss of life. Finally, the General stressed the importance of concentrating a huge military force which would be capable of acting offensively, while, concurrently protecting its lengthening lines of communications as it advanced toward a decisive victory.[51]

Consequently, upon assuming command of the Union troops in the Washington area, General McClellan immediately began to apply his enormous administrative and organizational talents to form and train the host which would soon become known as the celebrated Army of the Potomac. The General gave his creation a character and spirit which, notwithstanding many future disasters, it would retain throughout the war. In return, the soldiers of the Army of the Potomac idolized their charismatic commander in a manner never extended to any of his successors.[52]

Meanwhile, on July 3, 1861, immediately prior to the First Battle of Bull Run, the Federal high command created the Western Department. This new administrative entity included Illinois and the region between the Mississippi Valley and the Rocky Mountains, as well as western Kentucky (as soon as the situation in Kentucky clarified). Mr. Lincoln selected the "Pathfinder" of the American West, Major General John C. Fremont to command this enormous and important department. General Fremont's biographer, Allen Nevins, assessed the President's selection as follows:

That Fremont had never commanded more than the few hundred men of his California Battalion, and they briefly and controversially, might not be a crippling disability; very few American officers had led a larger body. That as Senator from California and first Republican Presidential candidate he had shown no political flair was not important; he had been a novice. What did matter was that Lincoln should ignore Fremont's erratic career. Fremont had indubitably proved himself an explorer of high distinction. Brilliantly intelligent, energetic, daring, and able to inspire expeditions with his own enthusiasm, he had united scientific skill with the ability to endure prolonged hardship. A pathmarker, not pathfinder, he had traversed, mapped, and described great areas of the West in a way that did the nation important service. His knowledge of mathematics, zoology, botany, astronomy, and geology outran that of other famous Western explorers; he wrote with a color and narrative interest that his best rivals hardly approached. The man who had climbed the Wind River Range, discovered Lake Tahoe, scaled the Sierras in midwinter, given the Golden Gate its name, and penned a book which guided the Mormons into Salt Lake Valley, deserved his first fame. The role he had played in the conquest and early government of California, while often indiscreet and at times calculating, contained some heroic pages; and his Presidential candidacy emphasized his rigid freesoil principles. Close scrutiny of his career, however, disclosed an impetuosity that had repeatedly brought him to the verge of disaster, a want of judgement that disturbed his friends, and a willingness to invade dubious ground for personal advantage.

Although cultured, sensitive, and quietly attractive, he had made an equivocal impression. Because he grasped at prizes, such as the civil governorship of California, which he had not honestly earned, he appeared a little the charlatan; because he tempted fortune in so many fields, sometimes failing tragically, as in the fifth expedition, and sometimes succeeding magnificently, as when he emerged from his famous court-martial to find the California senatorship and rich Mariposa estate in his hands, he seemed a little the adventurer. Though he did useful work in helping open the West, all his other labors had an illusory value. While some intimates of great discernment and honesty, like Jessie Benton, Horace Greeley, and Kit Carson, felt a lifelong devotion to him, other people thought that his character was au fond questionable. In 1860 he was still a hero to millions of Americans, the recent titular leader of the Republican Party, and a figure of international renown.[53]

The President, the General-in-Chief, and General Fremont agreed that the "Pathfinder's" first task should be to secure Missouri and, upon completion, move down the Mississippi Valley and take Memphis, Tennessee. But, for the moment, the Federal high command did not assign a prioritized list of specific objectives. Instead, Mr. Lincoln told the General, " 'I have given you carte blanche; you must use your own judgement and do the best you can.' "[54]

General Fremont reached St. Louis on July 25, 1861, where he "found the Western Department boiling with confusion, shortages, dissension, and perils." Fremont's principal force concentrations were as follows: a force of about 7,800 men at Springfield, Missouri, in the southwestern portion of the state, another force north of the Missouri River, and a third, weak force at Cairo, Illinois. Many of the troops were three month enlistees whose terms were about to expire. General Fremont could not send adequate reinforcements to all three of these concentrations, so he opted to reinforce the force at Cairo. As Allen Nevins noted, "beyond question Cairo was the more important position. Real danger existed that the rebels would sweep all lower Missouri, seize Cairo by a sudden stroke, carry Kentucky into the Confederacy, and rally their sympathizers in southern Illinois and Indiana." Meanwhile, as the "Pathfinder" ordered reinforcements to the confluence of the upper Mississippi and the Ohio, he directed the Springfield force to withdraw

to the rail terminus at Rolla where they could be modestly reinforced. But on August 10, the "proud, pugnacious, and head-
strong" commander of the Union forces at Springfield opted
instead to attack the Confederates at Wilson's Creek. The needless battle ended in a Union defeat and the death of a number
of Union troops, including their aggressive commander. As the
defeated Union forces retreated, "the immediate result was an
intensification of guerrilla warfare in central and northern Missouri and an augmentation of Confederate strength." From his
headquarters in St. Louis, General Fremont requested the Western governors to send additional troops and accelerated plans
for fortifying Missouri's principal river city. Thinking aggressively, however, the Western Department Commander planned
to use these troops to occupy the towns along the Missouri River,
while, simultaneously, concentrating his field army in Missouri
at Rolla in preparation for an advance upon Springfield. This,
in turn, would be the first step in a larger campaign to drive the
Southern forces from the southern and western portion of Missouri into Arkansas. From there, General Fremont intended to
move his force into Arkansas and down the Arkansas River to
its confluence with the Mississippi.[55]

Concurrent with these military developments, "two political
factions, destined to affect deeply the progress of the war, were
crystallizing among Missouri Unionists: a conservative, moderate party, the Claybanks, who believed in gradual action
against slavery; and a radical, uncompromising body, the Char-
coals, ready for vigorous and implacable attacks on it." The latter
group increasingly looked to General Fremont for leadership and
support. For his part, the General sincerely equated slavery with
secession and believed that "abolitionist principles were the
stamp of a true Union man." As such, he failed to recognize that
many individuals residing in the Border states were prepared to
support and defend the Union, but not join a crusade against
slavery. Further, against the background of this political
cleavage, General Fremont increasingly antagonized the politically powerful Blair family, one of the leading elements of the
Claybanks.[56]

It was in this politically polarized context that, on August 30,
1861, without coordination with the Lincoln Administration in

Washington, the Commander of the Western Department issued a proclamation extending martial law over the whole state of Missouri. Moreover, the General "drew a diagonal line from Leavenworth through Jefferson City, Rolla, and Ironton to Cape Girardeau as separating the areas of Unionist and secessionist control; declaring that all civilians caught in arms north of that line should be tried by court-martial and if found guilty, shot; and prescribed the extreme penalty for all persons found guilty of destroying railway tracks, bridges, or telegraph lines." Finally, he declared that "the real and personal property of Missourians who actively aided the enemies of the United States was confiscated to public use, and that their slaves would be freed." As Allen Nevins observed, while martial law may have been a military necessity, "even as a military measure, Fremont's proclamation was open to sharp objection." Executions "would simply invite reprisals" and "to begin the sweeping confiscation of secessionist property would create embittered resistance, not quiet it." But General Fremont's proclamation was much more than just "a military measure." It significantly escalated the definition of Federal war objectives to include the immediate, uncompensated abolition of slavery for certain categories of citizens. As such, it constituted "a sharp intrusion into the political field." Responding to his Western Commander's unauthorized act, on September 2, Mr. Lincoln sent General Fremont a letter outlining his objections to the proclamation. The President directed the General "to shoot no Confederate without Presidential approbation or consent, for if he did 'the Southerners would very certainly shoot our best men in their hands in retaliation.' " In a larger sense, however, the President was extremely concerned about the negative impact of the proclamation upon theoretically neutral Kentucky. Mr. Lincoln feared that unless reversed, Fremont's de-facto escalation of the war objectives would alienate the Kentuckians and drive them into the Confederacy. Consequently, notwithstanding the vocal support extended by Northern abolitionist elements for General Fremont's effort to strike a blow for emancipation, the President, already developing his own plan for the gradual and compensated abolishment of slavery, requested Fremont to modify the section of his proclamation dealing with emancipation of slaves and the confiscation of rebel property. The Western Department Commander responded to Mr. Lincoln's request by stating that he would modify his declaration only in response to a direct order from the President. Consequently, on September 11, President Lincoln rephrased his request into an order. Yet, despite the fact that General Fremont's proclamation was ultimately overturned, his "impulsive stroke had crystallized a mass of latent sentiment, and for the first time the idea that the conflict might result in a socio-economic revolution began to grip men's minds."[57]

As the confrontation concerning General Fremont's proclamation was developing, the situation in Kentucky was clarifying. Throughout the summer of 1861, Kentucky had clung to its precarious neutrality, but it was clear to all parties that the neutrality of the "Bluegrass State" could not be maintained indefinitely. Military operations between the Union and Confederate armies in the region between the Appalachians and the Mississippi would necessarily violate Kentucky's neutrality. The only element of doubt concerned which antagonist would violate Kentucky neutrality first. Both the Union and Confederate authorities recognized the importance of a number of locations in Kentucky. Columbus, Kentucky, the northernmost terminus of the Mobile and Ohio Railroad, was one such point. If seized by the Confederates, batteries on the high bluffs overlooking the Mississippi could prevent Federal warships from descending the river. Another important Kentucky site was Paducah, located about forty-five miles up the Ohio from its confluence with the Mississippi at the point where the Tennessee flowed into the Ohio and ten miles below the confluence of the Cumberland and Ohio Rivers. The Tennessee and the Cumberland, in turn, provided a waterway deep into Confederate territory. Louisville, one of Kentucky's and the Ohio River's most important cities, was also an important location. Similarly, the prospect of Confederate artillery batteries across the Ohio River from Cincinnati justifiably troubled the residents and shipping interests of the city. Indeed, it was a strategic imperative for the Union cause that the Federals prevent the Kentucky shore of the Ohio River from falling into Confederate hands.[58]

By late August, General Fremont recognized that events would render Kentucky's precarious neutrality anachronistic. Preparing for the inevitable extension of hostilities into Kentucky, the General selected Brigadier General Ulysses S. Grant to command the Union forces in southern Illinois and southeastern Missouri. Characterizing General Grant, Professor Nevins observed that,

> ... intimates knew he did possess invaluable qualities: integrity, singleness of purpose, hard common sense, industry, and above all an instinct for the enemy's jugular. He never lost his self-command or his cool combativeness. His taciturn inscrutability and his mixture of simplicity and strength threw an aura of mystery about him. ... And though he lacked the intellectual power of a Moltke, ... he possessed the faculty of sorting out from many facts the few that were critically significant. He was growing also in the asset which the Anglo-Saxon world has always esteemed most, strength of character. That is, he was growing in promptness, for once he made up his mind, he moved; in nerve, for in tight squeezes he kept his head; and in stubborn grit, for he never knew when he was beaten, and who could lose every battle till the last one. Modesty and magnanimity were inborn traits. ... Quick, clever men may supply the ideas, but it is the rarer man of character whose integrity, resolution, and clarity of view make them count.[59]

This thoughtful, tenacious officer, however, lacked the magnetism of personality and appearance so abundantly possessed by General McClellan. Yet, his record of accomplishments during the next four years would lead the British scholar, General J.F.C. Fuller to characterize Grant as "the greatest strategist of his age," the war's "greatest general." Similarly, Professor T. Harry Williams agreed with General Fuller, noting that, in addition to being a "brilliant theater strategist" and "a better than average tactician," General Grant "was head and shoulders above any general on either side as an over-all strategist, as a master of what in later wars would be called global strategy." Finally, unlike General McClellan, General Grant grasped the important relationship between the conduct of war, politics, and societal morale. He recognized that "sometimes in war generals had to act in response to popular or political considerations." But, while he was alert to the complexity of that relationship, again unlike General McClellan and, for that matter, the officer who would become his most trusted lieutenant, William T. Sherman, General Grant refrained from offering political advice to his civilian superiors.[60]

Like most Northerners, General Grant believed that "after one or two defeats," the Confederacy would collapse because "most Southerners were not really committed to the fight." When this assumption proved to be fallacious, the General realistically modified his expectations and recognized that the conflict had become a total struggle between two powerful nations for survival, a type of conflict which, as Bruce Catton wrote, was increasingly "the kind of struggle which Grant, more than any other Union officer, was fitted to conduct." Such was the man which General Fremont selected to command the area around Cairo, "the great strategical center of the West, the hub of communications, water and rail, leading to St. Louis, Pittsburgh, Knoxville, Chattanooga, Mobile, and New Orleans."[61]

General Grant's mission was to coordinate military activities in his department sector, "to clear southeastern Missouri of Confederate troops, and then to move into Kentucky and occupy the potential stronghold at Columbus" on the Mississippi, as well as Paducah on the Ohio. The Western command intended that these locations would serve as important staging areas for future operations toward Memphis and Nashville. Meanwhile, General Grant was to insure that "proper defensive works were completed at Cairo, at Birds' Point, at Cape Girardeau and at Ironton." For his part, however, the General had long ago recognized the importance of driving the enemy from southeastern Missouri and using Cairo and Paducah as a staging area for southward operations.[62] As Bruce Catton observed,

> ... the order spelled out a radical change in Federal policy; a change which may or may not have struck Grant at the time. Kentucky was still neutral, and the decision to violate or to continue to respect the state's neutrality was technically one for Washington to make. Actually, however, the decision would inevitably be made by some commander in the field. Fremont had already warned Washington that operations along the Mississippi would eventually involve the Kentucky shore; now he was ordering Grant to move into Kentucky and take possession of the bluffs at Columbus; and the effect which this might have on public sentiments in that all-important border state was wholly problematical.[63]

In the end, however, it was not the Union forces, but rather the Confederates who terminated Kentucky's neutrality. On September 4, 1861, Southern forces preempted the Union side and occupied Columbus, Kentucky. Seizing the initiative, General Grant immediately responded by occupying Paducah. Soon thereafter, Union forces from Ohio and Indiana occupied the Kentucky shore of the Ohio River, including Louisville. Based upon these new developments, General Fremont sent the Federal high command in Washington "an elaborate plan for a forward movement in Kentucky and astride the Mississippi, looking toward the capture of Columbus, the occupation of Nashville, and ultimately the capture of Memphis." But soon thereafter, renewed Confederate activity in Missouri and resultant concern in Washington forced the Western Department Commander to return his attention to the area west of the Mississippi. By the early autumn, however, the Lincoln Administration was having serious doubts concerning the "Pathfinder's" ability to command the Western Department. Finally, on October 24, 1861, as anti-Fremont pressure in Washington mounted, Mr. Lincoln yielded and ordered that General Fremont be relieved of command. Temporarily, Major General David Hunter would command, but General Fremont's permanent successor would be Major General Henry W. Halleck.[64]

General Fremont's removal and replacement was only one of the key command changes made by the Lincoln Administration in the autumn of 1861. The aged General-in-Chief, Winfield Scott, in ill health, troubled by a strained relationship with his principal eastern subordinate, General McClellan, and increasingly the target of criticism by McClellan, members of the Lincoln Administration, and Congress, decided to retire from active duty. Hence, on October 31, 1861, the brevet Lieutenant General was placed on the retired list. On November 1, President Lincoln named General McClellan as his replacement. Concurrently, General McClellan would continue to command the Army of the Potomac. As the General-in-Chief's flag passed to the youthful McClellan, General Scott and the President could congratulate themselves that, notwithstanding some reversals, under their stewardship the Union had seized the upper hand in the

Border states and had established the foundation for an effective blockade of the Southern coastline. These gains would be critical to the ultimate Union victory three and a half years later.[65]

CHAPTER II

Autumn 1861—Summer 1862

By the end of 1861, popular and Congressional pressure upon the President to escalate the Federal war objectives to include the immediate, uncompensated abolition of slavery mounted significantly. When the Congress met in December, the U.S. House of Representatives "refused to reaffirm the moderate Crittenden Resolution that the war was being waged for the Union alone." Similarly, Radical Republican Senators submitted a measure in the Senate calling for the "confiscation of rebel property." Indeed, while most Northerners, foremost the President, hoped that the Union armies would swiftly facilitate the end of the rebellion, many Radicals hoped that the war would last long enough to guarantee the abolition of slavery. In short, as Allen Nevins wrote, confronted by this mounting pressure, as the autumn of 1861 drew to a close, Mr. Lincoln "hammered into rough form a project which represented as bold a step as Jefferson had made in the purchase of Louisiana." As noted earlier, Mr. Lincoln "had long before concluded that some system of gradual emancipation at national expense, coupled with an effort to colonize the freed people abroad," promised to be the best way to approach the vexing slavery question. Consequently, he decided that the time had come to test the waters concerning the feasibility of such a scheme. Indeed, he reasoned that compensated emancipation "could arrest heedless Congressional action, facilitate the surrender of the Confederacy, and give notice that slavery everywhere must be regarded as a temporary and not a permanent institution." The President felt that the slaveowners in the Border states were likely to agree to the plan since they would recognize that emancipation was inevitable. Moreover, regarding the resettlement of liberated slaves abroad, Mr. Lincoln had maintained that there was " 'a moral fitness in returning to Africa her children whose ancestors have been torn away from her by the ruthless hand of fraud and violence;' or if Africa

offered no refuge, in sending them to another tropical land."
Finally, regarding the cost of compensated emancipation, the
President argued that " 'this is the cheapest and most humane
way of ending the war,' " since "the bill for a single half-day of
hostilities would pay for all of Delaware's slaves, with enough
left over to colonize them abroad." Thus, in early November,
the President made overtures to officials from Delaware concerning his plan for compensated emancipation. He requested
that these men "ascertain whether the legislature could be per-
suaded to free the slaves if the government paid for them at local
and individual appraisals." Mr. Lincoln hoped that, if his plan
was demonstrated to be feasible in that small state, the larger
Border states would follow Delaware's lead. During the next
several weeks, Lincoln's plan was discussed in Delaware, but by
early 1862, it was clear it would not be adopted by the state's
political leaders. Party rivalries, proslavery feelings, concern
about Congressional authority to buy the slaves, reluctance to
guarantee a debt based upon "a mere pledge of Federal faith,"
states rights, and apprehension concerning the feasibility of
"controlling race relations without slavery," all conspired to undermine the prospects for the adoption of President Lincoln's
plan. In short, the President's first experiment in solving the
slavery problem, while, simultaneously, keeping it separate from
the definition of Federal war objectives, failed.[1] But notwithstanding this initial setback, as Allen Nevins wrote, Mr. Lincoln,

> ... had adumbrated the boldest movement in the history of the Pres-
> idency. His conception ran beyond the mere liberation of four million
> colored folk; it implied a far-reaching alteration of American society,
> industry, and government. A gradual planned emancipation, a concom-
> itant transportation of hundreds of thousands and perhaps even millions
> of people overseas, a careful governmental nursing of the new colonies,
> and a payment of unprecedented sums to the section thus deprived of
> its old labor supply—this scheme carried unprecedented implications.
> To put it into effect would immensely increase the power of the national
> government and widen its activities. If even partially practicable, it
> would mean a long step toward rendering the American people ho-
> mogeneous in color and race, a rapid stimulation of immigration to
> replace the workers thus exported, a greater world position for the re-
> public, and a pervasive change in popular outlook and ideas. The at-
> tempt would do more to convert the unorganized country into an

organized nation than anything yet planned. Impossible, and undesirable even if possible? — probably; but Lincoln continued to hold his vision.[2]

Meanwhile, the emancipationist political pressure on the President to incorporate the liberation of the slaves into the definition of the Federal war objectives continued to mount. The President, however, continued to resist adoption of such a drastic step at that time, opting instead to repackage his gradual, compensated emancipation plan. In a message to Congress on March 6, 1862, the President asked the House of Representatives and the Senate to pass a joint resolution stating, " 'Resolved, that the United States ought to cooperate with any State which may adopt gradual abolishment of slavery, giving to such State pecuniary aid, to be used by such State in its discretion, to compensate for the inconveniences, public and private, produced by such a change of system.' " Discussing the Presidential initiative, Professor Nevins observed that Mr. Lincoln,

> . . . argued that the mere initiation of a gradual scheme in some or all of the Border States would do much to shorten the struggle, for it would cut off from Confederate leaders the hope that they could ever win that area. Other considerations played a part in his stroke. It enabled him to test the sentiment of slaveholders from the Chesapeake to the Missouri; it would temporarily quiet the radicals; and it advertised to the country two of his basic principles—that while the gradual extinction of slavery must be accepted, the work should be gradual, and the whole nation should bear the cost.[3]

While most mainstream political opinion applauded Mr. Lincoln's initiative, it was sharply criticized by the extreme elements at both ends of the political spectrum. Many of the same criticisms leveled earlier in the Delaware initiative were again expressed in the context of the March 6 joint Congressional resolution proposal. Again, ultra-Conservatives expressed concern about the fate of the former slaves following emancipation. Many suggested that, "after the President spent billions of dollars to buy freedom for the slaves, a great part of the freed Negroes would then come North, to be supported as paupers at public expense, or to compete with white laborers and thus take the bread from the white children's mouths." Indeed, Frank Blair, Jr. of the powerful Missouri political family argued that "emancipation would be a terrible mistake until arrangements could be made to colonize the Negroes abroad; they could not be sent back to Africa, but they could be shipped to areas south of the Rio Grande and settled under Federal protection." Finally, many individuals, both in the Northern states, as well as in Europe, maintained that "the idea of forcible colonization was immoral." Notwithstanding these criticisms, however, the House of Representatives and the Senate passed the proposed resolution on March 11 and April 2, respectively. The real test, however, would be in the Border state legislatures.[4]

The response in the Border states was far from encouraging. Summarizing the arguments of the opposition, Dr. Nevins wrote,

> One adverse argument was that Congress lacked constitutional authority to spend national funds to compensate slaveholders within selected States. Lincoln's supporters of course replied that such expenditures were justifiable under the war-making power. Opponents also argued that even if Congress did possess the power, it would never exercise it, but after cajoling the States into emancipation, would leave them in the lurch. Was the government about to become a huge Negro-trader? . . . Above all, border members repudiated the President's proffer as a gross invasion of State sovereignty, and an interference with their domestic institutions. This interpretation did wrong to Lincoln, who intended his plan not as an interference in State affairs, but as a system of cooperation between State and nation, with the States holding the decisive voice. But it appealed to a deep sense of pride.[5]

Beyond these "superficial arguments," deeper reservations were evident. The question of the monetary value of the slaves would be difficult to establish. Further, the Border leaders were perplexed over the issue of post-emancipation race adjustment. Indeed, many Northern workers were hostile to President Lincoln's plan since it raised the specter of black competitors. Recently, the entry of black workers into the shipyards at Baltimore had led to a strike. Conversely, agricultural interests in the Border states were concerned that President Lincoln's plan, if adopted, would disrupt their sector by sowing the seeds of "unrest among the slave population." In addition, emotions were always a factor in accounting for Border negativism. The Abolitionists were deeply resented in the Border states and the President's plan was perceived to be identified with Abolitionist elements. Moreover, Mr. Lincoln's argument that the gradual, compensated abolition of slavery in the Border states would deprive the Confederate states of the hope of being joined by their neighbors immediately to the North was resented by Border Unionists. Finally, the President's plan to resettle the liberated slaves abroad was coldly received in the international community and even Messrs. Seward and Chase, the Secretaries of State and the Treasury, respectively, expressed opposition to that element of Mr. Lincoln's plan.[6]

As the Border politicians and the international powers criticized the President's initiative to promote the gradual, compensated emancipation of the slaves and their resettlement abroad, the Radicals in Congress continued to press for the incorporation of immediate, uncompensated emancipation into the definition of Federal war objectives. In the early spring, Congress passed legislation "abolishing slavery in the Territories and the District of Columbia." The District bill provided for an average of up to $300.00 compensation for the owners of the 3,185 slaves residing in the District. In addition, the bill provided for the possible resettlement of the former slaves in Haiti, Liberia, or some other suitable place upon their consent. Notwithstanding his concern that the $300.00 limit would be viewed as too low by the Border states, that the Courts, not Congress, should establish the price of the slaves, that Maryland should first agree to the plan, and foremost, that the bill might undermine his own efforts to promote compensated emancipation in the Border states, on April 16, 1862, President Lincoln signed the bill into law. He noted that, despite his reservations, he was pleased to see slavery eliminated from the nation's capital and that the principles of resettlement and compensation had been affirmed. Shortly thereafter, in mid-May, however, Congress passed the bill abolishing slavery in the Territories without compensation. In doing so, Congress upheld the view that "no valid title to slave property" had ever existed in the Territories.[7]

Finally, as the Border politicians criticized the President and as Congress increasingly took the initiative concerning the slavery issue, like General Fremont the previous year, several Union field commanders felt it was a military necessity to address the slavery issue in their own way. On April 12, 1862, Major General David Hunter, commanding the Union forces which, as will be examined shortly, had established Federal control over portions of coastal South Carolina, Georgia, and Florida, issued an order "liberating the slaves in Union hands" within his department. Then, on May 9, 1862, General Hunter freed all the slaves in his entire department and, simultaneously, began recruiting blacks into the newly created First South Carolina Union Regiment. In doing so, General Hunter went far beyond the Fremont initiative and violated an area which Mr. Lincoln consistently maintained was his area of exclusive authority under the war powers provision of the Constitution. Hence, on May 19, the President revoked General Hunter's orders. The First South Carolina Regiment was disbanded, although one Company continued to perform "irregular garrison duty on St. Simon's Island." Meanwhile, in Kansas, another Union officer recruited the First Kansas Colored Volunteers, but his unit would not be "accepted by the government until early 1863." Finally, Major General Benjamin Butler, commanding the Union forces which, again as will be examined subsequently, had seized New Orleans, began enrolling free black volunteers into Union service. Although denied formal authorization by the War Department, "in rapid succession he took into his forces the First, Second, and Third Native Guards." In short, despite the Administration's reservations, many field commanders were pressing the limits regarding the enlistment of former slaves into the Union Army.[8]

As the pressure for the immediate emancipation of the slaves mounted, the President resolved to redouble his efforts to secure Border state approval for his gradual, compensated emancipation plan. In his proclamation revoking General Hunter's orders, the President requested the leaders of the Border states to reconsider their position regarding his proposed plan for ending slavery in the United States. He noted,

> I do not argue. I beseech you to make the arguments for yourselves. You can not if you would be blind to the signs of the times. I beg of you a calm and enlarged consideration of them, ranging, it may be, far above personal and partisan politics. This proposal makes common cause for a common object, casting no reproaches upon any. It acts not the pharisee. The change it contemplates would come gently as the dews

of heaven, not rending or wrecking anything. Will you not embrace it? So much good had not been done, by one effort, in all past time, as in the providence of God, it is now your high privilege to do. May the vast future not have to lament that you have neglected it.[9]

But the Radicals in Congress pressed forward relentlessly, challenging both the President's policy and assertion of exclusive authority to deal with the slavery question. During the early summer, 1862, the House of Representatives and the Senate passed the Second Confiscation Bill which had been stalled in committee. Discussing the provisions of the bill and its implications, Allen Nevins noted,

> Its direct provisions on confiscation were much less important than its frontal attack upon slavery. To be sure, the bill declared it the duty of the President to cause the seizure of all property of long categories of Southerners, and made all other persons who abetted the rebellion, sixty days after he gave public warning, equally liable to loss of their estates; Federal courts being empowered to dispose of forfeited property for the benefit of the Treasury. Obviously, the effectiveness of these clauses depended on Presidential cooperation. But much more important were the provisions that the slaves of all who supported the rebellion should be deemed legitimate war seizures, "forever free;" that the President might employ as many Negroes as he saw fit, and in such tasks as he deemed best; and that he might also colonize freedmen abroad.[10]

The bill came before the President in mid-July. Mr. Lincoln, of course, recognized that, with this act, Congress had directly challenged Presidential intentions to keep Executive control over the slavery issue. The President acknowledged the constitutionality of the act and that the Legislative Branch could "free a slave if that slave had been forfeited to the government by a traitor." President Lincoln, however, argued that his powers as Commander-in-Chief were larger than those of Congress with respect to the slavery question. He was also concerned about the mechanics of determining loyalty since the act only freed the slaves of those rebelling against national authority, but did not free the slaves of loyal citizens. In the end, however, the Chief Executive signed the bill, largely because of popular and political pressure. But Mr. Lincoln "never wavered in his belief that such vindictive measures should be avoided, for the nation must in time be restored as a truly fraternal union, a union of hearts, and he never abated his determination to keep the handling of slavery, which would lie at the core of national reconstruction, under his own control."[11]

The passage of the Second Confiscation Act, combined with the ever increasing pressure from individual members of the Republican Party, led President Lincoln to the inevitable conclusion that, if he did not achieve some immediate, even if limited success in implementing his gradual, compensated emancipation plan, he would have to abandon the effort or surrender leadership regarding the slavery issue to Congress. Consequently, he made his final, almost desperate appeal to the Border states. He noted that his policy had already given "dissatisfaction, if not offense, to many whose support the country cannot afford to lose. And this is not the end of it. The pressure is still upon me and is increasing." Appealing to the self-interest of the Border slaveowners, he noted that, if they hesitated, slavery would inevitably " 'be gone and you will have nothing in lieu of it. Much of its value is gone already! How much better for you, and for your people, to take the step which, at once, shortens the war, and secures substantial compensation for that which is sure to be wholly lost in any other event.' " Again, however, the President was to be disappointed as the Border leaders repeated the same arguments which the Chief Executive had heard since he first put forth the plan. Thus, with reluctance, Mr. Lincoln reconciled himself to defeat. As he looked back over his efforts, however, he probably reasoned that, "if Delaware had promptly accepted his proposal, selling her slaves for the $500,000 that Congress would have gladly distributed in bonds, the movement might have swept Missouri and Maryland along with it." But, alas, for better or worse, it was not to be.[12]

Meanwhile, during the late summer and autumn of 1861, as the President was contemplating the timing of his overture to Delaware and as the Northern people and politicians recovered from the shock and immediate panic following the disaster at Bull Run, there again rose throughout the North a demand for immediate action by the Federal authorities to crush the Southern rebellion. Mr. Lincoln, always sensitive to Northern public opinion, also advocated an early advance, in part to placate the Northern public and sustain morale. In addition, he continued to hope that a prompt, successful Union offensive would strengthen Southern moderates and enable them to displace the secessionists. His desire for action, however, was tempered by the experience of Bull Run. Not only did he recognize the importance of careful and complete preparation prior to any advance, a process then underway under General McClellan's guidance, Mr. Lincoln was also concerned about the Confederate capacity to suddenly concentrate dispersed forces by rail, as they had done at Bull Run, and defeat the advancing Union army. By late 1861-early 1862, however, the President concluded that the most effective counter to the threat of enemy concentrations was for all Union forces to advance simultaneously on all fronts. He reasoned that if several armies attacked Confederate held territory simultaneously, the Federals would possess a numerical advantage which would allow them to overwhelm the enemy on each line of advance. Should the Confederates utilize their advantageous interior lines of communications to concentrate their forces against any one of the advancing Union forces, the force against whom the concentration was directed could assume the defensive. Meanwhile, the other Union armies would have the opportunity to increase the speed of their advance, since they would be moving against an enemy force denuded of its strength in order to accomplish the concentration on another front.[13]

Building upon his recognition of the political importance of military action, as well as his conclusion that simultaneous advances were the best way to capitalize upon the Federal numerical advantage, while countering the Confederate advantage of interior lines of communications, President Lincoln, joined by General McClellan began to reformulate the national military strategy. The President and the General retained intact the maritime component of General Scott's original "anaconda plan." Indeed, the Washington high command reemphasized the strategy designed to cause the collapse of the rebellion by strangling the Confederacy into exhausted submission. Hence, Washington took steps to strengthen the heretofore ineffective naval blockade of the Southern coast, while, simultaneously, amplifying upon the continental component of General Scott's design for the limited territorial dismemberment of the Confederacy and the severance of the lines of communication between the Deep South and the trans-Mississippi states. In addition, it amplified upon the Presidentially ordered, but ill fated, Virginia offensive of July, 1861, which had been designed to more quickly trigger the collapse of the rebellion than Scott's plan, while, at the same time, boosting Northern popular morale and undermining the Confederacy's international standing. In the largest sense, however, the new Federal strategy continued to rest upon the assumption underpinning both the "anaconda plan" and the abortive Virginia offensive that escalating pressure, in the form of a series of successful, limited offensive operations by the Union forces, would eventually strengthen pro-Union moderates throughout the South and enable them to displace the secessionists and bring the South back into the Union. In brief, the Union high command now planned to launch a series of limited offensives onto Southern soil designed to seize specifically targeted geographic regions and centers which Washington felt were of strategic, logistical, economic, political, and/or psychological/symbolic significance to the Southerners. The President and General-in-Chief McClellan apparently still felt that the escalating pressure of the prompt seizure of such places, particularly when reinforced by the long-term threat posed by a reinvigorated Federal naval blockade of the Southern coastline, would strengthen pro-Union forces and enable them to displace the secessionists, thereby causing the collapse of the insurrection. The conquest of the Mississippi Valley, to which General Scott had attached exclusive continental priority in the original "anaconda plan," as well as the capture of the Confederate capital at Richmond, both of which the people of the North and their politicians attached importance to, were now only two of several places targeted by the high command. The capture of eastern Tennessee was now given increasing priority in Federal strategic planning since Union occupation of that region would liberate loyalist elements, contribute manpower to the Union cause, and cut the key rail line which traversed eastern Tennessee, linking Virginia with the Mississippi Valley. Indeed, the President hoped to encourage the pro-Union elements of north Georgia, east Tennessee and western North Carolina to make the region "a free mountain domain, a cancer in the Confederate vitals." Moreover, the capture of other strategically significant rail centers throughout the South also constituted important new targets in

the eyes of the Washington high command. In the trans-Mississippi portion of the Confederacy, the Federal leadership considered it important to secure complete Union control over
Missouri and, based upon a proposal by General McClellan, the
high command examined the possibility of launching an operation from Kansas southward toward Texas. Along the Southern
coast, the high command considered utilizing Union forces operating from the naval blockade bases to move inland and sever
those rail lines which ran close to the coastline. Moreover, since
several Southern port cities were obviously of considerable importance to the South and, hence, their capture and permanent
occupation by Federal forces would constitute a severe blow to
the Confederacy, these urban coastal centers became attractive
targets for Union amphibious operations. In addition, due to the
strategic location of many of these coastal cities, such as New
Orleans at the mouth of the Mississippi River, Union control
over these urban centers would facilitate efforts to capture those
adjacent regions deemed by Washington to be of significant
value to Richmond. Finally, in addition to contributing to implementation of the new high command's strategy of selectively
occupying Southern territory, the closure of the coastal ports
would significantly enhance the effectiveness of the Federal naval
efforts to deny the South access to the sea. In that way, the impact
of the loss of these population centers would be multiplied. General McClellan maintained that the main Federal effort should
be "made in the Virginia theater, with subsidiary operations
being conducted on the Mississippi and in Missouri and Tennessee." For General McClellan, the key target was the Confederate capital at Richmond. By contrast, Mr. Lincoln apparently
placed coequal emphasis on the conquest of the Mississippi, the
capture of eastern Tennessee, and the seizure of Richmond, although because of his proximity to the Virginia theater of operations, combined with his concern for the safety of the Federal
capital, the President gave disproportionate attention to the east.
As Allen Nevins noted,

> This was a grave error. The severest single stroke that could be dealt
> the Confederacy would be the seizure of the Mississippi Valley, sepa-
> rating Louisiana, Texas, and Arkansas from the rest of the South, and
> giving the Union the important railroad ganglia of Corinth, Jackson,

and Nashville. By comparison, a victory of McClellan in Virginia was unlikely to accomplish decisive results.[14]

Unfortunately, however, in their zeal to implement their national military strategy of simultaneously advancing on many fronts, dismembering the Confederacy, and selectively, but permanently occupying certain portions of Southern territory, both Mr. Lincoln and General McClellan tended to underestimate the logistical difficulties which their own armies would inevitably experience.[15]

As the Federal armies simultaneously moved toward these vital geographic regions and centers, they would, of course, encounter the defending Confederate field armies. As noted earlier, Mr. Lincoln recognized the political importance of successfully engaging the Confederate armies in battle, especially in the Virginia theater given the European, Northern, and Southern fixation on that area. He felt that battlefield engagements, even if militarily indecisive, were necessary to sustain Northern popular morale, retain support for the Administration's conduct of the war, undermine the Confederacy's effort to secure European diplomatic recognition and assistance, and enhance the political power of pro-Union moderates in the South, while, at the same time, undermining the prestige of the secessionist elements. By contrast, however, General McClellan attached little, if any, importance to these considerations in determining his operational plans. Indeed, he preferred to secure his military objective by maneuver and siegecraft, rather than by engaging the enemy in pitched battles, no matter how symbolically important. As T. Harry Williams noted, Mr. Lincoln,

> ... tried to impress on McClellan one of the great truths of war, especially of war waged by a democracy: that sometimes military movements have to be launched for political objectives, in this case, to sustain the Northern will to continue the war. What Lincoln was saying, with a special application to McClellan, was that unless a general did something to promise future victory, the people on whose support the war effort depended might become discouraged and give up the whole game. That is, without some action now there would be none later, no armies for McClellan or any general to lead, and no war. The relation between policy and war is one of the vital facts of war, especially of modern and democratic war.[16]

Moreover, General McClellan appears to have felt that the destruction of the principal Confederate field armies was not an absolute necessity for the collapse of the Confederacy. Rather, he seems to have concluded that the capture and permanent occupation of politically, strategically, logistically, economically, and/or psychologically and symbolically significant places, reinforced by the threatened strangulation effect of the Federal naval blockade, would themselves prove decisive and directly lead to the collapse of the Southern rebellion, irrespective of the continued existence of the Southern field armies. Conversely, General McClellan did not, at least initially, feel that the destruction of a well led, reasonably well equipped mid-nineteenth century field army was an impossibility. In short, as Russell Weigley observed,

> Though he had a hand in hastening Scott's retirement so he could become Commanding General himself, his military methods made McClellan more nearly the heir of Winfield Scott than any other general who followed in high command in the Union armies. Like Scott (during his celebrated campaign against Mexico City during the Mexican War) he hoped to reach his objective by maneuver rather than by fighting, and like Scott he chose a political objective, the enemy's capital city. He hoped that by capturing Richmond he would accomplish what Scott had done by capturing the City of Mexico, to convince the enemy of the military futility of the war, but without excessive bloodshed or bitterness.[17]

While General McClellan commented that " 'the war cannot be long, though it may be desperate,' " he also spoke of his desire to " 'crush the rebels in one campaign.' "[18]

Notwithstanding the growing impatience of the Northern public, the politicians, and even key members of the Lincoln Administration, including the President himself, the greatly anticipated simultaneous advances by the principal Union armies were postponed until the spring of 1862. The need for complete training, coordination, and good campaign weather all contributed to this postponement, but these considerations failed to satisfy the North's growing and increasingly vocal desire for the immediate suppression of the Southern rebellion. Although Mr. Lincoln recognized the need for complete preparation, he also continually emphasized that popular pressure for military action "was a real force and something that in a democracy the military had to take into account." When the principal armies did finally begin their advances during the spring, the field commanders in both the eastern and western theaters of operations opted for strategic turning movements.[19]

Meanwhile, throughout the winter of 1861-1862, as the main Federal armies prepared for their spring offensives, the Federal navy continued its effort to secure bases for its blockade operations along the Southern seacoast, as well as lay the groundwork for possible future inland operations. Following the fall of Port Royal, South Carolina in November, 1861, General McClellan considered launching an operation designed to seize Charleston, South Carolina, and Savannah, Georgia, as well as sever the coastal rail line connecting the south Atlantic states with Virginia. Although the chances of success were fairly good if the operation was quickly launched, ultimately, the operation was never undertaken. Meanwhile, in early February, 1862, a coordinated army-navy operation led by Major General Ambrose E. Burnside and Flag Officer Louis M. Goldsborough (Commander of the North Atlantic Blockading Squadron) was launched against Roanoke Island on the North Carolina coast. Reflecting the varying military/naval objectives sought by the controlling personalities involved,

> McClellan wanted Roanoke Island as a base of operations from which the Union could move against the Wilmington and Weldon railroad, but he needed naval cooperation to gain control of the sounds and the streams that led inland toward the railroad. Burnside agreed with this objective but also believed that the ultimate goal should be destruction of the Confederate forces in Virginia. To Goldsborough the island would provide a base to blockade the important interwater route to Norfolk. He realized the importance of the sounds, the Dismal Swamp, and the Albemarle and Chesapeake canals to Norfolk and southeastern Virginia.[20]

While the expedition did successfully take Roanoke Island and, subsequently, a considerable portion of eastern North Carolina, including New Bern and Fort Macon, was occupied, the railroad was neither cut, nor did the Union forces move resolutely against southeastern Virginia. Union control over the island, however, contributed to the Federal blockading effort and, further, contributed to the Confederate decision to abandon Norfolk in early May, 1862.[21]

Meanwhile, Fernandina, Florida was taken by Federal forces in mid-March and, on April 11, Fort Pulaski on the Georgia coast, several miles downriver from Savannah fell, although the city itself remained in Confederate hands until the end of 1864. Finally, most important of all, as a result of planning which had begun on November 15, 1861 in which the President had personally participated, on April 24, 1862, Federal warships successfully passed the Confederate held Forts Jackson and St. Philip near the mouth of the Mississippi, about seventy miles below New Orleans. Soon thereafter, the "Crescent City" fell to the Union forces. Indeed, "the fall of the largest port in the Confederacy was a severe blow, not only to its economic well-being but to the morale of the people at large." New Orleans soon became an important staging point for future Union operations in the Mississippi Valley.[22]

The Federal presence along the Southern coast, combined with the accompanying, though underused threat which that presence posed to coastal cities and areas inland, had a negative impact upon the morale of the Southern people, exacerbated internal Confederate tensions, and forced the Confederate high command to allocate valuable troops and scarce resources for coastal defense. Moreover, by early 1862, of the ten Southern seaports which possessed water or rail connections inland, six had been closed to Confederate shipping: New Orleans, Louisiana; Fernandina, Jacksonville, and Pensacola, Florida; Savannah, Georgia; and New Bern, North Carolina. Another, Norfolk, Virginia, would soon fall to the Union, leaving only three ports for use by the Confederates: Wilmington, North Carolina; Charleston, South Carolina; and Mobile, Alabama, all with relatively shallow harbors. The loss of these ports, combined with the establishment of Federal naval bases along the Southern coast, negatively impacted upon both the South's coastal maritime traffic, as well as its overseas trade. Yet, notwithstanding these important gains, the Federal naval blockade of the Southern coast remained far from effective in isolating the Confederacy from access to overseas commerce.[23]

Meanwhile, several considerations helped condition the Union line of advance west of the Appalachian Mountains. Geographically, there were five possible routes of advance into Confederate territory between the Appalachians and the Mississippi. Three were water routes: the Mississippi River itself, the Tennessee River, and the Cumberland River. These three routes possessed the enormously important asset of offering a relatively secure communications line for the advancing forces. The Tennessee was navigable to Muscle Shoals and, with high water, as far as Chattanooga. By contrast, however, the Cumberland was navigable only to Nashville.

> The Tennessee River, moreover, intersected the most important communication line between the Eastern and Western Confederacy, the Memphis and Charleston Railroad. This primary artery for traffic between the Mississippi and South Atlantic coast, running from Memphis east through southern Tennessee and northern Alabama, was cut or touched by the meandering river at several points. Gunboats with a few troops could disrupt it. They could also seal off Nashville, which lay on the Cumberland and was connected with the Memphis and Charleston by two railroads and a macadamized highway.[24]

The fourth line of operations was along the Louisville and Nashville Railroad and the Nashville and Chattanooga Railroad. From Chattanooga, a rail line passed through eastern Tennessee, connecting to Virginia, while another line went toward Atlanta and led to connections elsewhere throughout the Deep South. The fifth route followed the rail line southward from Columbus, Kentucky. In the trans-Mississippi area, however, the logistical opportunities were much less inviting. While the Federal forces possessed control of the Missouri River and the east-west railroad which ran north of the river, the rail lines which ran south and west from St. Louis extended for only a short distance. Beyond the terminal points of these lines, there were no clear avenues for movement southward. As will be seen, railroads proved to be significantly more vulnerable and, thus, inferior to rivers as dependable lines of communications for the advancing western armies.[25]

Of course, many of these avenues of approach into Confederate territory were blocked by the ill equipped, raw, undermanned, but enthusiastic Confederate forces, linked together by strategically located rail lines. For example, the Confederate forces held Columbus, Kentucky in considerable strength, thereby guarding the rail routes southward and blocking the Mississippi River. Similarly, Confederate forces located at Bowling Green, Kentucky blocked the Louisville and Nashville Railroad route. The vulnerable Forts Henry and Donelson guarded the Tennessee and Cumberland River approaches respectively. Finally, eastern Tennessee, an area of great importance in the strategic vision of the Federal high command, was relatively easy for the Confederates to defend because there were no logistically attractive avenues of approach from the Union controlled Ohio River.[26]

Another consideration affecting the Federal operational planning in the west in late 1861 and early 1862 was the divided command structure which had existed from the outset of the war. Since November 9, 1861, in the wake of the post Fremont command changes, Major General Henry W. Halleck commanded the Department of Missouri, encompassing the region from the Cumberland River westward, whereas on November 15, 1861, Major General Don Carlos Buell assumed command of the Department of the Ohio spanning the area from the Cumberland eastward to the Appalachian Mountains. The forty-six year old General Halleck entered the war with a national reputation as one of the United States' foremost military scholars. Totally devoid of the charismatic qualities abundantly possessed by the youthful, magnetic McClellan, General Halleck cut more the appearance of a university professor than a dashing military leader. General Grant characterized him as " 'a man of gigantic intellect and well studied in the profession of arms.' " Indeed, the General's record during the war testified to "his industry, understanding of general principles, and scholarly insight." Secretary of the Navy, Gideon Welles, however, provided an important, though somewhat harsh insight when he noted that the General " 'was a good scholarly critic of other men's deeds and ideas, but was incapable of originating or directing military operations himself. Excellent in grasp of theory, he was inert, muddy-headed, and erratic in action. He had an unmilitary cast of mind, and recoiled from direct control of armies.' " Even less generous were General Halleck's extreme critics who pronounced him to be "fussy, pedantic, and plodding," lacking "grasp and imagination," awkward, irresolute, confused, and timid. A graduate of West Point, General Halleck had served in

California with William T. Sherman during the Mexican War. He had been one of the key players in forming a civil government for California and had personally drafted much of its new constitution. Remaining in California following the war, he retired from the army and amassed a considerable personal fortune. Throughout, however, he continued his interest in the study of military science and history. General Halleck's prewar study of military science had led him to conclude that strategy should be seen as " 'the art of directing masses on decisive points.' " Consequently, General Halleck was initially derisive of the President's notions of simultaneous advances by all the Union armies as " 'hopeless military amateurism, because it ignored the indisputable maxim not to extend one's forces but to concentrate masses on decisive points.' " In General Halleck's eyes, decisive points were those geographic locations vitally necessary for the enemy to retain in order to sustain his war effort. Depreciating the necessity of destroying the enemy field armies, he believed that the war would be limited and the Confederacy would yield when the Union forces occupied those locations vital to the South. As such, like General McClellan, General Halleck did not feel that the destruction of the enemy field armies was a necessary prerequisite for victory. Rather, "the war might be won by the simple occupation of Confederate territory." In terms of theater operational planning and battlefield tactics, General Halleck, America's foremost student of Jomini, was thoroughly Jominian. Discussing this, his biographer, Stephen Ambrose, wrote,

> He learned that success in the art of war began with the choice of a base of operations. The ideal was an interior line of communications which emanated from a strong base and lay between the two wings of the enemy. From an interior line a soldier could, after the fashion of Frederick the Great, strike first one wing and then another before the enemy could join forces. Interior lines simplified supply and mobilization problems while facilitating concentration on the battlefield. And concentration, both strategically and tactically, was of primary importance to the Jominian system. The Swiss theorist stressed three basic principles, all of which revolved around the idea of concentration: The commander should bring his forces to bear on the decisive areas of the theater of war; strategically, he should manoeuvre to engage his masses against fractions of the enemy; tactically, he should attack with his masses against the decisive point on the battlefield.[27]

Finally, reflecting General Halleck's penchant for limited wars, the General entered the war with an "expressed distaste even for subsisting off the country, let alone spreading calculated ruin: 'The inevitable consequences of this system,' he said then, 'are universal pillage and a total relaxation of discipline; . . . and the ordinary peaceful and non-combatant inhabitants are converted into bitter and implacable enemies.' " As the war progressed, many of General Halleck's views would change, but in 1861 he was a very orthodox, classical military thinker. Concerning political issues, the General felt that, in a lengthy conflict particularly, Northern opinion would " 'become ultra anti-slavery, and . . . in the course of the war will declare for emancipation and thus add the horrors of a servile to that of a civil war.' " Hence, General Halleck felt that it was both politically, as well as strategically important for the Federals to hold the Border states. If they could be retained in the Union, " 'slavery will still be recognized and protected under the Constitution, and the door kept open for a compromise or reconstruction, if either should become possible.' " General Buell, akin to Generals McClellan and Halleck in his views on military strategy and operational planning, was a respected officer from the pre-war army, "austere, methodical, and painfully conscientious."[28]

The high command in Washington had directed General Halleck to consolidate Union control over Missouri and then prepare for an offensive down the Mississippi Valley. Meanwhile, from his new position as General-in-Chief, McClellan provided General Buell with guidance both as to the mission of his force and the direction of his advance. Despite General McClellan's acknowledgement that, under normal circumstances, General Buell would be expected to move along the Louisville and Nashville Railroad toward Nashville, both political and military considerations combined to make eastern Tennessee the priority target. While Mr. Lincoln emphasized the liberation of Union loyalists in that region, the General-in-Chief was particularly concerned that the railroad linking the western portion of the Confederacy with Virginia should be severed. This would prevent the Confederate authorities from moving troops from the west to Virginia in order to counter the Army of the Potomac's planned offensive against Richmond. Furthermore, Union possession of Knoxville would pose a threat to Virginia and, consequently, might force the Southerners to detach forces to protect Virginia's rear, thereby diluting the strength of their main body at Manassas.[29]

Although General Halleck, like General Buell, felt very uneasy about the division of Union command west of the Appalachians, he felt comfortable with both the Washington high command's overall national military strategy and the mission assigned to his forces. General Halleck felt that an offensive strategy, operating from a secure base with reliable lines of communications, designed to seize specific portions of Confederate territory, was an appropriate method for inducing the collapse of the rebellion. Thus, shortly after assuming command of the Union forces in the west, General Halleck began planning an advance up the Tennessee and Cumberland Rivers. Federal naval control over the rivers would provide the advancing Union forces with secure lines of communications back to their base of operations on the Ohio River. The immediate objective was the seizure of Forts Henry and Donelson on the lower Tennessee and Cumberland Rivers, respectively, and the severance of the strategically critical Memphis and Ohio Railroad. This, in turn, would deprive the defending Confederates of their strategically advantageous interior lines of communications before they could concentrate their forces to repel the advancing Union troops. The ultimate objective of the campaign, however, was the seizure of Nashville, Tennessee. The capture of the Tennessee capital would effectively turn the Southerners out of their positions at Bowling Green and Columbus, Kentucky. General Halleck also intended that another Union force would move into northwest Arkansas, while a third force moved against New Madrid and Island #10 on the Mississippi River. The General, however, felt that before he could advance southward across Kentucky into Tennessee, he had to have complete control over Missouri. The General lacked sufficient forces to commence two separate movements, one in Missouri and another up the Tennessee and Cumberland Rivers. Moreover, two separate advances conducted simultaneously within his department "would be on exterior lines, anathema to Jominian theory," and a violation of the principle of concentration of force.[30]

General Buell also recognized the promising strategic possibilities of a rapid Union advance up the Tennessee and Cumberland Rivers. Sadly for him, however, he also recognized that these inviting avenues were within General Halleck's department and outside his own. Within his own department, General Buell felt that the only practical avenue of advance was along the Louisville and Nashville Railroad to Bowling Green and thence to Nashville. An advance along this line, of course, would be rather slow due to the railroad destruction by the Confederates. As T. Harry Williams observed, after General Buell assumed command, he

> . . . saw rightly that he could not take East Tennessee by moving directly into it from the north. There were no railroads from his base at Louisville to the gaps opening into the mountains of East Tennessee; he would have to haul his supplies in wagons a long distance over poor roads. The logistics problem made it unlikely that Buell could get into the area or that if he got there, he could hold it. Buell presented McClellan a plan of his own to secure East Tennessee, a plan, in fact, to secure all Tennessee. He proposed simultaneous movements by his and Halleck's armies: Halleck to move from western Kentucky up the Tennessee and Cumberland rivers and Buell to move on Nashville. This would force the Confederates to fight or retreat. If they were defeated or forced out of their lines in Kentucky and Tennessee, the Confederates in East Tennessee would have to give up the region or be taken in flank. The Federals could walk in almost unopposed.[31]

The Washington high command, however, made clear their preference for a direct advance into east Tennessee over a movement toward Bowling Green. Characterizing Mr. Lincoln's reaction to General Buell's proposal, Professor Williams noted,

> Lincoln knew about Buell's desire to go after Nashville, but he understood that the General also intended a move into East Tennessee. Buell now told the President frankly that an advance on Knoxville would have to be entirely subordinate to an attack on the Confederate forces in his front. This announcement hit Lincoln hard. In a letter to Buell, he conceded that he was not competent to criticize the General's views, but said that he would rather have Knoxville than Nashville. Union seizure of Knoxville would cut an important artery of the enemy's communications, he contended, and free the loyalists of the mountains. Apparently Lincoln did not realize the comparative smallness of Buell's army, for he urged the General to attempt the impossible—advances against both Nashville and Knoxville.[32]

Shortly thereafter, on January 13, 1862, the President

> ... proposed that Halleck menace the Confederate forces in western
> Kentucky and on the Mississippi while Buell menaced those in eastern
> Kentucky and East Tennessee. The Confederates would have to weaken
> one point or another of their line and the Federals could break through
> the weakened point. We have the greater numbers, he told Buell, and
> we should threaten the enemy "with superior forces at different points
> at the same time. . . ."[33]

Hence, reluctantly, General Buell prepared to advance in two
directions, one in the direction which he preferred and another
toward Washington's priority target. Meanwhile, for the moment, General Halleck maintained that his forces were presently
able only to hold Missouri, but nothing more. He stated flatly
that "men could not be withdrawn from Missouri 'without risking the loss of the state.' " He stressed, however, that operations
west of the Appalachians could be better coordinated if they
were under one command rather than two.[34]

In mid-January, 1862, General Buell launched an advance toward eastern Kentucky and eastern Tennessee. Notwithstanding
the fact that his subordinate, General George H. Thomas, secured a victory at the Battle of Mill Springs, General Buell decided to suspend the advance in favor of his preferred movement
toward Bowling Green. This decision was due in large measure
to bad roads, but it deeply chagrined the high command, especially the President. Meanwhile, on January 20, having partially
secured the Union hold over Missouri, General Halleck submitted his plan for a general advance within his department to
General-in-Chief McClellan. As noted earlier, he advocated a
movement " 'up the Cumberland and Tennessee, making Nashville the first objective point,' " thereby forcing the Confederates
to evacuate Columbus and Bowling Green. Simultaneously, his
subordinate, Brigadier General John Pope would move against
New Madrid on the Mississippi. Finally, in Missouri, which General Halleck regarded as an independent theater of operations,
the Western Commander proposed sending a Union force toward
northeastern Arkansas, thereby severing the Confederate communications into Missouri and pushing the Southerners back
into Arkansas. The main effort for the proposed departmental
offensive was to be the operation on the lower Tennessee and

the Cumberland Rivers. Responding to inaccurate reports that the Confederates were heavily reinforcing western Kentucky and Tennessee, however, General Halleck decided to begin his campaign before he was completely ready. In an effort to strike before the Southern reinforcements could arrive, on February 1, 1862, General Halleck ordered Brigadier General Ulysses S. Grant to launch a quick coordinated naval and land assault to seize Forts Henry and Donelson and break the Memphis and Ohio Railroad. The tenacious, tough Grant proved to be an excellent choice to command the operation because, not only did he anticipate and fully support the planned operation, he would soon build a military reputation as a general willing to fight. On February 6, 1862, Fort Henry fell to General Grant's expeditionary force and, immediately thereafter, General Grant cut the Memphis and Ohio where it crossed the Tennessee, thereby severing the Confederates interior communications lines in western Kentucky and Tennessee. Then, on his own initiative, he moved immediately against Fort Donelson on the Cumberland which Generals Grant and Halleck appear to have viewed "as just part of the mopping-up process." Notwithstanding these early successes, however, General Halleck "remained apprehensive." He was concerned that the Southerners would immediately send massive reinforcements to Fort Donelson. A reinforced garrison at Donelson would occupy a "flank position," with secure lines of communications south via the Cumberland to Nashville. To help counter this threat, the Western Department Commander began reinforcing General Grant's army with troops from Missouri, Kansas, and Illinois. Indeed, he wanted to concentrate all available Union reinforcements, including General Buell's army, around General Grant's force on the Tennessee. General Buell, however, opted to continue his movement toward Bowling Green. Halleck denounced this as an operation which would be too slow to counterbalance the risk of a Confederate concentration against General Grant. In addition, the scholarly Halleck denounced Buell's insistence on maintaining his advance toward Bowling Green as an example of the theoretically inferior exterior line of communications type operation in which the two attacking forces, Grant's and Buell's, would be out of immediate touch with each other. This, in turn, would invite the enemy to concentrate against one force and then, after defeating that force, concentrate against the other. The President agreed with General Halleck.[35]

Despite the South's decision to evacuate Bowling Green and to send some reinforcements to Fort Donelson, while withdrawing the remainder to Nashville, the disagreement between Generals Halleck and Buell was postponed by the rapid fall of Fort Donelson on February 16, 1862.[36] With the fall of Fort Donelson, the Confederates lost over one quarter of their western army. Moreover, the fall of the fort was quickly followed by a second severance of the Memphis and Ohio Railroad, this time at the point where it crossed the Cumberland River, as well as the evacuation of Nashville on February 23. Thus, by late February, due in large measure to General Halleck's operational planning and the field initiative of General Grant, General Buell's forces were able to occupy the Tennessee capital, while those of General Grant held a line from Fort Henry to Clarksville, Tennessee. Farther to the west, along the Mississippi, shortly after the fall of Fort Donelson, the Confederates evacuated Columbus, Kentucky and on March 13, New Madrid fell to Union forces. Following his capture of New Madrid, the Federal commander, General Pope, moved against the next Southern stronghold on the great river, Island #10. In short, assessing the Federal position at this point, Allen Nevins observed,

> All Kentucky now seemed safe in Union hands, the Mississippi was open as far as Island No. 10 on the Kentucky-Tennessee border, and strong Union forces stood in central Tennessee. They held not only the rich manufacturing center of Nashville, with its flour mills, foundries, leather tannery, powder mill, and field-gun shop, but most of the Memphis branch of the Louisville & Nashville Railroad . . .[37]

Moreover, the Federals had forged the river fleets with which to further prosecute the war. Finally, the Union forces now held the strategic advantage of occupying a solid central position separating the two elements of the Confederacy's western forces.[38]

In this context, however, Generals Buell and Halleck soon resumed their disagreement concerning theater operations. The former preferred to concentrate both his own and General Grant's forces at Nashville and move immediately against the

Confederates located southeast of the Tennessee capital before they could be reinforced by Confederate forces from the Mississippi Valley and/or the Deep South. Conversely, the latter preferred to concentrate the Union forces around General Grant on the Tennessee, cut the Memphis and Charleston Railway east of Corinth, Mississippi, and destroy the key railhead at Corinth. Here, the Memphis and Charleston, the South's principal east-west artery, intersected the Mobile and Ohio Railroad. In short, if the Federals destroyed Corinth, they would sever the main rail tie linking the two separate elements of the Confederate army in the west, thereby forcing the defending Southerners to stand and fight in isolation or withdraw toward the Gulf of Mexico. Finally, General Halleck intended that Grant's force should destroy the rail heads at Humboldt and Jackson, Tennessee, both north of Corinth. While General Halleck favored the eventual permanent occupation of the area between the Tennessee and the Mississippi, for the moment he wanted to pursue a more limited goal. As Bruce Catton wrote, for the present, the expedition envisioned for General Grant's force

> . . . was to be a raid, pure and simple; at all costs Grant must avoid an engagement with superior forces, and it would be better to retreat than to risk a general battle. Having broken the railroads, Grant was to re-concentrate at Danville and was to move off toward the town of Paris, Tennessee, which lay west of the river on the line of the railroad running up from Memphis to the Tennessee River crossing.[39]

Later, however, the General expanded his plan to permanently occupy Corinth, thus transforming a raid into a penetration. Unable to agree upon a common course of action, the two generals began to implement their respective plans with the forces available within their own departments. General Buell advanced southeastward, away from General Halleck's forces, whereas General Halleck ordered his troops on the Tennessee/Cumberland River line to move directly southward, up the Tennessee, toward the Memphis and Charleston Railway. The General-in-Chief, George McClellan, approved the plans of both his western subordinates. Meanwhile, the Confederates, capitalizing upon their interior lines of communications, concentrated most of their troops in the western theater at Corinth in preparation for a counteroffensive. Notwithstanding their resolve to counter General Halleck's move south, however, they left a series of isolated strongholds garrisoned along the Mississippi River. This influenced Halleck to retain a large body of troops in the Mississippi Valley. The General remained anxious to take these strongholds and establish a permanent Union presence along the great river as far south as possible. His resolve to clear the Mississippi Valley, however, deprived the Tennessee River expedition of needed reinforcements.[40]

On March 11, 1862, President Lincoln made a series of important command changes. On that day, the President removed General McClellan from the position of General-in-Chief of the United States Army, while retaining him as the Commander of the Army of the Potomac. In addition, he placed General Halleck in command of the entire western theater of operations. The President decided not to immediately name a successor to General McClellan as General-in-Chief, opting instead to himself serve in that capacity on a de-facto basis for the next four months. Consequently, between March and July, 1862, the President, assisted by the Secretary of War, personally assumed responsibility for directing the Union armies in the field. In effect, this gave General Halleck a free hand in the west, responsible only to the general directives of the President.[41]

In his new capacity, General Halleck immediately ordered General Buell to leave a holding force in middle Tennessee and concentrate his forces with the main body of General Grant's Tennessee River expedition located at Pittsburg Landing, only about twenty miles from Corinth. Anticipating a very large battle against the Confederate forces concentrating at Corinth, the new Western Commander wanted an overwhelming force available for the expected, hopefully decisive confrontation. Hence, General Halleck directed the Tennessee River expedition to assume the defensive until it could be reinforced by General Buell's forces. Halleck emphasized, " 'My instructions not to advance so as to bring on an engagement must be strictly obeyed. . . . we must strike no blow until we are strong enough to admit no doubt of the results.' " On April 6, 1862, however, the Southerners launched a surprise attack against General Grant's army with their concentrated forces. Fortunately for the Union cause, at the time of the Confederate attack, General Buell's army was only seven miles away from General Grant's encampment. Caught offguard, General Grant quickly regained his balance and, with the help of reinforcements from General Buell, drove the Southerners from the field the following day. Unpursued, the Confederate force retreated to Corinth, a location which the Southern commander regarded as "the key to the war in the West because, 'if defeated here, we lose the Mississippi Valley and probably our cause.' " That same day, the Confederates suffered another reversal, this one in the Mississippi Valley, as General Pope's forces took Island #10, just below the Tennessee-Kentucky state line. Not only did this action open the Mississippi almost to Memphis, it effectively released troops which were quickly ordered to join Generals Grant and Buell on the banks of the Tennessee. Finally, on March 7, in Arkansas, the Union army defeated the Confederates at the Battle of Pea Ridge in the northwest corner of the state, thus further consolidating the Federal hold over Missouri.[42]

General Halleck now, for the first time, personally took field command over the advancing Union forces and directed the meticulous advance upon the Confederate railhead at Corinth. The General's focus remained the severance of the Memphis and Charleston Railroad and the permanent occupation of Corinth, not the destruction of the Confederacy's western army. Recognizing the futility of battle with such an overwhelmingly large Union force, the Southerners deceptively withdrew from the city on May 29-30. Although undramatic, the capture of Corinth marked the culmination of the first phase of the war in the West. The Confederates had been driven out of Kentucky and much of Tennessee. Not only had they been deprived of the resources of the region, the loss of middle Tennessee and the politically, administratively, logistically, defense industrially, and psychologically/symbolically important city of Nashville constituted a severe reversal for the authorities in Richmond. Furthermore, the loss of the strategically significant Memphis and Charleston Railroad, characterized as the " 'vertebrae of the Confederacy,' " very severely complicated the Confederacy's ties with the states

of the trans-Mississippi West. Indeed, the capture of New Orleans and Memphis by Federal naval forces in late April and
early June, respectively, left the Confederates with control over
only a small portion of the river and made their links with the
trans-Mississippi states " 'little more than theory.' " Finally,
once taken and fortified, Corinth would shield the Union efforts
to consolidate its hold over western Tennessee, while, simultaneously, like New Orleans and Memphis, providing an important
staging area and base for future Union operations against the
Confederates in the west. In short, although no longer the Washington high command's top priority, General Halleck's campaign
had greatly contributed to the attainment of General Scott's goal
of establishing permanent Union control over the Mississippi
and severing the Confederacy's internal lines of communications. Much of General Halleck's and General Grant's success,
however, was attributable to the availability of strategically located water lines of communications which, in turn, provided
the advancing Union forces with secure avenues for offensive
operations deep within the interior of the western Confederacy.
As the war continued, the opportunities for the Union forces to
utilize secure water lines of communications would diminish,
forcing them to rely upon alternative lines, especially railroads.
As experience would show, maintaining secure access to rail lines
of communications would become an overwhelming problem for
Union commanders.[43]

Following the fall of Corinth and the capture of Memphis,
many Union officers in the western theater were eager to continue the advance down the Mississippi Valley or to move upon
Chattanooga. Moreover, many felt that General Halleck's army
group should have energetically and relentlessly pursued the
Confederates as they retired to Tupelo, Mississippi. These officers looked forward to the prospect of decisively defeating the
Southerners in a battle of annihilation. General Halleck, however, rejected the idea of launching an immediate campaign in
northern Mississippi designed to destroy the retreating Confederate army. Halleck told his subordinates, " 'there is no object
in bringing on a battle if this object can be obtained without
one. I think by showing a bold front for a day or two the enemy

will continue his retreat, which is all I desire.' " He rejected the idea of a vigorous pursuit and a showdown battle, in part, because of logistical difficulties and the summer heat, but also because his whole approach to strategy depreciated the importance of destroying the enemy field armies as the precondition for final victory. Instead, General Halleck felt that the key to victory was the seizure of those geographic locations vital to the enemy and the conquest of his territory. Hence, the General opted not to hound the enemy army until it was destroyed, but rather to allow it to escape and, instead, consolidate the Union hold over its "conquest," while, at the same time, carefully preparing for the next phase of the war—further seizures of important geographical locations in the western theater. Consequently, General Halleck sent part of his consolidated army group west to establish communications with the recently captured city of Memphis. Halleck anticipated that naval forces, operating from New Orleans and Memphis, would soon complete the Union conquest of the Mississippi. Meanwhile, another portion of Halleck's army group, under the command of General Buell, was ordered to move eastward, along the Memphis and Charleston Railroad, rebuilding the railway as they advanced, intersect the Union forces which had already moved south from Nashville and held positions in middle Tennessee and extreme northern Alabama, and capture Chattanooga. The General reasoned that the capture of that city would inhibit a concentration of the Confederate forces in Mississippi and those located in eastern Tennessee. Indeed, if he had acted aggressively, General Buell's central position between the two enemy forces might have allowed him to have defeated each in turn. Moreover, General Halleck, erroneously in view of the existence of rail links to Virginia, felt that the Union occupation of Chattanooga would turn the Southerners out of east Tennessee. Of course, any movement aimed at the liberation of east Tennessee always elicited approval from the President. Finally, the occupation of Chattanooga would open the way for another campaign against another significant location—Atlanta. The portion of General Halleck's army group under the command of General Grant was assigned responsibility for guarding against a repeated Southern offensive from northern Mississippi. Finally, the Federal forces in the trans-Mississippi region were reinforced and ordered to consolidate Union control over northern Arkansas.[44]

As these events were occurring inland, on the Mississippi, immediately following the capture of New Orleans by Federal naval forces in the April, the Navy Department decided to send warships up the river to seize the remainder of the Mississippi Valley. Hence, in May, Federal ships ascended the river, captured Baton Rouge, but failed in their attempt to capture the strategic river city of Vicksburg, Mississippi. Consequently, they withdrew back downriver at the end of the month. In June, the ships of the West Gulf command returned to Vicksburg for another attempt, this time joined in late June by the upper Mississippi River flotilla, operating from the recently captured city of Memphis. Like the first operation, however, the second attempt by the Federal navy to take Vicksburg failed and the city remained in Confederate hands. Following the Union withdrawal downriver, the Southerners reoccupied Baton Rouge.[45]

Meanwhile, as the Union armies in the West were seizing Kentucky, as well as middle and western Tennessee, the President and many moderates, to say nothing of the Radicals, were becoming extremely impatient for a Union advance in Virginia. Mr. Lincoln favored an early southward overland advance against the Confederate forces located at Manassas, Virginia. He felt that such an advance had the advantage of protecting Washington, irrespective of whether the Union army met victory or defeat on the battlefield. Of course, Mr. Lincoln earnestly hoped for an overwhelming victory over the Southerners since he apparently still believed that such a victory in Virginia would not only bolster Northern morale, but, in addition, it would strengthen Unionist elements in the South, discredit the secessionists, and possibly prove decisive in causing the collapse of the Confederacy. While he initially considered the possibility of an advance along the lines suggested by the President, the Commander of the Army of the Potomac, General McClellan, felt very apprehensive about frontally assaulting an entrenched army, particularly since the General greatly exaggerated the size of the Southern force. Moreover, he reasoned that, even if the

Army of the Potomac successfully defeated the Confederates at Manassas, the Southerners would probably retreat southward and secure a new position, leaving the Federal army in possession of only the battlefield and the upper Potomac. Therefore, while General McClellan acknowledged the important psychological/symbolic effect of a field victory over the Southern forces near Washington, he emphasized that such a victory would be indecisive. It would neither ensure the destruction of the enemy army, nor, in itself, ensure the capture of Richmond. The Confederates, in a new position, but still with their backs to their own communications would have to be attacked again, perhaps several more times, until they could be forced back into the entrenchments around their capital. During the siege operations which would necessarily follow, the Army of the Potomac would invariably have to depend upon the James and York Rivers to provide the besieging force with a dependable channel of supplies. According to T. Harry Williams, what McClellan "wanted to do was to capture Richmond without fighting a battle, although his military sense should have told him that the occupation of the Confederate capital without defeating the Confederate army would be a barren achievement."[46]

Having rejected the idea of a frontal move against Manassas, General McClellan proposed an alternative plan based upon a surprise strategic turning movement designed to penetrate the Confederate rear. The General proposed to move the Army of the Potomac by water down the Potomac River, into the Chesapeake Bay, and then land it near the mouth of the Rappahannock River or at Fort Monroe at the mouth of the James. He would then move quickly inland and either take a position astride the Confederate line of communications between their main body at Manassas and their principal base at Richmond, or move directly upon Richmond, before the Confederates could retire from their advanced position in northern Virginia and concentrate their forces in defense of their capital. Since the Federal line of communications would be securely drawn from the sea, protected by Federal naval superiority, the proposed strategic turning movement would constitute a penetration, not a raid. In addition to secure communications, General Mc-

Clellan maintained that the proposed line of advance was much shorter than the overland route and would traverse terrain more favorable from the Union perspective. The General's proposed operation was, in many respects, similar to General Scott's campaign against Mexico City during the Mexican War, a decade and a half earlier, in which young McClellan, then a lieutenant, had participated. Like Scott, McClellan directed his campaign against the enemy's political capital. General McClellan apparently hoped that by seizing Richmond, he could replicate the impact of General Scott's capture of Mexico City and convince the enemy that additional resistance was futile, while, simultaneously, keeping casualties and bitterness on both sides to a minimum. Moreover, like Scott, McClellan intended to capitalize upon the Federal naval superiority to seize the element of surprise, amphibiously land troops, and thereby strategically turn the enemy position to the north. General McClellan's plans, however, had the advantage of placing Federal troops in a position to move quickly to sever the enemy line of communications and/or capture the enemy capital. But, unlike Scott's Mexico City campaign, the close proximity and direction of the Virginia rivers would enable the Union army to continue to securely draw supplies from the sea even after moving inland. Federal naval superiority along the Virginia rivers would also be operationally advantageous in that McClellan could use that superiority to amphibiously land additional troops behind the enemy lines and, thereby, tactically turn enemy defensive positions as the Army of the Potomac advanced inland. Likewise, General McClellan's proposed operation was similar to General Halleck's use of secure water communications to penetrate up the Tennessee and Cumberland Rivers and strategically turn the Confederates out of their positions at Columbus, Kentucky to the west, as well as middle Kentucky and Tennessee to the east.[47]

The Commander of the Army of the Potomac maintained that, under his plan, the Confederates would either be forced to abandon northern Virginia and retreat south via the roundabout route of the Shenandoah Valley or assume the tactical offensive and fight the Army of the Potomac in a position selected by the Federals. General McClellan felt confident that, through his plan, the Federals would acquire the territory between Washington and Richmond, as well as capture the city of Richmond before the Confederates could fall back from their forward position at Manassas to protect it. If, however, the Confederates anticipated the Federal penetration to cut their communications and quickly withdrew their forces to protect Richmond, General McClellan intended to lay siege to the city from the east or perhaps move to the south side of the James River and operate against the city from the south. He felt confident that eventually, as Federal pressure against Richmond mounted, the Confederates would be forced either to assume the tactical offensive and attack the Army of the Potomac in a Federally selected defensive position or abandon the city. In any case, General McClellan was confident that Richmond would fall. In losing Richmond, the Confederates would not only suffer the loss of their capital, given its significance as a communications, defense industrial, and supply center, its loss would constitute a severe material blow to the Southern war effort. Moreover, Richmond was rapidly assuming enormous psychological/symbolic importance in the eyes of both the Northern and Southern people, as well as to the European powers. Hence, its capture would yield disproportionately large political dividends for the Union cause. Geographically, the loss of Richmond would confirm Federal control over the Chesapeake Bay and Hampton Roads and possibly force the Confederates to abandon Virginia entirely. In short, General McClellan felt that his proposed strategic turning movement and penetration would yield precisely the type of decisive victory necessary to force the collapse of the Confederacy.[48]

The President appreciated the attractive military possibilities offered by a well executed penetration of the enemy rear, the severance of his lines of communications, and/or the capture of his capital. In reacting to General McClellan's plan, however, Mr. Lincoln was very uneasy concerning the fact that, when the Army of the Potomac left northern Virginia and moved south by water to strategically turn the Confederates, it would be beyond supporting distance to defend the Federal capital. Given that, the President feared that the Southern army might utilize its interior position and move directly upon Washington from its advanced position at Manassas near the Federal capital. General McClellan responded that, should the Confederates move against Washington, the capital's defenses were quite adequate to repel the attack. Meanwhile, by opting to attack Washington, the Southerners would forfeit Richmond to the Army of the Potomac. Even in the unlikely event that the Confederates were successful in seizing the Federal city, the occupation would necessarily be temporary, since the Army of the Potomac blocked their line of supply. Hence, they would soon be forced to abandon their raid on Washington, retreat up the Shenandoah Valley, abandoning eastern Virginia in the process. Conversely, with a water line of communications, General McClellan argued that the Army of the Potomac's own line of communications would be secure and the Federal occupation of Richmond would be permanent. Mr. Lincoln undoubtedly recognized that any Confederate seizure of Washington would be temporary, but he remained extremely worried about the political/psychological impact which even a brief Southern raid would have upon Southern and Northern public opinion, as well as the diplomatic position of the United States vis-a-vis the Confederacy abroad. In the largest sense, however, notwithstanding the theoretical correctness of General McClellan's viewpoint, the Commander of the Army of the Potomac clearly failed to allay the President's fears with the convincing reassurance that his proposed strategic turning movement would be executed with such swiftness as to allow the Federals to retain the initiative once it had been seized and, thereby, justify the risks inherently associated with an exterior lines operation like the one proposed.[49]

Finally, on March 8, 1862, after a great deal of discussion at the high command level, the President, with great reluctance, conditionally authorized General McClellan to begin implementing his proposed strategic turning movement no later than March 18. Mr. Lincoln qualified his approval by directing, in part, that the security of Washington be guaranteed by retaining a sufficiently large Federal force in the capital region. In this way, the President hoped to reduce the risks inherent in General McClellan's planned operation. On March 17, 1862, as the Confederate forces in the west began massing at Corinth, Mississippi for their attack upon the Union army at Pittsburg Landing, the first units of the Army of the Potomac left Alexandria for Fort Monroe, Virginia. General McClellan opted to land his forces at Fort Monroe in response to a Confederate redeployment from their advanced position at Manassas to a new position behind the Rappahannock River in early March. Although the General would now be unable to reach the Southern rear and position his army between the Confederates in northern Virginia and Richmond as he had originally planned, the Army of the Potomac Commander now intended to move his forces quickly up the peninsula between the York and James River and lay siege to Richmond. While denied access to the James due to the Confederate naval presence at Norfolk, the Union army did possess a secure line of communications along the York River and, hence, General McClellan decided to use the York as his primary line of supply as he ascended the peninsula. Finally, following the Confederate withdrawal from Manassas, the President ordered McClellan to leave behind sufficient forces to hold Manassas (as well as protect the capital) before moving his army to the peninsula.[50] Discussing McClellan's operational plan, Professors Beringer, Hattaway, Jones, and Still commented,

Seemingly McClellan would only have transferred the stalemate from the vicinity of Washington to that of Richmond. This change would, of course, give a significant psychological advantage to the Union, but what other success did it promise? The Union would have to besiege; but such a siege could not starve out the city because its extensive rail network could readily supply both the city and its defending army, a network McClellan could not possibly interdict from his Peninsula position. But the Union forces could conduct a traditional siege, digging diagonal trenches to provide protected approaches, and they could demolish the Confederate defenses systematically with vast quantities of artillery. This form of warfare the engineer-trained West Point graduates understood entirely and McClellan knew perhaps best of all, for he had observed the successful Anglo-French siege of the Crimean city of Sebastopol. The Union could expect to win such a campaign of material, just as the French and British had prevailed over the Russians after an eleven-month siege. Moreover, McClellan correctly believed that the Confederates would feel compelled to respond to this menace to their capital by taking the offensive against his army on the Peninsula. McClellan would then have gained one of the principal advantages of the turning movement, forcing the enemy to assume the tactical offensive against his prudently selected and prepared position. Of course, victory would give him no chance to trap the Confederate army, but even Napoleon had entrapped enemy armies on only two occasions.[51]

On April 1, 1862, a little less than a week before the Confederate surprise attack upon General Grant's Tennessee River expedition in the west, General McClellan, personally, left for Fort Monroe. By April 3, however, the high command back in Washington, encouraged by the General's enemies, concluded that he had not left a sufficiently large Union force in northern Virginia to protect Washington. Hence, the high command detained the Army of the Potomac's First Corps and redeployed it immediately north of Fredericksburg, Virginia in order to cover the Washington area. This, in turn, disrupted General McClellan's plans to move his main body directly upon the Confederate defenses stretching from Yorktown, on the York River, to the James, while, simultaneously, sending the First Corps up the York River, in an effort to turn the Confederate defenses. Without the missing corps, however, the cautious McClellan decided not to assault the Confederate defenses directly, opting instead to initiate siege operations. Given his numerical superiority at the outset of the siege, General McClellan probably should have attempted to smash his way through the Confederate line. During the month long siege, the Northern people, their political leaders, and the members of the Administration, including the President, became increasingly impatient for action and disgusted with what they felt was General McClellan's overcaution. Indeed, this resentment was increasingly generalized to all West Point trained professionals. In addition to emphasizing the political necessity for aggressive action, the President stressed that retention of the initiative was necessary to complement the simultaneous advance of the Union forces toward Corinth, Mississippi in the west. Meanwhile, the Confederates made use of the time to move their principal army in northern Virginia to the peninsula, east of Richmond, to meet the Army of the Potomac. Finally, in early May, fearing the possibility of a Federal amphibious landing behind their lines, the Confederates decided to abandon their position and, following an action at Williamsburg, withdrew up the peninsula.[52] Evaluating the initial phase of the Peninsular Campaign, Warren Hassler argued,

The decision of the Union government to withhold the First Corps from McClellan was a vital one for the Federal effort in 1862. . . . (Had it) not been detained, the Confederates would not have been given forty-five days in which to concentrate troops from all over Virginia and the South for a desperate defense of their capital. These six-odd weeks gave Lee and Davis time to assemble the largest Southern army ever marshaled during the war, and thus enabled Lee, in the decisive battles in front of Richmond, for the only time in the war, to confront the Federals with approximately equal numbers.[53]

General McClellan, now erroneously convinced that he faced an enemy of much greater size than his own Army of the Potomac, appealed to the Washington high command for reinforcements as he slowly pursued the Confederates up the peninsula. He anticipated a " 'decisive battle' " somewhere near Richmond and wanted his army to be at the maximum strength. By May 17, he reached a position immediately east of Richmond astride the swampy, soon to be swollen, and difficult to traverse Chickahominy River: two corps on the southwest side of the river and three corps northeast of the river. The Army of the Potomac remained in this awkward position until May 31 when the Confederates attacked the two corps located on the southwestern side of the Chickahominy. The General's decision to deploy his army in such a dangerous way was based on a series of considerations. First, his decision to push two corps across the river was, at least in part, based upon his desire to respond positively to the Administration's constant pressure for forward movement. Conversely, his decision to deploy his remaining three corps northeast of the river was based, in part, on his desire to draw supplies along the Richmond and York River Railroad line which extended from his supply depot at White House on the Pamunkey River, a tributary of the York. Given the Confederate evacuation of Norfolk on May 9-10 and the establishment of Federal naval control over the James to within a few miles of Richmond, however, General McClellan could have shifted his principal line of communications to the James River. He later claimed he wanted to do precisely that, but he was constrained by another factor. On May 17, the Washington high command informed the General that the First Corps, originally detained to help ensure the safety of Washington, would move overland, southward toward Richmond beginning on May 26 and, thereby, reinforce General McClellan's force, while, simultaneously, remaining capable of protecting the national capital. Hence, the Administration ordered General McClellan to extend his right wing north of Richmond to affect the juncture with the force advancing southward. General McClellan's pattern of deployment along the Chickahominy remains one of the greatest controversies of the entire war.[54]

Equally controversial was President Lincoln's decision on May 24, immediately prior to the scheduled departure of the First Corps overland toward its planned rendezvous with McClellan's force, to divert it to the Shenandoah Valley where it was to act in concert with other independently commanded Union forces to counter a Confederate diversionary movement in the area. The Confederates had reasoned that a sudden offensive against the Union forces in the Shenandoah Valley would cause the Federal high command to panic for the safety of Washington and lead them to detain the planned reinforcements for General McClellan's force. The Confederate diversion was successful in the sense that the Administration did halt the planned movement of reinforcements, opting instead to move them to the Valley. But, while there was panic in Washington at the news of the Confederate offensive in the Shenandoah and great excitement throughout the North, the Federal high command's decision was not motivated by panic, although concern for the national capital's safety was a consideration. Instead, the high command's decision to divert troops to the Valley reflected a desire to destroy the Confederate Valley force. Then, after completing this mission, the high command intended to return to its original plan and dispatch these forces to the Richmond area to help McClellan. Washington's plans to destroy the Confederate forces in the Valley, however, proved to be overambitious and the Southerners eluded destruction. Meanwhile, notwithstanding the diversion of the reinforcements whose route of transit had earlier necessitated the extension of the Union right wing north of Richmond, and despite the General's subsequent assertions that he would have preferred to have changed his base from the headwaters of the York River to the James, the Commander of the Army of the Potomac maintained his dangerous pattern of deployment astride the Chickahominy. Arguing that General McClellan was still required to keep forces on both sides of the Chickahominy even after the First Corps had been temporarily diverted to the Shenandoah Valley, Warren Hassler quoted General McClellan as stating, " 'that the order for the cooperation' " of the First Corps " 'was simply suspended, not revoked, and therefore I was not at liberty to abandon the northern approach.' " Transforming a dangerous situation into the setting for a potential disaster, on the night of May 30, a "furious rainstorm" hit the Richmond area. Describing the storm and its implications, Dr. Hassler has noted,

> It was the most savage storm that officers on both sides had ever seen. The terrible torrent and rising water endangered McClellan's bridges over the Chickahominy, threatening momentarily to sweep all of them away. If this happened, the two wings of his army would be isolated, thereby preventing him from reinforcing either wing if it were attacked in overwhelming numbers.[55]

Then, on May 31, the day after the Union occupation of Corinth, Mississippi, the enterprising Southerners took advantage of their successful diversionary operation in the Shenandoah Valley and attacked the two corps of the Army of the Potomac located on the southwest side of the Chickahominy. Fortunately for the Union cause, the Confederate attack was poorly managed and failed to dislodge the Northern troops.[56]

On June 8, after it became clear to the high command in Washington that it would be unable to destroy the Confederate forces in the Valley, the troops originally scheduled to reinforce General McClellan's army were ordered to resume their overland march and join the Army of the Potomac at the eastern gates of Richmond. Due to a variety of factors, however, most of this force was destined never to join McClellan's army near the Confederate capital. Meanwhile, however, the prospect of reinforcements approaching overland from the north, combined with the necessity to protect the army's lines of communications back to the Pamunkey, forced McClellan to retain one of his five corps northeast of the Chickahominy. Two other corps had been moved to the other side of the river to join the two corps which were already located there. Concurrently, by mid-June, General McClellan had begun to make contingency preparations for the establishment of a new supply base on the James should the line to the Pamunkey become untenable. By June 26, the President decided to unify the various independent commands operating in northern Virginia to form the Army of Virginia under the command of Major General John Pope from the western theater. As T. Harry Williams pointed out, "Pope had many of McClellan's faults in reverse. He was aggressive where McClellan was timid, rash were McClellan was cautious. Like McClellan, he could not judge realities. McClellan magnified dangers, Pope minimized or did not see them." Politically, General Pope was also General McClellan's opposite. While refraining from provocative comments concerning the definition of Federal war objectives, Pope advocated abandonment of the Administration's "soft war," conciliatory policies in favor of the "application of the harsh hand of war," designed, in turn, to "undermine the Southern will to remain out of the Union." In other words, in stark contrast to George McClellan and Henry Halleck, John Pope felt that punishment of Southern society, not just the seizure of key locations, should become a component of Union strategy. Soon after taking command of the Army of Virginia, Pope issued a series of harsh orders which clearly escalated the tone of the Union war effort in the east. Order Number 5 directed the troops of the Army of Virginia to,

> . . . subsist as far as possible on the country, giving vouchers for supplies taken; the vouchers to be payable at the end of the war, and then only if the owners proved they had been consistently loyal since the date of receipt. Order No. 6 declared that cavalry should dispense with supply trains and levy on the localities traversed for their needs. Order No. 7 notified the people of Northern Virginia that they would be held responsible for guerrilla outrages. If any railways, roads, or telegraphs were damaged, the inhabitants within a radius of five miles should be turned out to repair them, while any person detected in firing on Union soldiers from a house should be shot without civil process. Five days later Pope issued his still more draconian General Order No. 11. This required officers to arrest immediately all disloyal citizens of Virginia within reach, to give them a choice of taking the oath of allegiance or accepting deportation to the South, to treat all who returned across the line as spies subject to the death penalty, and to shoot all who violated their oath of allegiance.[57]

Notwithstanding the contradiction between General Pope's orders and his mild war policies, as well as the dubious legality of Order Number 11, the President did not countermand the new orders. The mission of General Pope's Army of Virginia was to shield the national capital from attack, defend the Shenandoah Valley and West Virginia, and operate in a southwesterly direction from Washington, toward Gordonsville, Virginia so as to threaten the Confederate lines of communication from Richmond to the Shenandoah Valley, thus drawing Southern troops from the Richmond area and, thereby, assisting the Army of the Potomac take the city.[58] According to T. Harry Williams,

> Pope's operation as stated in the order was to be primarily offensive in nature, and his main objective was the capture of Richmond. He was to move his army down through western Virginia and into the Valley, cleaning out the enemy there, and then to turn west against Richmond. At the same time McClellan was to close in on the capital from the east. What Lincoln had in mind, although naturally he did not lay out all the details in the order, was a pincer movement of the Army of the Potomac and the Army of Virginia that would snip off the Confederate army and the capital between them. When the two armies were in position to communicate or cooperate with each other, the question of the chief command was to be governed by the Rules and Articles of War, which meant that McClellan, the senior officer, would exercise control over Pope.[59]

The President was destined not to implement his plan to conduct a theater-wide convergence of General McClellan's and General Pope's armies in the Richmond area because the Confederates capitalized upon their interior communications to concentrate all available forces, including those previously operating in the Shenandoah Valley, and, on June 26, attacked the Federals east of Richmond. The Confederates hoped to destroy McClellan's army by striking at its communications which stretched eastward to the Pamunkey River, thereby forcing the Union commander either to fight for his line of communications or withdraw from the gates of Richmond while under attack. The Southern commander, General Robert E. Lee, then intended to assault the flank of the Army of the Potomac as it retreated down the peninsula toward Fort Monroe. The first part of the Confederate plan called for the destruction of the single Federal corps positioned northeast of the Chickahominy awaiting the promised reinforcements from the north and guarding the Army's line of supply back to the Pamunkey. In response to the Southern assault on his northern flank, General McClellan decided not to redeploy his main body north of the river in an effort to defend his line of communications, while, simultaneously, attempting to destroy the attacking Confederates. Instead, he abandoned his line of communications to the Pamunkey and established a new base on the James. In addition, instead of capitalizing upon the opportunity presented by the weakened Confederate defenses south of the Chickahominy to launch a concerted assault on Richmond, or even acting conservatively and remain in position, General McClellan, erroneously convinced that he was overwhelmingly outnumbered, withdrew his entire army to the banks of the James amid seven days of fierce fighting. Thus, while the Confederates had acted in accordance with General McClellan's original theoretical assumption that a Union strategic turning movement would force the Southerners to abandon northern Virginia, concentrate in defense of their capital, and assume the tactical offensive to relieve the threat to the city, in the largest sense, General McClellan's strategic turning movement failed to decisively defeat the Southern army or capture the Confederate capital. Instead, the Southerners had seized the initiative and pushed the Army of the Potomac back to the James River. Assessing the implications of the failure of the strategic turning movement to attain its goals, President Lincoln recognized that the Confederates suffered greater loss of lives and equipment than did the Army of the Potomac during the campaign. Moreover, given the war-making potential of the two sides, the Confederates could ill afford the losses.[60] Finally, evaluating General McClellan's position at the conclusion of the Seven Days Battles, B. H. Liddell Hart observed,

> By switching his base to the James River he not only secured his own communications, but placed himself menacingly close to Petersburg and the enemy's communications from Richmond to the South—the same position which Grant so painfully and expensively regained two years later. Thus McClellan still had the strategic advantage, perhaps more than before, of position for approach.[61]

But would the cautious McClellan take the same advantage of his position that Grant would two years later? From the Presidential perspective, the greatest adverse impact of the failure of the campaign was its psychological/symbolic impact upon both Northern morale, as well as the political configuration within the Southern states. In addition, the President also recognized the adverse impact of the failure of the Peninsular Campaign upon the diplomatic position of the United States vis-a-vis the Confederacy in countering the latter's efforts to gain European recognition and material assistance. Indeed, Mr. Lincoln correctly saw that, given the Virginia fixation of many Northerners, Southerners, and observers abroad, the failure of the Peninsular Campaign overshadowed the important, extensive operational successes gained by Generals Halleck and Grant in the western theater.[62] Summarizing the situation in early July, 1862, Allen Nevins wrote,

> Before the North stretched the prospect of a prolonged war, with all its implications: dismaying financial problems, the necessity of conscription, a harsher scrutiny of Administration shortcomings, a deeper schism on war aims between moderates and radicals, rising discontent and disloyalty, a starker danger of foreign intervention. Until thus suddenly ringed by failure, most Northerners had hoped to see the insurrection suppressed without a profound national upheaval. Now revolution faced them on every hand: a party revolution as factional strife boiled up, an economic revolution as war contracts, tariffs, and inflation spurred industry forward, a social revolution, even an intellectual revolution as millions began to think more responsibly and more nationally. From the beginning it had seemed likely that the war would mean the extirpation of slavery, the subordination of the South to the North and West, and a business domination of government; now this was certainty. Transcending all other changes was the fact that every new day of war demanded a larger mobilization of national energies, and that under this demand an organized nation was taking shape. . .[63]

CHAPTER III

Summer 1862—Autumn 1862

On July 11, 1862, after a four month period during which the President, assisted by the Secretary of War, had performed the duties of the General-in-Chief, Mr. Lincoln appointed Major General Henry W. Halleck to the vacant post. General Halleck would occupy the post of General-in-Chief until early 1864. During his stewardship, he gave the President military advice, but exercised very little command over theater operations. Most observers agree that General Halleck "delighted to counsel, but he hated to decide." Nevertheless, he was able to provide the President with the type of "technical information the President did not have and that he needed to solve certain military problems." Indeed, if Mr. Lincoln had "wanted only an advisor, he could not have chosen a better one than Halleck," but, in July, 1862, the President hoped that his new General-in-Chief would directly plan and command the unified Federal operations encompassing all the theaters of war. While he made attempts in that direction, his reluctance to command his theater generals would ultimately reduce his role to that of a "technical advisor to the President and a staff critic of the plans of field generals." Notwithstanding his failure as a central war director, however, the President retained General Halleck as the General-in-Chief because he apparently "valued Halleck's technical knowledge and respected his character."[1]

With the departure of General Halleck from the western theater, command responsibility over the west was divided between Generals Buell and Grant. General Buell was to continue his advance toward Chattanooga which he had commenced soon after the capture of Corinth. Summarizing General Buell's situation, Allen Nevins noted,

> He was ordered to repair the Memphis and Charleston railroad as he
> advanced and to use it as his line of supply—a line which left the ever-

extending flank of his communications exposed to raids from the south. As a result his advance grew slower and lost weight as it went, for the danger of his life-line being cut by the Confederate cavalry or guerrilla bands was ever present.[2]

Notwithstanding General Halleck's repeated directives to move as rapidly as possible toward Chattanooga, however, General Buell was eventually forced to halt his advance. As Professors Beringer, Hattaway, Jones, and Still observed,

Already harassed by guerrillas, he halted in August, when cavalry raiders interrupted his communications in the first major application of what became a fundamental and most effective Confederate defensive strategy. Adequately supplemented by the activities of guerrillas, cavalry broke the fragile rail lines in Buell's rear, burning bridges and tearing up track. Without rail communications and out of reach of river steamers, Buell refused to advance farther in such sparsely settled country with only primitive roads for supply.[3]

Meanwhile, as General Buell was supposed to be advancing toward Chattanooga, General Grant was to maintain his defensive stance in northern Mississippi. Union troops in Arkansas were to be reinforced, not only to help consolidate the gains already made in the trans-Mississippi region, particularly Missouri, but also to set the stage for additional territorial gains. In the Virginia theater, General-in-Chief Halleck was confronted with an exterior lines situation: General Pope's Army of Virginia, located in northern Virginia, and General McClellan's Army of the Potomac, positioned defensively on the banks of the James River, each unable to reinforce the other quickly. The Confederates occupied a central position between these two Union forces. Notwithstanding the scholarly Halleck's theoretical distaste for exterior lines type operations, the new General-in-Chief visited General McClellan, his former superior and now subordinate, at the Army of the Potomac's encampment on the James, in order to ascertain McClellan's intentions. The Commander of the Army of the Potomac expressed his conviction that the best way to decisively defeat the Confederates was to extensively reinforce his command for another advance against Richmond from the east or south. General McClellan proposed,

. . . to cross in force to the south side of the James and move on Petersburg, thereby severing a number of vital railroads from the deep

South to Richmond. Lee himself acknowledged that so long as the National Army was astride the James near Richmond, he could not weaken the Southern Army defending the capital in order to move northward toward Washington. Petersburg was then practically undefended.[4]

General Halleck, however, remained unconvinced that General McClellan would, even if reinforced with the maximum number of troops available to the Federal high command at that time, take the initiative and act aggressively to defeat the Confederates. The General-in-Chief concluded that without such action, only the risks inherent with an exterior lines operation would remain. In such case, the enterprising Confederates were likely to themselves seize the initiative and utilize their interior lines to strike at General Pope's Army of Virginia and McClellan's Army of the Potomac successively. Hence, on August 3, General McClellan was formally told that the Army of the Potomac would be withdrawn as quickly as possible from the peninsula and consolidated with the Union forces located in northern Virginia in preparation for a new offensive.[5]

General McClellan strongly protested the order arguing that the army was already in the best position to resume the offensive against Richmond. He further stated,

> Add to this the certain demoralization of this army, which would ensue, the terribly depressing effect upon the people of the North, and the strong probability that it would influence foreign powers to recognize our adversaries, and there appear to me sufficient reasons to make it my imperative duty to urge, in the strongest terms afforded by our language, that this order may be rescinded, and that, far from recalling this army, it be promptly reinforced to enable it to resume the offensive . . . . Here, directly in front of this army, is the heart of the rebellion . . . . Here is the true defense of Washington; it is here, on the banks of the James, that the fate of the Union should be decided.[6]

Partly agreeing with General McClellan, T. Harry Williams maintained that the Federal high command

> . . . would have done better to have left the army where it was. It was only twenty-five miles from Richmond and on a supply line that could always be kept open. It was closer to Richmond than it would be until 1864. Seldom if ever in military history has an army that near to an enemy capital retired without the enemy firing a shot at it. Lincoln would have made a wiser decision if he had kept the army on the James and removed McClellan as its commander. He should have replaced

> McClellan with a general who was not afraid to fight and who had some
> capacity to estimate the strength of the enemy. He could have given the
> command to Pope, who was soon to show that he had plenty of defects
> but who was pugnacious and who might have smashed his way into
> Richmond. There is no evidence that Lincoln considered keeping the
> army in the Peninsula and giving it a new leader. He was impressed
> with Halleck's learned and theoretical talk about the military error and
> the danger of having the armies of McClellan and Pope separated and
> the necessity of obeying the textbooks by uniting them. In a technical
> sense, the two Union armies were separated, which according to the
> books was bad, and there was an enemy force, the Confederate army
> at Richmond, between them, which according to the books was worse.
> Actually the Federal armies were not separated in a dangerous or stra-
> tegic sense, because the Federal navy controlled the water lines between
> Washington and the Peninsula, and some kind of cooperation was al-
> ways possible.[7]

Moreover, the Confederate armies in Virginia were not nearly
as strong as McClellan's inflated estimates suggested.[8]

As the General-in-Chief feared, however, with General Grant
on the defensive in northern Mississippi, General Buell, harassed
by enemy raids on his lines of communications, very slowly plodding eastward toward Chattanooga, and General McClellan passively awaiting the withdrawal of his army from the peninsula,
the Confederate high command seized the initiative both east
and west of the Appalachians. In Virginia, the Confederate commander, General Lee, decided not merely to passively guard
against another advance by General McClellan against Richmond from the east, while, simultaneously, defending against
the threat posed by General Pope's new army to the Virginia
Central Railroad which linked Richmond with the Shenandoah.
Instead, he and his lieutenants opted to employ only a portion
of the Southern forces then in the Richmond area to guard the
inert Army of the Potomac, while utilizing the remainder to
attack and, if possible, destroy the individual corps components
of General Pope's army before the latter could concentrate.
Meanwhile, on the Union side, the General-in-Chief informed
General Pope of his intention to withdraw the Army of the Potomac from the peninsula, combine it with the Army of Virginia,
and launch a new, offensive campaign. This decision by Washington, of course, negated a portion of General Pope's original
mission and eliminated, or at least significantly reduced the im-

mediate desirability for the Army of Virginia to maintain its advanced position. Moreover, remembering the experience of his western subordinate, General Grant, who was surprised by a concentrated enemy assault against his forces on the banks of Tennessee in the spring, General Halleck was justifiably concerned about the possibility that the Confederates might utilize their central position, quickly concentrate their forces, and attempt to destroy Pope's army before it could be joined by McClellan's forces. Specifically, General Halleck was concerned that the Confederates "could make a swift march through the Valley and come out on Pope's rear. Then Lee, arriving from Richmond and attacking from the south with General James Longstreet's corps, would have Pope in a vise." Hence, General Halleck continually urged General McClellan to withdraw his forces quickly from the peninsula, while, at the same time, counselling General Pope to act especially cautiously and be particularly vigilant against the danger of a sudden Confederate concentration in his vicinity before the Army of the Potomac had arrived. General Pope, however, remained buoyant and eager to engage the enemy. He was "absolutely convinced that bold action on his part would keep the Confederates on the defensive and that they would seek safety in retreat."[9] According to Kenneth P. Williams, the Commander of the Army of Virginia intended to

> . . . operate down the Orange and Alexandria Railroad toward Gordonsville and beyond, and also to make a move from Fredericksburg toward Hanover Junction, at least as a distraction. In this way he would keep Washington covered, and at the same time he would threaten the Virginia Central Railroad, the vital link between Richmond and the Valley.[10]

Given the aggressive inclinations of both General Pope and the Southern high command, a clash was virtually inevitable. Hence, on August 9, 1862, just north of Gordonsville, at Cedar Mountain, the Confederates clashed with those elements of the Army of Virginia which General Pope had ordered forward to provide cover while he concentrated and brought forward the remainder of his forces. Following the battle, however, recognizing that the opportunity to destroy the corps components of Pope's army individually before they could concentrate had passed, the Confederates withdrew to Gordonsville. Meanwhile, on the Union side, General-in-Chief Halleck again ordered General Pope to be cautious, pull back, and assume a defensive stance along the Rappahannock River line, while, simultaneously, Halleck ordered McClellan to make haste. In addition, General Halleck sent all available reinforcements to Pope's force. Finally, the Confederate high command had now become certain that the Union leadership had irrevocably decided to withdraw the Army of the Potomac from the peninsula. Consequently, the Southerners prepared to concentrate virtually all their available field forces in Virginia against General Pope's army and relieve the Rappahannock River area by forcing Pope back toward Washington before he could be joined by the Army of the Potomac from the peninsula. If such a combination were allowed to occur, the concentrated Union armies would greatly outnumber the Confederate forces in the area. Beyond this, the Confederate theater commander, General Lee, hoped to cross the Potomac and operate in Maryland and Pennsylvania. To accomplish this, General Lee planned to sever General Pope's line of communications which stretched from his advanced position at Cedar Mountain back to his forward supply base at Manassas via the Orange and Alexandria Railway. Thus, between August 18 and August 24, as the Confederates attempted to slip behind General Pope's flanks, Pope effectively countered their attempts. As this maneuver was taking place, the lead elements of the Army of the Potomac began arriving in northern Virginia.[11]

Recognizing that his opportunity to force Pope back toward the Potomac before he could be reinforced was quickly passing, General Lee decided to leave about one half of his army along Pope's front to function as a pinning force, while, concurrently, moving the other portion of his forces around the Union right and across the Federal communications line to Manassas and Washington. General Lee expected that, in response to his strategic turning movement, General Pope would quickly withdraw his army from its present position and move in the direction of Washington to recover his line of communications. Should this occur, General Lee intended to move that portion of his army originally utilized to pin Pope's army along the same route followed by the turning element. Although remaining alert to opportunities to advantageously strike at the Army of Virginia, General Lee expected only to liberate northern Virginia, but not to annihilate General Pope's army in battle. Thus, early on August 25, the Confederates began to implement their plan. By the following evening, half of General Lee's army stood across the supply line of the Army of Virginia. Quickly, the Confederates seized the large Union supply depot at Manassas, captured all the supplies they could transport, destroyed the remainder and, on August 27-28, deployed defensively immediately north of Manassas, adjacent to the old Bull Run battlefield of the previous year to await General Pope's probable attack. Meanwhile, concluding that General Lee had recklessly split his forces, General Pope decided not to immediately retreat to Washington, but rather to capitalize upon his interior position, assume the tactical offensive, and attack the turning element of Lee's army which blocked his supply line. Following the anticipated destruction of the Confederate turning force, General Pope then intended to turn upon and destroy the remaining portion of General Lee's army. Thus, on August 27, Pope withdrew from his advanced position and began to concentrate upon Lee's turning force at Manassas. Unfortunately for the Union cause, however, General Pope focused virtually all his attention on the Southern turning force now deployed defensively at Manassas and failed to adequately guard against the sudden concentration of Lee's forces by effectively obstructing the route of advance likely to be used by the reinforcing (formerly pinning) element of the Southern army. Meanwhile, back in Washington, General Halleck frantically urged General McClellan (who had arrived at Aquia Landing, Virginia, on August 24) to quickly bring forward the two corps of the Army of the Potomac which had recently arrived from the peninsula to assist General Pope in the approaching battle. General McClellan, however, failed to act accordingly and, hence, only the two corps of the Army of the Potomac which had arrived from the peninsula earlier and had already joined Pope's army would participate alongside the units of the Army of Virginia (as well as the IX Corps) in the coming battle. After some fierce preliminary fighting, on August 29, the main body of the Army of Virginia assaulted the Southern turning force in its strongly held defensive position above Manassas. Meanwhile, that same day, the reinforcing portion of General Lee's army arrived in the immediate proximity of the battlefield. Unaware of this development, General Pope remained very optimistic concerning the possibility of successfully destroying the Southern army. When the battle resumed the following day, suddenly, General Lee's recently arrived units decisively joined the battle and attacked the Union left flank. In heavy fighting, the Union troops were forced back to the site of their defeat at the First Battle of Bull Run the previous summer. Testifying to the defensive maneuverability of the mid-nineteenth century army, however, notwithstanding the fact that General Lee had about half of his army at right angles to the Union army, General Pope successfully redeployed his troops on the battlefield to cover his exposed right flank. Although he could still have been reinforced by fresh units from the Army of the Potomac which had recently arrived in the Washington area, General Pope opted to withdraw his badly mauled army eastward. This operation was performed in an orderly manner and, despite another clash between elements of the two armies on September 1, the Union army continued its retrograde operation until finally entering the safety of the Washington fortification network on September 3. Again, the Union army had been overwhelmingly defeated by the Confederates.[12]

Following the Union withdrawal into Washington, the badly shaken Federal high command moved to reorganize their defeated eastern forces. General Pope was now reassigned to new responsibilities in St. Paul, Minnesota, the short-lived, ill-fated Army of Virginia was dissolved, and its units were reintegrated into the Army of the Potomac. Moreover, despite a great deal of opposition from within his own Administration, the President, with considerable reservation, retained General McClellan as the Commander of the Army of the Potomac. Meanwhile, General-in-Chief Halleck correctly predicted that the Confederates would turn north and raid Maryland and Pennsylvania. The General-in-Chief, however, was concerned that General Lee might be planning to draw the Union army north in pursuit and then quickly double back and attack Washington. General

McClellan disagreed with General Halleck's fears and felt confident that the Southern army intended to continue north. Hence, he maintained that the Army of the Potomac could safely pursue the Confederates with all its forces. The President agreed that General McClellan should pursue the raiding Confederate army as quickly as possible. Although concerned about the impact of a Southern raid on Northern soil upon Northern, Southern, and European opinion, the President tended to feel that the principal cities of the North were in no real danger. "In their flank position northwest of Washington, McClellan's men precluded an enemy advance northward because Lee 'dares not leave them in his rear.' " Indeed, Mr. Lincoln quickly concluded that if the Confederates moved sufficiently far north, the Army of the Potomac could advance rapidly to sever Lee's supply line and force the Confederate General to assume the tactical offensive and fight to recover his communications against a Union army defensively deployed on Northern soil in a position of its own choosing. The President felt that General Lee's Northern raid might provide the Army of the Potomac with a "golden opportunity" to annihilate the Confederacy's principal army in the eastern theater, seriously damage the Confederacy's chances for European recognition, dramatically lift Northern morale, while, simultaneously, delivering a heavy blow to the morale of the South. Indeed, he felt that such a Union victory could possibly prove decisive in triggering the collapse of the Confederate government.[13]

Actually, as will be examined shortly, the Federal high command found itself confronted with a dual Confederate invasion of Northern territory by the South's principal eastern and western armies. Internationally, the Confederate authorities hoped that a successful invasion of the North, in the immediate wake of the recent dramatic Confederate military victories at the gates of Richmond and in northern Virginia, would conclusively demonstrate Southern military power and Northern military weakness and, thus, induce the European governments to recognize the Confederacy and help secure Southern independence. As Norman Graebner wrote, "diplomacy reflects the status of power, and Southern power never appeared greater than during the summer and autumn months of 1862." Dr. Graebner went on to note that,

> News of General George B. McClellan's retirement from before Richmond in the early summer of 1862 merely confirmed a general European conviction that the American Union was doomed. To European military experts, diplomats, and statesmen, Northern power seemed incapable of overcoming the defensive nature of the Southern military commitment. The North, Europe understood, enjoyed an immense industrial superiority, but the advantages of strategy, terrain, and leadership appeared to lie with the South. Confederate armies had no obligation to conquer the North, but only to beat off the Union forces. This they appeared capable of doing.[14]

Indeed, during the late summer of 1862, the European powers considered the possibility of some form of intervention into the conflict in America. While Russia rejected the idea of European intervention and maintained that, from its perspective, the political disintegration of the Union would be catastrophic, Napoleon III of France felt that the time had arrived to make European influence felt. Thus, the French Emperor told London that France was prepared to extend diplomatic recognition to the Confederacy if Britain would follow. The British government, however, was divided concerning the issue of recognition of the Confederacy and some form of intervention into the conflict. Suffering within the British textile industry was increasing due to the interruption in the flow of cotton from North America. Now, in the wake of General McClellan's reversal on the peninsula and General Pope's defeat at the Second Battle of Bull Run, the British, like all European observers, increasingly recognized that the conflict could be prolonged indefinitely. Hence, "a terrible transatlantic disaster" threatened to become an intolerable "endless international nuisance." From the perspective of British middle and working class opinion, a firm popular consensus against intervention remained absent "so long as the war lacked a high moral object (the abolition of slavery), and so long as it seemed uncertain that the North had the stamina and skill to fight to victory." While, for the moment, the politically weak British textile workers of Lancashire stood stubbornly behind the Union cause, as suffering in their sector of the economy increased, their commitment to the North could waver and their political voice within British politics might grow dramatically. Finally, as noted earlier, upper class British conservatives always leaned toward the South and were sympathetic to the idea of British recognition of the Confederacy, provided that the South could show that it could successfully defend its independence.[15]

On August 6, 1862, the British Foreign Secretary, Lord Russell, suggested to the Prime Minister, Lord Palmerston, that it might be appropriate to move toward recognition of the Confederacy and intervention in the conflict in October, 1862. Indeed, while Lord Russell felt that "further Confederate successes would force mediation on the North," he noted that " 'we must allow the President to spend his second batch of 600,000 men before we can hope that he and his democracy will listen to reason.' " The Prime Minister responded to the Foreign Secretary's views with caution. Mr. Palmerston had "consistently declared against any immediate effort at mediation as both useless and dangerous." Certainly he recognized the dramatic Confederate successes in the Virginia theater, but he was also aware of the Confederate reversals in the western theater. Hence, while in mid-September he wrote that if the Southern army captured Washington or Baltimore it might be appropriate for London and Paris to make their weight felt in favor of Confederate independence, he observed a few days later that he would "favor an offer of mediation only 'if the Federals sustain a great defeat.' " Finally, supporting the Prime Minister's caution, Earl Granville made known his doubts that, " 'if the war continued long after our recognition of the South, whether it will be possible for us to avoid drifting into it.' " In short, British involvement in the conflict in the United States could lead to war. Therefore, the last weeks of summer and the first weeks of autumn, 1862, would be critical regarding the prospect of European entry into the war. A dramatic victory by the Confederate field armies on Border or Northern soil could bring the South much needed, perhaps decisive assistance from the Great Powers. Conversely, only Union victories could deter European interference and keep the conflict confined to within the United States.[16]

Politically, Richmond hoped that a Confederate invasion of Northern territory would encourage the Border slave states, especially Maryland and Kentucky to join the Confederacy, as well as leave the impression throughout the North, South, and Europe that Washington was destined to be unsuccessful in forcing the South to remain in the Union against its will. It was hoped that this, in turn, could boost Southern morale, undermine Northern resolve to continue the conflict, as well as strengthen the forces favoring intervention on behalf of the Confederacy throughout Europe. Indeed, many in the Southern high command felt that a Confederate invasion of the North could provide a suitable backdrop for broaching a peace offer to the United States based upon U.S. recognition of the independence of the Confederacy. Even if the Lincoln Administration rejected such an offer, it might encourage the Northern people to express their opposition to the continuation of the war by electing peace candidates in the approaching elections. Already, the Administration was under attack from several political elements and many of its supporters feared an autumn electoral defeat. As Allen Nevins noted, the Lincoln Administration

> . . . had staked its prestige on the Peninsular thrust and rapid opening of the Mississippi, and in both areas had failed. Prices and taxes were rising . . . . Hatred of the draft was widespread. Arbitrary arrests and other invasions of fundamental civil liberties had created sharp resentment. Most disturbing of all in some States was the apprehension of an influx of liberated Negroes, which would take jobs away from white men, depress wages, and breed violence.[17]

Moreover, the high casualty lists further eroded the popularity of the Lincoln Administration. Many members of the electorate feared that, "what had begun as a national war to save the Union" was rapidly becoming "a Republican war to destroy slavery, create a strong centralized government, and hold the South in permanent subjection." Finally, in the Ohio, upper Mississippi, and Missouri Valleys, another reason for discontent was the perception that "the war was being used to enrich Eastern industrial, merchantile, and banking groups." The Administration's tariff policy appeared to be as harmful to agrarian interests as it was beneficial to industrial interests since it led to increased consumer prices, while, simultaneously, reducing the attractiveness of U.S. agricultural goods abroad. Moreover,

The trunk-line railroads, mainly owned by Eastern capitalists, were garnering a rich harvest from war traffic and the closing of the Mississippi. Agrarian groups complained of extortionate freight and elevator rates. All the while, of course, the Northwest shared the ardent longing of the whole nation for victory. To Westerners victory meant above everything else the clearing of the Mississippi. The East-West railways had not yet taken the place in men's imaginations so long held by the central river system.[18]

The "Peace Democrats" provided an alternative by advocating "an armistice, a national convention, and the restoration of the old Union under the old Constitution." Indeed, Western disaffection was deemed to be of such magnitude that some Southerners even entertained the hope of detaching the states of the upper Mississippi and Ohio Valleys from New England. Of course, attainment of these political goals was predicated upon avoiding a military defeat and, optimally, defeating and, if possible, destroying the main eastern and western Union armies while on Northern soil.[19]

Finally, the Southern military authorities felt that a Confederate invasion of the North also offered several inviting military enticements. Autumn on Northern soil would permit the Southern armies to feed both men and animals on the Northern harvest, while, at the same time, permitting Southern quartermasters to husband the South's crop yield for winter consumption. Moreover, an invasion of the North would allow Confederate recruiters to draw upon another source of manpower in their efforts to fill the ranks of the Southern army. The Confederate high command recognized, however, that eventually the agricultural resources of the raided areas would be exhausted and, without a dependable supply line to the South, the Confederate armies would inevitably have to withdraw to Southern soil for the winter.[20]

With these ambitions in mind, on September 4, 1862, General Lee led his forces across the Potomac, thus inaugurating his first invasion of the North. In addition to the generalizable politico-military goals discussed above, General Lee hoped to establish himself in Maryland, thus menacing Harrisburg, Pennsylvania, disrupting the east-west rail lines which traversed the region, and threatening Baltimore, Philadelphia, and Washington.

Moreover,

> Established in Maryland, Lee would occupy a flank position, threatening
> the flank and rear of any Union advance toward Richmond. "By cross-
> ing east of the Blue Ridge," Lee informed Davis, "both Washington and
> Baltimore would be threatened, which I believe would insure the with-
> drawal of the mass of the enemy's troops north of the Potomac." Even
> if forced back into Virginia, Lee intended to occupy a location that
> would either place him on the flank of the Union army if it moved on
> Richmond or give him a favorable situation with good communications
> to Richmond in case the Union Army of the Potomac should attack
> him. In this way he could protect Virginia and spend the fall in a place
> from which he could be driven only by a frontal assault. In expecting
> to remain so long unmolested north of the Potomac, Lee apparently
> counted on the reluctance of Union generals to make a frontal attack.[21]

As he advanced into Maryland, for a variety of reasons, Lee
distributed his army rather widely. Meanwhile, on September 6,
General McClellan, as usual convinced that he faced an army
much larger than his own, led the Army of the Potomac northward, leaving two corps behind in Washington to insure the
safety of the national capital. Reaching Frederick, Maryland on
September 13, the Commander of the Army of the Potomac
learned that the Confederates were widely dispersed and, hence,
he moved with unusual speed to interpose his army between the
divided components of General Lee's army. Recognizing the
danger, General Lee attempted to block McClellan's advance.
Although the Federal forces drove the obstructing Confederates
back at the Battle of South Mountain and despite the urging of
the President to move rapidly to " 'destroy the rebel army if
possible,' " the Union advance was slowed sufficiently to allow
General Lee to concentrate a portion of his forces. After considering various options, the Confederate commander decided
to make a defensive stand at Antietam Creek, just east of Sharps-
burg, Maryland, with the flanks of his army resting on the banks
of the Potomac and with a usable ford across the river to his
back. On September 15, the main body of the Army of the Potomac approached the Confederate position. General McClellan,
however, unnecessarily delayed attacking the Confederates on
the 16th, thereby not only wasting an opportunity to destroy a
portion of Lee's army before it could be reinforced, but also
providing the Confederate commander with additional time to

concentrate his forces. Finally, early on September 17, the Army of the Potomac stormed the defending Confederate positions. In the extremely heavy, day long fighting which followed, the Southerners were pushed back by the fierce Union frontal assaults. But, due in part to the timely arrival of additional Confederate reinforcements during the battle, as well as General McClellan's poor coordination of his corps on the battlefield and his unwillingness to commit his two relatively fresh corps at the critical moment in the fighting, the Southern line remained unbroken. The following day, the two armies remained in position. But, despite the fact that he still had a large body of fresh troops which had not been committed during the previous day's fighting, General McClellan refused to renew the engagement. Had he done so, it is possible that the Army of the Potomac would have destroyed Lee's army and, thereby, not only justified the enormous Union casualties suffered during the battle, the bloodiest single day in the war, but possibly triggered the fall of the Confederate government. General McClellan, however, reasoned that "the whole Union cause in the east rested on his army . . . and if he attacked and lost, the east would be at Lee's mercy." In any case, the night of September 18, General Lee began withdrawing his Southerners across the Potomac and, despite a timid pursuit by a small portion of the Army of the Potomac, the Confederates escaped southward into the Shenandoah Valley.[22]

Although it recognized the need for the Army of the Potomac to regroup and reequip, the Federal high command in Washington urged General McClellan to pursue the Confederates at the earliest possible moment. The General, however, ignored General-in-Chief Halleck's orders to cross the Potomac and remained north of the river until the end of October. Mr. Lincoln and General Halleck advised McClellan to move his forces east of the Blue Ridge Mountains, thereby, not only protecting Washington, but also, simultaneously, threatening the vital Virginia Central Railway and the Confederate line of communications to Richmond. The Commander of the Army of the Potomac, however, preferred to advance up the Shenandoah Valley. General McClellan feared that to advance along the route recommended by the high command would invite another Confederate invasion of Maryland or an attack upon the Union right flank or rear.

The President advised the General not to fear another invasion of Maryland, since such a Confederate offensive would again permit the Union forces to totally sever General Lee's supply line and possibly destroy his army as it attempted to recover its communications. Moreover, regarding the prospect of a Confederate assault upon the Union right or rear as it moved to sever Lee's line of communications, the President reminded General McClellan that he could base his own operations along the secure north-south line provided by the Potomac River and the other tributaries which flowed into the Chesapeake Bay, as well as the rail line which extended from Aquia Landing on the Potomac southward through Fredericksburg to Richmond. Finally, the President suggested that the Union army was in a good position to outrun the Confederates to Richmond or fight on favorable ground if Lee opted to move toward the Southern capital. General Halleck noted that, if the Army of the Potomac advanced via the Shenandoah Valley route, the line of advance would "expose Washington and again compel the government to keep a large force in the city." As with the Peninsular Campaign, McClellan would again "be operating on exterior lines." After considerable discussion, General McClellan eventually opted to advance along the line of operations recommended by the Washington high command. Thus, on the last days of October and the first days of November, the Army of the Potomac left behind one corps to guard the upper Potomac, crossed the river, and slowly moved southward along the eastern slope of the Blue Ridge. General Lee countered this move by leaving about half of his army in the Valley and moving the other half to block General McClellan's southward movement. Although later claiming that he intended to destroy the two elements of the Southern army in detail, he continued to fail to display sufficient aggressiveness, thereby further alienating the authorities in Washington. Therefore, on November 7, 1862, despite his continued tremendous popularity among the officers and men of the Army of the Potomac which he had founded over a year and a quarter earlier and led through the trials of the Peninsular and Antietam Campaigns, the Washington high command relieved George McClellan of his command of that army, thereby effectively terminating his military career. He was replaced by his friend, Major General Ambrose E. Burnside, Commander of the Ninth Corps.[23] An era in the life of the celebrated Army of the Potomac had ended and, although the President, General-in-Chief Halleck, and all Northerners hoped that the new Commander of the Army of the Potomac would provide a decisive victory, its time of trial had only begun.

Meanwhile, in addition to responding to the Confederate seizure of the initiative in the eastern theater of operations during the Second Bull Run and Antietam Campaigns, the Federal high command had to respond to the Confederate seizure of the initiative in the west. Concluding that it was impractical to move northward from the position which they held in northeastern Mississippi following the evacuation of Corinth, the Confederate leadership decided to leave a reduced force in Mississippi to guard that state against a southward drive by General Grant and take the main body of their western army to Chattanooga. From there, the Confederates intended to advance through middle Tennessee where they would be joined by additional Southern troops from eastern Tennessee. The Southern army would then attempt to strategically turn General Buell's position in northern Alabama by severing the rail line of communications connecting his force with his supply centers at Nashville, Tennessee and Louisville, Kentucky,[24] as well as by threatening the Ohio River cities. The Confederates hoped that this strategic turning movement would force Buell to abandon his forward position and fight for his communications somewhere in middle Tennessee. Should the Confederates successfully defeat Buell and, thereby, gain control over middle Tennessee, the Southern command hoped to then concentrate their entire western forces and move upon General Grant's army in west Tennessee. At minimum, the movement would serve to help protect the state of Mississippi and the lower Mississippi River from further immediate Union thrusts from the north, as well as secure the Confederate hold over Chattanooga. Accordingly, the Southerners commenced their operation on July 21 and, by the end of the month, as General Lee's plans against General Pope in the Virginia theater matured, the Confederates from northeastern Mississippi reached Chattanooga. Meanwhile, in mid-August, Confederate forces from eastern Tennessee moved northward into Kentucky, arriving in Lexington by the end of the month, thus establishing Confederate control over central Kentucky and threatening the Ohio River cities. In early September, the other Confederate element moved north from Chattanooga and, by mid-month, as the Army of the Potomac and General Lee's forces fought at Antietam, the western Confederates had penetrated into central Kentucky, further north than originally anticipated, cut the Louisville and Nashville rail line northeast of Bowling Green, and threatened the Ohio River Valley. In short, the Southerners had effectively turned General Buell's position.[25]

Responding to the Confederate strategic turning movement, General Buell, as expected, withdrew his forces from their original positions in northern Alabama, first to protect Nashville and then to Bowling Green. Thus, at the very least, the Southerners had relieved Chattanooga from the threat of Union capture. Of course, the North generally, especially the residents of the Ohio River cities of Cincinnati and Louisville were both outraged and quite alarmed by the prospect of a Southern invasion of the Ohio Valley. Consequently, General Buell came under intense pressure from Washington to immediately attack the Confederates blocking his supply route before they could combine with the other Confederate column, then located at Lexington. General Buell, however, was not enthusiastic about assuming the tactical offensive and assaulting the Southern army deployed across his communications line. Nor did he intend to retire in panic to the Ohio River to protect the river cities. The General recognized that the Confederate strategic turning movement was a raid, not a penetration, since the invading Confederates lacked a reliable supply line of their own. Hence, he felt confident that he could outlast the Southern force blocking the Louisville and Nashville railway and, eventually, they would be forced to themselves withdraw from their positions in search of forage. This, of course, would reopen Buell's communications to the Ohio River. In a larger sense, however, since the Confederates in Kentucky lacked a base analogous to that provided by the Shenandoah Valley for the Confederate invasion of Maryland, the raiding Southerners' lack of a secure source of supply would ultimately force them to abandon their Kentucky raid altogether. Hence, it was at least theoretically possible for General Buell to passively wait and starve the Confederates off his line of communications and out of Kentucky. The high command, however, would not permit the General to remain passive and insisted that it was politically imperative for him to immediately move against the invading forces and drive them from Kentucky and middle Tennessee.[26]

Meanwhile, as Buell predicted, the Confederates blocking the Louisville and Nashville did run short of supplies, as well as perhaps what Allen Nevins referred to as "grit in a crisis" on the part of the Southern commander, and withdrew northeastward, thereby rejecting an opportunity to, at least, raid Louisville or seize Nashville. Following the movement of the Southern force, General Buell moved his army to Louisville. Under intense pressure from the Administration to engage the enemy, General Buell then advanced against the still divided Confederate forces southeast of Louisville. On October 8, 1862, the Union army indecisively engaged a portion of the invading Confederate forces at Perryville, Kentucky. Immediately following the battle, the Confederate command concentrated its forces, but, in view of their numerical inferiority and precarious supply situation, the Southerners decided to end their invasion of Kentucky and withdrew to middle Tennessee via east Tennessee and Chattanooga. Meanwhile, General Buell made no real effort to pursue the defeated Confederates. In addition to logistical difficulties and concern about the safety of Nashville, General Buell noted that a retreating force can always move faster than its pursuer and it was extremely difficult to force a fleeing army to fight against its will. Buell preferred to take his army back to Nashville and prepare for a new campaign. The high command in Washington, as well as many other influential Northerners, already exasperated at Buell's passivity and his failure to decisively defeat the Confederates, sharply disagreed. Assessing General Buell's viewpoint, T. Harry Williams observed,

> Buell wanted to prepare some more before he fought. He insisted that the best way to secure East Tennessee was to operate on a line from Nashville. He was right. A Federal army in East Tennessee would have

supply difficulties unless it controlled a railroad to the outside. The railroad from Nashville to Chattanooga was the logical line of advance for Buell's army. The trouble with Buell was that he did not seem to sense any need for any celerity in movement on any line.[27]

By contrast, the President and General-in-Chief Halleck advocated a quick pursuit of the fleeing Confederates into east Tennessee so that the region, a priority area in the eyes of Washington, could be occupied by the end of autumn. Moreover, the high command felt that it would be easier to move against Chattanooga via east Tennessee, as opposed to a movement against that important city via Nashville. Finally, the Administration felt that a close pursuit of the retreating Confederates would significantly reduce the chances of the Southerners launching another raid into Kentucky. In view of the important differences of approach to operational planning in middle and eastern Tennessee and by now clearly out of patience, at the end of October, the Federal high command removed Don Carlos Buell from his command and replaced him with Major General Williams S. Rosecrans.[28]

Finally, as mentioned, when the Confederates launched their Kentucky raid, they left behind a force in northern Mississippi to watch General Grant and prevent him from either advancing southward or reinforcing General Buell's army. If the Federals sent troops from Grant's army to Buell's, the Confederates in northern Mississippi were supposed to clear western Tennessee of Union control. Thus, on September 2, due to erroneous information that the Union forces had abandoned Corinth, Mississippi and were joining Buell, the Confederate western command ordered their forces in northern Mississippi to advance toward Nashville, Tennessee. On September 14, as the Confederates in Kentucky were about to sever Buell's line of communications and the Antietam Campaign in Maryland approached its terrible climax, a portion of the Southern forces in northern Mississippi reached Iuka, Mississippi. Here, however, they learned that General Grant had not abandoned Corinth. Indeed, after securing permission from Halleck to regroup his forces "to protect his communications and the few places which it seemed essential to hold," the combative Grant now initiated his own plan for defeating the Confederates at Iuka. His complicated plan called for the convergence of two independent columns on Iuka, one from the northwest and the other from the south. Unfortunately for the Union cause, however, the plan miscarried and, on the night of September 19-20, the Confederates escaped southward. Elements of Grant's force then returned to Corinth, while the Southerners concentrated their forces for a coordinated assault upon that key railhead. On September 30, the concentrated Southern forces moved upon Corinth, assaulting the town on October 3 and 4, just a few days prior to Buell's clash with the Confederates at Perryville, Kentucky. Following stiff fighting, the repulsed Confederates withdrew and, notwithstanding a brief Union attempt to pursue the retiring Southerners, they escaped to Holly Springs, Mississippi. As Bruce Catton pointed out, the successful Union defense of Corinth was important to the war in the western theater, "because defeat at Corinth would in all probability cost the Union all of West Tennessee; and Grant's army might find itself hastening back to Kentucky ..." where the Union forces under General Buell were attempting to close with the enemy. To have suffered a major reversal in western Tennessee while the Southern army remained "on the loose near the Ohio River would be as heavy a blow as the Union cause could easily absorb."[29]

In short, the Confederates in Virginia and the west had, by means of their strategic turning movements into Maryland and Kentucky, accomplished their goals of relieving Union pressure on Richmond and Chattanooga, respectively. Moreover, the Southern armies ultimately assumed positions in Virginia and Tennessee at the conclusion of the Antietam and Kentucky campaigns, respectively, which promised to obstruct future Union drives against either of these two important cities. The Confederates had also partially achieved their logistical objective of subsisting off the Northern harvest. But, in the largest sense, the battlefield defeats, albeit militarily inconclusive, of the Confederacy's principal field armies within a three week period had extremely negative psychological and symbolic implications for Confederate political and international/diplomatic goals. General Lee's defeat at the Battle of Antietam provided the Union army in the east with its first major battlefield victory. Antietam, followed by the Union victory at the Battle of Perryville in Kentucky, deflated Confederate plans to extend a peace overture to the United States government and the Northern people while two major Confederate armies were positioned on the soil of the Border states. Moreover, the October and November mid-term elections failed to yield the crushing defeat for the Lincoln Administration for which the authorities in Richmond had hoped. During the campaigns, the Administration had been attacked by Radical Republicans, Regular Democrats, as well as by Peace Democrats upon whom the Southerners had placed their hopes. The Radical Republicans had called for the removal of General McClellan, immediate, uncompensated abolition of slavery, and the enlistment of black soldiers into the Union army. Regular Democrats had campaigned for General McClellan's retention, postponement of emancipation, and modification, non-enforcement, or repeal of the confiscation laws. As already noted, the Peace Democrats called for an immediate armistice and a negotiated settlement with the Southerners. Conversely, the Moderate Republicans and War Democrats had formed a Union coalition and many hoped that a "Union Party of national scope would soon emerge behind Lincoln—a party insisting on victory, but disclaiming any desire for utter subjugation of the South and a complete social revolution there," in favor of "gradual, compensated emancipation and a mild reconstruction policy." During the campaign, for the many reasons discussed earlier, extremists gained ground at the expense of Moderate Republicans, Regular Democrats, and War Democrats. With each Union reversal, the Radicals appealed for a harsher war policy, while the Peace Democrats called for conciliation. Clearly, Mr. Lincoln needed a victory; Antietam and Perryville, limited victories though they were, provided the Administration and its supporters with a much needed boost. When the votes were finally tabulated, the Administration forces suffered a clear reversal, but not a disaster. The outcome, however, did encourage the extremists at both ends of the political spectrum. But, given the circumstances, the Administration forces did reasonably well. Furthermore, the Confederate invasions of Maryland and Kentucky failed to detach the Old Northwest from the Union and "neither the Border states nor many of their citizens had taken the opportunity to enlist under the Stars and Bars." Finally, the highly visible Southern defeat at the Battle of Antietam, especially, made London pause and, ultimately, postpone recognition of the Confederacy. By the end of September, word of the Union victory at Antietam reached London and Lord Russell, "who had been the ministry's most vigorous spokesman for involvement," now began to modify his position. Moreover, Lord Palmerston, who had always been unenthusiastic about British intervention, observed that, "since mediation would favor the Southern position, its acceptance in the North hinged on Southern triumphs." With the recent Confederate reversals in Maryland and Kentucky, the Prime Minister maintained that it would be premature to intervene in the conflict in America and risk war with the United States at that time, since to do so would seriously jeopardize the British position in Canada and London's maritime commercial interests. Moreover, he stressed that any British move to intervene must be supported by Russia, as well as France. In short, the British Prime Minister concluded that the issue of British intervention " 'can only be cleared up by some more decided events between the contending armies.' " As Allen Nevins noted, "In a real sense, the double invasion" by the eastern and western Confederate armies, "represented the high tide of the Confederate cause. Never again would armies be as confident as those which almost simultaneously crossed the Maryland and Kentucky boundaries; never again would they have so good a chance of victory."[30]

Conversely, however, by early autumn, 1862, after a year and a half of heavy fighting and mounting casualties, the Federal government had been unsuccessful in its goal of crushing the Southern rebellion and restoring the Union. At sea, the Federal navy had attempted to isolate the Confederacy from access to maritime commerce and possible overseas support by establishing a naval blockade of the south Atlantic and Gulf coast, as well as by closing as many Southern ports as possible. Yet, notwithstanding much effort, the naval blockade remained ineffective in severing the South's communications with the rest of the world. On land, for about a year, Washington had amplified upon its earlier focus and had directed the eastern and western Union armies to advance simultaneously on their respective fronts in order to geographically dismember the Confederacy and selectively, but permanently occupy those portions of Southern territory which Washington felt the Southerners regarded as being of political, strategic, economic, logistical, and/or psychological/symbolic value. By the autumn of the second year of the war, however, the Federal government had been only partly successful in implementing this portion of its national military strategy. Union forces had, in varying degrees, consolidated their control over the Border states, as well as the area immediately adjacent to Washington. Within the Confederacy proper, the Union army had successfully penetrated through western Tennessee into the extreme northern portion of Mississippi. Finally, the Federals occupied a significant portion of middle Tennessee. In large measure, this advance had been made possible as a result of the excellent water lines of communications provided by the Tennessee, Cumberland, and Mississippi Rivers. Simultaneously, the Federal navy had taken New Orleans, thus leading to Union occupation of southeast Louisiana. In short, while no longer the exclusive priority which it once had been under the terms of General Scott's "anaconda plan," Union troops had captured much of the Mississippi Valley and virtually severed effective internal Confederate communication with the trans-Mississippi states. Finally, northern Arkansas had been penetrated by Union forces.[31]

These successes, however, had been purchased at the expense of extremely large amounts of blood and treasure, as well as time and effort. Most important, the vast bulk of Confederate territory remained under Confederate control and the morale, resolve, and popularity of the defiant secessionists to secure their independence from the United States appeared to remain high. Hence, it was becoming increasingly clear to many Union officers and political leaders that the Washington high command's national military strategy had only yielded a mixed record of indecisive, but symbolic battlefield victories and defeats, combined with the occupation of a small, but important portion of the Confederate territory and the establishment of a heretofore ineffective naval blockade of the Southern coast. These measures were clearly insufficient to decisively strengthen pro-Union Southern moderates and enable them to displace the secessionists, thereby causing the collapse of the Southern Confederacy. In the larger sense, however, the South was too self-sufficient for the strategy of enforced isolation to cause the Confederacy to exhaust its domestically produced war-making resources in a reasonable amount of time. Moreover, there were no specific geographic targets which were so imperative to the survival of the Confederacy that their loss would cause the Richmond government to collapse. Finally, in the largest sense, the South's commitment to the goal of political independence from the United States appeared in the autumn of 1862 to be too strong for any limited military strategy to yield decisive results.[32]

As the war continued with no end in sight, the attitudes of the Northern people, as well as their political and military leaders regarding the style with which the war was being fought and the national objectives which ought to be sought began to slowly undergo a transformation. After a year and a half of costly fighting, many Northerners began to have second thoughts about the moderate prosecution of the war with its emphasis upon shielding non-combatants and sparing their property (including slaves) from confiscation or destruction. Discussing this trend, Bruce Catton observed,

> The longer the war went on and the more it cost, the less willing were patriots on either side to recede from this position. The heroic dead, who were so tragically numerous and who had died for such diametrically opposite causes, must not have died in vain, and only total victory would justify what had been done. And because total victory was the only thinkable outcome, men came to feel that it was right to do anything at all that might bring victory nearer. It was right to destroy railroads, to burn factories and confiscate supplies of food or other raw materials, to seize or ruin any kind of property which was helpful to the enemy.[33]

Officers, such as General Grant, who had initially felt that the Confederate government would collapse after a few early defeats, now concluded that nothing but "complete conquest" would yield victory and that the war should be "pursued to the limit." Hence, by the summer and early autumn of 1862, Grant had concluded,

107

> I regard it as humane to both sides to protect the persons of those found at their homes, but to consume everything that could be used to support or supply armies. Protection was still continued over such supplies as were within lines held by us and which we expected to continue to hold; but such supplies within reach of the Confederate armies I regarded as much contraband as arms or ordnance stores. Their destruction was accomplished without bloodshed and tended to the same result as the destruction of armies. I continued this policy to the close of the war . . . . This policy I believe exercised a material influence in hastening the end.[34]

Similarly, even General Halleck was increasingly adopting a harder attitude, instructing General Grant that,

> It is very desirable that you should clear out West Tennessee and North Mississippi of all organized enemies. If necessary, take up all active sympathizers, and either hold them as prisoners or put them beyond our lines. Handle that class without gloves, and take their property for public use. As soon as the corn gets fit for forage get all the supplies you can from the rebels in Mississippi. It is time that they should begin to feel the presence of war on our side.[35]

Similarly, Major General William T. Sherman, an officer who began the war with extremely orthodox and scrupulous views regarding the definition and enforcement of foraging activities, began to liberalize and adopt a less restrictive policy. It should be noted, however, that in liberalizing their attitudes toward foraging, none of the Union leaders, including General Grant, had yet concluded that an army could cut loose from its line of communications and live off the enemy countryside.[36]

Finally, according to the future President, but then Brigadier General James A. Garfield, there "grew the conviction in the mind of every soldier that 'behind the Rebel army of soldiers, the black army of laborers was feeding and sustained the rebellion and there could be no victory until its main support was taken away.' " Hence, above and beyond the Congressional pressures which were being brought to bear upon the President regarding immediate emancipation, many Northern soldiers increasingly concluded that the emancipation of the slaves would be necessary in order to undercut the strength of the Confederacy. This, however, was not usually accompanied by the corollary conviction that the blacks should be made equal citizens. These Northerners merely wanted to free the slaves because their "bondage propped up the power of the Confederacy." In addition, the slavery question demanded attention since, "no matter where the Union armies went and no matter what they did, they met the Negro slave, and they had to do something about him simply because he was there. He represented a problem that could not possibly be postponed, and the inner sympathies of the men on whom the problem was being thrust made no difference at all." In short, for a host of reasons, by mid to late 1862, the Lincoln Administration concluded that the time had come, not only to replace the army's eastern and one of its western field commanders, the time had also come to fundamentally reconsider the definition of the national objectives and the national military strategy adopted to attain these objectives.[37]

CHAPTER IV

Autumn 1862—Summer 1863

Throughout the summer and the early autumn, President Lincoln began to reevaluate the Administration's position concerning the abolition of slavery and its relationship to the Federal government's national war objectives. As already traced, the first year and a quarter of the war witnessed the gradual growth of Radical influences within the Republican Party and Congress. Indeed, by the middle of the summer, 1862, the President feared "that if he did not adopt emancipation, the Congressional leaders would cut off appropriations for sustaining the war." Moreover, Mr. Lincoln concluded that, if he was to retain the leadership of his party, he would have to modify his position regarding gradual, compensated emancipation. Hence, during the summer of 1862, the President decided to seize the leadership of the abolitionist movement within the government. On July 13, the President privately and informally raised the topic with two members of his cabinet. Describing the conversation, Allen Nevins wrote that, in Mr. Lincoln's view, "the government had reached a crisis . . . it must make new military arrangements to meet the astonishing strength of the Confederacy, find a fresh inspiration to stimulate volunteering, and tap the reservoir of slave power." Hence, the President announced that he had " 'about come to the conclusion' " that the Administration would have to emancipate the slaves or lose the war. He felt that "it had become essential as a political measure, to keep the Republican Party behind him; a war measure, to cripple the South; a foreign policy measure, to align the humanitarian sentiment of the world, and especially Great Britain, with the North; and a measure to lift national morale." During the next several days, the Chief Executive drafted the historic Emancipation Proclamation. Finally, on July 22, President Lincoln announced to the cabinet that he had completed the draft. During the discussion which followed, Secretary of State Seward told the President,

> "I approve of the proclamation, but I question the expediency of its issue at this juncture. The depression of the public mind, consequent upon our repeated reverses, is so great that I fear the effect of so important a step. It may be viewed as the last measure of an exhausted Government, a cry for help; the Government stretching forth its hands to Ethiopia, instead of Ethiopia stretching forth her hands to the Government" His idea . . . was that it would be considered our last shriek on the retreat. . . . "Now," continued Mr. Seward, "while I approve the measure, I suggest, sir, that you postpone its issue until you can give it to the country supported by military success, instead of issuing it, as would be the case now, upon the greatest disasters of the war."[1]

The President immediately appreciated Secretary Seward's perspective and, certainly not wishing to have the proclamation publicly received as a desperate appeal by the dying Union for a slave rebellion, decided to withhold the announcement of the proclamation until the Union army could secure a highly visible battlefield success.[2]

During the following weeks, Mr. Lincoln attempted to emphasize that he was neither a spokesman for "Border Reactionaries" nor "Senate Abolitionists," but, instead, "his own master, prosecuting the war with a single eye to the maintenance of the Union." Along these lines, on August 22, 1862, Mr. Lincoln penned the following which was, in turn, published in the New York *Tribune* on August 25:

> I would save the Union. I would save it the shortest way under the Constitution. The sooner the national authority can be restored, the nearer the Union will be to "the Union as it was." If there be those who would not save the Union unless they could at the same time save slavery, I do not agree with them. If there be those who would not save the Union unless they could at the same time destroy slavery, I do not agree with them. My paramount object in this struggle is to save the Union, and is not either to save or destroy slavery. If I could save the Union without freeing any slave I would do it, and if I could save the Union by freeing some and leaving others alone I would also do that. What I do about slavery, and the colored race, I do because I believe it helps to save the Union; and what I forbear, I forbear because I do not believe it would help to save the Union. I shall do less whenever I shall believe what I am doing hurts the cause, and I shall do more whenever I shall believe that doing more will help the cause. I shall try to correct errors when shown to be errors; and I shall adopt new views as soon as they shall appear to be true views.[3]

The Union victory at Antietam set the stage for the announcement of the Emancipation Proclamation. At a cabinet meeting on September 21, the President stated,

"I think the time has come now. I wish it were a better time. I wish that we were in a better condition. The action of the army against the rebels has not been quite what I should have best liked. But they have been driven out of Maryland, and Pennsylvania is no longer in danger of invasion." When they were at Frederick, he said, he had promised himself and God that he would issue his proclamation as soon as they were driven out. "I am going to fulfill that promise. I have got you together to hear what I have written down. I do not wish your advice about the main matter—for that I have determined for myself."[4]

Notwithstanding the reservations of some members of Mr. Lincoln's cabinet, the proclamation was issued on September 22 and published in the press on the 23rd. It stated, in part,

That on the first day of January in the year of our Lord, one thousand eight hundred and sixty-three, all persons held as slaves within any State, or designated part of a State, the people whereof shall then be in rebellion against the United States, shall be then, thenceforward, and forever free; and the executive government of the United States, including the military and naval authority thereof, will recognize and maintain the freedom of such persons, and will do no act or acts to repress such persons, or any of them, in any efforts they may make for their actual freedom.[5]

In other words, the Emancipation Proclamation declared that the slaves in certain regions of the South were hereby freed. The areas exempted from the proclamation were: Tennessee, southern Louisiana, and western Virginia, all of which were under Union control. Similarly, the slaves residing in the Border states were not covered under the terms of the proclamation. Mr. Lincoln's action, however, did effectively escalate the national war objectives from the preservation of the Union to that, plus abolition of slavery without compensation in certain parts of the United States.[6]

In issuing the Emancipation Proclamation, Mr. Lincoln was exercising his war powers as Commander-in-Chief. As such, the President's "main interest" in issuing the proclamation "was not the liberation of a race (though he was fully conscious of this aspect) but the furtherance of the war effort and the preservation of the Union." Evaluating the significance of this historic document, Allen Nevins observed,

> Since the proclamation was an exercise of the war powers, what its legal effect would be after the war ceased was uncertain. As the President could issue a proclamation, so he, or a successor, could revoke it. It did not apply to those districts which the Union armies held on the date Lincoln designated, January 1, 1863; could not be enforced in those districts which they did not hold; and had no application whatever to the four border slave States. To this extent it is a fact that, as Seward said, the proclamation emancipated slaves where it could not reach them, and left them in bondage where it could have set them free. Lincoln himself continued to believe gradual emancipation better than summary liberation, and to cherish his plan for thus freeing the Negro in loyal areas.[7]

Notwithstanding this, however, the proclamation carried with it a variety of implications. First, after the proclamation took effect, the Union army became a liberating force as it advanced into Confederate territory. Second, the proclamation encouraged the slaves to take refuge behind Union lines. This, of course, had dual manpower implications, since it deprived the Confederate economy of much needed manpower, while it, simultaneously, increased the potential manpower pool available to Union army recruiters. Third, "the proclamation irrevocably committed the United States, before the gaze of the whole world, to the early eradication of slavery from those wide regions where it was most deeply rooted, after which all men knew, it could never survive on the borders. There could be no turning back." As such, however, it significantly transformed the image of black Americans. They were rapidly ceasing to be perceived as slaves and increasingly as refugees and future full citizens to be integrated socially, politically, and economically into society as equals. Similarly, "the proclamation placed the South on the moral defensive before the opinion of the Western world and made it difficult to maintain that the intent of the war was merely to achieve independence for the Southerners, when that meant slavery for blacks."[8] Consequently, as Professors Beringer, Hattaway, Jones, and Still commented,

> The Confederates no longer appeared before the world, and themselves, as champions of national self-determination; instead, they were forced to assume the character of suppressors of individual self-determination.

Southerners now appeared to the Western world as quintessentially es-
pousing an institution that most of the rest of Western civilization had
come to despise and had renounced. They were on the moral defensive;
the guilt over slavery and war which some had felt in 1861 now affected
more Southern consciences than before. . .[9]

Finally, the Lincoln Administration's decision to escalate the
national war objectives had important diplomatic ramifications
for the United States' attempt to dissuade the European powers
from recognizing and assisting the Confederacy, particularly
since it was juxtaposed against the recent show of Union military
strength at Antietam and Perryville. Indeed, after the announcement of the Emancipation Proclamation, those Britons who,
from the outset, had been sensitive to the anti-slavery implications of the war, including, "some of the aristocracy, and a multitude of the laboring millions . . . the hard-working, religious,
philanthropic sections of the well-to-do middle class," now felt
" 'a genuine veneration and even enthusiasm for President Lincoln.' " Slowly, the members of this body of opinion "made up
their minds that the North would end slavery and could win,"
and it, eventually, "became one of the impressive phenomena
of the war." But, while successful in its long-term goal of positively influencing British opinion toward the belligerents, as Norman Graebner pointed out, in the immediate wake of the
announcement of the proclamation, Lincoln's escalation of the
national war objectives had no real influence concerning the
British government's final decision not to intervene in the war.
Conservatives in Britain judged Mr. Lincoln's action to be "fool-
hardy and anticipated a servile insurrection." Conversely, while
Britain's workers, liberals, and abolitionists applauded the
Administration's action, "these groups had always favored the
Union cause." London finally decided not to recognize the Confederacy and/or intervene in the war, either directly, on behalf
of the South, or indirectly, in favor of the South by proposing
an armistice, largely because it never felt that that the Confederacy had enough strength to sustain a prolonged resistance
against a resolute North determined to preserve the Union. As
Sir George Cornewall Lewis declared on October 14, 1862, "the
South had not established a defacto independence, was not a
nation, and was hence not entitled on moral or legal grounds to

recognition." Three days later, he circulated a memorandum which contributed greatly to the British government's final decision to remain aloof from the struggle in the United States. Summarizing his argument, Allen Nevins wrote, Mr. Lewis

> ... pointed out that any mediation proposal would be made not to dispassionate men, but to heated and violent partisans; that an armistice could not be equal in effect on North and South, but must give the Confederacy an advantage; that determination on both sides was rocklike, and the North would be heatedly against compromise; that Washington would be sure to show its resentment in a fashion that might lead to hostilities; and that even if the North acceded, Britain and Europe would be utterly helpless in offering advice on boundaries, the slavery question, and other intricate matters. Implicit in Lewis' argument was his conviction that Great Britain could not afford to wage a costly and dangerous North American war.[10]

Finally, many recognized that, by raising emancipation to coequal status as a national war objective with the preservation of the Union, the Lincoln Administration made it virtually impossible to even approach a compromise peace with the rebellious states. The United States not only sought nothing less than total political objectives, it now added goals which, from the Southern perspective, were total socio-economic objectives also. Although there was one, last effort by France to involve Great Britain in an interventionist scheme in late October and early November, 1862, it failed almost from the outset. After November, the threat of European intervention passed away entirely.[11]

In retrospect, the Emancipation Proclamation significantly enhanced Mr. Lincoln's Presidential authority and prestige. As Allen Nevins noted, "two facts were now abundantly clear: Lincoln was running the war, the reins of power held tightly in his muscular grip; and he was determined to run it so that the North would keep the initiative on all fronts—military, economic, and moral." In September, 1862, however, the Northern reaction to the Presidential proclamation was mixed. The Radicals were temporarily pleased and, hence, for the moment, their constant criticism ceased. Conversely, Conservative opinion complained that "the proclamation altered the objects of the war, and that its direct result would be a heavy influx of Negroes into the free states." It should be noted that already Illinois and Indiana barred black immigrants and Ohio was considering similar barriers. In short, while the proclamation generated sympathy in certain quarters in Europe and enthusiasm among the Abolitionists of the Northeast, it antagonized many elements whose support the President needed in the upcoming mid-term elections. The army, of course, represented a cross-section of Northern society, with Radical, Moderate, and Conservative representation. Most analysts agree with Professor Nevins who observed,

> The safest generalization is this: that most Northern soldiers approved of the proclamation, but did so not so much from humanitarian motives as because their blood was now up, they wanted to win a decisive victory, and Lincoln's edict seemed to herald a relentless prosecution of the war. . . . But though the plain soldier, like Lincoln, thought of emancipation primarily as a war measure, in countless instances he also rejoiced in its enlargement of human freedom. As the Union troops in marching South studied the worst aspects of slavery, they quickly learned to hate it. When they saw the auction block, the whipping post, the iron gyve, when they glimpsed the field hand cringing under his master's gaze, when the fleeing slave bared his scarred back, or told a tale of young children wrenched from their mother's arms, they resolved that slavery must die.[12]

Finally, while assuring Congress of his commitment to begin enforcing the proclamation on January 1, 1863 if the Southerners did not end the rebellion before that date, Mr. Lincoln remained committed to gradual, compensated emancipation in those areas not covered under the terms of the Presidential proclamation. Hence, in his annual message to Congress at the outset of December, 1862, the President presented "an enlarged version of his old Border state plan." Mr. Lincoln "recommended that Congress should offer the several legislatures a constitutional amendment, to consist of three articles: first, providing compensation in Federal bonds for every State which should abolish slavery before 1900; second, guaranteeing freedom to all slaves who had gained it by the chances of war, but compensating loyal owners; and third, authorizing Congress to make some provision for colonizing freedmen abroad." Beyond this initiative, however, the President addressed himself not simply to the slavery question in isolation, but "with the far graver problem of race adjustment." Indeed, Mr. Lincoln,

. . . begged the people of the North to remember that they were as much responsible for the original introduction of slavery as the Southern people. He urged them not to give way to selfish fears that the freedmen would displace white workers. "If they stay in their old places, they jostle no white laborers; if they leave their old places, they leave them open to white laborers." He pleaded with them to abandon any mean prejudice against colored settlement in their communities. Equally distributed over the land, the Negroes would be but one colored to seven whites. "Could the one, in any way, greatly disturb the seven?"[13]

While the President was optimistic in his hope that his proposed Constitutional Amendment would be adopted and that, in turn, " 'would end the struggle now, and save the Union forever,' " he was to be again disappointed. Even members of his own cabinet predicted that the Administration supporters would not be able to muster the necessary two-thirds Congressional vote to send the proposal to the states for ratification and, even if they could, the states would not approve it. These predictions proved correct and the Presidential initiative met with almost universal disapproval.[14]

From the perspective of the Southerners themselves, in the aftermath of their battlefield victories of 1862, they were not about to abandon their struggle for independence and, hence, they dismissed both the President's Emancipation Proclamation and his proposal for a Constitutional Amendment. Consequently, on January 1, 1863, the Emancipation Proclamation took effect. As a corollary, the Administration quickly moved to receive former slaves into the Union army. The President felt that,

Even if unsuitable for field service, these former slaves could perform the duties of occupation of conquered territory and protection of communications from raiders and guerrillas. Since the Union devoted almost a third of its army to these security duties, such service provided ample scope for less demanding employment of black soldiers. More important, no plan could better implement the strategy . . . (of the Federal high command) . . . because, as Lincoln said, every recruit drawn from rebel territory subtracted from the Confederacy's productive population and was worth two in the North as "it adds one of us, and take one from the enemy." But soon the black troops evolved into effective fighting units engaged in all forms of combat. . . .[15]

In addition to their military utility and implications for the Southern economy, the increasing use of black soldiers had significant political implications since it gave the President much needed political support from the Radical wing of the Republican Party. Finally, the use of black troops was designed to have a negative psychological impact upon the Southern people, especially when combined with the psychological impact of the increasing pressure of the Federal naval blockade along the Southern coast and the gradual territorial dismemberment of the Confederacy. President Lincoln observed, " 'the mere sight of 50,000 armed and drilled black soldiers upon the banks of the Mississippi would end the rebellion at once.' " Apparently, Mr. Lincoln believed that a black force ''would arouse such fears of a general slave insurrection that Southern soldiers would break for home to protect their wives and children." As Bruce Catton noted, however, "the ex-slave as a soldier under discipline was much less to be feared than the ex-slave roaming the plantation country on his own hook, armed and under no discipline at all, full of hot resentment and for the first time in his life able to give his resentment unrestrained expression." In any case, by the conclusion of the war, black soldiers would compose just over 12 percent of the Union army.[16]

As spring, 1863 approached, recruitment of black soldiers into the Union army accelerated. In the west, however, many Union officers, "not only discouraged the Negroes from seeking Union protection, but by ill treatment forced them to return to their masters." For his part, the Western Commander, General Grant, did not feel strongly regarding the slavery question. For example, at the outset of the war, General Grant observed, " 'My inclination is to whip the rebellion into submission, preserving all constitutional rights. If it cannot be whipped in any other way than through a war against slavery, let it come to that legitimately. If it is necessary that slavery should fall that the Republic might continue its existence, let slavery go.' " Later, following the announcement of the Emancipation Proclamation and the Administration's decision to arm the former slaves, General Grant noted, " 'I would do all this whether the arming of the Negro seemed to me a wise policy or not, because it is an order that I am bound to obey and I do not feel that in my position I have a right to question any policy of the Government.' " While the General admitted that he " 'never was an Abolitionist, not even what could be called anti-slavery,' " he felt that " 'slavery was already dead and cannot be resurrected,' " Looking to the future, Grant observed that the blacks presently occupied "a peculiar status, somewhere between slavery and freedom" and that if they could demonstrate their value as free laborers and soldiers, they would eventually acquire full citizenship and voting rights. By late summer, 1863, after a number of black troops had joined the western army, General Grant came to the conclusion that the black troops "stood the hot climate better than whites, they preserved disciplines with less oversight, and 'all that have been tried have fought bravely.' " General Grant's principal lieutenant, William T. Sherman, however, said that he " 'would prefer to have this a white man's war and provide for the negroes after the time has passed.' " While acknowledging that, given his " 'opinions of negroes' " and " 'experience, yea, prejudice, I cannot trust them yet,' " he noted that " 'we are in revolution and I must not pretend to judge.' "[17]

As the Lincoln Administration escalated the national war objectives, the President and General Halleck began to review their military options for the remaining months of 1862. Indeed, this was the first real opportunity for the Lincoln-Halleck team to initiate national military strategy, since, up to now the new General-in-Chief had been reacting to the Confederate seizure of the initiative in July. In the largest sense, the President and General Halleck gradually concluded that the Confederacy had maintained itself sufficiently long that any single, highly visible Union battlefield victory and/or Union occupation of any specific place, group of places, or block of territory, no matter how significant, would probably not, in itself, prove sufficient to trigger the collapse of the Confederacy. Indeed, as General Halleck observed in April, 1863,

> The character of the war has changed very much with the last year. There is now no possible hope of reconciliation with the rebels. The Union party in the South is virtually destroyed. There can be no peace but that which is forced by the sword. We must conquer the rebels or be conquered by them. The North must conquer the slave oligarchy or become slaves themselves, the manufacturers mere "hewers of wood and drawers of water" to the Southern aristocrats.[18]

Hence, Washington ceased to predicate its national military strategy upon the assumption that the limited, though escalating occupation of specifically targeted locations throughout the South, reinforced by the long-term strangulation impact of the Federal naval blockade, would decisively strengthen pro-Union Southern moderates and enable them to displace the secessionists and terminate the insurrection. Instead, the high command now decided to significantly increase the pressure upon the Southern people collectively in order to force them to sucumb directly to the will of the Federal government. Consequently, between late 1862 and early 1864, Washington attempted to progressively weaken the Confederacy in a variety of interconnected ways. At sea, the high command, of course, continued its effort to isolate the South by means of the naval blockade. On land, the Washington leaders prepared for the gradual, relentless, territorial conquest, dismemberment, and permanent occupation of the entire South for the duration of hostilities, not just specifically identified locations. Indeed, the high command reasoned that the occupation of progressively larger portions of the South would serve not only to weaken the Confederacy by depriving the Richmond government access to the agricultural, industrial, transportation, administrative, and manpower resources of that region, it would strengthen the Union cause by allowing the Union forces to utilize those resources. This strategy, in turn, was complemented by the Federal policy of recruiting black soldiers into the Union army described above. Furthermore, General Halleck reasoned that, by seizing strategic locations throughout the South, the Union armies would deprive the Confederate field armies of their " 'base of operations,' " thereby leaving " 'the Confederates up in the air.' " Thus, in keeping with his overall military philosophy, the General-in-Chief believed that by seizing and permanently occupying the Confederacy's bases of operations, the Southern armies would not have to be defeated in the field, but, instead, would themselves disintegrate as Richmond would be unable to supply them. In short, the Federal high command in Washington reasoned that increasing maritime isolation, the Union occupation of increasingly large portions of territory and resources, especially bases of operations, and the disruption of its internal communications, combined, would progressively deprive the Confederates of their reservoir of war-making resources, while, simultaneously, the morale of the Southern people declined proportionately. Finally, in conducting their offensive against the Confederates the General-in-Chief instructed his subordinates to " 'live upon the enemy's country as much as possible and destroy his supplies. This is cruel warfare, but the enemy has brought it upon himself by his own conduct.' " By gradually weakening and ultimately breaking the military power of the Confederacy, the high command hoped to convince the people of the South that their struggle for independence was hopeless, that they should cease resistance, and reenter the Union on terms established by Washington.[19]

By the autumn, 1862, General-in-Chief Halleck had convinced the other members of the Federal high command that the decisive theater of operations lay in the west; it would be here that the war would be won or lost. Initially, the President still favored an immediate effort to capture eastern Tennessee. He continued to emphasize his determination to liberate pro-Union loyalists and gain Union (while denying Confederate) access to the area's resources, as well as to sever the Confederacy's internal rail communications, linking the west with Virginia, which traversed the region. Gradually, however, the President joined the General-in-Chief and concluded that the Mississippi Valley should receive priority. By successfully opening the great river, the Union would obtain several benefits. First, they would completely and visibly sever the Confederacy's communications with the trans-Mississippi states. Second, continued closure of the river had political ramifications. Agitation promoting the establishment of a Northwest Confederacy was intensifying and strengthened by the fact that the Confederacy continued to obstruct the flow of river traffic. The conquest of the Mississippi would open the river to Northern shipping, thereby diffusing secessionist extremism in the states of the upper Mississippi and Ohio Valleys. Third, the conquest of the Mississippi would provide the Union cause access to the Valley's resources. Access to cotton, as well as the reservoir of black manpower, would directly contribute to the success of the Union cause, while, simultaneously, indirectly contributing by denying these resources to the rebels. Fourth, since possession of the river had acquired great psychological/symbolic importance to the people of both the South and the North, especially those residing in the Ohio, Missouri, and upper Mississippi Valley, the opening of the Mississippi to the Gulf would negatively impact upon Southern morale, while, at the same time, elevating the morale of the Northern people and enhancing the political position of the Lincoln Administration, especially in the Old Northwest. Finally, fifth, the conquest of the river would open the way for further conquests in either direction from the Valley. If the Mississippi were in Union hands, the right flank of the Union army under General Rosecrans advancing through middle Tennessee toward Chattanooga would be more secure. Furthermore, following the conquest of the Mississippi Valley, General Halleck intended to seize other strategic locations in the Deep South and, he reasoned, control of the Mississippi Valley would facilitate future offensive operations. In short, under the guidance of the General-in-Chief, the Mississippi Valley again resumed the priority status it had held earlier under the provisions of General Scott's "anaconda plan." In contrast to earlier strategies, however, the new high command's renewed emphasis on the conquest and permanent occupation of the Mississippi Valley was no longer exclusively a vehicle to isolate the rebellious states, forcing them to exhaust their own war-making resources, and, in the process, enhancing the political power of Southern moderates so that they could, in turn, displace the secessionists. Nor was it viewed as part of an escalating effort to apply intensifying military pressure on the South by seizing a number of important specific locations throughout the South, again in an effort to strengthen Unionist elements and enable them to eclipse the secessionists and terminate the insurrection. Instead, it was now seen as a preliminary step in the conquest of the entire South, as well as the continental element of the Union blockade, all designed to break the military power of the Confederacy and force the Southerners to sue for peace.[20]

With respect to the Virginia theater, by autumn, 1862, both

the President and the General-in-Chief had begun to conclude that any Union attempt to take the Confederate capital at Richmond by siege or storm would be futile. First, the Union Quartermaster General expressed doubts as to his department's capacity to supply the Union army in a prolonged siege operation outside Richmond. Second, the Richmond communications network was so extensive and difficult to sever that isolation of the city would be virtually impossible. Unless the city's communications were cut, the siege would probably be doomed to last for several months. Third, the network of field fortifications which had been constructed around Richmond were too powerful to allow the city to be taken by assault. Fourth, the high command feared that a Union siege of Richmond would actually allow the Confederates to scale down the number of defending troops committed to the defense of the city and permit their deployment elsewhere in Virginia or in the west. Hence, the President and General Halleck came to feel that there was no realistic possibility of taking Richmond by force. Therefore, by January, 1863, following another disastrous move toward Richmond in December, to be examined subsequently, the Washington political/military leadership decided to abandon the capture of Richmond, or for that matter any other specific place in Virginia, as the goal of their operational planning in the eastern theater. Instead, the high command would direct that the object of all future campaigns in Virginia would be the destruction of General Lee's army. Specifically this meant that the Army of the Potomac should try to keep General Lee's army occupied and await a favorable opportunity to strike a decisive blow against the Confederate force. One way to accomplish that mission was to threaten General Lee's communications, while not jeopardizing the Union lines of supply, and to try to engage him in as advantageous a circumstance as possible. Indeed, already the President had leaned in that direction when he had expressed his conviction during the autumn, 1862 that, if Lee invaded Maryland, the Army of the Potomac might be able to cut his line of communications with the South and force him to fight at a disadvantage on ground selected by the Union army. By the winter, 1862–1863, this focus on Lee's army, not Richmond, would become established as the focus for operational planning in the Virginia theater.[21]

Mr. Lincoln and General Halleck, of course, recognized that the new emphasis upon the Confederate army, not Richmond, which they would adopt at the end of 1862 for the Virginia theater, had important political overtones. Given the Northern public's Virginia fixation and its hunger for a decisive battle culminating a successful Union military campaign, the President continued to feel that a field victory over General Lee's army, even an indecisive one, would yield disproportionately large political dividends and serve to dramatically uplift Northern morale more than a field victory in any other theater of operations. Conversely, the high command felt that the damage to Northern morale would be less in the event of a failure to defeat Lee's army than would be the damage caused by a prolonged siege of the Confederate capital. But, while the new focus on General Lee's army would be more satisfying to the Northern people and politicians, the new mission and objective of the Army of he Potomac created tension between that Army's commanders and the high command in Washington. The Commanders of the Army of the Potomac resented having to abandon what they felt was an attainable objective, a siege of Richmond, and substitute it with the unpromising task of destroying Lee's field army. This resentment was redoubled when placed in the emotional context of the politically charged, ongoing, agonizing reappraisal of the record of the popular, former Commander of the Army of the Potomac, George McClellan, and the conduct of the Peninsular Campaign. Certainly the President recognized that the prospect for the Union destruction of General Lee's army was unpromising, but he also felt that the prospects for successfully besieging Richmond were even less promising. In the largest sense, however, Mr. Lincoln and General Halleck concluded that Virginia was unlikely to be the decisive theater of the war and, hence, downgraded it in importance compared to the west.[22]

It was in this context that General Halleck and the President again attempted to apply the principle of simultaneous advances in coordinating the late autumn, early winter offensives by the Union armies in the three main theaters of operations: Virginia, middle Tennessee, and the Mississippi Valley. As early as August 3, 1862, the members of the Administration had discussed initiating a final effort to clear the Mississippi Valley. The Acting Secretary of the Interior, supported by the Secretary of the Treasury, proposed the idea of recruiting a special force to open the river. The General-in-Chief supported the idea of moving vigorously to clear the valley, but was troubled by the plan to use newly raised troops. Hence, for the moment, the plan was shelved. In any case, the Washington high command's attention was soon to be monopolized by the Confederate invasions of Maryland and Kentucky. By autumn, however, the President personally began to plan an operation to finally clear the valley, optimally, before the end of the year. Mr. Lincoln planned to reinforce the Federal garrison at New Orleans in order to effectively create a new field army capable of moving northward, up the Mississippi, to Vicksburg. As B. H. Liddell Hart pointed out,

> Vicksburg, roughly midway between Memphis and the mouth, was the main key to the Mississippi. Not only did it stand on high ground overlooking the river, the first high ground below Memphis, but it was the only rail and river junction between Memphis and New Orleans. From Vicksburg a line ran eastward through Jackson, forty-five miles distant, where it intersected the main north and south (to New Orleans) line and then continued east through Meridian where it intersected the parallel line which ran from Corinth down to Mobile. And on the west bank of the Mississippi opposite Vicksburg, a line ran westwards towards Shreveport in western Louisiana. Thus Vicksburg was not only the nodal point of the communications in the Southern States but the naval cord which connected the newer trans-Mississippi area of the Confederacy with the parent body.[23]

Consequently, on November 19, 1862, about the time the Federal high command relieved Generals McClellan and Buell of their respective commands, it named Major General Nathaniel P. Banks, a Massachusetts politician and veteran of the Shenandoah and Second Bull Run Campaigns, to assume command of the Department of the Gulf with headquarters at New Orleans. General Banks' mission was first to clear the river to Vicksburg and then to advance up the Red River into northwestern Louisiana and on to Texas. General Banks arrived in New Orleans in mid-December, whereupon he moved a portion of his force upriver and recaptured Baton Rouge. His next target was Port

Hudson, a naturally strong position which the Southerners had carefully fortified. Port Hudson, in turn, was the southern gateway to both the Red River Valley, as well as Vicksburg, two hundred miles to the north.[24]

Meanwhile, the President also planned to send an expedition down the Mississippi to Vicksburg from the north which, he hoped, would ultimately cooperate with General Banks' force moving upriver from the south. The origins of this expedition dated back to September, 1862, when Major General John A. McClernand, a prominent Illinois War Democrat and veteran of the Tennessee River expedition, visited the President in Washington and proposed that a new army be recruited by McClernand and that, in cooperation with the navy, he independently lead it down the Mississippi and capture Vicksburg. After taking Vicksburg, McClernand proposed to either move across Mississippi and Alabama and capture Atlanta or move into the trans-Mississippi West toward Texas. The idea of a pincer movement by McClernand and Banks along the Mississippi appealed to Mr. Lincoln and, hence, on October 20, 1862, General McClernand was ordered to Illinois, Indiana, and Iowa " 'to organize the troops remaining in those states and to be raised by volunteering or draft, and forward them with all dispatch to Memphis, Cairo or such other points as may hereafter be designated by the General-in-Chief, to the end that, when a sufficient force not required by the operations of General Grant's command shall be raised, an expedition may be organized under General McClernand's command against Vicksburg, and to clear the Mississippi river and open navigation to New Orleans.' " The order concluded by stipulating that " 'the forces so organized will remain subject to the designation of the General-in-Chief, and be employed according to such exigencies as the service in his judgement may require.' " The order, however, left unclear whether General McClernand was to be independent or under the command of the Department Commander, General Grant.[25]

Meanwhile, as Mr. Lincoln and General McClernand were developing their plan for an independent movement down the Mississippi, General Grant was developing his own plans. While there were rumors that Washington was planning some sort of operation commanded by McClernand, General Grant was not officially informed of the McClernand expedition. Consequently, "all that Grant knew was that he himself was expected to plan and execute a new offensive, with the capture of Vicksburg and the final opening of the river as the objective, and he modeled his campaign on the formula that had been so successful down to date." General Grant planned to move his force, known since mid-October, 1862 as the Army of the Tennessee, parallel to the Mississippi, but inland (east) from it. As early as the latter part of October, General Grant had proposed to General Halleck,

> Destruction of the railroads to all points of the compass from Corinth ... and the opening of the road from Humboldt to Memphis. The Corinth forces I would move to Grand Junction, and add to them the Bolivar forces except a small garrison there. With small re-enforcements at Memphis I think I would be able to move down the Mississippi Central road and cause the evacuation of Vicksburg and to be able to capture or destroy all the boats in the Yazoo river.[26]

General Grant's proposal accurately reflected the concerns which many Union officers sensed regarding the high command's strategy emphasizing the conquest and permanent occupation of Confederate territory. To hold the railway network in western Tennessee against Confederate raiders would effectively immobilize the Union army. Hence, Grant proposed to hold only that portion of the railway which was necessary to facilitate a further advance and abandon the remainder. The General-in-Chief did not reply to General Grant's proposal, but it was an important step in the intellectual development of the latter.[27]

On October 26, 1862, General Grant proposed concentrating his forces in northern Mississippi and then advancing toward Jackson, Mississippi. The capture of Jackson would strategically turn Vicksburg, forcing the Confederates to abandon the isolated city. Grant intended to use railways as his line of communications. During the early phase of the campaign, General Grant planned to draw his supplies from Columbus, Kentucky, 180 miles away. Once he reached Grenada, Mississippi, however, he intended to change his base to Memphis and supply his army relying upon the Mississippi and Tennessee Railroad which linked Memphis with the Mississippi Central at Grenada. By November 2, he had begun to mass his forces at Grand Junction, Tennessee. The following day, General-in-Chief Halleck authorized Grant to advance, noting, " 'I hope for an active campaign this fall.' " Meanwhile, in early November, General Grant, still officially in the dark regarding the high command's planned Mississippi River expedition to be commanded by General McClernand, but quite concerned due to the multitude of rumors regarding the planned offensive, requested clarification from the General-in-Chief. For his part, General Halleck was extremely uneasy about the role which the President had defined for General McClernand. Hence, the General-in-Chief opted to quietly sabotage McClernand. Capitalizing upon the clause in General McClernand's instructions which held that McClernand could use all the troops not needed by General Grant, General Halleck cryptically told Grant, " 'You have command of all troops sent to your department and have permission to fight the enemy where you please.' " Most analysts agree with Bruce Catton's observation that "Halleck could not tell Grant what was up, but he obviously wanted him to get his campaign developed well enough so that it would take precedence over anything McClernand might be contemplating." On November 20, General Grant moved southward along the Mississippi Central. Meanwhile, General Sherman, one of Grant's principal lieutenants in the western theater, brought his forces from Memphis and, by December 5, had joined Grant at Oxford and College Hill, Mississippi.[28]

At this point, however, General Grant was compelled to totally revise his operational plan. First, it became clear that there were not enough locomotives to allow the Mississippi Central rail line of communications to support the concentrated Army of the Tennessee as it advanced southward. Second, the General-in-Chief apparently remained concerned about the McClernand complication and seems to have felt that it was important to integrate operations along the Mississippi River with Grant's movements in the north central portion of the state of Mississippi. Consequently, General Halleck suggested that the railroads not be put into " 'operation south of Memphis' " and

" 'operations in north Mississippi must be limited to rapid marches upon any collected forces of the enemy feeding as far as possible upon the country.' " Finally, General Halleck wrote, " 'The enemy must be turned by a movement down the river from Memphis as soon as sufficient force can be collected.' " As Bruce Catton observed,

> Considered in light of what Grant knew at the time, this was nothing less than astounding. All spring and summer, Halleck's emphasis had always been on repairing and using the railroads. When Grant suggested that the network near the Mississippi border be abandoned Halleck had failed to approve, and Grant had set out, with Halleck's blessing, on an offensive which was directly dependent on railway transportation. Now he was being told that the railroads were not to be relied on, and his plan of campaign was being turned inside-out.[29]

In view of these considerations, General Grant concluded that, if there was to be an expedition down the Mississippi from Memphis, he wanted General Sherman to command it. Consequently, on December 8, 1862, Grant informed General Halleck that he intended to divide his force into two elements and launch a two-pronged assault on Vicksburg. General Sherman was to take one division back to Memphis where it would be reinforced by the troops which McClernand had already recruited and had been sent forward to Memphis, as well as the gunboats of the Mississippi River flotilla. Grant would remain with his other two divisions in northern Mississippi. General Grant planned to lead an overland advance southward along the rail line in person, attacking and pinning the enemy in northern Mississippi. If Grant defeated the Confederates or they retreated, he intended to advance upon Vicksburg, via Jackson. Simultaneously, General Sherman was to lead his sizable force down the Mississippi River from Memphis and assault the Southern defenses located immediately above the city. Grant expected that, while his force pinned the main Southern army in northern Mississippi, Sherman would be able to take Vicksburg via the river route. Conversely, if the Confederates concentrated against General Sherman's force on the river, General Grant intended to move quickly upon the Confederate rear. Thus, General Grant hoped that these two forces would be mutually supportive and ultimately successful in capturing Vicksburg and opening the Mississippi River. Following the intended fall of Vicksburg, General Grant expected the Confederates to fall back toward eastern Mississippi, where he felt they could be brought to battle. General Sherman left Memphis on December 20, 1862, arrived in the Vicksburg vicinity on December 26, and unsuccessfully assaulted the Confederate defenses at Chickasaw Bluffs on December 29.[30] General Sherman made another attempt to overcome the defending Southerners by attacking Hayne's Bluff, located a short distance up the Yazoo River, on December 31, but that assault also failed. Meanwhile, about the time General Sherman's force left Memphis for Vicksburg, but unknown to Sherman, General Grant had been forced to cancel his overland movement against Vicksburg's rear because Confederate cavalry raids had destroyed his forward supply base at Holly Springs, Mississippi and disrupted his line of communications, forcing him to withdraw northward to the Tennessee-Mississippi border. Like General Buell earlier, General Grant now experienced the extreme vulnerability of rail lines of communications to disruption by enemy cavalry and guerrilla operations, as compared to the relatively secure and dependable water communications provided by the Tennessee River during his expedition southward the previous spring. Consequently, Grant resolved not to predicate future military operations on vulnerable rail lines of communications if alternative options were available. With his supply lines severed, General Grant's troops were compelled to forage, but they soon found that there was plenty of food available. Grant later observed, " '. . . had I known the demoralized condition of the enemy, or the fact that central Mississippi abounded so in all army supplies, I would have been in pursuit of Pemberton (the Confederate commander) while his cavalry was destroying the roads in my rear.' " In short, while Grant felt compelled to halt his southward advance and retire northward, he undoubtedly began as early as January, 1863 to question the axiom "that an army of invasion must retain a firm connection with its own base . . . in a land that produced a surplus of food." Meanwhile, on January 2, 1863, General McClernand arrived in the Vicksburg area and assumed command over the river expedition, reducing Sherman to a subordinate position. General

Sherman, however, suggested that, rather than standing inert in the Vicksburg area, the river force could move against Arkansas Post which posed a threat to the communications lines of the Union Mississippi River expedition. General McClernand agreed and, on January 11, the Post was taken. Following the destruction of the Confederate fortifications, the Union troops returned to the Mississippi line. As B. H. Liddell Hart pointed out,

> McClernand had contemplated a further move up the Arkansas River in order to pounce on Little Rock, the base and headquarters of the Confederate forces operating in northern Arkansas, which still threatened Missouri. Although not mentioned in Sherman's memoirs—probably out of deference to Grant—it would appear from the records that this move was suggested and advocated by him. Such an exploitation of the army's water-borne mobility promised, if successful, to extinguish the trans-Mississippi effort of the Confederacy, and also the danger of interference with the Mississippi communications of the Union army while operating against Vicksburg, a danger already damped down by the capture of Arkansas Post. At the least a pounce on Little Rock would distract the Confederates' attention, now concentrated on Vicksburg. In assessing the merits of this still-born project it is just to remember that the Union army, after reverting to a rigid maintenance of their main objective, lay confronting Vicksburg ineffectively for nearly six months, and that the trans-Mississippi forces continued to be a thorn in the Union side even after the capture of Vicksburg.[31]

Notwithstanding the success of the useful Arkansas Post operation, General Grant remained uncomfortable with the prospect of General McClernand in command along the river. For that reason, combined with his reservations about using rail lines of communications to attempt another advance through north central Mississippi, Grant transferred his entire force to the Mississippi, concentrated the Army of the Tennessee immediately north of Vicksburg, and assumed personal command over the entire campaign. Here, however, Grant was to devote the winter pondering how to circumvent the Confederate defenses above Vicksburg which had demonstrated their invulnerability against General Sherman's recent, costly assaults. As he did so, he engaged in a series of projects which he later said were designed to " 'consume time, and to divert the attention of the enemy, of my troops, and of the public generally.' "[32]

In the Virginia theater of operations, the new Commander of the Army of the Potomac, Major General Ambrose Burnside, proposed to concentrate his forces near Warrenton, Virginia as if to attack the portion of the Confederate army located at Culpepper (the other portion being located in the Shenandoah Valley, southeast of Winchester). He then intended to abandon his line of communications along the Orange and Alexandria Railroad, quickly shift the bulk of his army to Fredericksburg, and advance southward, overland, toward Richmond, using the relatively secure Richmond and Potomac Railroad to link his army with its supply base at Aquia Landing on the Potomac. As Stephen Ambrose observed,

> Burnside claimed the movement would give better protection to Washington than an advance along the Blue Ridge Mountains. He was obsessed with the cry of "On to Richmond" and later declared the capture of the city "should be the great object of the campaign, as the fall of that place would tend more to cripple the Rebel cause than almost any other military event, except the absolute breaking up of their army."[33]

The new Commander of the Army of the Potomac felt that this threat to the Confederate communications and capital would induce General Lee to shift the portion of his divided forces located east of the Blue Ridge Mountains at Culpepper eastward to oppose the Union advance. Should that occur, Burnside hoped to destroy that portion of Lee's force before it could be reinforced. The General-in-Chief, however, had reservations about General Burnside's plan. He believed that the new Commander of the Army of the Potomac should have advanced according to the plan which the high command had suggested to General McClellan prior to McClellan's removal — "moving 'on the interior line to Richmond' from his present position, 'hugging closely to the Blue Ridge,' watching its passes, prepared to fight." Discussing General Burnside's plan, Warren Hassler observed that the scheme "had much to recommend it."

> The ten-mile-long segment of the R. F. & P. between Aquia Creek Landing and Fredericksburg was far safer and less vulnerable than the long, circuitous Orange & Alexandria. Then, too, operating on the Fredericksburg line would place the Federal army directly between the enemy and Washington — a favorite defensive move for the safety of the capital which was supported by the administration. A disadvantage of Burn-

side's plan was that, once at Fredericksburg, a number of rivers inter-
vened between the Federal army and Richmond. Also, to be successful,
Union intentions would have to be masked from Lee up to the last
moment. Once Burnside began his movement it had to continue without
interruption, and was undertaken with the understanding that bridging
material would be sent to Fredericksburg in time to enable the army to
cross at that point as soon as it arrived.[34]

For his part, the President, apparently not having yet finally and
irrevocably concluded that Lee's army and not Richmond should
be the exclusive objective of the Army of the Potomac, reluctantly approved of Burnside's plan, noting, " '. . . it will succeed
if you move very rapidly, otherwise not.' " On November 15,
1862, General Burnside began implementing the plan and, by
November 17, the lead elements of the Army of the Potomac
arrived across the Rappahannock River from Fredericksburg. At
that time, Fredericksburg was lightly held by the Southerners.
Poor weather, combined with a delay in the arrival of pontoons
with which to cross the river, however, prevented the immediate
seizure of the city. General Burnside would not allow his leading
corps to cross the river until the pontoons had arrived due to
concern that the Union forces might become isolated and be
destroyed on the south side of the river. Meanwhile, on November 21, half of General Lee's Confederates arrived on the south
side of the Rappahannock, with the other half of Lee's army
enroute to Fredericksburg from the Shenandoah Valley. The
reinforcing element, however, did not arrive until much later,
thereby providing Burnside with a lost opportunity to quickly
move up the Rappahannock, cross the river, and place the entire
Army of the Potomac between the two divided portions of the
Confederacy's principal eastern army. Conversely, had he been
able to quickly cross the Rappahannock at Fredericksburg en
masse before the Confederates could be reinforced, he possibly
could have overwhelmed the portion of Lee's army defending
the city. Finally, between December 10 and 12, as General Lee
hurriedly completed the concentration of his army, the main
body of the Army of the Potomac finally crossed the Rappahannock at Fredericksburg. On December 13, 1862, General
Burnside threw the Army of the Potomac frontally against the
virtually impregnable Confederate defensive position. The result

was a terrible, tragic disaster for the Union army. Lee's defenders held and inflicted extremely heavy losses on the Union attackers. On the night of December 14, the badly mauled Army of the Potomac withdrew to the north side of the Rappahannock. Its survival in the aftermath of this serious defeat, as with the survival of the Union army following its defeat at the Second Battle of Bull Run, again confirmed the high degree of resilience of the mid-nineteenth century army, despite extreme reversals.[35]

Following the disaster of Fredericksburg, as discussed earlier, the Washington high command, long troubled concerning the vexing problems associated with maintaining Richmond as a theater objective of the Army of the Potomac, decided to officially revise its focus in Virginia. The President and the General-in-Chief now stipulated that, henceforth, the Army of the Potomac should "abandon Richmond as an objective and adopt as the 'first object' of a Virginia campaign 'the defeat or scattering of Lee's army which threatened Washington and the line of the upper Potomac.' " Hence, they directed the Army of the Potomac to attempt to cross the Rappahannock River, incurring as few casualties as possible and " 'occupy the rebel army south of the Rappahannock,' " but prevent the Confederates from retreating into the Richmond entrenchments. In the largest sense, however, the high command "recognized the remoteness of the likelihood of a decision in Virginia" and would have preferred to have transferred troops to the west to reinforce efforts to conquer the Mississippi Valley. For his part, General Burnside was not destined to remain in command of the main Union army in the east. On January 25, 1863, just two and a half months after his appointment to command the Army of the Potomac, General Burnside was relieved of that command and replaced by Major General Joseph Hooker.[36]

Finally, in the third principal theater of operations, middle Tennessee, the high command ordered the new commander of General Buell's old army, now known as the Army of the Cumberland, General William Rosecrans, to quickly occupy the eastern portion of Tennessee and sever the rail line which traversed the region and connected Virginia with the west, at Chattanooga, Cleveland, or Athens, Tennessee. General Rosecrans, however,

135

delayed in carrying out the order to advance from his position at Nashville because of repeated cavalry raids upon his line of communications along the Louisville and Nashville Railroad. Like his predecessor, General Buell, and, more recently, General Grant, General Rosecrans experienced the high vulnerability of rail lines of communications, as compared to water lines, to raids by Southern cavalry and guerrillas. Unlike Grant, however, who could alternatively utilize the Mississippi River to approach his geographic objective, General Rosecrans was forced to depend upon the railroad to communicate with his base of supply. In addition to the problem of maintaining his communications, General Rosecrans delayed his advance because he wanted to fully prepare his army for what he hoped would be a decisive battle of annihilation of the Confederate field army somewhere south of Nashville. The Washington high command, however, became increasingly impatient with Rosecrans' delay. In a communication to the General, General Halleck attempted to explain the reasons for the high command's eagerness to have the Army of the Cumberland take the offensive. As T. Harry Williams reported,

> The President had said to him time and again, Halleck wrote, that there were imperative reasons why the enemy must be driven over the Tennessee River at the earliest moment. Lincoln had not told him what the reasons were, but Old Brains (General Halleck) knew. The government feared that the friends of the South in England would make an attempt at the January meeting of Parliament to force the government to intervene in the war on the side of the Confederacy. If at that time the Confederates were in possession of middle Tennessee, the supporters of intervention would have an argument that the South was gaining in the war and that England ought to get in on the winning side. Federal possession of middle Tennessee, said Halleck, might be the turning point in Northern foreign relations. Referring to Lincoln's feelings about the possibility of foreign entrance into the war, Halleck said: "You can hardly conceive his great anxiety about it."[37]

General Halleck summarized the high command's views by noting that "a victory before the opening of Parliament would be of more value than 'ten times that success at a later date.' " Finally, on December 26, 1862, in the wake of the army of the Potomac's terrible defeat at Fredericksburg and as General Sherman's force arrived before the defenses above Vicksburg, General Rosecrans led the Army of the Cumberland southward against the Confederates concentrated at Murfreesboro, Tennessee. On December 31, 1862, as General Sherman made his second, ill fated assault upon the Vicksburg defenses, the principal Union and Confederate armies in middle Tennessee clashed a few miles northwest of Murfreesboro at the Battle of Stones River. In the extremely bloody fighting, the Southerners bent the Union right back 90 degrees, but the maneuverability and defensive firepower of the mid-nineteenth century army again asserted itself and the Army of the Cumberland held. Finally, following a day of suspense after the initial clash, the fighting resumed on January 2, 1863, after which the Confederates withdrew to Tullahoma, about 36 miles to the south. The Army of the Cumberland occupied Murfreesboro on January 5, but did not pursue the retreating Confederates. Rosecrans' army had won a victory "in a very narrow sense," since the enemy had retreated, but General Rosecrans had failed to annihilate the Confederate army as he had hoped or occupy a major portion of Confederate controlled territory.[38]

Although the triple Union offensives in late 1862 had threatened the Confederates in all three principal theaters of operations, thereby preventing Richmond from transferring large bodies of men from a quiet theater to one which was threatened, all three offensives had failed to attain their objectives. Moreover, General Burnside's offensive in the Virginia theater had ended in a bloody disaster and General Rosecrans' indecisive battlefield victory had been purchased at a high cost in Union lives. Fortunately for the Union cause, the abortive Mississippi Valley offensive had been considerably less costly than the Union offensives in Virginia and in middle Tennessee. Politically, the obvious failures of General Grant's campaign in the Mississippi Valley and General Burnside's campaign in Virginia, combined with backlash Northern resentment as a result of the Emancipation Proclamation, caused a serious decline in Northern morale. In this context, as Professors Beringer, Hattaway, Jones, and Still commented,

> The reverses sustained by the Republican Party in the fall elections two months earlier seemed but the beginning of the consequent misfortune. On January 3, 1863, Governor Oliver P. Morton of Indiana warned

Secretary of War Stanton that his state legislature intended "to pass a joint resolution acknowledging the Southern Confederacy, and urging the states of the Northwest to dissolve all constitutional relations with the New England states. The same thing," he added, "is on foot in Illinois," . . . Iowa was also in a demoralized condition. Shocked by the emancipation policy and encouraged by their party's successes at the polls the preceding November, Democrats held numerous peace meetings throughout the state in January 1863. . . . It is no wonder that Lincoln said, as Orville H. Browning recorded in his diary, "The Almighty is against us, and I can hardly see a ray of hope."[39]

While, as Allen Nevins observed, "the precise strength of disloyalty was for three reasons difficult to measure: a clear definition was impossible; its worst manifestations were kept secret; and its vigor fluctuated from place to place and day to day," from Washington's perspective, the situation was extremely serious. Conversely, the operations of late 1862 raised Southern morale and, notwithstanding the defeat of the Confederate forces at Stones River, Southern confidence remained high throughout the winter. Given all this, it can be easily understood why Mr. Lincoln was extremely grateful to General Rosecrans for providing the Administration with a timely, though bloody victory.[40]

Following the failure of the simultaneous advances of late 1862, during the relative quiet of the winter of 1863, the Federal high command began to lay its plans for the coming spring, 1863 campaigns. Politically, Congress was becoming increasingly polarized. As Allen Nevins noted,

The Republican Jacobins . . . interpreted the military defeats and the election as requiring much more drastic and pugnacious action. Democrats and Border Republicans, on the other hand, interpreted them as requiring a return to strict interpretations of the Constitution and the single war-object of restoring the Union. More fighting, more confiscations of rebel property, more liberation of slaves, and full use of colored fighters—these were the demands vociferated by extreme Republicans. An instant stoppage of arbitrary arrests, a repudiation of emancipation as unconstitutional, or inexpedient, and a halt in the head-long progress toward despotism—these were the ultimatums of extreme Democrats.[41]

Clearly, the Administration needed a military victory and needed it as soon as possible. But, conversely, as Professor Nevins also observed,

The North in 1863 held four tremendous advantages: first, its possession of a chief of state who was indisputably the greatest American of his time; second, its ever-growing superiority in manpower, natural resources, all phases of economic life, and money; third, its open ports, largely undamaged rail and river transportation system, and its unoccupied territory; and fourth, the moral superiority that a combatant of slavery could assert over a defender of slavery, although all did not agree on the weight of this. These advantages were sternly impressive, but they were not irresistible.[42]

Most of the Union field forces were distributed into four principal armies: the Army of the Potomac in Virginia, under the command of Major General Joseph Hooker; the Army of the Cumberland in middle Tennessee, commanded by Major General William Rosecrans; the Army of the Tennessee immediately north of Vicksburg on the Mississippi River, under Major General Ulysses S. Grant; and the Army of the Gulf on the lower Mississippi, under Major General Nathaniel Banks. In addition, a very large number of Union troops were scattered along the coast, as well as performing garrison and guard duties behind the lines. Unfortunately for the Union cause, however, notwithstanding the efforts of General Halleck from Washington, the operations of these four armies remained poorly coordinated and marched "not as parts of a well-organized machine, each general assisting and supporting his fellow generals, but largely as individual entities, each general acting alone." Conquest of the Mississippi Valley remained the highest priority for Washington, with the conquest of eastern and middle Tennessee second, operations in the Virginia theater third, and activity in Missouri and Arkansas of lowest priority. The President and General Halleck felt that the moves designed to capture Vicksburg and the operations in middle Tennessee would be mutually supporting. Moreover, the high command hoped that the campaign in middle Tennessee would support an independently conducted, but poorly coordinated Union drive against eastern Tennessee. In contrast to the west where the high command's focus remained on territorial conquest, in the Virginia theater, the President and the General-in-Chief reiterated that the destruction of General Lee's army, not the capture of Richmond, was the primary mission of the Army of the Potomac. To do this, General Halleck advised the new Commander of the Army of the Potomac, General Hooker, to conduct turning movements which would occupy the Confederates, thus preventing them from reinforcing their armies in Tennessee or Mississippi, as well as possibly yielding a favorable opportunity to successfully engage Lee's forces and provide the Administration with a much needed battlefield victory in the highly visible Virginia theater. Overall, however, the high command appears to have continued to expect very little from the Army of the Potomac, opting instead to concentrate Union efforts upon the west where the Confederates were weaker and the Union cause had enjoyed earlier successes. As General Halleck observed, " 'in my opinion, the opening of the Mississippi River will be to us of more advantage than the capture of forty Richmonds.' " As Stephen Ambrose observed, until Vicksburg finally fell, "every movement in the west was considered only in terms of its effect on Grant's offensive against the place."[43]

In the priority Mississippi Valley theater of operations, General Grant's problem remained how to turn Vicksburg's defenses and sever the rail line linking Vicksburg and Jackson, Mississippi, thereby compelling the city's Confederate defenders to surrender, evacuate the city by a roundabout route, or assume the tactical offensive and attack the Union army astride the city's line of communications. Eventually, after experimenting with a variety of options and notwithstanding General Sherman's advice to "transport the whole army to Memphis, then march down the railroads to Vicksburg's rear," as Grant had originally planned to do during the autumn of 1862, General Grant decided to move his army downriver and maneuver against the city from the south. General Grant felt that a movement along the lines suggested by General Sherman would be interpreted by the North as a Union defeat, leading, in turn, to further demoralization. As General J.F.C. Fuller pointed out,

> From the first, Grant was fully aware of the feasibility of passing a force down the river and past the Vicksburg batteries, in spite of the fact that his line of communications would be under constant fire. The advantage of such an approach was obvious, namely, once the Vicksburg bluff was passed he could land anywhere he chose on the eastern bank, and operate northwards and in rear of Vicksburg. Another advantage was that by establishing a base south of Vicksburg, he could, if required,

co-operate with General Banks. . . . The disadvantages of this approach were not only the constant threat to Grant's line of communications, which I have already mentioned, and the danger of being caught between two fires when once in rear of Vicksburg, but that the exceptionally heavy winter rains prohibited such a move for several months.[44]

But, at the outset of spring, Grant moved. Throughout April, the General dispatched two of the three corps of the Army of the Tennessee down the west side of the river to a position below Vicksburg. Here, the two Union corps were joined by the ships of the Mississippi River flotilla which had passed beneath the Vicksburg river defenses on the night of April 16. The Navy's contribution to the campaign was significant, since the river flotilla "not only allowed supplies to be moved south of Vicksburg, but also provided protection to the transports which ferried Grant's army to the east bank and brought other supplies across from the west bank." On April 30, amid a diversionary raid by Federal cavalry through Mississippi to Baton Rouge, Louisiana, and demonstrations north of Vicksburg by General Sherman's corps, which General Grant had left behind, all designed to confuse the Confederate defenders, General Grant ferried his two corps across the Mississippi to the east bank. He then quickly brought Sherman's corps south, such that, by early May, the Army of the Tennessee had been concentrated on the east bank of the Mississippi River at Bruinsburg, below Vicksburg. General Grant had initially intended to hold his army in position, while sending one corps farther down river to cooperate with the Army of the Gulf under General Banks which was supposed to be proceeding upriver from Baton Rouge toward Port Hudson. Then, once the Mississippi Valley below Vicksburg to the Gulf was securely in Union hands and he had a secure line of communications southward, Grant intended to concentrate both the Armies of the Tennessee and the Gulf for the final drive on Vicksburg. Indeed, the President felt that "it was vital" that Grant's and Banks' armies be united, since, Washington feared, not to do so would provide the Confederates with the opportunity to concentrate their forces and crush the two Union armies separately. As will be discussed shortly, in early May, the Army of the Potomac would suffer another defeat in Virginia and the high command feared that a disaster on the Mississippi River could spell the end of the United States. On May 2, however, General Grant learned that General Banks' Army of the Gulf was not in position. Back in late January, 1863, General Banks had attempted to move his forces up the west bank of the Mississippi, past the Confederate stronghold at Port Hudson, to the Red River. Unfortunately for Banks, however, his force failed to successfully traverse the difficult terrain. On March 13, David Farragut, Commander of the West Gulf Squadron, moved a portion of his naval forces past Port Hudson, sustaining heavy losses in the process, whereupon they blockaded the Red River. Since both Vicksburg and Port Hudson depended upon the Red River Valley for supplies, the resultant gains justified the cost of the operation. With Farragut's ships blockading the Red River, General Banks would have been better advised to have remained at Port Hudson, where the Confederate garrison could not have long held out. In the judgement of most historians, "his best usefulness lay in aiding Grant's movement to clear the Mississippi." But, instead, Banks moved his forces into the Louisiana hinterland and, by early May, when General Grant expected to rendezvous with the Army of the Gulf, the latter was at Alexandria, Louisiana, in about the center of the state. This, of course, left General Grant and the Army of the Tennessee in an awkward position. If he opted to wait for Bank's force to return to the anticipated rendezvous position, the Confederates would have time to concentrate and reinforce their forces in west central Mississippi. Moreover, Grant's supply line remained vulnerable. Conversely, if he opted to advance, his increasingly lengthening line of communications would become ever more precarious.[45]

It was in this context that General Grant opted to make one of the boldest movements of his life. He decided to cut loose of his line of communications and operate without a base. The General believed that his troops could forage from the countryside, but ammunition would have to be carried. Hence, he directed that all wagons be loaded primarily with ammunition. Indeed, the unforaged, fertile region through which the Army of the Tennessee would pass promised an abundance of food and fodder, since local planters had largely substituted these crops for cotton. But, the General's decision to sever his communications lines meant that his turning movement would be a raid, not a penetration as originally intended. This implied that his army would, of necessity, have to keep moving, since to halt in any specific location for a long period of time would exhaust the available sources of supply and force the raiding army to disperse. Conversely, however, the absence of communications lines would be an advantage in the sense that it would be impossible for the enemy to cut his army off from its base and force it to fight for its communications. As one analyst put it, "he protected himself against an attack in the rear by leaving himself without a rear to be attacked." General Grant, however, did not intend to be without a line of supply for long. The General planned to move swiftly between the Confederate forces concentrated at Vicksburg and those which were concentrating at Jackson, Mississippi. He then intended to destroy the latter before moving upon the former.[46] As General J.F.C. Fuller noted,

> By so doing he would not only protect his rear when the time came for him to advance westwards against Vicksburg, but he would simultaneously cut Vicksburg off from its base of supply. In short, his idea, rather than plan, was to manoeuvre against the Vicksburg line of communications in order to isolate the fortress, and, simultaneously, destroy that force of the enemy which was so placed that it could operate against his rear.[47]

Advancing rapidly, by mid-month, General Grant's army occupied a position astride the railway linking Jackson and Vicksburg, whereupon, on May 14, two corps of the Army of the Tennessee attacked and took Jackson, driving the Confederate forces northward, while the Army's third corps guarded against an advance by the Confederates based at Vicksburg. Fearing that the two separated Confederate forces would move north and unite, Grant immediately turned west and moved two of his corps against the Confederate forces located just east of Vicksburg. The third corps, Sherman's, remained near Jackson to keep the recently defeated Confederate force, now located north of Jackson, from attacking the Union rear. In addition to watching the Confederates, General Sherman's corps destroyed the city's industry, as well as its railroad assets, thereby making a Confederate advance westward more difficult. Meanwhile, on May 16, the two Union corps moving toward Vicksburg clashed with the

Confederate force covering Vicksburg at the Battle of Champion's Hill, along the rail line east of the city. Following their defeat in this encounter, the Confederates withdrew into the city's defenses. The entire Army of the Tennessee, including General Sherman's corps, followed and, on May 19, it unsuccessfully attacked the city. On May 22, Grant again stormed Vicksburg, but was again unsuccessful in taking the city. Hence, the Army of the Tennessee began a siege operation. Its position was now quite strong. Upon investing Vicksburg, General Grant had reopened a secure line of communications with the North via the Mississippi. Moreover, although on the strategic offensive, the Army of the Tennessee now enjoyed the benefits of the tactical defensive. On the one hand, the Confederates trapped inside Vicksburg had no choice but to surrender or assume the tactical offensive and attempt to break out against Grant's entrenched army. On the other hand, to be successful in relieving the city and its trapped garrison from the ouside, the Confederate relief force (the embryo of which was the force which had been driven north of Jackson on May 14) would have to attack the Union army of observation which General Grant had positioned to cover his rear. Meanwhile, recognizing that it would be inappropriate for the Army of the Tennessee to join Banks' Army of the Gulf as had been originally expected, the Washington high command directed General Banks to join Grant's army at Vicksburg. The General-in-Chief firmly told General Banks, " 'The OPENING OF THE MISSISSIPPI RIVER has been continually presented as the FIRST and MOST IMPORTANT object to be attained. . . . Operations up the Red River (or) toward Texas . . . are only of secondary importance, to be undertaken AFTER we get possession of the river, and as circumstances may then require.' " On May 14, General Banks finally agreed and returned to the Mississippi. On May 23-24, with the support of Admiral Farragut's ships, General Banks' forces encircled Port Hudson. Upon learning that General Banks had taken his army to Port Hudson and not Vicksburg as directed, General-in-Chief Halleck was livid. He informed General Banks that "the Port Hudson operation was a glaring violation of the principle of concentration and in 'direct violation' to orders. He told Banks that the manoeuvre was 'so opposed to military principles I can hardly believe it true,' and added he had so often demonstrated 'the peril of separate and isolated operations, that it would be useless to repeat them.' " General Halleck emphasized that, "the moment Vicksburg fell, Port Hudson would follow." General Banks, however, remained at Port Hudson and, on May 27, in an effort to hasten the capture of the town, he launched a "furious, but ill-coordinated assault." The attack tragically failed and Banks' army commenced siege operations. On June 14, the General again attempted to hasten the capture of Port Hudson by launching an assault upon the city's defenses, but this offensive, like the first attempt, ended in failure. Finally, on July 4, 1863, the Confederate commander at Vicksburg surrendered the city, as well as his entire army—one of the Confederacy's principal field armies. The Confederate troops were paroled, rather than sent north as Union war prisoners. General Grant opted for the parole arrangement because he believed it would expedite surrender, while, at the same time, avoiding overburdening the Northern prison facilities. Immediately following the surrender of Vicksburg, General Grant sent General Sherman with a large detachment against the Confederate relief force. Quickly, Sherman pushed this body back to Jackson and, on July 16, took Jackson for a second time, driving the Confederates farther eastward. Neither Halleck, Sherman, or Grant felt that the retiring Confederates should be pursued. Sherman then carefully destroyed the rail lines which emanated from Jackson, thus preventing Jackson from again becoming " 'a place for the assemblage of men and material with which to threaten the Mississippi River.' " Meanwhile, as General Halleck had predicted, less than a week after the fall of Vicksburg, on July 8, Port Hudson surrendered to General Banks. Thus, the Union conquest of the Mississippi was finally completed and " 'the Father of Waters' " again went " 'unvexed to the sea.' "[48]

Many people throughout the North felt, and certainly all hoped, that the conquest of the Mississippi Valley and the opening of the legendary "Father of Waters" in the summer of 1863 would, in itself, prove sufficiently decisive to produce the collapse of the rebellion. The Confederacy was now visibly severed into two parts and, perhaps more important, the South had lost one of its principal field armies. Moreover, not only did the South lose access to the river and the resources of the Mississippi Valley, the North could now itself capitalize upon these resources. Finally, of great significance to the peoples of the Ohio, Missouri, and upper Mississippi Valleys, Union control over the lower Mississippi to the Gulf of Mexico would, theoretically, allow goods to again be shipped to and from the Old Northwest through the port of New Orleans, as had been the case in the pre-war years. Notwithstanding these hopes and expectations, however, the Union conquest of the Mississippi Valley did not prove decisive in producing the collapse of the rebellion. In the largest sense, the Union war objectives were now of such total political, economic, and social magnitude for the South that the loss of the Mississippi Valley, or any other single geographic region, either alone or in combination with a major field defeat, would be insufficient to cause the Southerners to abandon their quest for political independence and the preservation of the antebellum socio-economic order. Beyond this, the Union conquest of the Mississippi Valley simply did not prove to be as significant in enhancing or damaging the military, economic, or logistical position of either of the two antagonists as many had expected. Logistically, for practical purposes, the Confederacy had been divided into two parts for over a year since the Union capture of Memphis, Tennessee, and New Orleans, Louisiana. Consequently, the Southern states east of the Mississippi and those of the trans-Mississippi Confederacy had long operated as separate "self-sufficient" entities. Thus, after the fall of Vicksburg, they survived adequately with supplementary shipments occasionally smuggled across the Mississippi. Commercially, traffic on the lower Mississippi failed to revive to its pre-war level. Indeed, although military supplies were able to securely traverse the river, commercial traffic was harassed as Southern partisans fired on the steamboats plying the great waterway. Perhaps the decline of river traffic was inevitable, however, since the rise of railroads linking New England and the mid-Atlantic states with the region west of the Appalachians had begun to affect the flow of commercial traffic even prior to the Civil War. Militarily, notwithstanding the loss of one of the Confederacy's main field armies and the implications of that loss for Southern attrition, as subsequent events would clearly demonstrate, the South still had a great deal of military power remaining. In addition, as Professors Beringer, Hattaway, Jones, and Still observed,

> True, the Union gained in substance the use of the river for commercial navigation and easy access to the Red River for any advance into Louisiana; but the Union also acquired a liability—more territory to be guarded. Instead of Confederate troops protecting Vicksburg, Union troops now had to stand duty there. The Union army had to defend a long frontier between Memphis and Baton Rouge . . . if only because of the traditional importance of Mississippi River commerce and the prestige of having opened the river. After the fall of Vicksburg the Union employed at least fifteen thousand men along with gunboats of the Mississippi squadron to defend nonmilitary commerce on the river.[49]

In the final analysis, probably the greatest gains derived from the completion of conquest of the Mississippi Valley were psychological and political, rather than military, logistical, or economic. The great military stalemate between the Confederacy and United States appeared to many to be broken in the Union's favor. Hence, Union control of the Mississippi produced an upward surge in Northern morale, while, conversely, yielding a decline in the morale of the Southern people. But, as Bruce Catton observed, "the capture of Vicksburg was a beginning, not an end. Occupation of the Mississippi Valley meant nothing in itself. It made possible the final conquest of the Confederacy, but it called for more aggressiveness rather than less."[50]

Meanwhile, in middle Tennessee, throughout the winter of 1863, the Army of the Cumberland, under the command of Major General William Rosecrans, remained inactive at Murfreesburo. Although the high command repeatedly urged the General to threaten the Confederates located a short distance to the south, General Rosecrans delayed. Instead, he attempted to secure his line of communications which was constantly threatened by Confederate raiders. Indeed, the Southern cavalry served as a persistent threat to Rosecrans' rail communications back to Louisville in the Ohio Valley. Moreover, the Confederate horsemen controlled the surrounding countryside, thus, not only ameliorating their own supply problems, but, simultaneously,

147

partially denying the Union army access to the surrounding agricultural resources and, thereby, rendering it even more dependent upon its fragile rail line of communications.[51]

With the arrival of spring, the President and General-in-Chief Halleck became doubly impatient for the Army of the Cumberland to advance against the enemy, thus synchronizing the forward movement of all three of the principal Union field armies. In accord with the theory of simultaneous advances, the high command reasoned that the Army of the Cumberland would have a good chance of success against the Confederates, since Richmond was already diverting troops from middle Tennessee to the Mississippi theater to oppose the Army of the Tennessee's offensive against Vicksburg. At the very least, Washington felt that action in middle Tennessee would tie down the Confederates and prevent them from reinforcing their army opposing Grant on the Mississippi. But Rosecrans refused to be hurried, justifying his reluctance to move with a variety of arguments. First, logistically, he maintained that his supply reserve and line of communications were not sufficiently secure. Second, politically, Rosecrans' generals reasoned that the Union victory at Stones River the previous December had saved the Union. Now, with success in neither the Mississippi Valley nor in the Virginia theater certain, a premature Union advance in middle Tennessee would risk national disaster. A Union battlefield defeat in middle Tennessee would depress Northern morale, lift Southern morale, and possibly again raise the specter of European recognition of the Confederacy. Third, militarily, General Rosecrans challenged the universal applicability of the theory of simultaneous advances which the President had long advocated. The General reasoned that the Confederates might abandon middle Tennessee in order to save Vicksburg. If the Army of the Cumberland advanced, the Southerners might rapidly fall back, destroying the rail lines of communications, foraging the countryside thoroughly, and harassing the advancing Union forces with their cavalry, thus significantly slowing the Union pursuit. The enemy could then assume a naturally defensive position along the Tennessee River, draw down their forces, and send the surplus to the Mississippi Valley or Virginia. In short, General Rosecrans

argued that the best way to prevent the Confederates from reinforcing other theaters of operations was through inactivity in
middle Tennessee, not through simultaneous advances.[52]

Finally, in late June, General Rosecrans led the Army of the
Cumberland southward against the enemy. Rosecrans still sought
a decisive battle and the destruction of the Confederate army
in middle Tennessee, but, partly as a result of his experience at
Stones River, he wanted to avoid a costly frontal assault. Hence,
he opted to use a portion of his force to threaten the Confederate
left, while his main body would maneuver against the Southern
right. Fearing that their communications might be severed, the
Confederates retreated to Chattanooga on the Tennessee River
where they took up a defensive position. Hence, by early July,
about the time Vicksburg fell, General Rosecrans successfully
maneuvered the Confederates out of middle Tennessee with a
minimum of casualties.[53]

Meanwhile, in the Virginia theater, the new Commander of
the Army of the Potomac, Major General Joseph Hooker, boast-
ing that his reconditioned, reinvigorated force was the "finest
army on the planet," formulated plans to launch a major offensive against Lee's Confederates, still located at Fredericksburg,
Virginia. General Hooker possessed an overwhelming numerical
superiority, in part, because his Confederate counterpart, General Lee, had sent two divisions to southeastern Virginia. After
considering a number of alternatives, General Hooker planned
a movement designed to turn General Lee's "left flank, reach
his rear, and compel him to attack to recover his communications." He claimed that his objective was not " 'to drive the
enemy, but to bag him.' " Specifically, Hooker planned to "catch
Lee between two powerful Union forces, each nearly equaling
his whole army," The new Commander of the Army of the Potomac intended to send three of his corps up the Rappahannock
River, cross that river six miles above the confluence of the
Rappahannock and the Rapidan, cross the Rapidan, and move
upon Lee's rear. Meanwhile, the other four corps of the Army
of the Potomac would pin the Confederates in position by threatening Fredericksburg and the nearby fords across the Rappahannock. Indeed, Hooker planned to have three of these corps

demonstrate against Lee's right in the hope that the Confederate commander would interpret the demonstration to be the principal threat and concentrate his forces accordingly. Meanwhile, joined by at least one corps originally assigned the pinning mission, the turning force would descend upon Lee's rear. Hence, General Hooker, with short, relatively secure lines of communications, would be in a position to sever Lee's lines and annihilate him between the two elements of the Army of the Potomac. On April 27, General Hooker began the operation and, by April 29, the General had over half of his army in position to advance upon Lee's rear, while his pinning force occupied Lee's front. General Hooker now confidently concluded that Lee's army " 'must either ingloriously fly, or come out from behind his defences and give us battle on our own ground, where certain destruction awaits him.' " Unfortunately for the Union cause, however, after this promising start, General Hooker decided to halt his turning force near Chancellorsville, several miles west of Fredericksburg. Subsequently, General Hooker would reinforce the turning element of his army with two of the three corps assigned to the pinning force. Ultimately only one corps (reinforced with one division) would continue to attempt to pin Lee's army at Fredericksburg, whereas six corps would be deployed with the main body of the Army of the Potomac in the Chancellorsville area. Seizing the initiative, the daring Lee responded by placing a holding force at Fredericksburg to watch the Union pinning force, while he led his main body west to engage Hooker's turning force near Chancellorsville. Once there, Lee divided his main body into two wings and, on May 2, used one wing to tactically turn Hooker's right flank, while the other wing held Hooker's front. The Confederate tactical turning movement was quite successful and, because of a major tactical blunder by Hooker, the two wings of Lee's main body reunited on May 3. Meanwhile, apparently dazed by recent events, General Hooker ordered his forces around Chancellorsville to withdraw to a defensive position just south of the Rappahannock River. Meanwhile, the one reinforced Union corps which had served as the Federal pinning force at Fredericksburg had itself launched an offensive drive on May 3 and had pushed Lee's holding force westward from the city. In response, Lee now left a holding force at Chancellorsville to watch Hooker's defensively deployed main body and turned on the Union corps advancing from Fredericksburg. On May 4, Lee successfully attacked the aggressive Union troops and pushed them against Rappahannock. Consequently, on the night of May 5–6, having lost both the initiative and his confidence, General Hooker ordered the Army of the Potomac to withdraw north of the river. The Confederate army in Virginia had again triumphed, but, similarly, the Army of the Potomac had again escaped intact.[54]

Following the battle, the Union and Confederate armies resumed their respective positions north and south of the Rappahannock which they had maintained throughout the winter of 1862–1863. The President and the General-in-Chief accepted the stalemate in Virginia and told General Hooker to merely try to keep the Confederate forces along the Rappahannock River line occupied and concentrated, thus preventing General Lee from reinforcing the Southern armies in middle Tennessee and in the Mississippi Valley, while, at the same time, protecting Washington and the upper Potomac. For now, General Hooker was to remain north of the Rappahannock. Meanwhile, General Lee's army was reinforced by the divisions which had been detached earlier, as well as by replacements to compensate for the recent battlefield losses. Moreover, the morale of Lee's entire army was extremely high following the great Southern victory at Chancellorsville. General Lee incorrectly felt that the Union army intended to quickly launch another offensive south of the Rappahannock and this erroneous conclusion partially conditioned his actions for the next few weeks. The Confederate commander "did not realize that Lincoln and Halleck viewed Virginia as a theater of secondary importance, had little hope of successful attack on his army, and did not wish to push him back to Richmond and besiege the city." But, as a result of this erroneous estimate of the situation, combined with the continued, though dimming Southern hopes of European assistance, as well as a desire to create a diversion in the east to help relieve the pressure on the Southern forces in the west, ease Confederate supply problems by utilizing the Northern harvest, undermine Northern morale by operating on Northern soil, and optimally defeat the Union forces in battle or raid a major Northern city, General Lee decided to launch a preemptive campaign designed to foil the expected Union movement south of the Rappahannock. Since the Army of the Potomac was too strong to attack directly, as Professors Beringer, Hattaway, Jones, and Still wrote,

> Lee therefore decided to use his Valley base to turn Hooker back; he also wished to "create an apprehension for the safety of their right flank and the Potomac," in the hope of diverting Federal troops from the "line of their operations in the South." As he had the previous fall in the Antietam campaign, he also planned to supply his army from untapped resources in the North, leaving most of Virginia to be gleaned for winter needs. He certainly expected to have to fight a battle if he crossed the Potomac, but, unconstrained to defend a particular line, he could select a strong position and let Hooker come to attack him.[55]

Indeed, the Confederate commander hoped to inflict a major defeat upon the Army of the Potomac on Northern soil, threaten Washington, Baltimore, and Philadelphia, and, thus, hopefully, contribute decisively to the termination of the war on terms favorable to the Confederacy.[56]

Hence, in early June, General Lee began to slowly move his army along the south side of the Rappahannock to the Shenandoah Valley and, thence, via the Shenandoah and Cumberland Valleys, through western Maryland, into central Pennsylvania. As he moved his army north, he took steps to hold the mountain passes which controlled the eastern approaches to these two valleys. Meanwhile, General Hooker quickly became aware of Lee's movement northward and suggested to the high command in Washington that the Army of the Potomac cross the Rappahannock and attack the Confederate army's rear, still located at Fredericksburg, or move directly upon Richmond. The President and General Halleck, however, emphatically rejected these two alternatives and reiterated the high command's conviction that the proper objective of the Army of the Potomac was Lee's army, not Richmond. Consequently, they directed General Hooker not to take the Army of the Potomac south of the Rappahannock, but rather to move north as Lee moved north. Indeed, the President and the General-in-Chief preferred an energetic offensive designed to inflict a severe defeat upon Lee's army and, possibly, destroy it. The high command felt that Lee's invasion of central Pennsylvania was the best opportunity the Union army in the east had since the war began over two years ago. Washington felt that General Lee's forces would be more vulnerable than they had been during the Antietam Campaign, thus creating an even better opportunity than the one which Washington felt McClellan had wasted the previous autumn. This was precisely the type of mistake that the high command had hoped General Lee would make. Both the President and the General-in-Chief hoped that, if properly utilized, this opportunity would allow the Army of the Potomac to break the stalemate which had long existed in the Virginia theater in its own favor. Hence, Mr. Lincoln and General Halleck advised General Hooker to move west and try to cut General Lee's army in half as the latter moved northward in an elongated fashion far from its supply base. Alternatively, the high command reasoned that the Army of the Potomac could cut Lee's line of communications as he moved north and block his line of retreat, forcing him to assume the tactical offensive and assault the Army of the Potomac on ground chosen by General Hooker for its tactical defensive merit. Either way, the Administration hoped that prompt action would produce a highly visible, perhaps decisive victory in the east. But, whereas the President and the General-in-Chief viewed Lee's invasion of central Pennsylvania as a golden opportunity, the people of the Northeast were quite alarmed at the prospect of the Confederacy's best army operating north of the Potomac. Consequently, in response to the Confederate threat posed to the eastern cities, the high command authorized the Army of the Potomac to move north and east of the Blue Ridge Mountains so as to protect the northeast's urban centers. Meanwhile, predictably, as Lee's army moved north, the gray leader scattered his forces quite widely. Then, on June 28, Lee learned that General Hooker had not only moved north of the Potomac, he was in position to threaten the Southern rear. Lee recognized that the Army of the Potomac "might thrust west across the Blue Ridge or South Mountain, ensconce itself in the Cumberland Valley across his line of retreat, and seize the initiative." Hence, Lee decided to concentrate his forces and move them eastward "as if closing on Baltimore, so as to keep Hooker also on the east" side of the Blue Ridge and South Mountain.[57]

By late June, Washington had lost confidence in General Hooker's ability to command the Army of the Potomac as it approached a major, possibly decisive battle on Northern soil. Consequently, on June 28, with the Army of the Potomac located around Frederick, Maryland, the Washington high command relieved General Hooker of his command and replaced him with Major General George G. Meade. The high command told the new commander of the Army of the Potomac,

> You will not be hampered by any minute instructions from these head-quarters. Your army is free to act as you may deem proper under the circumstances as they arise. You will, however, keep in view the important fact that the Army of the Potomac is the covering army of Washington as well as the army of operation against the invading forces of the rebels. You will, therefore, maneuver and fight in such a manner as to cover the capital and also Baltimore, as far as circumstances will admit. Should General Lee move upon either of these places, it is expected that you will either anticipate him or arrive with him so as to give him battle.[58]

With these instructions, with the lead elements of General Lee's army at the Susquehanna River opposite Harrisburg and Columbia, Pennsylvania, and with the main body of the Southern army located to the west of Chambersburg, General Meade assessed the situation. As Kenneth P. Williams wrote,

> It should not have been difficult for Meade to estimate the situation and come to a sound decision. Three courses were open to Lee: (1) He could continue up the Cumberland Valley in order to join Ewell's corps, which Meade knew was making for Harrisburg. (2) He could bring the other two corps of his army through one of the gaps in the mountains that formed the eastern barrier of the Valley, recalling Ewell, and with his concentrated army threaten Baltimore and Washington and force the Army of the Potomac to battle. If this maneuver were adopted the march toward Harrisburg would be of a diversionary nature, meant to frighten Washington and lead the authorities to waste some good field forces by sending them to defend the Pennsylvania capital. (3) He could halt his main body under the protection of the mountains and let Ewell return from his raid toward the Susquehanna. Of the three possibilities the last seemed the most unlikely because Lee was living off the country and could not stay long in one position. Furthermore, what satisfaction would this procedure have given to the men who had marched so hard and the people at home who were expecting so much of their invincible

154

brigades? There would be nothing for the army except some days of good living and the chance to see what the Yankees were like at home; for the people at home there would be nothing but the stories their soldiers told in their letters. Nor would this course stimulate foreign recognition. Nevertheless from "opposite Williamsport" Lee wrote to Davis the night before he crossed the river that he might have to return without any other achievement than forcing the Federals to cross to the north bank of the Potomac, and thus delaying any plan that they might have for a summer campaign. On the other hand, if Lee adopted the second plan he would certainly come through the Cashtown gap, because it led to Gettysburg, where several important roads converged. Thus Meade's proper decision would seem to have been this: to move northward, keeping his army well in hand, so as to be able to fall upon any part of Lee's army that might venture through the Cashtown Gap and destroy it before it could be supported, and to engage Lee beyond the termination of the mountains if he continued toward Harrisburg.[59]

Based upon the situation as he knew it, as well as his instructions from Washington, the new Commander of the Army of the Potomac quickly selected a good defensive position at which to fight or fall back upon, if necessary, while, simultaneously, ordering the lead elements of his army toward Gettysburg. General Meade reasoned that Gettysburg was strategically important because "it was the first point in General Lee's eastward march across the South Mountains where roads led southward toward Baltimore and Washington." On July 1, 1863, the Confederate commander attempted, but with only very limited success, to defeat the lead portion of General Meade's army before it could be reinforced at Gettysburg. General Meade, in turn, hurriedly brought the remainder of his army forward and soon both armies were fully concentrated. General Halleck approved General Meade's decision to establish a strong defensive position immediately south of Gettysburg, but was concerned that Gettysburg itself was too far east. The General-in-Chief noted,

Lee might turn the army's left flank, . . . interpose on Meade's supply line and entrench between the Union army and Washington. Then Meade would have to attack Lee, not vice versa. Manoeuvre had been the key to Lee's previous victories and Halleck saw no reason for the Virginian to discard the Jomini method in favor of a direct attack. Longstreet (commander of one of Lee's corps) proposed that precise plan to Lee, but his chief decided—over Longstreet's protest—to fight where he found the enemy.[60]

Meanwhile, on July 2, the Confederates unsuccessfully assaulted the Union left flank, with supporting assaults elsewhere along the Confederate line. By the next day, the Army of the Potomac held a strong defensive position and had withstood two days of stiff fighting. On that day, July 3, 1863, General Lee launched a major frontal assault upon the center of the Army of the Potomac, while, simultaneously, his cavalry was supposed to descend upon the Union rear. The frontal attack, the celebrated "Pickett's Charge," ended in a tragic disaster for the gallant Southerners, while the Union cavalry drove the Southern horsemen off about one mile east of the main battle. Immediately following the repulse, General Meade was urged to launch an instant counterattack, but lacking both the will and a concentrated, fresh reserve force available for immediate commitment, the General refused to seize the initiative. As Allen Nevins observed, if General Meade "had shown the imprudence exhibited by Lee and Jackson at Second Manassas and Chancellorsville he might have routed the Confederates and ended the war; but it is difficult to fault his caution."[61]

The Confederate army remained on the battlefield the following day preparing for their withdrawal, but again the Commander of the Army of the Potomac refused to attack. That evening, amid a heavy rainstorm, the Southern army retreated. Meanwhile, General Meade issued a congratulatory order to his troops, the conclusion of which looked to the future stating, " 'Our task is not yet accomplished, and the commanding general looks to the army for greater efforts to drive from our soil every vestige of the presence of the invader.' " Commenting on General Meade's order, however, the President reportedly observed, " 'This is a dreadful reminiscence of McClellan. The same spirit that moved McClellan to claim a great victory because Pennsylvania and Maryland were safe. The hearts of ten million people sunk within them when McClellan raised that shout last fall. Will our Generals never get that idea out of their heads? The whole country is our soil.' " Upon receiving word that Vicksburg had fallen on July 4, and with General Lee's army in full retreat following the Union victory at Gettysburg on July 3, Mr. Lincoln felt that a decisive moment in the war was at hand. He told the

General-in-Chief, " 'Now, if General Meade can complete his work, so gloriously prosecuted thus far, by the literal or substantial destruction of Lee's army, the rebellion will be over.' " Meanwhile, on July 6–7, Lee's defeated army arrived at Williamsport, Maryland, on the north bank of the swollen Potomac River. Lacking bridges, the Confederates had no choice but to entrench themselves with their backs to the river as they hastily attempted to improvise a bridge over which to cross to safety. Meanwhile, both the President and the General-in-Chief urged General Meade to follow up the victory at Gettysburg and destroy the retreating Confederate army. With General Lee's army at Williamsport and no route of escape immediately available, Mr. Lincoln felt that the destruction of the Confederate army was virtually certain. On July 12, the Army of the Potomac cautiously approached Lee's position. As Kenneth Williams observed,

> ... Meade could have held a strong defensive position with a part of his command, while he crossed sufficient force over the Potomac— keeping the two parts within supporting distance—to seize the south bank of the river and make bridging impossible for Lee. Such a maneuver seems to turn on the location of Meade's pontoons. After the army had crossed into Maryland in June the bridges were dismantled and shipped to Washington for safe keeping. On July 5, forseeing their use in the pursuit of Lee, Meade wisely telegraphed General Benham, "Put your bridge trains and troops in motion at once for Harper's Ferry." Four days later Benham, at his ordered destination after overcoming many difficulties, reported, "The two bridges are in the canal, and ready to be towed anywhere they may be needed up the river." Thus Meade had the ability to move a part of his army over the river. What an aggressive commander could have accomplished by throwing part of his superior force to the other side of the Potomac can be imagined.[62]

But, unfortunately for the Union cause, General Meade, having only a little over a week earlier witnessed the futility of frontally assaulting an enemy in a prepared position, concluded that General Lee's position was too strong to be attacked. Thus, on the night of July 13–14, Lee's army escaped over the river and began the trek up the Shenandoah Valley. Meade crossed the Potomac on July 17 and by July 22, his main body was just east of the Manassas Gap through the Blue Ridge Mountains. Even after Lee crossed the Potomac to Virginia, General Halleck told the

Commander of the Army of the Potomac, "to pursue and lacerate the Army of Northern Virginia (Lee's force), keeping between the enemy and Washington and living off the country." General Meade did send a portion of his army through the gap in an effort to hit Lee's flank as his force passed west of the Blue Ridge, but again Lee managed to slip away. By late July, 1863, the Confederates had crossed the mountains farther to the south and had taken up a position around Culpepper, Virginia. Meanwhile, the Army of the Potomac took up a position a few miles to the northeast on the north side of the Rappahannock River. The two armies would remain in these positions for about a month and a half.[63]

Assessing the results of the Gettysburg Campaign, the President was extremely critical of General Meade's handling of operations following his battlefield victory in Pennsylvania. Immediately following the Battle of Gettysburg, the President had observed that General Meade's activities appeared " 'to be connected with a purpose to cover Baltimore and Washington, and to get the enemy across the river again without a further collision, and they do not appear connected with a purpose to prevent his crossing and to destroy him.' " On July 14, upon learning that the Confederates had successfully escaped across the Potomac to Virginia, Mr. Lincoln disgustedly observed, " 'We had them within our grasp. We had only to stretch forth our hands and they were ours. And nothing I could say or do could make the army move.' " Indeed, President Lincoln felt that in missing " 'the best opportunity we have had since the war began,' " General Meade failed to " 'appreciate the magnitude of the misfortune involved in Lee's escape ... the war will be prolonged indefinitely,' " Possibly, however, in his zeal to capitalize upon the strategic possibilities opened by Lee's defeat at Gettysburg, the President was too optimistic concerning the Union ability to overcome the tactical realities obstructing prospects for the annihilation of General Lee's army by the Army of the Potomac at Williamsport. Conversely, General Meade seemed to see only these tactical realities and ignored both inviting tactical and strategic possibilities beckoning an aggressive effort to destroy Lee while he was caught in an extremely disadvantageous position.[64]

Although the President was visibly and understandably disappointed with the outcome of the Gettysburg Campaign, on
balance, the high command's strategy emphasizing the conquest
of territory in the region west of the Appalachians, especially the
Mississippi Valley, while, simultaneously, reducing the importance of the Virginia theater and awaiting a mistake by Lee, had
yielded large dividends. During the last days of June and the
first week of July, the Confederates had been maneuvered out
of most of middle Tennessee and now held only Chattanooga
and the eastern portion of the state. Simultaneously, the North
celebrated the fourth of July, 1863 with the surrender of Vicksburg and one of the Confederacy's principal field armies. This
success was immediately followed by the surrender of Port Hudson, Louisiana, thus completing the Union occupation of the
entire Mississippi Valley. Finally, in the east, Lee had committed
the type of operational and tactical mistakes in launching and
conducting the Gettysburg Campaign which the high command
had hoped for. Operationally, Lee had erred by launching his
preemptive invasion of the North based, in part, upon the mis-
taken assumption that the Army of the Potomac would again,
soon move south of the Rappahannock River. Tactically, at Gettysburg, on July 3, Lee had frontally thrown a significant portion
of his army against the Union center with predictably disastrous
results. As news of the Union victories at Gettysburg, Vicksburg,
and in middle Tennessee successively broke, the morale of the
Northern people soared, while that of the Southerners plummeted
dramatically. Yet, notwithstanding these great victories, the
North still had many months of bloody sacrifice remaining before the Southerners would abandon their quest for independence and the victories of July, 1863 would be complete.[65]

CHAPTER V

Summer 1863—Winter 1864

By midsummer, 1863, in the aftermath of the Emancipation Proclamation and against the background of vigorous Federal efforts to recruit blacks into the Union Army, Northern newspaper editors and politicians increasingly focused upon the issue of reconstruction. Conservative opinion "denied the right of any state to leave the Union." Accordingly, just as "no state can commit treason . . . and no state can give its citizens authority to commit treason," the present conflict was viewed by Conservatives as a "struggle not to reduce the states to submission, but to compel the obedience of rebellious individuals." Meanwhile, notwithstanding the fact that the rebels were acting on behalf of the states and that citizens loyal to the United States had been displaced, the states themselves remained full members of the Union. They still possessed "full rights as states" and, upon their liberation, they should not be looked at or "governed as territories." Rather, upon liberation, the people of the states "should of their own motion proceed to reorganize the state government on the basis of the state constitution which existed prior to the outbreak of the war." Moreover, as one Conservative politician put it, " 'multitudes of magistrates, state and Federal functionaries, are ready to resume their functions the moment the rebel military duress is removed.' " Conversely, Radical opinion, in the words of one Radical newspaper, held that,

> . . . the revolt of a State against the authority of the general government destroys its political rights under the Constitution, and reduces its territory to the condition of the unorganized public domain. It forfeits all its rights. . . . There is no longer a State of South Carolina, a State of Georgia, etc. The territories and their inhabitants still exist, and the general government has lost none of its rights of superior jurisdiction over them. . . . It is equally clear that the seceded States can never come back into the Union until they have been reorganized and reofficered in all their departments. Every vestige of their treason must be repudiated . . . Having framed Constitutions, it will be competent for

161

them to apply for readmission to the Union, and Congress may receive them or continue to hold them in the condition of Territories until satisfactory assurance shall be given that the people have returned to a sentiment of loyalty.[1]

In a larger sense, however, as Allen Nevins observed, the Radicals

. . . hoped to destroy the former balance of the Constitution, if they could, in two ways—by making legislative power paramount over executive power, and by substituting national authority throughout the South for State authority. The States had formerly been regarded as sovereign, with rights that were not to be invaded by Congress except in areas specified or implied in the Constitution; hereafter the seceded States were to be regarded as completely under the foot of Congress, without any rights whatever that Congress did not grant them. It was not true that . . . the Acts of Secession were inoperative and void, and therefore left the States intact in all their rights; the . . . States had ceased to exist constitutionally once they seceded.[2]

As one of the principal Radical leaders, Charles Sumner, argued,

. . . the former State governments had been vacated (a word used by the men who dethroned James II in 1688), the Constitution became for the time being the supreme and only law. "And the whole Rebel region, deprived of all local government, lapses under the exclusive jurisdiction of Congress, precisely as any other territory; the military entitled to govern it while fighting endured, but Congress alone empowered to exercise civil authority." Virginia, Mississippi, and South Carolina were not States—they were merely territory. "The whole broad Rebel region is tabula rasa, or 'clean slate.'"[3]

While Senator Sumner did not maintain, as did some of his Radical colleagues, that the boundaries of the Southern states might be reconfigured, he forcefully argued that Congress should decide the fate of the South. Looking to the socio-economic future, Radical leaders proposed large scale property transfers to the former slaves. Only in that way, they stressed, could the power of the Southern aristocracy be broken. Indeed, many Radicals feared that unless emancipation was combined with property transfer, the South would attempt to establish a form of serfdom from which "such a revised slaveocracy might conceivably challenge the political and economic dominance of the new Northern alliance of freesoilers, Republicans, and industrial progressives." As such, the Radicals feared most that the Administration might conclude a compromise peace which would "do less than full justice to the Negro demands for unslackened progress toward social, political, and eventually economic equality."[4]

President Lincoln's views were very similar to those of the Conservatives. It should be remembered that in his inaugural address in March, 1861, Mr. Lincoln had put forth the interpretation that the Union was a perpetual entity and that the Southern states could not leave the Union of their own will. Hence, the rebellion was an act of individuals, not the states. That rebellion " 'neither destroyed nor impaired the rights or obligations of statehood, nor even any rights and obligations of their co-citizens who remained loyal.' " As such, early in the war, the President asserted that he intended to organize loyal state governments as soon as the Union armies had liberated their respective territories. In short, the Chief Executive wanted to avoid "a needless debate on the constitutional status" of the Southern states. Indeed, from the outset of the war, the President quietly encouraged loyal Southerners to, in turn, encourage their fellow loyalists throughout the South to elect state governments and send representatives to Congress, as soon as that became feasible. In the early autumn, 1862, immediately after the preliminary announcement of the Emancipation Proclamation, he had urged both military and naval authorities, as well as local state politicians in Louisiana, to restore state government and send a delegation to Congress before January, 1863. Indeed, Louisiana did elect a Congressional delegation in 1862 and that delegation was seated in Congress on February 17, 1863. On August 5, 1863, the President wrote to General Banks, the military commander in Louisiana, that,

> I would be glad . . . for her to make a new Constitution recognizing the Emancipation Proclamation, and adopting emancipation in those parts of the State to which the proclamation does not apply. And while she is at it, I think it would not be objectionable for her to adopt some practical system by which the two races could gradually lift themselves out of their old relation to each other, and both come out better prepared for the new. Education for young blacks should be included in the plan.[5]

Meanwhile, the President took similar steps in Tennessee. On March 4, 1862, he appointed a Military Governor and, by the late autumn, was encouraging the loyalists in Tennessee to follow a course similar to that recommended to the loyalist elements of Louisiana. But, notwithstanding preliminary efforts, the loyalists of Tennessee agreed that eastern Tennessee must be liberated before a permanent civil government would be restored. Finally, by the end of 1863, preliminary steps had been taken toward restoration of civil government in Arkansas. Moreover, hints of pro-Union sentiment in those portions of the South still under Confederate control gave the President reason for optimism concerning the early reconstruction of those states still in rebellion. Thus, as Allen Nevins observed,

> ... by the opening of Congress as the winds of December blew over Capital Hill in 1863, steps looking toward reconstruction and reentrance into the Union had been taken in three States.The President was plainly anxious to make it easy for any considerable body of loyal citizens to erect a civil government, and to send men knocking at the door of the House. ... Lincoln was plainly determined to exercise the powers of the Presidency to the fullest in the work of reconstruction. He was willing to accept Congress as partner; he repeatedly emphasized the fact that although a State might elect Representatives and Senators, Congress alone could admit them. But he was insistent that while rebellion might destroy the old structure of society in a State, and its old Constitution, it could not destroy membership in the Union, which was perdurable.[6]

Needless to say, however, the Radicals were troubled by the President's quietly effective efforts to implement his interpretation of reconstruction.[7]

On December 8, 1863, in his annual message to Congress, the President took another step toward implementation of his plan for the reconstruction of the Southern states. The message contained a proclamation of amnesty, under the terms of which a "full pardon" was extended,

> ... to all those who had participated in the rebellion, except those who had been civil or diplomatic officers of the Confederacy, those who had abandoned judicial stations, seats in Congress, or commissions in the Army or Navy of the United States to aid the rebellion, and those who had been officers above the rank of colonel in the Confederate Army, or lieutenant in the Confederate Navy. Persons guilty of maltreating prisoners of war were also excepted. This pardon, which carried with it a restoration of all rights of property except as to slaves, and except where the rights of third parties had intervened, was conditional upon the acceptance and maintenance of an oath of allegiance.[8]

The wording of the oath of allegiance was politically controversial, since it used the wording " 'henceforth faithfully protect and defend the Constitution.' " This clashed with the Radical desire to make the oath retroactive. Mr. Lincoln regarded "the resumption of allegiance and the grant of pardon" for the maximum number of Southerners as a critical element in his effort to reestablish loyal governments in each of the Southern states. Beyond this, according to the President's plan,

> Whenever, in any of the ten seceding States south of Virginia, one-tenth of the total number of persons who had cast votes in the 1860 Presidential election of that State had taken and kept the oath of allegiance, and held each the status of a legally qualified voter, they might reestablish a republican State government. This should then be recognized as the true government of the State, and should receive all the benefits of the constitutional provision for protecting and safeguarding every member of the Union.[9]

The President maintained " 'that, in constructing a loyal State government in any State, the name of the State, the boundary, the subdivisions, the constitution, and the general code of laws, as before the rebellion, be maintained, subject only to the modifications made necessary by the conditions hereinbefore stated. . . .' " Finally, while Mr. Lincoln acknowledged that only Congress "could determine whether members sent from any State could be admitted," he clearly maintained that the Executive Branch would play the leadership role in determining the direction of reconstruction policy.[10]

The President's terms demanded very little from the Southerners except that they acknowledge that slavery was dead. Indeed, under Mr. Lincoln's plan, not only would the Southern states resume their place in the Union without political penalty, the congressional strength of the South would actually increase. The three-fifths formula for counting slaves which had been agreed to at the Constitutional Convention in 1787 "would become moot, enabling the South to count its entire population" in determining its representation in the U.S. House of Representatives. The President hoped that his generous reconstruction policy would especially appeal to the partially conquered states of Tennessee, Arkansas, Louisiana, and Florida. He hoped that, in these states, he could build Unionist sentiment, which, in turn, would serve several purposes. First, it would provide the Administration with additional political support in the prosecution of the war effort. Second, it was designed to appeal to Conservative sentiment in the North, thereby further politically strengthening the Administration. Third, it was designed to diminish "civilian resistance and guerrilla warfare in occupied areas." Finally, the President hoped to provide the remainder of the South with a positive example which would induce the Southern people to lay down their arms and resume their place in the Union. While the President's reconstruction policy did yield some positive results, there was significant opposition to his plan in both the North and the South. In the North, predictably, Radical Republicans opposed the President's policy as being too lenient on the South. Conversely, the Confederates "were virtually unanimous" in their rejection of the President's policy, although the reasons for their rejection tended to vary. The confirmation of the abolition of slavery, however, did challenge one of the Confederacy's primary war aims.[11]

Within weeks, the Radicals in Congress began to muster their forces in opposition to the Presidential plan. By the spring of 1864, when two representatives from Arkansas applied for admission to the Senate, "the Senate asserted 27 to 6 that the rebellion had not been so far suppressed in Arkansas as to entitle the state to representation in Congress." Soon thereafter, Congress passed the Wade-Davis bill. Describing this piece of legislation and its implications, Allen Nevins wrote,

First, the President should appoint a provisional governor for each State declared to be in rebellion. Second, as soon as military resistance ended, the governor should enroll the white male citizens and offer them an oath to support the United States Constitution. Finally, when a majority of registrants had signed the oath, the governor should arrange the election of a State constitutional convention. This was perhaps a reasonable program, although Lincoln thought of inaugurating reconstruction on a ten-percent basis rather than a majority basis. But the Wade-Davis legislation proceeded to lay down additional tests of penalizing character. One, a requirement that the new constitutions cancel all debts incurred in aid of the rebellion, was perfectly equitable. It would impoverish some Southerners, but they deserved their losses. Quite different was a draconian stipulation that the constitutions should forbid all men who had held high office under the Confederacy, or military rank above a colonelcy, to vote for a legislator or governor, or occupy these positions. No former office-holder or person who had voluntarily borne arms against the United States could take the oath, and no one who did not take the oath could vote for the constitutional convention. This would proscribe the ablest and most experienced leaders in the South. Worse still, in theory and practice, was a demand that the constitutions abolish slavery. This was plainly unconstitutional, for Congress had no power to deal with slavery inside the States. It was also unwise, for if slavery were thus abolished by national action, the nation might be expected to take steps to aid and protect the freedmen for which it had made no preparatory study, and possessed no adequate machinery. The Wade-Davis bill provided that, whenever a State constitution embodying these iron provisions had been adopted by a majority of the registered voters, the President, with prior Congressional assent, should recognize the government so established as competent to send men to Congress and choose Presidential electors.[12]

Obviously, the Wade-Davis bill was unacceptable to the President. Not only did it overturn the ten-percent formula which he had announced only a few months earlier, it reflected a harsh, retaliatory policy toward the South which, Mr. Lincoln believed, would be counterproductive to the long-term political integration of the Union. Hence, when the bill arrived for his signature on July 4, 1864, he killed it through pocket veto.[13]

The Presidential pocket veto elicited a statement by Messrs. Wade and Davis, the so-called Wade-Davis Manifesto, which was published in a number of Northern newspapers. The Manifesto called upon the Congress " 'to check the encroachments of the Executive on the authority of Congress.' " The authors of the document went on to note that Mr. Lincoln " 'must understand' " that the support extended by Congress, " '. . . is of a cause and not of a man; that the authority of Congress is paramount and must be respected; that the whole body of Union men in Congress would not submit to be impeached by him of rash and unconstitutional legislation; and if he wishes our support, he must confine himself to his executive duties—to obey and to execute, not to make the laws—to suppress by arms armed rebellion, and leave political reorganization to Congress.' " Then, after asserting the doctrine of Congressional predominance in reconstructing the Union, the Manifesto ominously suggested that the American people " 'consider the remedy' " for the Executive Branch's " 'usurpations and, having found it, fearlessly to execute it.'" Although this sharp attack upon the President proved counter-productive to both the Radical cause and the authors of the Manifesto, it did bring to center stage what would soon become a national debate concerning reconstruction.[14]

Finally, as the reconstruction issue was maturing into open confrontation, the final steps were being taken to completely outlaw slavery in the United States. Abandoning the concept of gradual, compensated emancipation as dead, the Administration threw its weight behind a Constitutional Amendment banning slavery in the United States. In April, 1864, the Senate passed the following draft amendment to the Constitution:

> Article XIII, Section 1. Neither slavery nor involuntary servitude, except as a punishment for crime whereof the party shall have been duly convicted, shall exist within the United States or any place subject to their jurisdiction. Section 2. Congress shall have the power to enforce this article by appropriate legislation.[15]

The House of Representatives, however, waited until January 31, 1865 to adopt the measure which Mr. Lincoln then signed that sent to the states for final ratification.[16]

Meanwhile, as these political developments were maturing, in late summer, 1863, the Federal high command began a reassessment of its operational emphasis in the various theaters. As was the case earlier, the Washington high command again decided to accept the stalemated balance in the Virginia theater. Both the President and the General-in-Chief concluded that, if the Army of the Potomac could not destroy Lee's army immediately following the latter's defeat at Gettysburg, the Union army certainly stood little chance of destroying it after it had time to recover from the battle. Hence, the high command returned to its pre-Gettysburg theater operational focus and, expecting little or nothing from the Army of the Potomac, assigned the Virginia theater of operations a low priority compared to the west. General Meade was merely to try and occupy Lee's attentions and keep the Confederate army in Virginia fully employed, thus preventing Richmond from detaching troops for use in the west. He was to attempt to do the maximum damage to Lee, while sustaining as little damage to his own force as possible. If the Confederates were too strong to be assaulted directly, as the high command was prepared to admit, then General Meade was to indirectly occupy them by maneuver. Finally, should General Lee make a mistake, the high command expected General Meade to be ready to to fully exploit the opportunity. Like his predecessors, however, the Commander of the Army of Potomac felt uncomfortable with the mission of occupying Lee's army and awaiting a mistake by the able Confederate commander. At least initially, General Meade preferred the more attainable mission of capturing Richmond. He felt that it was possible to cut Richmond's communications from the south and southwest, which would, in turn, force the Confederates either to evacuate the city or fight the Army of the Potomac on ground selected by the latter. Thus, General Meade maintained that, if Richmond were the objective, the best avenue of approach to the Confederate capital would not be overland from the north, but rather via the peninsula from the east, as General McClellan had originally suggested in 1862. He maintained that the overland route to Richmond was devoid of tactical advantages as rivers became natural barriers to the southward advance. Moreover, the overland route tended to raise vexing logistical problems for the attacking force. Indeed, General Meade felt that General Lee wanted him to move against Richmond by the overland route so that the wily Confederate could cut the Union line of communications and fight the Union army under advantageous conditions. Finally, especially after his great defensive victory at Gettysburg, General Meade felt that the tactical power of the defense was significantly stronger than the tactical offensive. In short, whereas the high command had long since rejected Richmond as the objective in the Virginia theater, preferring instead to focus on Lee's army, General Meade still preferred to direct his army's attentions upon the Confederate capital. In the end, however, the high command was in no mood to rediscuss the mission of the Army of the Potomac or the merits of various avenues of approach to Richmond, particularly in the emotion charged context of a reassessment of General McClellan's Peninsular Campaign. Already, many were suggesting that General McClellan would be selected by the Democratic Party to run against Mr. Lincoln in the 1864 Presidential campaign. Hence,

Washington firmly reiterated that the mission of the Army of the Potomac was to occupy the attention of Lee's army and, should the opportunity again present itself, engage it at an advantage and, if possible, destroy it.[17] On September 9, 1863, the President wrote,

> To avoid misunderstanding, let me say that to attempt to fight the enemy slowly back into his intrenchments at Richmond, and then to capture him, is an idea I have been trying to repudiate for quite a year. My judgement is so clear against it that I would scarcely allow the attempt to be made if the general in command should desire to make it. My last attempt upon Richmond was to get McClellan, when he was nearer there than the enemy was, to run in ahead of him. Since then I have constantly desired the Army of the Potomac to make Lee's army and not Richmond, its objective point. If our army cannot fall upon the enemy and hurt him where he is, it is plain to me it can gain nothing by attempting to follow him over a succession of intrenched lines into a fortified city.[18]

Meanwhile, in the west, following the opening of the Mississippi River, General-in-Chief Halleck continued to view the Mississippi Valley as the primary and decisive theater of the war. Furthermore, he continued to view the war in the western theater "as one of position, of securing and holding places followed by concentration of forces." General Halleck felt that the best operational plan would be to utilize the north-south Mississippi line as a base for future eastward or westward Union campaigns. He maintained that this would allow the Union armies to fully exploit their interior position. The high command had looked forward to the conquest of the trans-Mississippi portion of the Confederacy and, therefore, now favored the conquest of the west before launching an eastward offensive movement from the great river. Militarily, General Halleck correctly postulated that the Southern forces located in the trans-Mississippi portion of the Confederacy were weaker than those in the region east of the Mississippi. Furthermore, a successful conquest of the trans-Mississippi region would relieve pressure on Missouri and, thus, release a significant portion of the Union forces committed to garrison duty in that state for utilization elsewhere. Economically and politically, the conquest of the trans-Mississippi Confederate states was attractive to the Administration because it would appeal to the Northeastern textile manufacturing interests by providing a significant amount of cotton, while, at the same time, opening the area to agricultural development relying upon freed laborers. Conquest of the trans-Mississippi Confederacy was also politically appealing in that it would permit the Lincoln Administration to reconstruct the state governments of Louisiana, Arkansas, and Texas along desired lines. This would not only provide the Administration with additional supporters, it would appeal to the President's conservative allies, as well as provide those Southerners still in rebellion with an attractive example which would hopefully induce them to lay down their arms and resume their place within the Union on the lenient terms established by the President. Finally, the reassertion of Federal control over Texas, especially, would strengthen the United States' diplomatic position via-a-vis France whose troops had occupied Mexico City on June 7, 1863 as part of Paris' larger effort to make Mexico the centerpiece of a new French Empire in the Western Hemisphere.[19]

Thus, the General-in-Chief ordered that Union forces in the Mississippi Valley prepare for a campaign in western Louisiana, Arkansas, and eventually Texas. Although the high command's trans-Mississippi focus had much to commend it, the trans-Mississippi emphasis suffered from a number of problems. First, the sheer geographic expanse of the trans-Mississippi portion of the Confederacy made a campaign of military conquest of the region unpromising. Second, the campaign would require a vast amount of manpower and material resources which could have been more profitably utilized in other theaters of operations. Third, the commander of the expedition, General Banks, lacked the military talent to expeditiously bring the campaign to a successful conclusion. Fourth, the emphasis on conquest of the trans-Mississippi Confederacy meant the virtual suspension of most offensive Union operations elsewhere in the Mississippi Valley. This, in turn, would provide the enterprising Southerners with an opportunity to seize the initiative east of the Mississippi. General Halleck, however, hoped to retain at least a measure of the initiative elsewhere in the west by redoubling the Union efforts to clear eastern Tennessee and capture Chattanooga. Consequently, he ordered the inert Union forces in eastern Kentucky to move into eastern Tennessee, while, simultaneously, protecting Kentucky, generally, and the Louisville and Nashville railway, especially, from Confederate raids. Halleck intended that this advance would be mutually supported by a new offensive movement southward by General Rosecrans' Army of the Cumberland designed to take Chattanooga and cut the railway linking Virginia and Atlanta. In the final analysis, however, the problems inherent in the effort to conquer the trans-Mississippi region would outweigh the promise and the effort would, ultimately, culminate in the abortive Red River Campaign west of the Mississippi and the Confederate seizure of the initiative east of the river.[20]

Actually, the General-in-Chief had preferred General Rosecrans to continue his advance without interruption following his well executed maneuver during the last week of June and the first week of July, 1863, which had pushed the Confederates back to Chattanooga. General Rosecrans, however, halted and, despite constant pressure from Washington encouraging him to advance, the Army of the Cumberland remained in position for about six weeks. During this period, the army gathered supplies, repaired railroads, and waited for area's crops to ripen. Although time consuming, these preparations were important because Rosecrans intended to cross the Tennessee River just below Chattanooga and strategically turn the Confederate left with the main body of the Army of the Cumberland, while a small portion of his force occupied the Southern attention by demonstrating on the north bank of the river, directly across from the main body of the Confederate army located at Chattanooga. "With no base such as that which Lee had in the Shenandoah Valley, the Federal army again would be out of touch with its own communications depending as in the first advance, on what the army could carry with it, living off the country, and on what wagons could bring by a circuitous route through rugged country over bad roads."[21]

General Rosecrans began his strategic turning movement on August 16, 1863. Initially the operation went as planned and, by September 4, General Rosecrans had a considerable portion of his turning force across the Tennessee River and in position to sever the Confederate line of communications which extended southward from Chattanooga. To accomplish this, however, Rosecrans' turning force would have to traverse the rugged mountainous country which stood between the Tennessee River and the railroad which linked Chattanooga and Atlanta and which served as the Confederate line of communications. Simultaneously, a small Union force from eastern Kentucky, under the command of General Burnside, had advanced into eastern Tennessee and, at the outset of September, had captured Knoxville, thereby satisfying the high command's long held desire to liberate the pro-Union loyalists residing in that region and sever the rail line linking Virginia with the west. The latter, in turn, served to prevent the Southern high command in Richmond from reinforcing the Confederate defenders in northern Georgia with reinforcements from General Lee's army in Virginia via the direct rail line from the "Old Dominion." Instead, reinforcements would have to arrive via the much more roundabout route through the Carolinas and Georgia. On September 8, the Confederate command, recognizing the immediate threat to its communications posed by Rosecrans' turning force and Burnside's occupation of Knoxville, ordered the evacuation of Chattanooga. From the Northern perspective, the capture of Chattanooga and Knoxville provided the Union forces with a vital base for future operations into the Deep South. Simultaneously, of course, it deprived the Confederacy of a critical line of communications connecting Virginia and northern Georgia, as well as the coal fields and other war resourses provided by Tennessee's eastern region. Upon learning of the Confederate evacuation of Chattanooga, General Rosecrans erroneously concluded that the Confederates were fleeing southward, down the railway toward Dalton, Georgia. Hence, the Union commander ordered one corps to immediately occupy Chattanooga and proceed southward along the rail line in pursuit of what was perceived to be the retreating Confederates. Another corps was to cross the mountains at Stevens' Gap, about eighteen miles southwest of Chattanooga, and proceed along the road in a southeasterly direction toward Lafayette, Georgia. Finally, a third corps was to cross the mountains about forty-five miles south of the city and use cavalry to break the rail lines south of the expected Confederate position.[22]

Contrary to General Rosecrans' sanguine estimate of the situation, the Confederates had, indeed, withdrawn southward, but not along the railway. Instead, they had moved about twenty-five miles south of Chattanooga to Lafayette, immediately east of Stevens' Gap through which one Union corps was to pass. Moreover, Richmond had directed that the Confederates in north Georgia be reinforced in a nation-wide concentration of forces which drew troops from as far away as Virginia. The Southerners intended not only to counter the advance of the Army of the Cumberland, in addition, Richmond had concluded that middle Tennessee offered the most promising opportunities for a Southern counter-offensive. Hence, the Southern command intended not just to push Rosecrans "back to secure their communications, but to employ their superior numbers to carry out their long-discussed major offensive against this weakest of the principal Union lines of operation." Indeed, "Rosecrans, commanding the smallest of the major Union offensive armies, was perhaps the only Union commander to confront such superior numbers in a major battle during the war." Moreover, with the corps components of the Army of Cumberland widely dispersed as they crossed the mountains, and, therefore, too isolated to provide mutual support should any one of them be suddenly attacked, the Confederates were in an excellent position to destroy a significant portion of General Rosecrans' army in detail. Fortunately for the Union cause, however, the Confederates moved irresolutely, while, at the last moment, General Rosecrans awoke to the danger confronting the Army of the Cumberland and rapidly concentrated his forces. On September 20, 1863, following some very sharp, but indecisive action between the two armies, the Confederates launched a fierce, concerted attack against the Army of Cumberland at the Battle of Chickamauga. During the battle, General Rosecrans' right collapsed and the General, along with a significant portion of his army, retreated to Chattanooga, leaving the commander of the Union left, Major General George H. Thomas, in sole command of the remaining Union forces in the battle. General Thomas held out for the remainder of the day, withdrawing from the field that night. General Thomas' "sterling leadership was a decisive factor in preventing a disastrous Union defeat. Here he earned the title of 'The Rock of Chickamauga,' for, though all the troops had fought valiantly, it was Thomas who provided the necessary determination and inspired leadership." The Confederates followed the mauled Federals back to Chattanooga and occupied the high ground opposite the city which dominated both the main rail line and the Tennessee River. These, in turn, were vital if General Rosecrans was to retain control of the city. Indeed, the Army of the Cumberland's only remaining supply route was the roundabout hill route on the north side of the Tennessee River. But, notwithstanding the severe shortage of supplies which was to quickly develop for the Union defenders at Chattanooga, the Army of the Cumberland held the city. Again, the Union forces at Chickamauga had "demonstrated the defensive power of a Civil War army, not only to resist attack but also to maneuver so as to survive even a major breakthrough in its line of battle." Conversely, "having suffered defeat but a few months earlier and having just been turned out of two positions," the Confederate army again demonstrated the "recuperative power" of a mid-nineteenth century army.[23]

The Washington high command reacted to the Union defeat in northern Georgia and Rosecrans' withdrawal to Chattanooga by ordering a counter-concentration to reinforce and relieve the besieged Army of the Cumberland. The high command felt that "it was extremely important to the Union cause that Rosecrans should hold Chattanooga because its possession kept the Confederates out of all Tennessee and broke their western railroad connections." Mr. Lincoln felt that, if Chattanooga could be held, "the rebellion would die—it could only 'eke out a short and feeble existence, as an animal sometimes may with a thorn in its vitals.' " Hence, General Grant and other commanders were directed to send troops to Chattanooga, but initially, the President and the General-in-Chief were reluctant to draw forces from the Army of the Potomac. In accord with the high command's theory of simultaneous advances, Mr. Lincoln and General Halleck felt that Richmond's decision to transfer troops from Lee's army in Virginia to northern Georgia in order to implement the Confederacy's national troop concentration immediately prior to the Battle of Chickamauga, provided the Army of the Potomac with an opportunity to attack Lee's weakened army. But General Meade was discouraging about the prospects of a successful offensive campaign against Lee's forces. He maintained that the defensive firepower of the Confederate army in Virginia, even in its present weakened condition, was still too overwhelming to invite assault by the Union forces. Thus, again accepting the Virginia stalemate, the high command reluctantly withdrew two corps from the Army of the Potomac and sent them west to reinforce the Army of the Cumberland. The eastern troops departed for their new assignment in middle Tennessee on September 24, 1863.[24]

On October 16, the President named General Grant to be the new commander of the Division of the Mississippi which united under one command all the troops between the Appalachian Mountains and the Mississippi, except those in Louisiana which remained under separate command. Most immediately, this new western command arrangement placed General Grant in direct charge of the Union forces at Chattanooga and Knoxville. In this theater of operations, the Washington high command expected General Grant to raise the siege of Chattanooga and consolidate the Union hold over eastern Tennessee. Grant, in turn, quickly elected to relieve General Rosecrans of command of the Army of the Cumberland in favor of the hero of the Battle of Chickamauga, Major General George Thomas. General Grant, himself arrived in Chattanooga on October 23 as General Thomas prepared to implement a plan which significantly eased the Army of the Cumberland's logistical problems. On November 4, the Confederates, located on the high ground around Chattanooga, felt sufficiently secure to draw down their forces and send a significant portion to eastern Tennessee in an effort to drive the Union force under General Burnside out of the region. Following an indecisive engagement in mid-month, the Southerners threatened Federally occupied Knoxville which, of course, aroused the Washington high command's anxiety. Meanwhile, as Union reinforcements arrived from Virginia and the Mississippi Valley, the stage was set for a Union effort to break the siege of Chattanooga. Reviewing the situation, the General-in-Chief concluded that,

Since Burnside could barely feed the troops he had, no more should be
sent to Knoxville and although Sherman (the new Commander of the
Army of the Tennessee upon General Grant's elevation to the Command
of the Division of the Mississippi) was marching toward Chattanooga,
it was inadvisable to concentrate more soldiers than necessary in the
city because it also was plagued by a food shortage. Instead of allowing
Sherman to join him, Grant should send him on a raid to Atlanta,
Bragg's (the Confederate commander) supply depot. If Sherman could
destroy Atlanta, Bragg would have to retreat. The plan was an expression
of the Jominian idea of manoeuvre and of Halleck's belief that, in the
west, places were more important than armies; Old Brains would
prefer the capture of Atlanta to the destruction of Bragg's army. Grant,
however, decided against Halleck's strategy and refused to change
Sherman's orders.[25]

Hence, General Sherman and the Army of the Tennessee proceeded to Chattanooga. Following a series of preliminary operations on November 23 and 24, in which sharp fighting
occurred between Union and Confederate forces, on November
25, 1863, the Union army decisively attacked the Confederates
and drove them from their position atop Missionary Ridge overlooking Chattanooga. The Army of the Cumberland's assault
upon Missionary Ridge, supported, in turn, by the assaults of
the Army of the Potomac detachment and General Sherman's
Army of the Tennessee, was "the war's most notable example of
a frontal assault succeeding against entrenched defenders holding high ground. It resulted from confusion, luck, and a lackluster
Confederate effort." The routed Confederates finally rallied below Chickamauga Creek in northern Georgia. Following his
victory at Missionary Ridge, General Grant " 'effectively
destroyed' " the rail line linking the Confederate forces in north
Georgia with those recently dispatched to eastern Tennessee.
Simultaneously, he sent General Sherman with a sizeable force
to eastern Tennessee to reinforce the Union troops already there
and, if possible, " 'destroy' " the Confederates who were threatening Knoxville. Although failing to destroy the Southern army,
Sherman's advance did succeed in forcing the Confederates to
withdraw to a position northeast of the city, where they remained
throughout the winter of 1863–1864. General Grant noted that,
" 'had it not been for the imperative necessity of relieving Burnside, I would have pursued the broken and demoralized retreat-

ing army as long as supplies could have been found in the country.' "[26] For his part, General Sherman wanted to quickly relieve Burnside and then withdraw from Knoxville, rather than tie troops down garrisoning eastern Tennessee. While enroute to Knoxville, Sherman wrote Grant,

> That any military man should send a force into east Tennessee puzzles me. Burnside is there and must be relieved, but when relieved I want to get out and he should come out too. I think, of course, its railroads should be absolutely destroyed, its provisions eaten up or carried away and all troops brought out. Cumberland Gap should be held simply as an outpost of Kentucky.[27]

In any case, Chattanooga and eastern Tennessee were now securely in Union hands. Although Mr. Lincoln may have underestimated the Confederacy's endurance when he wrote that it could not last long without control over the region, the loss of Chattanooga and east Tennessee was a very serious blow to the South. As Allen Nevins wrote,

> Again and again, in this war, strategic operations had to be related to two considerations of a non-military character. One was their effect upon public sentiment, party movements and decisions at the polls; the other was the agricultural and industrial situation. It had been highly important for the Union army to take and hold Chattanooga before the November elections. Had it lost its grip upon the city and been forced back to Nashville, a heavy depression would have settled upon the Northwest. Now a sense of elation pervaded the great area from Ohio to Kansas. It was equally important for the powerful western forces to gain the prospect of any early subjugation of Georgia. That State, with its resources of grain and livestock (to say nothing of mills and factories), had been one of the main supports of the Confederate armies; but now, long before a new harvest could ripen, Union forces would push their way into its very heart. These were facts upon which the sorely tried Army of (the) Tennessee could base comforting reflections in the long winter months ahead.[28]

Moreover, as General Fuller pointed out, militarily, the capture of Chattanooga provided the Union forces with a base of operations "from which an army could operate against the rear of Lee's forces in Virginia."[29]

Finally, following the conclusion of the Chattanooga-Knoxville Campaign, the new Commander of the Army of the Tennessee, General Sherman, proposed a plan which would further secure Union control over the Mississippi Valley, "so that the Mississippi might remain peaceful" during the approaching spring, 1864 campaigns, while, simultaneously, releasing many of the troops presently assigned to garrison responsibilities for further duty elsewhere. Specifically, Sherman was concerned that,

> Although the Confederacy had been permanently severed down the Mississippi line the cut had not been wide enough to prevent the Confederate edges closing in while Grant was operating anew along the Tennessee line. Vicksburg itself was immune from Confederate encroachments, but in eastern Mississippi the Confederate forces based on Meridian had drawn in close enough to the Mississippi to be unpleasant company and an ever-present menace to the free navigation of the great river.[30]

For some time, General Sherman had been, in his words,

> ... convinced that we should hold the river absolutely and leave the interior alone. Detachments inland can always be overcome or are at great hazard, and they do not convert the people ... with the Mississippi safe we could land troops at any point, and by a quick march break the railroad, when we could make ourselves so busy that our descent would be dreaded the whole length of the river.[31]

Sherman's plan was "to strike a quick blow at these forces and roll them back eastward, while Banks from New Orleans similarly rolled back the Confederate forces west of the Mississippi." Sherman proposed that he lead his infantry force from Vicksburg, on the Mississippi, to Meridian, one hundred and fifty miles to the east. Meanwhile, as General Sherman's force distracted the Confederates, a Union cavalry force would move upon Meridian from Memphis, if possible, defeating the Southern cavalry en route. General Sherman and the Memphis cavalry force would rendezvous at Meridian, destroy the arsenal and railroad, and defeat the Confederate army in eastern Mississippi. Thus, in late January, Sherman's force began its advance, arriving in Meridian on February 14, 1864, whereupon it destroyed all the Confederate supplies available, as well as twenty-five miles of railroad in all directions. Indeed, General Sherman reported to General Halleck that he had destroyed " 'a full hundred miles of railroad . . . and (made) a swath of desolation fifty miles broad across the state of Mississippi which the present generation will not forget.' " The cavalry force, however, was defeated en route to Meridian by its numerically inferior Confederate counterpart and never joined Sherman's force. Hence, on February 20, Sherman's raiding infantry left Meridian for Vicksburg, their mission only partially successful. This operation, however, would set the tone for future operations by General Sherman's armies.[32]

Meanwhile, in the Virginia theater, by the first of October, General Lee had become aware that two corps of the Army of the Potomac had been transferred from Virginia to Chattanooga. Hence, the Confederate commander decided to launch another offensive against the weakened Union army. On October 9, General Lee began an operation in which he attempted to strategically turn the Army of the Potomac's right and take a position between it and the Federal capital as he had done during the Second Bull Run Campaign. General Meade, however, kept his army concentrated and withdrew in good order, refusing to "halt at any position where there was any danger of his west flank being enveloped (as had happened to Pope and Hooker)," thus denying the Confederates any "opportunity for a successful attack." Finally, the Army of the Potomac took up a position at Centreville, Virginia, near Washington. Conversely, General Lee, without a rail line of communications and forced to keep his army concentrated in the presence of the enemy, thus eliminating the option of living off the countryside, opted to withdraw behind the Rapidan River. His army arrived south of the river one month after commencing the latest operation, with General Meade's army in slow pursuit. The Confederates now began to disperse and prepare for the winter. The Commander of the Army of the Potomac would have preferred to have done likewise, but, under intense pressure from the Washington high command, he attempted one last maneuver. In late November, 1863, General Meade formulated a plan to move his entire army swiftly down and across the Rapidan, turning the Confederate right rear, thus positioning itself between the dispersed Confederate corps and, hopefully, destroying them individually before they could concentrate. Unfortunately for General Meade, however, the movement down the Rapidan did not proceed as smoothly as expected and the Confederates were able to concentrate their forces and entrench themselves along Mine Run Creek in preparation for Meade's expected assault. General Meade's forces arrived on November 28, but after a careful reconnaissance and attack preparations, the General wisely decided to call off the offensive and withdraw his forces to the north side of the Rapidan. Simultaneously, unknown to the leadership of the Army of the Potomac, General Lee planned an enveloping assault on the Union position. But, when the Southern attack commenced on December 2, the Army of the Potomac had already retired. Both forces then settled into winter quarters, thus confirming the Virginia stalemate for another season. General-in-Chief Halleck was "exasperated," but President Lincoln, "proving more realistic accepted the situation philosophically."[33]

In short, by late 1863 and early 1864, most Union and Confederate general officers had concluded that it was virtually impossible to destroy a competently led, reasonably well equipped army in battle. As Professors Hattaway, Beringer, Jones, and Still observed,

> Lacking the ability to win a total victory in battle or to conduct an effective pursuit, Union forces had to occupy the enemy's territory. This meant that they had to contend with the nearly insurmountable problems of operating over long lines of communications in a thinly populated but hostile and huge country as they conducted a national war without decisive numerical superiority against adequately armed and competently led Confederate armies.[34]

After over two and a half years of extremely heavy and sustained fighting, the Union armies had conquered only a relatively small portion of the South. The Deep South and the Carolinas had only experienced a limited amount of fighting and even Mississippi, which had endured many months of conflict, was still partly under Confederate control. Moreover, "the conquest of the Mississippi had conferred no significant military or logistical benefit," the Union naval blockade "remained only a serious nuisance" for the South, and most of the vast trans-Mississippi Confederacy "remained beyond the scope of Union control." Most importantly, the Confederate field armies remained effective and the military stalemate in Virginia continued. Notwithstanding the heavy Confederate manpower losses experienced during the second half of 1863, especially at Gettysburg and Vicksburg, "conscription and volunteering had brought enough new men into the armies almost to make up the losses sustained in the summer and fall campaigning." Southern morale had definitely suffered during the second half of 1863, but, at this point, the decline did not appear to be a decisive factor. Finally, during the remaining year and a half of the war, the Confederate "economy became more self-sufficient, and the administration of government became more centralized and uniform." In short, clearly, the South "had retained the capability to not only preserve its own existence, but in doing so to threaten its adversary's determination to continue to struggle." Thus far, the Union armies had achieved only "limited successes."[35]

Moreover, the Union armies had initially been successful in penetrating deeply into Southern territory when they had been able to utilize strategically positioned rivers as lines of communications. Their problems dramatically intensified, however, when the river lines of communications ceased to be available and the Union armies were forced to rely upon rail communications. As the Federal armies were compelled to increasingly depend upon these fragile rail lines, the Confederates resorted more and more to raiding the Union rear in order to disrupt the Union advance. The first of these raids had been applied to General Buell's advance on Chattanooga during the summer of 1862, following the Union capture of Corinth, Mississippi. Later in 1862, advances by Generals Rosecrans and Grant had been halted by extensive and systematic use of Confederate cavalry raids against Union rail lines of communications. Indeed, "it had taken about a year and a half to advance the one hundred airline miles from Nashville to Chattanooga and another half year to consolidate the gain." Certainly, this experience did not offer great hope to those Union generals forced to rely upon rail lines to support the conquest of the remainder of the South. Indeed, the most successful western theater commander, General Grant, became convinced that there existed "almost insuperable obstacles to supplying the Union armies over great distances by railroad." The enemy had shown that he could destroy the railroad as he retreated, forcing the Union armies to rebuild the rail lines as they slowly followed. Of course, the Confederates could still utilize their own interior rail lines of communications to shift troops to threatened theaters, thereby forcing the Union commanders to constantly guard against a sudden Confederate troop concentration and counter-offensive. Furthermore, the Confederate cavalry and guerrilla raiders could cut the rail lines behind the advancing Federals as soon as the latter reconstructed them, thereby forcing them to detach large bodies of troops to protect the railroads linking the army with its source of supply. The same problems were encountered in defending territory already occupied against Southern raiders, thereby forcing the detachment of more troops from the field armies. Already, the Union army "employed a third of its soldiers garrisoning territory and guarding communications." These considerations, combined, eventually stalled the Union advance. Moreover, the problem would be increasingly exacerbated with the capture and occupation of additional territory and the lengthening of communication lines, especially now that water lines of communications were no longer available and only rail lines provided avenues for deeper penetrations into the Deep South. In short, it appeared that Southern raiding forces "were too formidable" and the logistical problems which had earlier immobilized Generals Buell, Grant, and Rosecrans raised serious questions concerning the ability of the Union armies to conquer a region as vast as the Confederacy. Thus, if, as many feared, the Union armies could not annihilate the Southern armies on the battlefield, capture them, as at Fort Donelson or at Vicksburg, or seize and permanently occupy the territory upon which they depended to sustain themselves, how was the Confederacy to be defeated and the rebellion crushed? This was the dilemma which confronted both the Federal high command and the theater commanders in the winter of 1863–1864.[36]

CHAPTER VI

Winter 1864—Summer 1864

Ulysses S. Grant, the officer who had already emerged as the hero of the war in the western theater, would now emerge as the architect of the new strategy which would break the military stalemate between the United and Confederate States. During the winter of 1864, Congress revived the rank of Lieutenant General, previously held permanently only by George Washington and by brevet by Winfield Scott. In early March, 1864, General Grant was promoted to the revived rank on a permanent basis. Consequently, as the United States Army's ranking officer, General Grant became the new General-in-Chief, while the former General-in-Chief, Henry Halleck, was appointed to the newly created subordinate post of Chief of Staff. Major General William T. Sherman succeeded General Grant in command of the Union armies in the west. Already, for over a year and a half, however, General Grant and his close colleague, General Sherman, had reflected upon the problems of vulnerability of overland lines of communications and occupied territory to enemy raids. Consequently, by the time of his promotion, General Grant's ideas regarding a new strategic approach had matured.[1]

General Grant concluded that the primary goal of Union military operations should be the destruction of the Confederacy's principal field armies: General Lee's army, located in northern Virginia, and the Southern forces situated in northern Georgia. The General was, however, realistic about the improbability of annihilating these enemy armies in a single battle. As such, General Grant agreed with his predecessors that the most promising way to end the rebellion was to deprive the Confederacy of the resources necessary to sustain its field armies. Hence, Grant retained the naval blockade component of the earlier Union strategies which had consistently sought to isolate the South from overseas maritime commerce. In addition, the Union forces would continue to occupy the entire Mississippi Valley, thus severing one segment of the Confederacy's internal communications network and, thereby, contributing to the further isolation of the South. The maritime and continental isolation of the Confederacy was, in turn, still designed to compel the South to rely upon and eventually exhaust its domestic war-making resources. It will be recalled that, when General Scott had originally suggested his plan in 1861, he had intended that this should be the exclusive element of Federal war strategy and, upon the establishment of the maritime and continental blockade, the Union forces should wait for it to strangle the rebellion. It had been President Lincoln and General Scott's successor, General McClellan, who had decided to expand the continental component of Federal war strategy to include the seizure and permanent occupation of a number of significant locations throughout the South. Like General Scott, the President and General McClellan had believed that, when enough military pressure was applied, pro-Union moderates in the South would displace the secessionists and return the South to the Union. It will be further recalled that, by late 1862, Mr. Lincoln and General McClellan's successor as General-in-Chief, General Halleck, agreed to escalate the limited military strategy heretofore pursued, which had, in turn, been predicated upon the existence of powerful pro-Union elements in the South. Recognizing that the Union Party in the South was powerless against the secessionists, the Federal high command opted to progressively conquer the entire South, thereby, gradually weakening and, eventually, eliminating the South's capacity to resist Washington's will and compelling the Southerners to sue for peace. This national military strategy, in turn, had been combined with the subsequent formal announcement of lenient peace terms, designed, in turn, to induce the Southerners to abandon their struggle for independence and rejoin the Union. The new General-in-Chief, General Grant, remained committed to defending that portion of the South which had already been occupied during the first three years of the war. In accord with the assumptions underpinning his predecessor's strategy, this would continue to permit the Union forces to utilize the resources of these captured areas, while, simultaneously, denying those resources to the enemy. But beyond maintaining territorial control over the areas already occupied, General Grant proposed that no additional Southern territory be permanently held. Instead, General Grant proposed a national military strategy which envisioned the systematic, simultaneous movement of several Union armies, not just cavalry, to raid deeply into those portions of the South which remained under Confederate control. These raiding armies were to break up the South's internal rail communications network and destroy those resources necessary to sustain the Confederate war effort: foundries, armaments factories, textile mills, etc. In a sense, General Grant was copying the enemy raiding oriented strategy which had been so successful in immobilizing the Union overland advances by disrupting the lines of communications of the individual Union armies. General Grant, however, intended to enlarge this approach to a national scale and not just sever the lines of each of the enemy field armies, but to strike at the communications network which linked the Confederacy together, as well as the war economy necessary for the Richmond government to sustain those armies. Deprived of necessary supplies, it would become impossible for the Confederacy's principal field armies to remain cohesive and they would, therefore, disintegrate without necessitating further Union conquest of Southern territory. Operationally, drawing upon his earlier experience during the Vicksburg campaign, General Grant intended that the Union raiding armies would live off the enemy country. Not only would this allow the Union raiders to free themselves from the fragile rail lines of communications which had proven so vulnerable to attacks by Southern cavalry and guerrillas, by living off the enemy countryside, the Union forces would consume agricultural resources which would otherwise be utilized by the enemy. General Grant intended that the remaining agricultural resources should be destroyed, thus denying them to the Confederate cause. In short, General Grant's use of raiding, not conquering armies followed the "path of least resistance." It avoided the liabilities associated with protecting additional occupied territory and depending upon ever lengthening, extremely vulnerable rail lines of communications. Moreover, successful implementation of this strategy was not predicated upon the destruction of the Confederacy's principal field armies in battle. Instead, it concentrated upon the most vulnerable elements of the enemy's defenses: his logistical infrastructure and his war-making resources. This, combined with the simultaneous timing of the Union advances, would disrupt Richmond's ability to concentrate its forces in threatened theaters and eventually destroy its capacity to field armies at all. Thus, the continental component of the new General-in-Chief's strategy eliminated the focus of his predecessors upon the additional permanent acquisition of Southern territory, in favor of maintaining territorial gains already made and conducting large-scale Union raids upon enemy territory. His approach, however, retained the goal of progressively denying the enemy access to his own resources and logistical infrastructure, "thus crippling his armies by means of deprivation."[2] The difference was, unlike the strategy heretofore pursued by Mr. Lincoln and the Union high command, the newly appointed General-in-Chief, General Grant, predicated the offensive element of his strategy on area denial, rather than additional area control.

Even before he was named to be the General-in-Chief, General Grant had recommended to the Washington high command that two individual armies commence two separate raids into the interior of the Confederacy. As early as the summer of 1863, immediately following the fall of Vicksburg, General Grant had proposed that the Federal high command transfer their field forces from the Mississippi Valley to the Gulf of Mexico and use them to attack Mobile, Alabama. Following the capture or, at least, investment of Mobile, the Union army could then proceed up the Alabama River, through Selma and Montgomery, into Georgia, toward Atlanta. There, it would optimally be in position to intersect or directly cooperate with the Army of the Cumberland which was to, simultaneously, move southward from the Tennessee River against the Southern forces located in northern Georgia. The Washington high command, however, did not adopt Grant's suggestion, opting instead to allocate a large portion of the Union forces in the Mississippi Valley to the expedition designed to assert Union control over the trans-Mississippi portion of the Confederacy. Later, immediately following the Battle of Missionary Ridge, General Grant revived the "Mobile project." Discussing this, Bruce Catton commented,

> Grant believed . . . that an immediate advance toward Atlanta was out of the question, since it would be necessary before making such a move to accumulate at least six months' supplies for men and animals in Chattanooga. At the same time, simply to hold Chattanooga while these supplies were being brought forward would take only part of the army, "and instead of holding the remainder in winter quarters he (General Grant) proposes to employ them in an offensive campaign against Mobile and the interior of Alabama." This return to the Mobile plan marked a new step in Grant's development as a soldier. During the summer he had argued for this move but he had never really pushed it; it was as if he had had to give his mind time to make itself up. Now he saw this plan as the completely logical sequel to victory in Tennessee. He had at last reached the point where he could see that final triumph for the Union depended on crowding a beaten force without respite, permitting no breathing spell in which the weaker antagonist could regain his balance and repair damages—using the superior power of the North, in short, to apply unrelenting pressure of a sort the Confederacy had not the resources to resist.[3]

Finally, by the spring of 1864, General Grant had returned to the two-pronged advance concept which he had suggested during the summer of 1863.[4]

General Grant reasoned that the proposed Alabama River expedition would accomplish several goals. First, it would close the port of Mobile, the Confederacy's last significant port on the Gulf of Mexico, thus, considerably enhancing the effectiveness of the Federal naval blockade. Second, the proposed expedition would serve as a strategic turning movement directed against the Southern army located in northern Georgia confronting the reinforced Army of the Cumberland. Since the expedition would act as a raiding force, it could utilize, but not depend upon the water lines of communications provided by the Alabama River for supplies. Hence, while moving up the river and, especially, after leaving its banks, as the army proceeded into Georgia, the expedition could forage off the countryside and remain unencumbered by lines of communications. This, in turn, would allow it to elude those Confederate forces located in its path of advance. It would be very difficult to pin and destroy such a raiding army, since, without a line of communications, it could move in virtually any direction. Moreover, the Confederate forces in the Deep South would be confronted by two simultaneously advancing Union armies: the Army of the Cumberland, advancing southward from the Tennessee River, and the Alabama River expedition, advancing northeastward from the Gulf coast. Even if the Confederates concentrated against one of the two armies, the Union army under attack could strike a defensive stance and simply hold the line or maneuver knowing that the other Union force was advancing rapidly upon the Confederate rear. If the Southerners focused the attention of their forces in northern Georgia upon halting the southward movement of the Army of the Cumberland, their forces in eastern Mississippi and central Alabama would probably be incapable of preventing the Alabama River expedition from threatening and possibly taking Atlanta. This, in turn, would mean not only the loss of the supply base of the Confederate forces opposing the advance of the Army of the Cumberland, it would place them in a vise between the Army of the Cumberland to their front and the Alabama River expeditionary force to their rear. Third, as the Union army advanced up the Alabama River and into northern Georgia, the Alabama River force could destroy the Confederacy's remaining east-west rail connections, thereby effectively isolating both Mississippi and Alabama, as well as the remaining Confederate forces located in these two states, from the rest of the Confederacy. Lee's army and the Confederate forces defending northern Georgia would, thus, be permanently denied the resources of the western Confederacy. From another perspective, however, since the states of Mississippi and Alabama would be effectively isolated from the remainder of the territory under Confederate control, but not permanently occupied, these states would be transformed into a de-facto buffer area separating the Federally controlled Mississippi Valley from the remainder of the states of the Deep South and the mid-Atlantic region. This would further secure previous Union conquests and possibly reduce the necessity to maintain such a large contingent of troops to protect these areas, thereby permitting these troops to be utilized elsewhere. Fourth, by destroying the rail infrastructure as it advanced from Mobile toward Atlanta, the Alabama River expedition could strike a "crippling blow" at the defense industrial resources located in the area, while, at the same time, seizing Montgomery, the cradle of the Confederacy, and Atlanta, one of the most important cities in the South. Fifth, an advance up the Alabama River into Georgia "would practically limit the tactical theater to Virginia, the Carolinas, and Georgia." Conversely, if the authorities in Richmond decided to defend the Deep South against the Army of the Cumberland and the Alabama River expedition, General Lee's army would be forced to " 'abandon Virginia and North Carolina,' " thus, allowing the Federals to assert control over these contested areas. Finally, the spectre of a large-scale Union army raiding throughout the Deep South would have a positive impact upon Northern morale and perhaps an even greater negative impact upon the morale of the Southern citizens and the soldiers defending the Confederate cause.[5]

In addition, following the conclusion of the Chattanooga-Knoxville Campaign in November, 1863, but prior to his appointment as General-in-Chief, General Grant proposed that a raid be launched in North Carolina concurrently with the proposed Alabama River offensive. General Grant suggested that a 60,000 man raiding army move from southeastern Virginia into the interior of North Carolina, destroying the north-south rail lines which traversed the state. The Union expedition could then seize the important port city of Wilmington, North Carolina from the rear. Since General Grant intended that the operation be a raid, no territory in the interior of North Carolina was to be permanently occupied. Moreover, while the Union raiding army would be able to draw supplies from New Bern, North Carolina, until Wilmington was captured, Grant envisaged that the Union raiders would not be dependent upon any particular line of communications. Instead, he felt they should live off the country. He argued that the North Carolina raid would serve a variety of purposes. First and most important, it would further destroy the logistical infrastructure of the Confederacy. Second, the North Carolina expedition would serve as a large-scale strategic turning movement designed to sever the communications linking General Lee's army and the Confederate capital at Richmond with the Confederate troops and the war-making resources located in South Carolina and Georgia. As a result, Virginia would be effectively isolated and, eventually, the Confederates would be forced to abandon the state. Third, the Union raiders could destroy those war-making resources located in their path of march, while, simultaneously, liberating slaves, thus further reducing the manpower and material resources available to the Confederacy. Fourth, like the Alabama River expedition, the proposed North Carolina raid would probably cause many Southern soldiers to desert from the Confederate field armies and return home to protect their families and property. This would further weaken the Southern field armies. Finally, Wilmington, one of the Confederacy's last and most important windows to Europe, would finally be permanently closed, thereby further increasing the effectiveness of the Federal naval blockade. Certainly, the proposed Alabama River expedition and North Carolina raid, combined with ongoing operations in northern Virginia and immediately south of Chattanooga, would place the Union armies on exterior lines of operations. General Grant argued, however, that this was unavoidable and the disadvantages associated with such a situation would be partly negated by the fact that all four of these major field armies would be advancing simultaneously.[6]

Ultimately, neither the Alabama River expedition, nor the North Carolina raid were implemented as Grant had proposed them. The troops which would have been used for the former were permanently tied down in the abortive Red River Campaign and there were simply not enough troops in the west to support the trans-Mississippi, Alabama River, and northern Georgia campaigns, simultaneously. Moreover, discussing the high command's reaction to General Grant's Alabama River expedition proposal, T. Harry Williams wrote,

> ... if the army at Chattanooga was weakened to build up the force destined for Mobile, there was always the possibility that the Confederates might be able to recover East Tennessee. Grant's scheme violated the strategic principle of doing one big thing at a time. Lincoln saw the weakness in the plan and vetoed it. Halleck informed Grant that no operation would be permitted that endangered East Tennessee. Expressing Lincoln's thoughts, Halleck pointed out that Chattanooga was

a central position for the armies of both sides. If the Confederates held it, they could menace Tennessee and Kentucky. If the Federals held it, they could protect the two states and operate from it on central, interior lines against the long Confederate defence periphery.[7]

Similarly, the President and General Halleck raised manpower questions with respect to the North Carolina raid. The Washington high command neither wanted to weaken the Army of the Potomac, nor had a surplus 60,000 men available to commit to the projected raid into North Carolina. In addition, with respect of the North Carolina operation, the President and General Halleck failed to recognize that General Grant's principal objective in proposing the raid was to destroy an important portion of the Confederacy's rail infrastructure, as well as close the port of Wilmington. Hence, Mr. Lincoln and General Halleck misinterpreted Grant's proposal as merely a variation upon General McClellan's spring, 1862 Peninsular Campaign designed to seize Richmond from the east. As such, they felt that it ran all the risks associated with any exterior lines type operation. Indeed, just as the spectre of the loss of Chattanooga and eastern Tennessee haunted the Federal high command, the threat of a Confederate dash on Washington or the upper Potomac still bothered the Administration. In the largest sense, the Washington political/military leadership failed to recognize the logistical vulnerability of the Confederacy and insisted that Lee's army remain the direct focus of the Virginia campaign.[8]

Abandoning the proposed North Carolina raid as politically infeasible, but remaining hopeful concerning the prospects for launching the Alabama River expedition, General-in-Chief Grant formulated his operational plan for the spring, 1864 campaign. As General J.F.C. Fuller observed, General Grant's "central idea was concentration of force from which he intended to develop a ceaseless offensive against the enemy's armies and the resources and morale of the Confederacy." The General-in-Chief planned for the principal Union armies east of the Mississippi River to attack simultaneously, thereby preventing the Southerners from detaching troops and reinforcing threatened sectors or "sending men on furlough or to work in the fields or the workshops, as had frequently been done during the intervals between battles in the past." As Grant emphasized, " 'the enemy has not got army enough' to resist the pressure that would be exerted if all the major Union armies moved in proper coordination." Like his predecessor, General Halleck, General Grant felt that the west, not Virginia, was the decisive theater of the war, since operations in the western areas would determine the fate of the South's main army, General Lee's Army of Northern Virginia. Hence, General Grant planned for General Sherman to move southward from Chattanooga with a large army group, composed of the Army of the Cumberland, the Army of the Tennessee, and the force from Knoxville, the Army of the Ohio, to engage the Confederate forces in northern Georgia. General Sherman's mission was to: keep the Southerners in his theater fully occupied so that Richmond could not detach troops from Georgia for use in Virginia, "break up" the defending Confederate army, take Atlanta, and destroy the Confederacy's economic and logistical resources in north Georgia. Originally, General Grant had still hoped to coordinate the long planned Alabama River expedition with Sherman's advance. As discussed earlier, this operation would have supported the southward movement of Sherman's army group, while, simultaneously, disrupting the Confederate war-making resources and infrastructure, before the two forces united around Atlanta. Indeed, in an effort to gather the necessary forces to begin the raid up the Alabama River, as Bruce Catton noted, General Banks was ordered,

> ... to conclude his Red River campaign as quickly as possible, turn over that territory to Steele and the navy, abandon all of Texas except for an outpost on the Rio Grande, reduce the number of troops on the lower Mississippi to the smallest possible total, and in all of these ways to collect at New Orleans at least 25,000 men, to which force Grant would add 5,000 more from Rosecrans' force in Missouri. Banks then was to move against Mobile, and "it will be impossible for him to commence too early."[9]

Ultimately, however, the Alabama River operation failed to commence at all. Thus, General Sherman's campaign in northern Georgia was unsupported and, thereby, made more difficult because of the absence of another Union effort directed against the Confederate rear. In any case, Grant planned that, following the capture of Atlanta and the "break up" of the defending

Southern force in northern Georgia, Sherman would then conduct a raid into the Deep South, most likely to the Gulf of
Mexico, destroying the South's remaining east-west rail net, as
well as all available war and agricultural resources. During the
initial portion of the campaign, prior to the fall of Atlanta, Sherman's army group would be tied to a line of communications
extending by rail to Chattanooga. During the second, raiding
phase of his campaign, however, following the fall of Atlanta and
the destruction of the Confederate army in northern Georgia,
Sherman's force was to cut free of its supply lines and live off
the country until reaching the ocean and the support which the
Federal navy would provide. General Grant also wanted the
Union forces along the Mississippi River to conduct concurrent,
distracting raids of their own. Finally, according to General
J.F.C. Fuller, the "whole idea" of General Sherman's offensive
was to "operate against Lee's communications and once he had
cut them to make use of them to operate against Lee's rear."
Hence, according to General Fuller, Grant "saw clearly that,
whilst Chattanooga was the back door to Virginia," General
Lee's "rear was his objective."[10]

At the same time General Sherman's army group advanced
into Georgia, the Union forces in the Virginia theater were to
attempt to defeat Lee's army in battle or, more realistically, isolate it from its immediate sources of supply. The Army of the
Potomac, still under the command of the victor of Gettysburg,
Major General George Meade, was to advance and fully engage
Lee's army. General Meade's primary mission was to destroy or
isolate that army, but, should he fail in these extremely ambitious
assignments, he was to tie Lee down, thereby preventing the
Confederate commander from detaching troops for use elsewhere. Grant hoped "to bring Lee to decisive battle someplace
between the Rapidan-Rappahannock line and Richmond." But
his celebrated instructions to General Meade were, " 'Wherever
Lee goes, there you will also go.' " This, of course, quite
literally coincided with Mr. Lincoln's long held views concerning the Army of the Potomac's proper mission. Grant considered
the possibility of the Army of the Potomac cutting free of its supply line and moving against General Lee's left. His goal would

have been to sever Lee's and Richmond's line of communications, while, simultaneously, pushing the Confederates back into their isolated capital. The Union forces could then reestablish their own communications with the North and await the outcome of a siege. Ultimately, however, General Grant rejected this duplication of his Vicksburg Campaign plan as too risky and opted instead to attempt to move around General Lee's right. This would allow the Army of the Potomac to remain in contact with a relatively secure line of communications throughout the campaign, as well as remain in position to protect Washington. Moreover, if Lee's right were successfully turned, he would become separated from his supply center at Richmond. Meanwhile, as the Army of the Potomac engaged General Lee's army and General Sherman began his effort to cut Lee's army off from its warmaking resources in the Deep South, two other Union armies were to make additional attempts to deny Lee access to his immediate sources of supply in Virginia. A separate Union force was assigned to quickly advance up the James River from Ft. Monroe toward Richmond in a "surprise, waterborne turning movement," designed to isolate and optimally take Richmond. Grant planned for the James River expedition first to sever the rail lines of communication which extended to the south from the Confederate capital and then to advance upon the city itself. A movement directly upon Richmond was important because, in addition to the enormous symbolic significance of the city in the eyes of both the Northern and Southern people, General Lee's army drew a large portion of its supplies from the Confederate capital. Richmond, itself, in turn, depended heavily upon the rail network connecting it with the Carolinas and the Shenandoah Valley for its supplies. Hence, as Bruce Catton wrote, "to take Petersburg (immediately to the south of Richmond), or to break the connection between Richmond and Petersburg, was accordingly to strike a powerful blow at Lee's rear and at the line of supplies that kept his army alive, and so what happened on the south side of the James meant almost as much as what Meade's army did below the Rapidan." General Grant expected that the James River expedition,

> ... could overwhelm the small Confederate contingent near the Confederate capital, cut its rail communications to the south, and, if not

take the city, at least beleaguer it by occupying the south side of the James. To save Richmond, Lee would have to rush reinforcements from his army, enabling Meade, against his much-weakened opponent, to push rapidly south, cutting the railroads north of the city and either forcing its evacuation or beginning a siege that would sever almost all of Richmond's communications.[11]

Apparently from the outset of the campaign, General Grant felt that, if the Army of the Potomac was unable to decisively defeat Lee's army in battle or successfully turn Lee's right and move between him and Richmond, and, instead, the Confederates withdrew into the Richmond defenses, he would unite the Army of the Potomac and the James River force (the Army of the James) on the James River and lay siege to Richmond from the east and south. Finally, General Grant planned to have another, separate Union force advance up the Shenandoah Valley, occupy the upper Valley, cut off the flow of supplies from that fertile region to both Richmond and Lee's army, destroy the railways around Gordonsville, and then move east and unite with General Meade's Army of the Potomac.[12]

Comparing the Virginia and Georgia campaigns, as Professors Beringer, Hattaway, Jones, and Still pointed out, General Sherman's campaign

> ... paralleled Grant's against Lee but with several important differences. First, Sherman did not have to win battles, for the public had no such expectation from him. Second, he had to move more slowly than Grant because he lacked water communications, possessed only one base, and had to rebuild and fortify the railroad as he advanced. Third, just as Grant feared Lee might detach troops to reinforce Johnston (the Commander of the Confederate forces in northern Georgia), Sherman felt a similar but less acute apprehension that Johnston might send men to strengthen Lee. And, unlike Grant in the early stages of his campaign, Sherman had no hope of distraction in Johnston's rear; that had been the goal of the aborted Mobile landing.[13]

In short, the new General-in-Chief had formulated a single, comprehensive, national, integrated operational plan designed to disrupt the enemy's ability to field armies and, hence, indirectly, but effectively destroy those armies as organized, cohesive entities without necessarily annihilating them in battle.

Finally, while General Grant felt that these planned Union operations in the Virginia and western theaters would ultimately yield victory, the General-in-Chief felt that, unless the Union armies had crushed the rebellion or, at least, were in a position where victory was virtually certain prior to the November, 1864 Presidential elections, there was a strong possibility that Mr. Lincoln would be defeated in his bid for a second term. Throughout his Presidency, Mr. Lincoln's political position had been very closely tied to the outcome of Union military operations. Looking back over the first three years of the war, Allen Nevins observed,

> Lincoln's prestige had sunk to its nadir after the failure of the Peninsular Campaign and Pope's defeat just outside Washington at Second Manassas (Bull Run). The Democrats were embittered by his decisive removal of McClellan, and Radical Republicans had fallen into a deep depression that inspired fierce demands after Fredericksburg for a reorganization of the Cabinet. Had the United States possessed a government of British type, its Ministry might have fallen. Antietam and the Emancipation Proclamation had lifted the President's standing; Chancellorsville unquestionably depressed it again.[14]

Then, "as the summer began, the military factor came into play on the side of the Administration." Indeed, "in the Northwest, the moral effect of Vicksburg was incalculable; in the East, Meade's repulse of Lee, though without proper sequel, was still a potent victory."

> The rejoicings of Union men over Western success in the summer of 1863 were to be temporarily halted as autumn began with a stunning Confederate blow at Chickamauga. But the mood of victory had been too firmly fixed to be shattered. After Vicksburg and the capture of Chattanooga, it was impossible to persuade reasonable Middle Westerners that the war was a failure. The costs were appalling, but the salvation of the Union would repay all sacrifices—and that salvation now seemed certain. Nor were the victories of the day confined to the battlefields, for triumphs of policy had equal magnitude. It had become so clear that all risk of Anglo-French intervention was past, that men ceased to worry about it.[15]

Indeed, undoubtedly reflecting the summer, 1863 military successes, the Republicans and War Democrats did well in the autumn, 1863 elections and, when Congress gathered in early December, they held "decisive control of the Senate and a clear though not emphatic majority in the House." Meanwhile, the Administration received another boost as General Grant's victory at Missionary Ridge restored the prestige which the Administration had lost as a result of Rosecrans' defeat at Chickamauga.[16]

Notwithstanding these hopeful trends, however, the President was "anxiously uncertain" about his prospects for reelection. He was fully aware of the volatile nature of both the Republican and Democratic Parties in the spring of 1864.

> Peace Democrats were willing to end the war even without saving the Union; War Democrats were determined to end the war on a full restoration of the Union and on no other fixed condition whatever. In opposition to them, the Moderate Republicans stood for the Union, Emancipation, and a rapid reconstruction on mild terms; the Radical Republicans demanded Union, Emancipation, and a delayed reconstruction on steel-hard terms or rather penalties. A variety of shades of opinion might be distinguished under these four areas, but they suffice for a broad classification. If the Peace Democrats ever gained overwhelming strength in the North and Northwest, the Union was lost. If the Radical Republicans conquered majority opinion, they would insist upon nominal union in spiritual disunion.[17]

Of these four loose groupings, the President could really count on only one, the Moderate Republican element. To maintain himself, he had to unite those elements with the War Democrats into a new Union Party. Yet, while many War Democrats had, in the past, supported the President on key issues, still respected his abilities, and "rejoiced over his charitable attitude toward the conquered Southerners," they would have preferred another man to lead the Union cause. Indeed, many War Democrats accepted the viewpoint that "the principle of one-term Presidencies ought to be firmly established," noting that "nobody since Andrew Jackson had served two terms and eight men in succession had held the White House for four years or less." In short, if Lincoln were to win reelection, he would have to possess sufficient strength within the Republican Party to be renominated and then receive enough support from War Democrats to ensure reelection. In the spring, 1964, that appeared to be a very formidable task. But, if Mr. Lincoln failed to be reelected, many feared that the Union cause would sink to defeat. Consequently, as the General-in-Chief formulated his operational plans for the spring and summer, 1864, he recognized that his actions would have significant political ramifications which, in turn, could seriously effect the outcome of the war. In the immediate sense, Grant was sensitive to the fact that "the Northern public counted on the new Lieutenant General to take on Lee, the South's best general, who had threatened Washington and twice raided north of the Potomac." Hence, for that, as well as other reasons, the General-in-Chief took the field with the Army of the Potomac, rather than remain in the western theater, which he regarded as the decisive arena, or in Washington, as had his predecessors had done since the war began in 1861. In the larger sense, however, General Grant recognized that his operational plan for the 1864 campaign would have to produce successes quickly if he was to attain what he felt was an important ingredient to victory—to "magnetize the North into supporting Lincoln."[18]

In early May, 1864, almost simultaneously, operations began in Virginia and northern Georgia. The 118,000 man Army of the Potomac, under General Grant's personal direction, moved across the Rapidan River in an effort to turn Lee's right without bringing on an immediate engagement in the tangle of the Wilderness. Lee, however, quickly parried the Union movement and, on May 5–7, his 64,000 man army clashed with the Federal host in a fierce contest around Wilderness Tavern, near the Chancellorsville battlefield of the previous year. While the Army of the Potomac failed either to destroy Lee's army in battle or sever its line of communications with Richmond, the Union forces did successfully pin Lee's army, thereby preventing the Southerners from detaching forces and deploying them elsewhere in Virginia or against Sherman in northern Georgia. Immediately following the battle, the Army of the Potomac again attempted to keep Lee from disengaging his forces, while, simultaneously, attempting to move around the Confederate right in an effort to place themselves between Lee's Confederates and the Southern army's base of operations at Richmond. Again, however, the Army of the Potomac was stopped before reaching its objective, this time at Spotsylvania, whereupon the two armies entrenched. Meanwhile, as the Army of the Potomac engaged Lee's forces, General Grant learned that, after enjoying an initial success, the Army of the James had encountered difficulties. Thus far, the

James River expedition had totally failed, neither severing the rail lines south of Richmond, nor taking the Confederate capital as Grant had hoped. But, the General-in-Chief remained cautiously hopeful.[19]

In response to these developments, General Grant modified his campaign plan and decided to commit the Army of the Potomac to a direct attack against Lee's army at Spotsylvania. In doing so, he hoped to "placate the public and possibly to gain a significant victory in battle." He hoped that the Army of the Potomac would break Lee's lines, split his army into two parts, sever the Virginia Central Railroad linking Richmond with the Shenandoah Valley, and optimally destroy Lee's entire force. Given Grant's experience at the Battle of Missionary Ridge outside Chattanooga, where the Army of the Cumberland had frontally attacked the entrenched Confederates and driven them from their strong positions, compared to General Meade's experience at Gettysburg, Grant was more optimistic than was General Meade concerning the prospect for a successful frontal assault. At the very least, Grant felt that by retaining the initiative via direct assaults, he would keep General Lee's army pinned in position at Spotsylvania. By keeping the pressure on the Confederates north of Richmond, General Grant still wanted to prevent the Southerners from diverting troops to other threatened sectors. In addition, as J.F.C. Fuller noted,

> . . . had he attempted to manoeuvre Lee out of his position, which he might have done, he would have forced Lee back towards Butler (the Commander of the Army of the James and leader of the James River expedition). This was the very thing he did not want to do, for by holding him as far away from Butler as he could, he facilitated his advance along the James River, which was causing as great a consternation in Richmond as Jackson's in the Valley had to Washington two years before (during the Peninsular Campaign), which shows the wisdom of this distracting movement.[20]

Simultaneously, as the Army of the Potomac attempted to smash through Lee's lines, General Grant ordered General Sheridan and the Union cavalry to move around the Confederate right, defeat any Southern cavalry encountered en route, sever the Virginia Central and the Richmond and Potomac Railroads, relieve as much pressure on the James River expeditionary force as possible, and then join the latter force. As General Fuller observed,

> The objects of this raid were: to attack Lee's line of supply—his rear; to draw the Confederate cavalry away from the Army of the Potomac, and to reduce traffic from Fredericksburg forward. Critics of it frequently overlook the fact that Butler was ... under orders to move against Richmond. Had Butler occupied Petersburg, as he should have done, then damage to the railways in rear of Lee would almost certainly have compelled Lee to fall back or risk starvation.[21]

Thus, on May 10, General Grant repeatedly, but unsuccessfully attempted to break through the Confederate entrenchments at Spotsylvania. Eventually, however, recognizing the futility of continued frontal assaults and discouraged about the prospects of the James River force breaking out of its position and performing its mission, Grant again modified his theater campaign plan.[22]

The General-in-Chief resumed his effort to move the Army of the Potomac around Lee's right. Indeed, he was able to move about halfway to Richmond before being halted by General Lee's forces on May 23 along the North Anna River. Summarizing General Grant's position at this point, General Fuller noted,

> Once again Grant's manoeuvre had succeeded strategically, but tactically it had failed. It had moved Lee out of his entrenchments, but it had not brought him to battle in the open; far from it, for the works Lee now occupied had been constructed during the previous winter and were formidable in the extreme, and there can be little doubt that from them Lee should have assumed an offensive. Grant's situation was an anxious one, and realizing the difficulty and cost of an assault, and no longer having to consider Butler, who was bottled up at Bermuda Hundred, he determined on another flanking movement.[23]

Consequently, in late May, General Grant again attempted to slip the Army of the Potomac around the Confederate right, unite it with some of the elements of the James River force which would be moved north of the James, and compel Lee to fight in the open. The wily Confederate, however, again blocked the Union forces, this time at Cold Harbor, a location east of the Confederate capital, near the position which the Army of the Potomac had occupied two years earlier during General McClellan's Peninsular Campaign. Here Grant could draw supplies via the water lines of communication utilized by General McClellan in 1862. On June 3, General Grant again frontally assaulted the Confederate entrenchments in an effort to keep General Lee's army fully engaged and, thus, preclude the possibility of the Confederates detaching forces and utilizing them elsewhere. In addition, General Grant apparently hoped to achieve a battlefield victory which would, optimally, end the war or, at least, open the way to Richmond. In doing so, Grant apparently hoped to also elevate Northern morale, enhance Mr. Lincoln's reelection prospects, and impress the Europeans by showing that victory was within the Union reach, prior to the commencement of a protracted siege of Richmond. Unfortunately for the Union cause, however, again the Army of the Potomac was thrown back with heavy losses. Meanwhile, as the efforts of the James River expedition and the Army of the Potomac failed to reach the General-in-Chief's maximum hopes, on May 15, the third Union force, the army which was supposed to have advanced up the Shenandoah Valley, had been defeated at the Battle of New Market and had retreated northward.[24]

By this point the "total casualties in the campaign were proportional to the forces engaged, each side diminished by about 50 percent of its initial strength." Union morale, however, probably declined more than did Southern morale because the soldiers of the Army of the Potomac "acutely felt the futility of assaulting entrenched positions." Indeed, the "Northern reservoir of manpower was not inexhaustible, even apart from the moral consideration that extensive losses in battle might destroy the relatively fragile Northern will to continue the war." Moreover,

> The heavy casualties not only disenchanted the Northern public with battles but also hurt President Lincoln's reputation with both the people and his own party. Victory seemed as far away as ever. To many, Grant appeared to have done no more than hopelessly reach McClellan's 1862 position.[25]

As a result, the Federal high command "faced the problem of maintaining public morale and will to win, when expensive victories thus far had produced no results and could produce none comparable to Vicksburg or Chattanooga." As Professors Hattaway and Jones noted, it was in this context that,

Rather than making the Northerners realize the failure of past operations and that battles were merely incidents of movements against communications, the safer approach was to sustain morale by showing that the victories had been productive, thus justifying the heavy casualties of the Wilderness and Spotsylvania. Though he may have been weakening in his conviction that Confederate losses were as great as his own, Grant took this as a basis for his justification. In part at least, and perhaps entirely, an authentic belief on his part, Grant's thesis used the battles and the Confederate losses to explain the failure of the Confederates to assume the offensive. . . . Thus, Grant shrewdly turned against Lee the Confederate general's prestige in the North and Lee's successful offensive maneuvers against earlier commanders of the Army of the Potomac. Lee's failure to take the offensive was evidence of the beneficial effects of the initial battles of the campaign. These battles had reduced the formidable Confederate army, which had twice invaded the North, merely to cringing behind breastworks, unwilling to fight fairly, and unable to prevent the siege of its capital. After the war, Grant summed this up well in his attrition thesis: "Lee had to fight as much as I did, . . . every blow I struck weakened him, and when at last he was forced into Richmond it was a far different army from that which menaced Washington and invaded Maryland and Pennsylvania. It was no longer an invading army. The Wilderness campaign was necessary to the destruction of the Southern Confederacy."[26]

As General Grant explained to General Halleck in early June, the Confederates " 'act purely on the defensive, behind breastworks, or feebly on the offensive immediately in front of them, and where in case of repulse they can instantly retire behind them.' " Conversely, according to General Grant, the Army of the Potomac was, " 'not only confident of protecting itself without entrenchments, but . . . can beat and drive the enemy wherever and whenever he can be found without this protection.' "[27]

Following the Battle of Cold Harbor, General Grant concluded that he would not be able to separate Lee's army from its base of supply at Richmond or smash his way into the city " 'without a greater sacrifice of human life' " than he was " 'willing to make.' " Not only did General Grant recognize the futility of continued frontal assaults against prepared Confederate positions, the Army of the Potomac was running low on men. Richmond's elaborate lines of communications, however, remained intact. Consequently, Grant again revised his campaign plan. The General decided to dispatch a large portion of the Union cavalry westward to sever the Virginia Central Railroad which linked Richmond with the Shenandoah Valley, while, simultaneously, drawing Lee's cavalry behind him. At the same time, the Union army in the Valley was to resume its movement up the Valley and destroy the rail lines, as well as, if possible, destroy the James River canal. Upon completion of their respective missions, the cavalry force and the Valley army were to link up and move east, ultimately uniting with the Army of the Potomac. Meanwhile, following a brief delay in order to provide the cavalry with sufficient opportunity to move west, Grant intended to suddenly move the Army of the Potomac south of the James River and take Petersburg, Virginia before Lee could reinforce the city. The planned strategic turning movement would, hopefully, allow the Army of the Potomac to reach Lee's rear where it could cut the rail lines extending southward and southwestward from the Confederate capital. Following the seizure of Petersburg, Grant intended to "turn the enemy works . . . in front of Butler (the Commander of the Army of the James) at Bermuda Hundred, and then advance on Richmond." Grant hoped that by breaking Lee's line of communications with the Deep South, the Confederates would be forced to "leave the safety of Richmond and fight the decisive engagement that Grant wanted," optimally upon ground selected by the Union military leaders.[28]

On June 12, after his cavalry raiders had departed westward drawing the Southern cavalry behind them, Grant secretly disengaged from General Lee's army and executed the planned surprise strategic turning movement. The two lead corps of the Union army arrived near Petersburg on June 15, but the entire operation was halted at that point due to bad execution by the Federal corps commanders, combined with an excellent Confederate defensive reaction in the Petersburg area. Following unsuccessful Federal attempts to take the town between June 16–18, both sides entrenched themselves, thus beginning a nine month trench warfare stalemate. As Bruce Catton noted, General Lee's army

... would never again see northern Virginia, nor would the Army of the Potomac see the Potomac again. There were fixed in position, almost totally immobilized, and henceforth for month after dreary month they would see little more than the desolate trenches, the heavy forts that were built at every weak point, setting the pattern of trench warfare

> with its eternal round of shelling and sharpshooting and day-by-day discomfort of heat and dust and thirst, with its occasional furious small fights for small advantages. Richmond was a good many miles away, and yet in reality the entire layout of works was the defense of Richmond—a twenty-five mile set of trenches and forts that began up near White Oak Swamp, east of Richmond, came down across the James, crossed Bermuda Hundred neck, crossed the Appomattox, and then swung south in a long arc just east of Petersburg, the lower end of the arc curving toward the west.[29]

In reaching this impass, however, the Union army had again failed to sever Richmond's rail links extending to the south and west connecting the Confederate capital with the Deep South. Thus, "the rickety Confederate supply organization managed to feed both Lee's army and the Richmond population during this siege." Meanwhile, on June 11–12, the Union cavalry raiders were forced to turn back at Trevilian Station before they could complete their mission. Finally, reacting to the threat which the Union army in the Shenandoah Valley posed to Richmond's communications, the Confederate high command had detached one corps from General Lee's army and sent it west. This Confederate force not only prevented the Union Valley army from performing its mission, it pushed it westward.[30] These operations concluded the Wilderness-Petersburg Campaign which "blemished" General Grant's reputation. As Professors Hattaway and Jones wrote,

> In six weeks of incessant struggle he had lost over 60,000 men. The Confederates had not tabulated their losses but they had amounted to at least 30,000. It is likely that each army lost approximately the same percentage of its forces. Thus, instead of being remembered for the sophistication of his strategy and as an economizer of lives by always taking the enemy in the rear, Grant became known as a butcher of men who advocated the head-on collision. Rather than viewed as the architect of a successful strategy of exhaustion, because of this campaign Grant has been perceived by many evaluators as a practitioner of the strategy of annihilation, victorious, if at all, only after paying a hideous human toll.[31]

Meanwhile, as it became increasingly clear that Grant's Virginia Campaign would culminate in a siege of Richmond, the Chief of Staff, General Halleck, reminded General Grant that, in his opinion, siege operations would tend to " 'exhaust us more than they injure the rebels, for it would require 2 men outside to keep 1 in Richmond.'" General Halleck noted that, since it would be virtually impossible to permanently isolate the Confederate capital, a siege of Richmond should be avoided. Rather, the Chief of Staff reminded the General-in-Chief that General Lee's " 'army, not Richmond, is the true objective point of the campaign.'" Moreover, Halleck was particularly concerned about the prospect of a siege operation against the Confederate capital from the east and south. If General Lee's army remained intact, the wily Confederate could leave a small portion of his army to hold Richmond and move the remainder upon Washington or the upper Potomac as he had done so successfully in 1862. In order to reduce this possibility, the Chief of Staff advocated that the Army of the Potomac remain north of the James River.[32] Hence, if siege operations were to be commenced at all, General Halleck argued that the Army of the Potomac should lay siege to Richmond,

> . . . from the northwest with one flank resting on the James where "you will hold the canal, and can, with your cavalry, control the railroad lines south of the James River.'' . . . He suggested that Grant's line of communications be due north, along the Richmond, Fredericksburg, and Potomac Railroad. The siege from the northwest would take place "over favorable ground'' and toward the side of the city "most favorable for an attack, as the Tredeger Iron Works, the arsenal, the waterworks, and all the flouring mills lie on the northwest side of the city, and exposed to bombardment from that direction.'' Except to say that Grant's flanks would be "pretty safe,'' the Chief of Staff did not allude to another obvious advantage—in a northwest position Grant's army would be closer to the Shenandoah Valley than Lee's.[33]

General Halleck's worst fears soon materialized when the Confederate corps which had been detached from Lee's army to the Shenandoah Valley moved northward after pushing aside the Union force which had been moving upon Lynchburg. The Confederate high command hoped that pressure in the direction of the national capital at Washington and the upper Potomac would induce the Union high command to withdraw troops from the Army of the Potomac besieging Petersburg. In early July, the Confederates raided into Maryland and, on July 11, they threatened Washington itself before returning to the Valley. As General

Ballard wrote, the "moral effect" of the temporary Confederate capture of Washington during the summer of a Presidential election year "would have brought down both the President and Grant in ruins." An enemy sack of Washington "would have been taken as a convincing proof of the Democrats' assertion that the 'war is a failure . . .' " Thus, Ballard may have been quite correct when he observed, "The people were prepared to undergo necessary sacrifices, but would find it hard to forgive the quite unnecessary sacrifice of their capital." Meanwhile, on July 10, immediately prior to the Confederate raid on Washington, the President,

> . . . informed Grant that the government had no force fit or large enough to take the field against Early (the Commander of the Confederate raiding force). Washington could probably be held against an attack, Lincoln said, but Baltimore could not. Lincoln then told Grant what he thought the General should do: "Now, what I think is, that you should provide to retain your hold where you are, certainly, and bring the rest with you personally, and make a vigorous effort to destroy the enemy's forces in this vicinity. I think there is a fair chance to do this, if the movement is prompt. This is what I think upon your suggestion, and is not an order." Again, as in 1862, Lincoln was thinking in offensive terms about the Confederate force in the Valley. He was not worried as much about the safety of Washington as he was about the possibility of running down the invaders and removing finally the enemy menace in the Valley area.[34]

In response to the Confederate movement up the Valley, the General-in-Chief sent two corps to Washington to strengthen its defenses, as well as those of the upper Potomac, but did not return to the capital city himself. Grant felt that for him to personally leave Petersburg and go to Washington "would be interpreted by the Northern people and the enemy as a sign of weakness." Like Mr. Lincoln, however, General Grant also felt that the "objective of the campaign" should be the "destruction rather than the repulse" of the Confederate threat from the Shenandoah Valley. Unfortunately, for the moment, the Federal command structure in northern Virginia was too decentralized for an effective offensive campaign against the Southern forces in the Valley. Later that same month, the Southerners again crossed the Potomac and raided Maryland and Pennsylvania. But General Grant remained adamant that the Confederate diversionary effort in the Shenandoah Valley should not distract from the main effort in the Petersburg area. Hence, he continued to attempt to sever Richmond's southward communications by extending his lines and by launching cavalry raids. As J.F.C. Fuller noted,

> The railways vital to the supply of Lee's army may be divided into two groups, namely, those entering Richmond and those entering Petersburg; with the Richmond and Petersburg railroad in between. The first group comprised the Richmond and York River and the Fredericksburg railroads—now of little use, and the Virginia Central and Danville railroads, which were vital; the second—the City Point and the Petersburg and Norfolk railroads, already in Grant's hand, and the Weldon and Southside (or Lynchburg) railroads, the first of which was of high value, for it linked Petersburg to Wilmington. Once the Petersburg lines were captured, the bulk of the Confederate traffic would be thrown on to the Danville railway, which was incapable of carrying all of it. Grant's plan was, therefore, to occupy the Weldon and Southside railways in order to compel the evacuation of Petersburg; and then, by turning the Confederate works west of Bermuda Hundred, operate against the Danville railway, the occupation of which would not only force the surrender of Richmond, but sever Lee from Wilmington and the Atlantic, and consequently cut him off from European supplies. It is true he could still retire into the interior, or unite with Johnston (the Confederate commander in northern Georgia), but without an administrative base, and his vital supply base was Europe, he would soon have been reduced to bow-and-arrow warfare.[35]

Unfortunately for the Union cause, however, neither the extension of the Union lines, the cavalry raids, nor the one frontal effort to break through the Confederate lines by means of mining operations were to prove successful in severing Lee's rail communications southward and/or ending the stalemate. By keeping the pressure in the Petersburg area up, however, the Army of the Potomac made it difficult for the Confederates to detach any more troops to reinforce their diversionary effort in the Shenandoah Valley or for operations against General Sherman's army group in the west. But all of this, particularly the raids on Washington and later Pennsylvania, coming at a time when the Northern people were still very depressed over the terrific casualties sustained during the recent weeks in Virginia, only served to further depress Northern morale and undermine their confidence in the Lincoln Administration as they approached the autumn Presidential elections.[36]

Notwithstanding the frustrations experienced by General Grant in Virginia during the spring and early summer of 1864, from the perspective of the General-in-Chief's overall operational plan, the Army of the Potomac had, through hard fighting, successfully prevented the Confederate high command from transferring troops to what the Union leadership regarded as the decisive theater of operations, northern Georgia.[37] Meanwhile, in early May, coinciding with the Battle of the Wilderness in Virginia, General Sherman led his almost 100,000 man strong army group, consisting of the Armies of the Cumberland and the Ohio, as well as his and Grant's old command, the Army of the Tennessee, south against the numerically inferior Confederates located in northern Georgia. During the next several weeks, the two armies maneuvered, with Sherman successfully turning the Southerners out of a series of entrenched positions. In the process, the two antagonists fought only one battle, the Battle of Kennesaw Mountain, on June 27. Throughout, General Sherman fulfilled his assigned mission of keeping the Confederates in his theater of operations sufficiently occupied to prevent them from transferring reinforcements to Virginia to oppose Grant's southward advance. By July, General Sherman's force had approached its geographic target, Atlanta, the "gate city of the South," whereupon, insofar as was possible, he severed the rail lines connecting Atlanta with Virginia, thereby reducing the possibility of the sudden arrival of Confederate reinforcements from the Petersburg area. On July 20, 22, and 28, 1864, the Confederates, under new theater leadership, clashed with Sherman's army group in very heavy fighting just outside the city at the Battles of Peachtree Creek, Atlanta, and Ezra Church, respectively. In each of these contests, the Union forces prevailed, with the Southerners sustaining comparatively heavy casualties. Yet, the Southerners continued to hold the city.[38]

Thus, by August, 1864, with the Army of the Potomac bogged down in siege operations outside Petersburg, Virginia, the Confederates actively threatening the upper Potomac and the Federal capital from the Shenandoah Valley, and Atlanta still in Confederate hands following weeks of tedious maneuvering and the recent battles outside the city, all at an enormous cost in blood and treasure, the Northern people were becoming weary of the war. Many concluded that, even if it were possible to defeat the Confederacy, it might not be worth the enormous cost. Reflecting the dissatisfaction with the Lincoln Administration's handling of the war effort, Radical elements of the Republican Party met in Cleveland on May 31 and nominated the fifty-one year old "Pathfinder," John C. Fremont, for President. According to Allen Nevins,

> The brief platform, Radical from beginning to end, promised a sweeping reversal of Lincoln's policies, and an acceleration of government action against slavery. One resolution, insinuating Administration indifference to governmental integrity and economy, promised strict regard to both. It contained a forcible assertion that as the war had destroyed slavery, the Federal Constitution should now be amended to prohibit its reestablishment, and "to secure to all men absolute equality before the law." Another plank demanded that civil liberties be protected against infringement outside of areas under martial law. A third called for a constitutional amendment restricting Presidents to a single term. The most important resolutions declared that control of Reconstruction belonged to the people through their representatives in Congress, not the Executive, and asked that the lands of rebels be confiscated and distributed among soldiers and actual settlers. Clearly, the document was not a practical program of action, but an extremist manifesto. This tiny splinter-party hoped not to elect any man, but to ally itself with malcontent Republicans in defeating Lincoln and his moderate aims.[39]

Although Fremont's chances of being elected President were slim, in a tight election between Mr. Lincoln and the Democratic nominee, even a small vote for Fremont could influence the outcome of the race. A few days after Fremont accepted the nomination, the mainstream Republican Convention was opened in Baltimore. While it was virtually a foregone conclusion that Mr. Lincoln would be renominated, there was a real danger that, unless the President managed to secure the active support of the Radicals, the factionalism within the Party would defeat him. Finally, the slate of candidates became complete when, in August, the Democrats met in Chicago and selected Major General George B. McClellan, the founder and first Commander of the Army of the Potomac, as their standard bearer for the 1864 Presidential election. Moreover, the "peace faction" of the party managed to get the Convention to adopt a resolution which stated, " 'After four years of failure to restore the Union by the experiment of war . . . humanity, liberty, and the public welfare demand that immediate efforts be made for a cessation of hostilities . . .' " Thus, notwithstanding General McClellan's expressed commitment to continue the war, the Democrats clearly emerged as the party of peace in the 1864 campaign.[40]

By August, within this political context and against what appeared to be a rising tide of Northern discontent caused by the high level of battlefield casualties, accompanied by the lack of any dramatic successes against the Confederate armies, Mr. Lincoln entertained "grave doubts" concerning his reelection chances. Furthermore, he, as well as many others, felt that his failure to secure reelection would probably lead to the final defeat of the efforts to restore the Union. President Lincoln believed that, if General McClellan were to win the election, his victory would have been secured " 'on such grounds that he cannot possibly save it (the Union)' " after taking office. Hence, in the event of defeat in the November election, the President resolved to try to " 'cooperate with the President-elect as to save the Union between the election and the inauguration,' " since, in his opinion, that would be the old Union's last chance. In doing so, irrespective of the final result, President Lincoln told the members of his cabinet, " 'At least, I should have done my duty, and have stood clear before my own conscience.' "[41] If the Confederates could hold out a bit longer without suffering any really significant, highly visible reversals in the field, it was still quite possible for them to emerge victorious from America's terrible ordeal.

CHAPTER VII

Summer 1864—Winter 1865

The mid-summer and early autumn of 1864 was one of the most momentous times in the history of the United States; indeed, the fate of the republic hung in the balance. But then, dramatically, the tide of war began to shift clearly in favor of the Union. First, the port of Mobile was finally closed by the Federal naval forces. Earlier, immediately following the capture of New Orleans in the spring of 1862, Admiral Farragut had wanted to move against Mobile and, as noted earlier, General Grant had long advocated the capture of Mobile Bay as the prelude to his proposed Alabama River expedition. Finally, on August 5, 1864, Admiral Farragut took control of Mobile Bay. On August 23, Fort Morgan, at the entrance to the Bay, was overcome, although, for the next three quarters of a year, the city of Mobile itself remained in Confederate hands. Between January and April, 1865, a coordinated Union army-navy force operated against the city, resulting in its eventual capture on April 12, 1865, long after it had ceased to have strategic significance in the Union war effort.[1]

Meanwhile, on August 25, following a lengthy artillery bombardment of Atlanta, during which "the ground shook night and day from the roar of 223 cannon," General Sherman quickly moved his forces south of the city and severed the rail lines which were vital for continued Confederate possession of the city. Without communications, the Southerners had no viable choice but to abandon the city. Hence, on September 1, 1864, the Confederate army evacuated Atlanta and regrouped south of the city. The following day, General Sherman informed Washington that Atlanta was in Union hands. The fall of Atlanta was, of course, of enormous importance, since, with its fall, the Confederacy lost one of its major cities, an important rail hub, and a key supply center. As B. H. Liddell Hart wrote,

For Atlanta, . . . had a three-fold strategic value—apart from its moral value, which grew with the effort to hold it. First, as one of the few manufacturing centres for munitions—a term wider than "ammunition"—in the agrarian Confederacy; its foundries and machine-shops furnishing a high proportion of the material without which the war could not be maintained. Second, as the greatest rail centre of the South; thither converged and thence radiated outward the main lines connecting the Atlantic seaboard with the western parts of the Confederacy. If these were already curtailed, the value of Alabama's resources had increased thereby, and not least that of the newly created ordinance works at Selma. Third, because Atlanta was the inner back gate, as Chattanooga was the outer, to the Atlantic states of old foundation, which were the foundation of the hostile power and will. And the last line of nature's battlements was that which covered Atlanta. Once the Atlanta gate could be opened the heart of the Confederacy would lie open to a mortal thrust.[2]

Professors Hattaway and Jones pointed out, however,

The existence elsewhere of another east-west railway link did, however, limit Atlanta's importance. This still unbroken line ran through Macon, some 100 miles south of Atlanta. Although Union forces had closed the port of Mobile, the major manufacturing centers of Selma and Augusta remained untouched and still enjoyed uninterrupted rail connections. The fall of Atlanta hurt the Confederate logistics badly but not fatally.[3]

Finally, notwithstanding the capture of Atlanta, the Confederate army which had been defending the city was not destroyed. Rather, it had escaped intact to fight again. On balance, perhaps the greatest impact of Atlanta's fall was symbolic; its capture by Sherman's army group had enormous psychological significance to the people of both the North and the South. This, in turn, had tremendous political and military ramifications for both antagonists. In the North, General Sherman's capture of Atlanta provided the Northern people with a highly visible field victory and, thus, significantly lifted their morale. Moreover, Sherman's victory gave the Lincoln Administration tangible evidence to place before the Northern electorate that General Grant's strategy was, indeed, working and that real progress was being made.[4] Conversely, as Professors Beringer, Hattaway, Jones, and Still observed, throughout the South,

. . . the fall of Atlanta produced exactly the opposite effect. Desertion rates, already serious, now multiplied as the needs of destitute families at home were reinforced by a soldier's presumption of the inevitable outcome of the war to persuade him that there was no more point in risking his life for a lost cause. It was no longer possible to augment military power by the strength of national will, nor was it possible to stiffen civilian determination by exciting victories on the field. The basic purposes of government are to protect lives and property, but as casualty lists lengthened, the letters from home grew more urgent, and the Union armies seemed more aggressive, it became clear that Confederate armies were doing neither. Why, then, a Confederacy? Thousands of soldiers and civilians asked themselves that question and concluded that "their interests could best be protected by rejoining the Union:" accordingly, they waged war with less enthusiasm than heretofore. After Atlanta, the bottom was about to drop out of the Confederate tub.[5]

Finally, in the Virginia theater, although the stalemate in the Petersburg area continued, Union forces made significant progress in the Shenandoah Valley. As T. Harry Williams noted, following the Southern raid on Pennsylvania, General Grant,

... realized that he would have to unify the command system in the Washington area by putting the troops in the capital and the adjacent departments under the control of one general. Early (the Confederate Commander of the Shenandoah Valley army) was still in the Valley and was sure to strike again. Only a central command of all the forces around the city could prevent a recurrence of the confusion prevailing in the recent raid. If Early could make periodic sweeps at Washington and escape each time because of the divisions in the Federal command system, Grant would always have to be detaching troops from Petersburg to chase after the Confederates. He would never be able to corner Lee. Furthermore, Grant knew that if Early got close to Washington again Lincoln would become dissatisfied with the defense setup for the capital.[6]

Consequently, in early August, 1864, the General-in-Chief unified the confused command structure in northern Virginia. Grant placed Major General Philip H. Sheridan in command of the troops in Washington, northern Virginia, Maryland, Pennsylvania, and West Virginia. General Sheridan's mission was to destroy the Confederate field forces in the Shenandoah Valley, destroy the rail lines and the James River canal which connected Richmond and the Confederate army with the Shenandoah Valley, and destroy the crops in the area so as to prevent them from being utilized by the increasingly hard pressed Southerners. General Grant summed up his instructions to General Sheridan by stating, " 'Give the enemy no rest, and if it is possible to follow

215

to the Virginia Central road, follow that far. Do all the damage to railroads and crops you can. Carry off stock of all descriptions, and negroes, so as to prevent further planting. If the war is to last another year we want the Shenandoah Valley to remain a barren waste.' " Meanwhile, the Army of the Potomac remained active in the Petersburg area in an effort, not only to break the defenses and/or sever the rail lines of communications which extended southward from the town, but also to prevent General Lee from reinforcing the Confederate forces in the Valley and, optimally, to force Lee to recall the Valley force to assist in the defense of Petersburg. If the latter occurred, General Grant instructed General Sheridan to aggressively pursue the retiring Southerners. Throughout September, culminating in mid-October, fighting continued in the Shenandoah Valley and, ultimately, the Confederates were compelled to suspend operations in the area. Following in the wake of the closure of Mobile Bay and the fall of Atlanta, Sheridan's victory in the Shenandoah Valley further depressed Southern morale, elevated Northern morale, and significantly helped secure Mr. Lincoln's reelection. On September 22, 1864, the Radical favorite, John C. Fremont, withdrew from the Presidential race. As Allen Nevins noted,

> Fremont, a lifelong Abolitionist at heart, had withdrawn primarily because he thought that McClellan's candidacy on a platform which offered longer life to slavery must at all cost be defeated. "The Chicago platform is simply separation," he wrote. "General McClellan's letter of acceptance is re-establishment with slavery." Both were intolerable. "The Republican candidate, on the contrary, is pledged to the re-establishment of the Union without slavery . . ." Fremont would do what he could to prevent a Democratic victory, and he realized that Republican unity was a paramount necessity.[7]

Notwithstanding Fremont's withdrawal, however, while Mr. Lincoln obtained an overwhelming 212 electoral votes, compared to General McClellan's 21, only 400,000 popular votes separated the two candidates. Hence, even a relatively small shift in the voting patterns in the larger states could have altered the results of the election. Clearly, Mr. Lincoln owed his reelection to Admiral Farragut, General Sherman, General Sherdian, and the architect of the overall operational plan for the 1864 campaign, General Grant. Conversely, "for many Southerners, Lincoln's reelection dashed their hopes of victory, and they became increasingly willing to abandon the struggle." From another perspective, as General Grant commented to the President, " 'The election having passed off quietly, no bloodshed or riot throughout the land, is a victory worth more to the country than a battle won.' "[8]

Meanwhile, following the loss of Atlanta, the Confederates moved west and north of the fallen city and threatened Sherman's rail line of communications. In assuming their position parallel to Sherman's supply line, the Confederates possessed good communications with the interior of Alabama which remained in Southern hands. In response to the Confederate flank position, Sherman was forced to lead a portion of his force north to protect his line of supply. Wisely eluding Sherman, however, the Confederates fell back, but continued to threaten the Union rail line linking Atlanta with the north. Even before the Confederates began to threaten his line of communications, General Sherman recognized the vulnerability of his advanced position in Atlanta, noting, " 'I've got my wedge pretty deep, and must look out that I don't get my fingers pinched.' " Immediately after the fall of Atlanta, General Sherman had looked forward to beginning the second phase of the campaign, when he would cut loose from his fragile rail lines of communications back to Tennessee and raid across the South. Originally, Generals Sherman and Grant had discussed moving the Union forces along a number of alternative routes: to Mobile, to the mouth of the Apalachicola River, or to Savannah. Upon reaching any of these locations, his forces could be resupplied by the Federal navy. From Washington, the Chief of Staff, General Halleck, argued in favor of a movement toward Montgomery and then down the Alabama River to Mobile, on the Gulf of Mexico. He asserted that such a movement would "prevent Confederate raids into Mississippi, Tennessee and Kentucky, while depriving the Southerners of the grain, iron and coal of Northern Georgia, Alabama, and Mississippi." General Halleck further maintained that a raid across Alabama would destroy the logistical base of the remaining Confederate forces in the Deep South and, thereby, limit their power to conduct raids on the Union positions. Eventually, however, with the General-in-Chief's approval, General Sherman decided to make Savannah the terminus for the raid. He argued that " 'the possession of the Savannah River is more fatal to the possibility of Southern independence,' " since the Confederacy " 'may stand the fall of Richmond, but not all of Georgia.' " He reasoned that Georgia was now serving as "the granary of the South, since its severance from the western states," and, hence, it was imperative that the Confederacy continue to have access to these agricultural resources. Finally, as Lloyd Lewis noted, by marching to Savannah, Sherman's army would be in position to move "up the coast to help the Army of the Potomac finish Lee at Richmond." Indeed, by early November, he indicated to one of his subordinates that he hoped to move through the Carolinas to Goldsboro from which he would be in position to threaten Lee's army. For the moment, however, Sherman's army was to destroy the rail lines of communications and all war-making resources in the area through which his army would pass. In addition, General Grant told his principal western lieutenant, " 'As far as arms can be supplied, put arms in the hands of negro men. Give them such organization as you can.' " But, while the General-in-Chief's strategy of destroying the South's infrastructure and war-making resources had "political implications" in the sense that "its ultimate objective" was to indirectly "cause a political change" by "removing the military props from the Confederate policy of independence" and, thus, induce the Southerners to abandon their struggle, General Sherman added a dimension to his proposed raid through Georgia which he hoped would directly impact upon the will of the Southerners to continue the war.[9]

During the first three years of the war, General Sherman gradually developed a coherent approach to the origins and implications of the Southern rebellion, as well as the most appropriate methods by which the secessionist movement should be suppressed. The rock upon which Sherman's convictions were based was his powerful aversion to political anarchy. As B.H. Liddell Hart wrote, "his hatred of anarchy was not inspired by an abstract motive but by the essentially practical one that only in a state of order are prosperity and progress possible." Hence, in

Sherman's eyes, "order was merely the means to the end—progress.'' Order, in turn, was attainable only through adherence to the law. Sherman recognized that moral law, while perhaps, theoretically the best guide, was open to individual interpretation and, thus, was impractical as a societal standard. Sherman emphasized that there must be one law for all, a law enacted and enforced by a strong national government.[10] Hence, this "ardent nationalist" repeatedly stressed that, in the United States, the supreme law was embodied in the Constitution and "all must obey" that law, " 'without stopping to enquire why.' " Turning from the abstract to the specific Sherman recalled that, prior to 1861, the Southerners,

> ... had a government so mild and paternal that they gradually forgot they had any at all, save what they themselves controlled; they asserted an absolute right to seize public moneys, forts, arms, and even to shut up the natural avenues of travel and commerce. They chose war—they ignored and denied all the obligations of the solemn contract of government and appeal to force . . . .[11]

Thus, from General Sherman's perspective, "the South had without cause flounted a legal authority" and in breaking the laws of the United States and, indeed, by attempting to destroy the Union, the secessionists had brought political anarchy to the United States. Consequently, General Sherman believed that the war was "for the maintenance of authority" and not "a crusade to free the slaves or alter significantly the pattern of race relations." At the outset of the war, Sherman argued that " 'the question of national integrity and slavery should be kept distinct, for otherwise it will gradually become a war of extermination—a war without end.' "[12] Hence, for him the great lesson that this " 'war against anarchy' " must teach all Americans, but especially the Southerners, was that " 'obedience to law, absolute—yea, even abject,' " was the duty of all citizens. But the General stressed that the lesson must be complete. Along these lines, he "pointed out the dangers of reviving the obstructive power of any section or area until the whole was subdued." He wrote, " 'I would deem it very unwise at this time, or for years to come, to revive the State governments of Louisiana, etc., or to institute in this quarter any civil government in which the local people have much say.' " He went on to note that the interests of the nation " 'demand the continuance of the simple military rule after all the organized armies of the South are dispersed, conquered and subjugated.' " Indeed, General Sherman stated bluntly,

> I would not coax or even meet them half way but make them so sick of war that generations would pass before they would again appeal to it .... The people of this country have forfeited all right to a voice in the councils of the nation. They know it and feel it and in after-years they will be better citizens from the dear-bought experience ....Let them learn now, and learn it well, that good citizens must obey as well as command.[13]

Sherman felt that any compromise with the Southerners "would only lead to a renewal" of problems later. He maintained that policies which appeared to " 'court peace' " would only be interpreted by the Southerners as indications of Northern " 'weakness.' " Instead, Sherman's formula for victory was to, " '. . . make this war as severe as possible, and show no symptoms of tiring till the South begs for mercy; indeed, I know, and you know, that the end would be reached quicker by such a course than by any seeming yielding on our part.' " In short, General Sherman maintained that the outcome of the war "rested in the wills of the Southern people and not in the bodies of their troops," since the latter flowed from the former. Hence, the General "deliberately aimed at the non-combatant foundation of the hostile war spirit instead of at its combatant roof." He believed that, ultimately, any successful Union strategy would have to convince the Southerners that their dreams of independence were hopeless. This, as T. Harry Williams concluded, was "warfare conducted for a psychological end, war against the enemy state sheltered behind its armies."[14]

General Sherman felt that a nation's willingness to make war "rests on the economic and psychological security of its people and that if these supporting elements are destroyed all resistance may collapse." As B.H. Liddell Hart wrote, Sherman

> . . . perceived that the resisting power of a modern democracy depends more on the strength of the popular will than on the strength of its armies, and that this will in turn depends largely upon economic and social security. To interrupt the ordinary life of the people and quench

> hope of its resumption is more effective than any military result short of the complete destruction of the armies. The last is an ideal rarely attained in the past, and increasingly difficult since the appearance of nations in arms.[15]

Indeed, as Professors Beringer, Hattaway, Jones, and Still noted, given the total nature of Union war objectives and the impracticality of garrisoning a hostile South in perpetuity, "regardless of whether the Union destroyed the enemy's armed forces and occupied its territory, it could not win 'so long as the enemy's will has not been broken.' " Based upon these assumptions, General Sherman intended to use his raid from Atlanta to Savannah to break the Southern popular morale—their will to continue to resist—by letting the people of the South, " 'old and young, rich and poor, feel the hard hand of war' " and, thereby, " 'see what war meant.' " He observed that his objective was " 'to whip the rebels, to humble their pride, to follow them to their inmost recesses, and make them fear and dread us.' " By demonstrating " 'the vulnerability of the South' " and making " 'its inhabitants feel that war and individual ruin were synonymous terms,' " Sherman hoped to demonstrate to the Southern people, as well as to all observers, that neither the Confederate government nor its armies could defend the territory of the South or protect its citizens against the power of the Federal government. At the outset of his raid across Georgia, Sherman told Grant,

> I propose to act in such a manner against the material resources of the South as utterly to negative Davis' boasted threat .... If we can march a well-appointed army right through his territory, it is a demonstration to the world, foreign and domestic, that we have a power which Davis cannot resist. This may not be war but rather statesmanship, nevertheless it is overwhelming to my mind that there are thousands of people abroad and in the South who reason thus: If the North can march an army right through the South, it is proof positive that the North can prevail .... Now Mr. Lincoln's election, which is assured, coupled with the conclusion thus reached, makes a complete, logical whole. Even without a battle, the result operating upon the minds of sensible men would produce fruits more compensating for the expense, trouble and risk.[16]

Hence, Sherman, an officer who began the war by refusing to allow his troops to do any foraging, now bluntly stated that, " 'you cannot qualify war in harsher terms than I will. War is cruelty and you cannot refine it . . . . You might as well appeal against the thunder-storm as against these terrible hardships of war.' " He noted that, " 'If the people raise a howl against my barbarity and cruelty, I will answer that war is war and not popularity-seeking.' " He maintained that, since " 'war is cruelty,' " it is " 'no use trying to reform it, the crueler it is, the sooner it will be over.' " But, while stressing that " 'war is at best barbarism,' " Sherman's strategy was not without limits. He noted, " '. . . to involve all—children, women, old and helpless— is more than can be justified. Our men will become absolutely lawless unless they can be checked . . . . I always feel that the stores necessary for a family should be spared and I think it injures our men to allow them to plunder indiscriminately.' " In short, General Sherman believed that, once the Southerners recognized that Federal authority was too powerful to resist and that war was too terrible to be a viable solution to political problems, they would cease to support the secessionist movement and that, combined with the disruption of the Confederacy's logistical and war-making resources inherent in Grant's strategy, would lead to the termination of organized resistance. In a sense, General Sherman's strategy was the negative incentive complementing the positive incentive provided by Mr. Lincoln's policy of liberal reconstruction for those Southern states no longer in rebellion. Sherman planned to bring the horrors of war home to the Southern people.[17]

While perhaps unique in the degree to which he developed his ideas regarding war into a coherent philosophic approach, General Sherman was not alone in experiencing a hardening of his attitudes toward the South during the long conflict. For example, General Sheridan reported with great satisfaction that, because of his campaign in the Shenandoah Valley, " 'the people here are getting sick of war.' " Similarly even General Halleck, who, it should be remembered, began the war with strict, orthodox views concerning its conduct, experienced a hardening of attitude. His transformation began during the summer of 1862 when he urged Generals Pope, Buell, and later Banks to live off the country with " 'payment or nonpayment . . . determined on hereafter.' " By April, 1863, he told General Rosecrans to "make the

Confederates feel the hard hand of war," to "live off the land and take food and supplies from the 'openly hostile' without benefit of compensation." Halleck further noted that this policy should be applied "to those who took no partisan interest in the conflict; if a citizen were not pro-Union he must be against it." By 1864, General Halleck's transformation was virtually complete. Consequently, commenting on Sherman's campaign in Georgia, the Chief of Staff urged General Sherman to exhibit a style of warfare which both he and Sherman had outspokenly deplored at the outset of the war. He observed,

> . . . I am fully of opinion that the nature of your position, the character of the war, the conduct of the enemy (and especially of non-combatants and women of the territory which we have heretofore conquered and occupied), will justify you in gathering up all the forage and provisions which your army will require, both for a siege of Atlanta and for your supply in your march farther into the enemy's country. Let the disloyal families of the country, thus stripped, go to their husbands, fathers, and natural protectors, in the rebel ranks; we have tried three years of conciliation and kindness without any reciprocation; on the contrary, those thus treated have acted as spies and guerrillas in our rear and within our lines . . . . We have fed this class of people long enough. Let them go with their husbands and fathers in the rebel ranks; and if they won't go, we must send them to their friends and natural protectors. I would destroy every mill and factory within reach which I did not want for my own use . . . .[18]

General Halleck added, " 'I do not approve of . . . burning private houses. . . . That is barbarous. . . . But I approve of taking or destroying whatever may serve as supplies to us or to the enemy's army.' " Finally, by the end of the year, the Chief of Staff bitterly wrote Sherman, " 'Should you capture Charleston, I hope that by some accident the place may be destroyed, and if a little salt should be sown upon its site, it may prevent the growth of future crops of nullifcation and secession.' " [19]

While, as Bruce Catton wrote, General Grant "had no liking at all for the cruel weight which modern warfare puts on the civilian, on all who are helpless and luckless enough to stand in its path, and he never wasted any words talking about it; . . . he could order the weight applied without the slightest hesitation when it seemed to him to be necessary." In the largest sense, however, like Mr. Lincoln, and in contrast to his principal lieutenant, General Sherman, General Grant felt that the people of the South must ultimately want to return to the Union. Hence, commenting on General Sherman's views concerning the occupied South, Grant noted that his views did " 'not fully coincide with the General as to policy that should be adopted toward these people.' " The General-in-Chief's views coincided with those of the President; he argued for a tenacious national military strategy designed to destroy the Confederacy's capacity to make war, combined with liberal " 'terms held out that by accepting they could receive the protection of our laws.' "[20]

While General Grant felt that it would eventually be desirable for General Sherman's army to sever its line of communications and raid across Georgia to the Atlantic, as noted earlier, the General-in-Chief had originally intended that General Sherman should commence his raid only after destroying the Confederate army in northern Georgia. But, while General Sherman had successfully taken Atlanta, the Southern army had escaped destruction. In view of this, General Grant repeatedly expressed his desire to see the Confederacy's main western army "broken up" before the planned march to Savannah began. Indeed, by the late summer, 1864, having recently experienced the negative political ramifications of the Confederate raid on Washington and the upper Potomac by the Southern forces in the Shenandoah Valley, both General Grant and the President were especially sensitive to the political risks associated with another Confederate raid toward the Ohio River. Likewise sensitive to the possibility that the Confederacy's main western army could move northward into middle Tennessee and Kentucky if he left the Tennessee River line unprotected, General Sherman detached a sizable force under General Thomas and sent it back north of the Tennessee River. Here it was to coordinate with other Union forces already there to keep the previously occupied areas secure. On October 1, 1864, General Sherman told the General-in-Chief that, if the Confederates put themselves in a vulnerable position, he would attack them, but, if they "circled out through Alabama on a swing toward Tennessee, it would be better to let Thomas receive him, 'and for me to destroy Atlanta and march across Georgia to Savannah or Charleston, breaking roads and doing irreparable damage. We cannot remain on the defensive.' "

Sherman told General Thomas that the Southern army " 'may follow me or turn against you. If you can defend the line of the Tennessee . . . it is all I ask.' " Indeed, by early November, General Sherman had finalized his plans to protect against a Confederate raid northward into Tennessee and Kentucky. On November 3, he wrote to General Halleck that indications suggested that the Confederates intended to " 'invade middle Tennessee, for the purpose of making me let go Georgia.' " He went on to note, however, that in view of the sizable force under General Thomas north of the Tennessee River line, " 'I therefore feel no uneasiness as to Tennessee, and have ordered Thomas to assume the offensive in the direction of Selma, Ala . . . .' " If the Confederates attacked General Thomas' force, however, General Sherman had advised his lieutenant to exercise caution, but also, if possible, to destroy the Confederate army. Should that occur, Thomas was directed to vigorously pursue the remnants and, thus, prevent them from concentrating upon Sherman's raiding force. Sherman further advised that the Union forces along the Mississippi River " 'leave the Mississippi to be watched by gunboats and local garrisons, and push with about 15,000 men for the Alabama River and Selma.' " These multiple efforts were designed to divert attention from General Sherman's main raid, while, simultaneously, destroying the remains of the Southern infrastructure and war-making resources in Mississippi and Alabama. As for General Thomas, he felt adequately confident of his strength to reassure General Sherman, " 'I will undertake to clear the rebels out of West Tennessee' " (i.e. Confederate cavalry raiders) and " 'draw off enough' " of the Southern defenders " 'from you to enable you to move anywhere in Georgia.' " Examining Sherman's arrangements, however, the General-in-Chief remained uneasy and still told Sherman, " 'If you can see a chance of destroying (the Confederate) army attend to that first and make your other move secondary.' " Sherman, however, stood firm and, on November 2, 1864, the General-in-Chief finally authorized his Western Commander to " 'go as you propose.' " But, while General Grant finally gave his approval, the President remained concerned about the safety of Sherman's army as it detached itself from its line of communications to

Chattanooga and, living off the countryside, raided across Geor-gia to the Atlantic. The General-in-Chief reassured the President concerning the basic invulnerability of a well-led, even moderately well equipped mid-nineteenth century army, espe-cially when performing a raiding mission. As a raiding army, it would be without ties and, consequently, it could maneuver in any direction in order to avoid destruction. Looking to the con-clusion of General Sherman's raid, at this time, General Grant anticipated that, upon reaching the Atlantic, Sherman's army would take up a position around Augusta, Georgia, draw its sup-plies from the Savannah River, and, from that position, "per-manently dissever the Confederacy ensuring the continued dis-ruption of the transportation network."[21]

In mid-November, 1864, William T. Sherman led his 62,000 man force out of the partly destroyed city of Atlanta on their celebrated march across Georgia to Savannah. As. B.H. Liddell Hart wrote,

> . . . it was with a just assurance of Thomas' security that Sherman turned his face to the east. None the less it was a supreme act of moral courage. To leave the enemy in his rear, to divide his army, to cut himself adrift from railroad and telegraph, from supplies and reinforcements, and launch not a mere raiding force of cavalry but a great army into the heart of a hostile country—pinning his faith and fortune on a principle which he had deduced by reasoning contrary to orthodoxy. And with nothing to fortify his spirit beyond that reasoning, for his venture was to be made under the cloud of the dubious permission of his military superior, the anxious fears of his President, and the positive objections of his advisers. If it requires great moral courage under such gloomy conditions to launch an army to an attack from a secure base, how much greater the effort and strength of will required to launch an army "into the blue"—knowing that the nearest point, Savannah, where he could hope to renew touch with his own side, was three hundred miles dis-tant.[22]

The timing of Sherman's departure was significant since it oc-curred in the immediate wake of Mr. Lincoln's reelection. As Lloyd Lewis wrote, "the news of Lincoln's triumph would dismay the South, and at that precise moment Sherman would add to their consternation by bursting upon Georgia with devastation." In plotting his line of march, Sherman attempted to confuse the enemy by moving between Augusta and Macon, Georgia. Regarding the conduct of his army, however,

> Before "going into the very bowels of the Confederacy," where he proposed "to leave a trail that (would) be recognized fifty years hence," Sherman issued detailed regulations. Soldiers, he ordered, would "forage liberally on the country during the march," but "must not enter the dwellings of the inhabitants, or commit any trespass, but during a halt or a camp they may be permitted to gather turnips, potatoes, and other vegetables, and to drive in stock in sight of their camps." To corps commanders alone he "intrusted the power to destroy mills, houses, cotton-gins, etc." In so doing, he ordered them to follow this principle: "In districts and neighborhoods where the army is unmolested no destruction of such property should be permitted; but should guerrillas or bushwhackers molest our march, or should the inhabitants burn bridges, obstruct roads, or otherwise manifest local hostility, then, army commanders should order and enforce a devastation more or less relentless according to the measure of such hostility." The rule differed for the needs of the army. In addition to food, the soldiers could take "horses, mules, wagons, etc." for the needs of cavalry, artillery, quartermasters and commissaries, but "leave each family a reasonable portion for their maintenance." The army also planned to gather able-bodied Negroes along the way. Such careful rules reflected the laws of war, but Sherman probably did not expect his men to adhere strictly to them once the march began.[23]

As he predicted, General Sherman did " 'make Georgia howl.' " Destruction of the primary target, Georgia's rail network, was " 'performed better than usual.' " Discussing the implications of the raid for the Confederacy's communications network, Professors Hattaway and Jones commented,

> Sherman's march produced a devastating effect on Southern logistics. Confederate supply already had received a serious blow just before the 1864 campaign began. The Chickamauga-Chattanooga campaign had "lost one of the main railroad supply lines from Georgia to Virginia" and gave up "much of the niter and nearly all of the copper production" of the Confederacy. For the 1864 campaign the Confederate armies possessed a sufficient supply of adequate shoes and clothing, though barely so. The total amount of food and fodder was also adequate but "the cotton states had surpluses while Virginia was in short supply." This meant dependence on the railroad for interregional shipments. Despite rapidly deteriorating rolling stock and rails, the railroads in 1864 equalled the task but were "stretched to their utmost capacity; if rail transportation were disrupted, the war effort would grind to a halt." Sherman's raid succeeded in "knocking the Confederate war

effort to pieces.'' By concentrating on the destruction of the railroads
he conducted ''the most lethal onslaught possible.'' Though most
powderworks survived his raid, ''Sherman thoroughly smashed the
Macon-Savannah Railroad and thus permanently severed Lee from his
south Georgia subsistence and from the ordnance production of
Columbus and Macon.''[24]

Finally, on December 10, 1864, Sherman's raiding army reached
the Atlantic coast near Savannah. Three days later, on December
13, Ft. McAllister fell and, soon thereafter, the Confederates
abandoned Savannah. Sherman quickly occupied the city and
telegraphed the President, '' 'I beg to present you as a Christmas
gift, the city of Savannah, with one hundred and fifty heavy guns
and plenty of ammunition, and also about twenty-five thousand
bales of cotton.' '' For the next few weeks, Sherman rested and
reequipped his army before commencing his last campaign of
the war.[25]

Meanwhile, on November 21, the Confederacy's western army,
located in northern Alabama, moved into Tennessee. The objective of the western Confederate command was to "draw Sherman back" from his raid and "defeat the Federals in the
mountains." The commander of the Southern host, however,
intended not merely to raid Tennessee, but rather to reconquer
it and, from there, threaten Kentucky and the cities of the Ohio
River. As such, the Confederates would be required to engage
and defeat the defending Union forces under General Thomas,
as well as establish a secure supply line to sustain a long-term
penetration of middle Tennessee. The Confederate command
reasoned that, if they could move quickly enough, they might be
able to destroy the widely scattered Union forces in detail. Indeed, until the theater commander, General Thomas, concentrated his 55,000 man force around Nashville in early December,
the main Union concentration was the 32,000 man force located
near Columbia, Tennessee. On November 27, the Confederates
made contact with the Federals at Columbia, but rather than
assault the Union position directly, the Southerners wisely attempted to turn the Union forces. Though unsuccessful in cutting the Union army's line of communications and blocking its
retreat, the threatened turning movement forced the Federals to
retire northward to Franklin, Tennessee. On November 30, 1864,

the Confederate pursuers opted against another turning operation and hurled their forces against the entrenched Union defenders at Franklin in "piecemeal, uncoordinated, and fruitless attempts to break through." Moreover, despite considerable Southern casualties, the Confederate command persisted in ordering assaults. Following the battle, the Union army withdrew northward where it joined General Thomas and the remainder of the well supplied Union army entrenched around Nashville. Indeed, the Union position outside the Tennessee capital was quite strong, with the Union flanks protected by gunboats patrolling along the Cumberland River. Meanwhile, General Sherman refused to be drawn back to Tennessee in response to this latest Confederate offensive. Instead, he continued his operation toward Savannah and left General Thomas to deal with the western Confederate field army.[26]

By December 2, the advance units of the Confederate army arrived outside Nashville. Confederate morale, however, showed serious signs of depression, undoubtedly exacerbated by the recent, heavy losses at Franklin, the frosty weather, and the army's inadequate clothing and equipment. Indeed, under the circumstances, General Thomas probably could have merely waited and let the numerically inferior Confederates suffer from the cold weather until they voluntarily retreated south. Such passivity, however, was politically impossible given the position taken by the high command in response to the Confederate invasion of a region which had not been threatened for over two years,

The President expressed his concern about the enemy's position at Nashville before Sherman reached the coast, a movement about which Lincoln had reservations. The outcome of Sherman's campaign was still doubtful. So Grant became vulnerable to criticism, because the effectiveness of his strategy since the fall of Atlanta had yet to be proven. And Grant, no more than Lincoln, wanted "the mortifying spectacle . . . of a rebel army moving for the Ohio River" just as Congress was convening. Even if this embarrassing situation did not develop, the President worried that Hood (the Southern commander) would hold Thomas at Nashville and detach part of the Confederate forces and operate "against other important points." Reports also reached headquarters that a rebel force might invade eastern Kentucky . . . . Grant's primary concern was that Hood would turn the Nashville position, in spite of Thomas' report that "iron-clads and gun-boats are so disposed as to prevent Hood from crossing the river."[27]

In addition, General Grant reasoned that, with the Confederate force so far from its source of supply, the Nashville situation presented " 'one of the finest opportunities' " for destroying one of the Confederacy's principal armies. If successfully destroyed, the Confederacy could " 'never replace it.' " Hence, the General-in-Chief impatiently told General Thomas to attack the Confederates immediately, since they " 'cannot even stand a drawn battle so far from his supplies of ordinance stores. If he retreats and you follow, he must lose his material and much of his army.' " Finally, on December 15–16, after much prodding by an increasingly impatient and exasperated Federal high command, General Thomas successfully attacked and defeated the Confederates at the Battle of Nashville. Indeed, the battle completed the process of destruction of the principal Confederate army in the Deep South which had begun with the battles around Atlanta and had been accelerated with the needlessly heavy casualties at the Battle of Franklin. Hence, at the Battle of Nashville, General Thomas "came close to fighting a battle of annihilation" which many had sought throughout the four years of war in America. Two weeks after its defeat at Nashville, the broken remnants of the shattered Confederate force arrived in northern Mississippi, virtually incapable of further service to the Southern cause.[28]

Assessing the situation at the end of 1864, superficially, the balance of power appeared to have shifted only slightly, but in a deeper sense, the balance had clearly shifted in favor of the Union cause. At sea, while the Federal naval blockade contributed to the erosion of the economic welfare of the South, its impact was selective. The evidence tends to suggest that, while the Federal blockading force gradually increased in size, as long as Southern ports remained under Confederate control, Southern blockade-runners were able to get through. Indeed, "although the number of blockaders on the Wilmington station grew, the number of blockade-runners captured or destroyed remained approximately the same." Interestingly, most blockade-runners "were more concerned with bringing in goods that sold well than in meeting the needs of the war effort." The Confederate authorities in Richmond, however, did not appear to have been overly concerned about this situation, suggesting, in turn, that the South did not remain as dependent upon the import of foreign war material as many had assumed they would be at the outset of the war. As has been recently observed, "the industrial revolution experienced by the Confederate states helps explain this almost blase attitude toward the blockade. To have a chance to win, the Confederacy had to industrialize, and it did . . . . Although the Confederacy did not obtain self-sufficiency, it made extraordinary progress." In short, as Professors Beringer, Hattaway, Jones, and Still noted,

> Clearly, Confederates could get whatever they wanted or needed through the blockade, if they wanted it badly enough. To do so, they had to regulate the trade by law or price, and they eventually adopted both methods. Davis complained of ruinous charges, as he did in other economic contexts; but had Confederates been willing to pay more for cargo space, they would have gotten more, and quickly. That they did not pay more, and that their own figures indicated that the blockade remained relatively ineffective as late as December 1864, argues that they had sufficient domestic supply available to preclude the necessity of draconian measures to increase foreign supply. Private blockade-runners, whether grudgingly or not, did provide vast supplies, augmented by the eleven vessels that the Confederacy owned outright or in three-fourths share.[29]

But, while the Federal naval blockade failed to cripple the Confederacy's material ability to sustain the war effort, it did have an important impact in other areas. For example, it negatively impacted upon Southern coastal maritime traffic. Moreover, although relatively neglected, the ever-present Union option of landing amphibious forces along the Atlantic coast and threatening the Southern port cities, as well as the Confederacy's vulnerable coastal rail lines, forced Richmond to commit increasingly scarce manpower resources to coastal defense, which might have been effectively utilized elsewhere. Beyond its impact upon manpower, however, the Federal naval blockade had a significant impact upon Southern morale. The naval blockade had a direct impact upon both the price and the availability of foreign consumer goods. Moreover, the reorientation of the Southern economy to sustain the war effort, indirectly caused by the blockade, also had an adverse impact upon the daily lives of the Southern people. Perceived hardships, in turn, gradually contributed to undermining the will of the Southerners to continue to make the sacrifices necessary to win their independence.[30]

Similarly, on land, the balance sheet was mixed. In terms of territory controlled, the balance had shifted very little. Indeed,

> . . . in December 1864, with Sherman's army confined to the Savannah area, Union forces had almost completely evacuated Georgia, holding little or no more of the state than they had when Sherman began his campaign in May. The situation differed little in Alabama, though the Union navy had closed Mobile Harbor; and in Mississippi the Union had not acquired much new territory since the fall of Vicksburg, though Union forces had conducted several raids since the fall of the city on July 4, 1863. In the vast Confederate area west of the Mississippi no substantial territorial changes had occurred in 1864, and Price's (Confederate) raid into Missouri had created a serious commotion in that state. So, except for broken railroads and the damage done along the path of Sherman's raid and the smaller diversionary spring and summer raids in northern Mississippi, the Union did not leave much evidence of Sherman's crucial campaign and its concomitant operations. Except in Virginia, the Confederacy had lost little territory since May, and even there the Union had added only a small portion of the state to the area it dominated.[31]

But, as noted earlier, General Grant's strategy specifically precluded the occupation of additional territory. Instead, Grant's focus had been to destroy the Confederacy's infrastructure and war-making potential. In this respect, Generals Sherman, in Georgia, and Sheridan, in the Shenandoah Valley, had performed a major service. For months prior to General Sherman's celebrated march to the sea, trains in the South had become "slower, sound locomotives fewer, good mechanics rarer, and breakdowns and wrecks more numerous." Indeed, by the summer of 1864, the Confederate rail system "had deteriorated so badly that, while Lee's army and the citizens of Richmond had been short of food, Georgia's granaries, as the other end of an open freight-line, had been overflowing." As Allen Nevins concluded, "the railroads of the South were cursed by too many gauges; too little fresh equipment; lack of repair facilities; excessive corporation selfishness and other weaknesses—all compounded by the want of any thoughtful, coherent system for their utilization." General Sherman's march through Georgia eliminated what remained of Georgia's infrastructure, but even then, the Confederacy's final loss of rail links to Georgia and the Deep South "did not have an immediate effect on Confederate logistics." The "ramshackle Confederate logistic organization, displaying an amazing resilience, continued to make adequate provisions for the armies." Thus, notwithstanding the deteriorating logistical situation, "the Confederacy provided its armies with food and clothing, albeit often in barely adequate and sometimes inadequate quantities, and with a sufficiency of weapons and ammunition." In short, for the moment, "the main Confederate armies continued to receive needed supplies," although, given the damage to the South's communications network, there were serious questions concerning Richmond's ability to sustain the Confederate armies for another year of hostilities. Finally, General Thomas' victory at Nashville contributed significantly to the Union war effort by effectively destroying one of the main Confederate field armies. But General Lee's celebrated army, though seriously weakened, remained a formidable force. In short, the Confederacy's military position at the end of 1864 was certainly not totally hopeless. Certain military options remained open if the South wished to avail itself to them.[32]

But, just as the naval blockade indirectly undermined Southern will to continue the war by creating economic hardships at home, General Sherman's capture of Atlanta and march across Georgia, General Sheridan's devastating operations in the Shenandoah Valley, General Thomas' decisive battlefield victory in Tennessee, all reinforced by President Lincoln's reelection, combined to psychologically depress the morale of the Southern people even further, crippling their "will to win." Indeed, from as early as mid-1863, "internal will became an ever important indicator of declining Confederate strength." As Professors Beringer, Hattaway, Jones, and Still have observed,

> . . . the production of too much cotton and not enough food crops, like the decline in railway service and the constraints of the blockade, severely affected the home front, already heavily taxed through inflation and diminished in manpower because of the needs of the army and of war production. These costs and hardships, like the casualties in battle and the gloom occasioned by defeats, depressed civilian morale. Many of the deficiencies of Confederate supply affected civilians more than the armies and aggravated hardships inseparable from such a bloody

and costly war . . . . The defeats, shortages, reduced standard of living, and change of war goals, as well as the war's length, obviously placed a severe strain on the Confederates' dedication to their cause. The high degree of dependence of Confederate morale on military events meant that setbacks on the battle front usually had a significance far beyond the military importance of the loss of a battle or a fragment of territory. A succession of defeats and territorial losses, though not representing militarily consequential conquests of the South's vast land area, worked steadily to depress morale and confidence in victory . . . . the depression of the people and their desires for peace deepened after the fall of Atlanta and the start of the siege of Petersburg, and by 1865 morale was beyond recovery. The armies had not yet surrendered, but the people were beaten.[33]

These attitudes, in turn, were transmitted to the troops serving in the Confederate armies via the Confederate postal service and Southern newspapers. In this context, B.H. Liddell Hart wrote,

It was not merely that Sherman's unchecked progress through the heart of the Confederacy had been a visual proof to the people of their helplessness and a physical blow at the stomachs of people and army alike. But by making the non-combatants suffer it had sent a wave of pacifism and despair through the land, and the echoes unnerved the combatants. Man has two supreme loyalties—to country and to family. And with most men the second, being more personal is the stronger. So long as their families are safe they will defend their country, believing that by their sacrifice they are safeguarding their families also. But even the bonds of patriotism, discipline, and comradeship are loosened when the family is itself threatened. The soldier feels instinctively that if he was at home he could at least fight for the immediate protection of his family, work to gain food for it, and at the worst die with it. But when the enemy is closer than he is, the danger and his fears are magnified by his remoteness. Every letter, every rumor is a strain on his nerves and on his sense of duty. It is the supreme deadliness of the rear attack as conceived and executed by Sherman—against the rear of a people, not merely of an army—that it sets the two loyalties in opposition and so imposes a breaking strain on the will of the soldier.[34]

This concern, combined with inadequate rations, clothing, and other supplies, irregular pay, depression within the ranks concerning the loss of comrades in battle and due to disease, and overarching doubts concerning the South's ability to achieve its independence by force of arms, led a very large number of Confederate soldiers to question the wisdom of continuing the fight for what increasingly appeared to be a lost cause. Consequently, beginning in the late summer of 1864 and accelerating throughout the autumn and winter of 1864–1865, the Confederate soldiers began to desert en masse, reducing the Southern armies east of the Mississippi by about forty percent by spring. The end was near for the Confederacy.[35]

CHAPTER VIII

Winter 1865—Spring 1865

Planning the direction of the spring, 1865 campaigns, the General-in-Chief, Ulysses S. Grant, felt that the main focus of the Union effort to crush the Southern rebellion should continue to revolve around the operations of General Sherman's army. Abandoning his original intention to position Sherman's force around Augusta, Georgia, so that it would be able to permanently logistically sever the Atlantic coast portion of the Confederacy from the Deep South, General Grant briefly considered the possibility of bringing Sherman's forces by water to Virginia so that they could be united with the Army of the Potomac and together they could destroy General Lee's army. The General-in-Chief, however, rejected the maritime transit alternative as too difficult, as well as due to anticipated problems associated with supplying both General Sherman's army and the Army of the Potomac in the Richmond area simultaneously. Hence, in accord with General Sherman's original desires and with General Halleck's encouragement, the General-in-Chief finally directed Sherman to launch another overland raid upon the Confederate infrastructure and war-making resources, this time through the Carolinas, before joining the Army of the Potomac in Virginia, where the latter continued to watch Lee's army. Then, after concentrating his armies, General Grant intended to use these forces to destroy General Lee's Confederates.[1]

Plotting the course of his raid, as with the march from Atlanta to the sea, Sherman hoped to confuse the Confederates by leaving doubt as to whether his initial target would be Augusta, Georgia or Charleston, South Carolina. The General finally opted to march upon neither of these two cities, but rather to move between them to Columbia, South Carolina, destroy the railroad, and then move into North Carolina, making contact with the Federal navy via Wilmington, North Carolina, prior to moving upon Weldon or Raleigh. Sherman wrote the General-in-Chief, " 'I feel confident that I can break up the whole railroad system of South Carolina and North Carolina, and be on the Roanoke, either at Raleigh or Weldon by the time spring fairly opens.' "[2]

Examining the implications of his raid through the Carolinas for the Confederate forces operating against the Army of the Potomac in Virginia, Sherman observed that General Lee would be forced to " 'come out of Richmond or acknowledge himself beaten.' " General Sherman anticipated that General Lee would probably attempt to exploit his interior position between Sherman's own army and the Army of the Potomac and swiftly turn on Sherman's force. In such case, General Sherman expected to " 'force him to attack me at a disadvantage, always under the supposition that Grant would be on his heels; and if the worst came to the worst I could fight my way' " to the Atlantic. Thus, General Grant and his principal lieutenant, General Sherman, adhered to the indirect approach to the defeat of the Confederacy. After the march through the Carolinas had begun, Sherman summarized the overall implications of his campaign by noting,

> The utter demolition of the railroad system of South Carolina and the utter destruction of the enemy's arsenals at Columbia, Cheraw, and Fayetteville are the principles of the movement. These points were regarded as unaccessible to us, and now no place in the Confederacy is safe against the Army of the West. Let Lee hold on to Richmond and we will destroy his country, and then what use is Richmond?[3]

Similarly, in another context, he observed, " 'Richmond is not more vital to his cause than Columbia and the heart of South Carolina.' " Thus, the march through the Carolinas was designed to cut Lee off from his sources of supply in the Deep South, a point which Sherman emphasized when he observed that his campaigns were " 'as much an attack on Lee's army as though I was operating within the sound of his artillery.' " Finally, Sherman intended that his raid through the Carolinas would again underscore the political dimension of the strategic approach which he repeatedly stressed. As with his march from Atlanta to Savannah, Sherman intended to further undermine Southern morale by bringing the war home to the people of the Carolinas.

In the larger sense, however, the General wanted to again demonstrate to all Americans, Northern and Southern, as well as to the Europeans that no place in the Confederacy was beyond the reach of the Union army. He sought to graphically show everyone that the power of the Federal government and its military arm was overwhelming and that the Union cause would inevitably prevail.[4]

Meanwhile, during the autumn of 1864, General Grant had revived a modified version of the North Carolina project which he had proposed to the Federal high command immediately prior to his appointment to the position of General-in-Chief, but which had been abandoned due to opposition from Mr. Lincoln and General Halleck. Grant now planned to use a coordinated army-navy force to close the port of Wilmington, North Carolina, the Confederacy's last major window to the sea and, since 1863, the South's most significant base for blockade-running operations. By mid-December, after a slow start, a combined force arrived off Cape Fear, but the initial attack upon Fort Fisher guarding the gateway to Wilmington failed. A new expedition was quickly organized and, on January 13, 1865, the Union forces launched a second attack upon the fort. Two days later, the fort fell to the Union forces. Meanwhile, between mid January and the outset of February, Sherman moved his army north from Savannah on his raid into the Carolinas. In order to help provide support, with General Sherman's encouragement, General Grant transferred 20,000 men from Tennessee to reinforce the Union force outside Wilmington. Grant intended that this force should seize the city, " 'give General Sherman material aid, if needed on his march north,' " as well as " 'open a base of supplies for him on his line of march' " and open rail communications with Goldsboro, North Carolina. By opening a line of communication for Sherman's raiding army, his movement would be transformed into a full penetration. Meanwhile, on February 17, General Sherman's army reached Columbia, South Carolina, already ablaze with a fire of unknown origins and fanned by high winds. As a result of this fire, about two-thirds of the city was destroyed. Sherman's army remained for two days in the ruins of the South Carolina capital waiting for the high winds to calm prior to destroying the Treasury office and the arsenal. Shortly after Columbia fell to Sherman's army, Wilmington fell to the Union forces located on the North Carolina coast. By March 11, Sherman reached Fayetteville, North Carolina and, following a last ditch fight with the defending Confederate forces in mid-March, the victorious Sherman proceeded to Goldsboro, North Carolina to resupply. Here, on March 23, Sherman's army united with the Federal forces from the North Carolina coast. Meanwhile, after holding out for two years against concerted Federal efforts to take Charleston, South Carolina from the sea, in response to Sherman's operations inland, the Southerners abandoned the city where the war had begun a little less than four bloody years earlier. By now, however, Charleston had little except symbolic importance to the remains of the Confederacy since its inland rail communications had been destroyed by Sherman's host and the city left isolated from the interior.[5]

General Sherman's march through the Carolinas completely devastated the Confederacy's infrastructure. Moreover, the fall of Wilmington and Charleston finally cut the Confederacy's links with the outside world. Indeed, although General Lee's army in Virginia continued to receive provisions until its surrender in April, 1865, the Confederate supply network could not have sustained the concentrated Southern field armies much longer with its rail network destroyed and its principal ports captured. Thus, while certain factories continued to produce war material, these items piled up in warehouses since they could not be transported to the troops in the field. More important, Southern morale continued to plummet and desertion from the Confederate army increased. The Southern armies were rapidly disintegrating and ceasing to be viable fighting instruments.[6]

As the main Union effort was being orchestrated in the Carolinas, General-in-Chief Grant ordered a series of movements in Alabama designed to destroy the remains of the Confederacy's infrastructure and war-making resources in the Deep South. Grant ordered reinforcements be sent to the Union army outside Mobile so that it could finally take the city and move up the Alabama River as had been originally intended. The General stressed, " 'It is important to prevent as far as possible, the planting of a crop this year and to destroy their railroads, machineshops, etc. It is also important to get all the negro men we can before the enemy put them in the ranks.' " In addition to the main expedition up the Alabama River from Mobile, the Federals planned a series of supporting cavalry raids from the Mississippi toward Selma, Alabama. Finally, General Grant directed General Thomas to send a large cavalry raiding expedition southward from the Tennessee toward Selma. These cavalry raids, especially the latter, were designed to support the Alabama River expedition by striking at the enemy rear, while, simultaneously, destroying as much of the remaining Southern rail network, warmaking industry, and resources as possible. Since Mobile did not fall until the final days of the war, the work which was supposed to have been performed by the Alabama River expedition was accomplished by the cavalry force which was despatched southward from the Tennessee. Commencing the raid on March 18, the Union horsemen moved to Selma and thence to Georgia. In the process they destroyed "almost all of the South's remaining industrial capacity: ironworks, foundries, machine shops, rolling mills, collieries, factories, niter works, arsenals, a navy yard, a powder magazine, steamboats, locomotives and railroad cars, and untold quantities of quartermaster, commissary, and ordnance stores."[7]

Meanwhile, as the winter and spring, 1865 campaigns progressed, the President attempted to provide guidance concerning both the terms and conditions under which hostilities might be terminated. In his December 6, 1864 message to Congress, Mr. Lincoln observed that " 'no attempt at negotiations with the insurgent leader could result in any good' " as long as the Confederates insisted upon the dissolution of the Union. The President did note, however, that " 'some of them, we know, already desire peace and reunion.' " Expressing hope that this opinion would increase, he commented that " 'they can, at any moment, have peace simply . . . by laying down their arms and submitting to the national authority under the Constitution.' " Remaining questions could then be resolved by the electorate, the legislature, the courts, etc. The President, however, was adamant concerning the slavery issue and expressed his determination to enforce the Congressional acts, as well as the Emancipation Proclamation. As Allen Nevins wrote, "that Lincoln keenly desired to incorporate the Thirteenth Amendment in the Constitution was no secret, but he now made it absolutely clear. The extinction of slavery in the United States had not been in doubt for some time, but it was well to have it once more made a fundamental object." Finally, Mr. Lincoln kept the option of a general pardon and amnesty open, but noted, " 'the time may come—probably will come—when public duty shall demand that it be closed; and that in lieu, more rigorous measures than heretofore shall be adopted."[8]

Having set forth his position, the President remained open to, and even indirectly solicited the opinions of the Confederate leadership in order that he might capitalize upon any available opportunity to terminate the rebellion. In late December, 1864, the President's political ally, the elderly Francis P. Blair, went to Richmond under a pass signed by Mr. Lincoln and met with Confederate President Davis. Mr. Blair and Mr. Davis agreed concerning the utility of peace talks, but disagreed concerning the key issue of the status of the Union. On the President's instructions, Mr. Blair emphasized the indivisibility of the Union and the importance of restoring peace to " 'the people of our common country.' " Mr. Davis, however, expressed his desire to " 'secure peace to the two countries,' " the Confederacy and the United States. As Bruce Catton observed, "in the gap between these two concepts there was all the difference between a war won by the Federal government and a war won by the Confederacy." Notwithstanding the apparent impasse, however, the Southern leadership decided to follow-up on the apparent Presidential overture. Thus, in late January, Confederate Vice President Alexander Stephens, Confederate Assistant Secretary of War and former U.S. Supreme Court Justice John Campbell, and Mr. R.M.T. Hunter, the President pro tempore of the Confederate Senate, entered the Union lines with a letter addressed to General Grant expressing their desire to meet with Mr. Lincoln in Washington concerning the possible termination of the war. Upon receipt of the Southerners request, General Grant requested instructions from his civilian superiors in Washington.

In response, the Administration despatched a representative, Major T.T. Eckert, to ascertain the intentions of the Southerners. If they were prepared to accept the abolition of slavery within the context of a restored Union, they were to be escorted to Fort Monroe where they would meet with the Secretary of State. Conversely, if they were unwilling to accept these conditions for negotiation, then the preliminary talks were to be completely broken off. Meanwhile, the President directed General Grant to " 'let nothing which is transpiring change, hinder or delay your military movements or plans.' " Major Eckert interviewed the Southern delegation and ascertained that they were constrained by Mr. Davis' stipulation that negotiations were designed to secure peace between " 'two countries,' " not within one. In order to prevent the collapse of the negotiations before they had really begun, General Grant injected his presence. On February 1, he telegraphed the Secretary of War and stated, unofficially and confidentially, that, based upon his conversation with Mr. Stephens and Mr. Hunter, " 'their intentions are good and their desire sincere to restore peace and union.' " He further observed,

> I fear now their going back without any expression from any one in authority will have a bad influence. At the same time I recognize the difficulties in the way of receiving these informal commissioners at this time, and do not know what to recommend. I am sorry, however, that Mr. Lincoln cannot have an interview with the two named in this dispatch, if not all three now within our lines.[9]

General Grant's suggestion that there might be some flexibility in the Southern position regarding reunion was reinforced by a new note from the Southerners in which they expressed willingness to discuss peace with President Lincoln or other appropriate officials on terms " 'not inconsistent with the essential principles of self government and popular rights upon which our institutions are founded.' " Based upon these hopeful signs, President Lincoln told General Grant that, " 'I will meet them personally at Fortress Monroe as soon as I can get there.' " The President did meet with the Confederate commissioners, but the two sides failed to reach an agreement.[10] As Bruce Catton observed,

> Davis' emissaries made the mistake of thinking they could negotiate their way to the sort of compromise the Confederate armies could no longer win for them, and they were somewhat stunned to learn that

> Lincoln would not compromise at all. He was ready to be most liberal about the way in which submission might take place, but not about submission itself; flexible about the arrangements for reunion and abolition but totally inflexible about the idea that the union was going to live and slavery was going to die forever. A mere yearning for peace was not enough. Here was the final gateway where the determination to make the war mean something worth its terrible cost met and blended with the determination that had made the war so costly and the victory at last so complete. . . . Peace depended on Southern acceptance of reunion and abolition . . . Obviously, the President wanted no reprisals; it was equally obvious that he was not going to get the Southern acceptance he wanted until military victory was absolute. But if the voluntary end of armed resistance became unconditional, almost any conditions the South wanted could be arranged on other points.[11]

About a month after the Hampton Roads conference, at the end of February, Confederate Lieutenant General Longstreet met under a flag of truce with Union Major General Ord concerning a prisoner exchange, but, during their conversation, the issue of the termination of hostilities arose. It was suggested that a military convention between the commanders of the opposing armies might be a useful device by which peace could be restored. Consequently, the two subordinate generals discussed the possibility of arranging a meeting between their respective army commanders to further discuss the possibility of such an arrangement. As a result of this conversation, on March 3, General Grant received a note from General Lee which stated,

> Lieutenant General Longstreet has informed me that in a recent conversation between himself and Major General Ord as to the possibility of arriving at a satisfactory adjustment to the present unhappy difficulties by means of a military convention, General Ord stated that if I desired to have an interview with you on the subject you would not decline, provided that I had the authority to act. Sincerely desiring to leave nothing untried which may put an end to the calamities of war, I propose to meet you at such convenient time and place as you may designate, with the hope that upon an interchange of views it may be found practicable to submit the subjects of controversy between the belligerents to a convention of the kind mentioned. In such an event I am authorized to do whatever the result of the proposed interview may render necessary or advisable.[12]

As with the earlier overture, General Grant immediately transmitted the text of General Lee's letter to Washington and requested instructions. Grant noted that he had promised to reply by noon the following day—the moment the President was to be inaugurated for this second term at the Federal capital. The high command quickly responded with a message signed by the Secretary of War, but, in fact, written by Mr. Lincoln himself. The message read,

> The President directs me to say to you that he wishes you to have no conference with General Lee unless it be for the capitulation of Gen. Lee's army, or on some minor, and purely military, matter. He instructs me to say that you are not to decide, discuss or confer upon any political question. Such questions the President holds in his own hands; and will submit them to no military conferences or conventions. Meanwhile you are to press to the utmost your military advantages.[13]

Unfortunately, copies of this directive were not sent to the other principal Union army commanders. In any case, General Grant sent word to General Lee that the proposed meeting concerning a military convention would not take place. But, while the President was, as always, determined to control the direction of postwar political issues, he remained equally determined to resist the Radicals who were intensifying their pressure to impose a draconian peace upon the South.[14] On March 4, 1865, Mr. Lincoln concluded his Second Inaugural Address by enunciating one of the most immortal statements of his Presidency:

> With malice toward none; with charity for all; with firmness in the right, as God gives us to see the right, let us strive on to finish the work we are in; to bind up the nation's wounds; to care for him who shall have borne the battle, and for his widow, and his orphan—to do all which may achieve and cherish a just, and lasting peace, among ourselves, and with all nations.[15]

In late March, 1865, General Grant invited the President to visit his headquarters with the Army of the Potomac, still located near Petersburg, Virginia. Mr. Lincoln accepted and, on March 23, the Presidential party left Washington aboard the steamer River Queen, arriving at City Point on the James River the following evening. The President remained with the army until April 8, when he began his final journey to Washington. While at City Point, Mr. Lincoln met twice with Generals Grant and Sherman (the latter having journeyed from North Carolina to confer with the General-in-Chief and the President), as well as with Admiral Porter, jointly. In their informal conversations, the President further clarified his views concerning the termination of the war. The Chief Executive made it clear that he wanted to " 'let'em up easy.' " Recalling the meetings, General Sherman reported, " 'his earnest desire seemed to be to end the war speedily without more bloodshed or devastation and to restore all the men of both sections to their homes.' " Lincoln remained firm, however, in his commitment to ending the war only on the basis of a restored Union and the abolition of slavery. According to General Grant, the President told his lieutenants that, at the Hampton Roads conference, two months earlier, he had and continued to have only two conditions: " 'One being that the Union should be preserved and the other that slavery should be abolished; and if they were ready to concede these two points he was almost ready to sign his name to a blank piece of paper and permit them to fill out the balance of the terms upon which we would live together.' " Similarly, Admiral Porter reported that General Sherman stated that his army was in a position to command any terms from the opposing Confederates and they would have no alternative but to yield. Mr. Lincoln, however, " 'was very much decided about this matter and insisted that the surrender' " of the Confederate forces " 'must be obtained on any terms.' " In another context, Admiral Porter recalled, " '. . . he wanted peace on almost any terms. . . . His heart was tenderness throughout, and as long as the rebels laid down their arms, he did not care how it was done.' " According to General Sherman, in emphasizing his willingness to extend liberal terms in order to end the war as quickly as possible, the President presented some ideas concerning the role of the state governments which, as Allen Nevins noted, "did not seem altogether compatible with the guarded language which Lincoln used elsewhere." General Sherman wrote,

> Mr. Lincoln was full and frank in his conversation, assuring me that in his mind he was all ready for the civil reorganization of affairs at the South as soon as the war was over; and he distinctly authorized me to assure Governor Vance and the people of North Carolina that, as soon as the rebel armies laid down their arms, and resumed their civil pursuits, they would at once be guaranteed all their rights as citizens of a common country; and that to avoid anarchy the State governments then

in existence, with their civil functionaries, would be recognized by him as the government de facto till Congress could provide others.[16]

As Lloyd Lewis remarked, the President had, on at least two earlier occasions, authorized Sherman to "deal with civilian authorities" and, hence, the statements attributed to the President in his conversations at City Point "did not seem strange to Sherman." Moreover, Sherman had become sympathetic to the notion of dealing with the state governments if that was the best way to avoid anarchy and ultimately to restore Federal authority. Finally, General Sherman had always acted generously and mercifully toward the Southerners as soon as they had ceased resistance. Irrespective of the accuracy of Sherman's recollections or the degree to which his own view did or did not coincide with the views of the President regarding this particular issue, as Bruce Catton wrote,

> What Sherman also got, unfortunately, was a fuzzy notion of what he himself as a soldier was supposed to do about it. Grant had been firmly notified, by Stanton and by Lincoln, that he was not to do anything more than impose terms on Lee for the surrender of Lee's army. Sherman saw it differently. He went away with the feeling, not only that he knew how the President's mind was working, but that he himself was authorized to deal with the civilians once Johnston's army (the Confederate forces opposing him in North Carolina) surrendered.[17]

Moreover, General Sherman apparently did not understand the fury of the views of the Radical wing of the Republican Party which was forcefully pressing for a draconian peace which would permanently break the socio-economic position of the ante-bellum Southern aristocracy. This failure to properly grasp his own role with respect to the Confederacy's civilian authorities would contribute to the enormous difficulties in the days ahead as the Confederacy collapsed. Lastly, the President offered guidance concerning the disposition of the individuals who had held key civilian positions in the Confederate government. The President reportedly said, " 'we will leave the door open; let them go! We don't want to be bothered with them in getting the government to running smoothly.' " The President was said to have expressed the same views at a cabinet meeting in Washington on April 14, only a few hours before his assassination.[18] Discussing that cabinet meeting, Allen Nevins wrote,

There was talk of what would happen to the leaders of the Confederacy. All agreed it was best to have as few "judicial proceedings" as possible. Yet could they go completely unpunished? Dennison, the Postmaster General, is quoted as asking the President, "I suppose, Mr. President, you would not be sorry to have them escape out of the country?" Mr. Lincoln replied slowly, "I should not be sorry to have them out of the country, but I should be for following them pretty close, to make sure of their going."[19]

Meanwhile, as the President visited the General-in-Chief and his principal deputies, General Sheridan led a raid from Winchester, in the Shenandoah Valley, to Richmond. On route, General Sheridan's raiders destroyed railway bridges and track, as well as large portions of the James River canal, thus, seriously reducing Richmond's access to supplies from the fertile Shenandoah. Conversely, however, Sheridan did not complete his destruction before turning east and heading for the Army of the Potomac outside Petersburg. By the end of March, Sheridan's force had joined the Army of the Potomac, whereupon, General Grant, concerned that Lee's Southerners might attempt to unite with those Confederate forces opposing General Sherman in North Carolina or withdraw into the mountains and commence guerrilla operations, as well as anxious to cut Lee's communications, directed Sheridan to cut the railroads leading south from the Richmond/Petersburg area. General Grant wrote, " 'I feel extremely desirous of not only cutting the lines of communications' " between Lee's army and those Confederates opposing Sherman, " 'but of having a large and properly commanded cavalry force ready in case the attempt is made' " to concentrate the Southern forces in the eastern theater. In addition, General Grant apparently felt that it was important that the eastern armies alone destroy their antagonist for the previous four years before they were joined by Sherman's westerners, if that were at all possible. General Grant later wrote,

The Western armies had ... conquered all the territory from the Mississippi River to the State of North Carolina, and were now almost ready to knock at the back door of Richmond, asking admittance. I said to him (Lincoln) that if the Western armies should be even upon the field, operating against Richmond and Lee, the credit would be given to them for the capture. ... It might lead to disagreeable bickerings between members of Congress of the East and those of the West in some of their debates. Western members might be throwing it up to the members of the East that in the suppression of the rebellion they were not able to capture an army, or to accomplish much in the way of contributing toward that end, but had to wait until the Western armies had conquered all the territory south and west of them, and then come on to help them capture the only army they had been engaged with.[20]

Sheridan's operation was quite successful and, at the Battle of Five Forks on April 1, 1865, the Union forces severed the rail line extending southwest from Petersburg. This, in turn, threatened both Lee's rear and Richmond's last communications link with the South. Grant quickly followed up on April 2 with a highly successful assault upon Lee's entrenchments in which the Union troops broke through the Southern lines and penetrated to the Appomattox River, thus, cutting General Lee's force in two. As a result of these reversals, the Confederate commander was compelled to abandon both Petersburg and the long defended Confederate capital at Richmond and retreat westward. The Union forces pursued Lee's army, a portion in his immediate wake and another portion remaining in a position between the North Carolina Confederates and Lee's retreating forces. General Grant's goal, however, was not to pursue Lee and harass his rear, but rather to move ahead of the Southerners and block their path of retreat.[21]

On April 4, as the Northern troops pursued the Southerners westward, Mr. Lincoln, accompanied by a guide, Admiral Porter, and ten sailors, entered Richmond, the city which Confederate President Davis had left barely forty-eight hours earlier. The city, occupied by Union troops only hours before, was still partially ablaze with fires set by the retreating Confederates and racked with confusion. Mr. Lincoln stayed in Richmond that day, spent the night aboard ship in the James River, outside the city, and returned to Richmond for a second visit on April 5. While in the city, the President, at his own request, met twice with Mr. John Campbell, one of the Confederate commissioners with whom he had met at Hampton Roads two months earlier. At the initial Lincoln-Campbell meeting in Richmond, Judge Campbell expressed resignation that the South had lost the war and that the President should now " 'consult and counsel with her public men and her citizens as to the restoration of peace, civil order, and the renewal of her relations as a member of the Union. . . .' " Consequently, at their second meeting, the President called for,

> . . . restoration of national authority, and promised no retreat by the executive on the slavery question, and no cessation of hostilities short of an end to the war, plus the disbanding of all hostile forces. He stated that other propositions not inconsistent with the major points would be considered by the North. Lincoln said that confiscated property would be returned to the people of a State which should immediately withdraw its troops and halt its support of the rebels. Of course, that did not refer to slaves.[22]

Following reassurances by Judge Campbell that the Southerners would not oppose these terms, the President allegedly confided that he was considering a plan "to call the Virginia Legislature, 'the very legislature which has been sitting up yonder,' pointing to the Capital, 'to vote the restoration of Virginia to the Union.' " Assessing Judge Campbell's recollections of the President's observation, Allen Nevins asked, "Is this what Lincoln really said? Or did he, in exacting, carefully-chosen words, qualify the role of the Virginia Legislature? Certainly, at any rate, it was a departure in policy to suggest making use of the Virginia Legislature in any form." In any case, on April 6, upon returning to City Point, Mr. Lincoln wrote to General Weitzel, the Union Commander at Richmond, the following,

> It has been intimated to me that the gentlemen who have acted as the Legislature of Virginia, in support of the rebellion, may . . . now desire to assemble at Richmond, and take measures to withdraw the Virginia troops, and other support from resistance to the general government. If they attempt it, give them permission and protection, until, if at all, they attempt some action hostile to the United States, in which case you will notify them and give them reasonable time to leave; and at the end of which time, arrest any who remain. Allow Judge Campbell to see this, but do not make it public. . . .[23]

On the same day Mr. Lincoln wrote to General Weitzel, the President wrote to General Grant concerning the possibility that the individual states might withdraw troops from the rebel army. The President wrote,

> Judge Campbell thought it not impossible that the Rebel legislature of Virginia would do the latter if permitted, and accordingly I addressed

a private letter to General Weitzel, with permission for Judge Campbell to see it, telling him that if they attempt to do this to permit and protect them, unless they attempt something hostile to the United States, in which case to give them notice and time to leave and to arrest any remaining after such time. I do not think it very probable that anything will come of this, but I have thought best to notify you so that if you should see any signs you may understand them. From our recent dispatches it seems that you are pretty effectually withdrawing the Virginia troops from opposition to the government. Nothing I have done, or probably shall do, is to delay, hinder or interfere with you in your work.[24]

Meanwhile, Mr. Campbell took preliminary steps to call the Virginia Legislature together.[25]

As these events were transpiring in the former Confederate capital, General Grant was relentlessly pursuing the remnants of General Lee's once formidable host. The Confederate delay at Amelia Court House on April 4-5, however, proved fatal to the Southern army's position since it permitted General Sheridan's cavalry, with infantry support, to move ahead of Lee and cut his line of retreat. Meanwhile, the remainder of the Union infantry maintained the pressure on the Confederate rear. On April 6, a large portion of the Confederate rear guard was captured at Sayler's Creek. On April 7, estimating that Lee's position was now hopeless, General Grant wrote the gray commander that he felt it was his duty " '. . . to shift from myself the responsibility of any further effusion of blood, by asking of you the surrender . . .' " of the Confederate Army of Northern Virginia. Lee responded that, " 'though not entertaining the opinion you express on the hopelessness of further resistance on the part of the Army of Northern Virginia (General Lee's army), I reciprocate your desire to avoid useless effusion of blood, and therefore, before considering your proposition, ask the terms you will offer, on condition of its surrender. . . .' " On April 8, adhering to the President's directive of March 3 which had instructed the General-in-Chief to confine the subject of any conferences with the Southerners to purely military matters, General Grant wrote to his counterpart that any meeting between the two commanders must be to arrange the surrender of Lee's army. " 'I would say that, peace being my great desire, there is but one condition I would insist upon, namely that the men and officers surrendered shall be disqualified from taking up arms against the Government of the United States until properly exchanged. . . .' " General Lee wrote back that he did not feel that his situation was sufficiently untenable to warrant surrender, but he did seek a " 'restoration of peace.' " On the morning of April 9, 1865, as the Union army nearly surrounded the Southern forces at Appomattox Court House, General Grant notified General Lee that, while it was beyond his authority to negotiate a peace settlement, he also hoped that peace would soon be restored. He added, " 'by the South laying down their arms they will hasten that most desirable event, save thousands of human lives, and hundreds of millions of property not yet destroyed. . . .' " At this point, General Grant could have ordered the final annihilation of the remnants of General Lee's army, but the General-in-Chief hoped that further blood need not be shed and that Lee would surrender and influence the remaining Confederate forces still under arms elsewhere in the South to do likewise. As Bruce Catton wrote, even after a showdown battle which would have successfully destroyed Lee's army, "there would be survivors to take to the hills, rally others to them, and wage a guerrilla warfare that would cost the country more than it could ever pay. Grant wanted a victory that could be turned into a lasting peace . . ." On the morning of April 9, General Lee assessed his position, judged it hopeless, and requested that hostilities be suspended pending his surrender.[26]

Thus, on April 9, 1865, almost four years after the great Civil War began, Generals Lee and Grant met at Appomattox Court House to arrange for the surrender of the once seemingly invincible pride of the South, Lee's Army of Northern Virginia. General Grant's terms were as follows,

> The officers to give their individual paroles not to take up arms against the Government of the United States until properly exchanged; and each company or regimental commander to sign a like parole for the men of their commands. The arms, artillery and public property to be parked and stacked, and turned over to the officers appointed by me to receive them. This will not embrace the side-arms of the officers, nor their private horses or baggage. This done, each officer and man will be allowed to return to his home, not to be disturbed by U.S. authority so long as they observe their paroles and the laws in force where they may reside.[27]

In addition, while not formally entered into the instrument of surrender, General Grant agreed to " 'let all the men who claim to own a horse or mule to take the animals home with them to work their little farms.' " Assessing General Grant's generous terms, clearly the General-in-Chief went beyond the scope of his authority as defined in the President's March 3 directive. Essentially, the General-in-Chief had extended a pardon to all the officers and men of Lee's army, irrespective of rank. Hence, no member of that army from its commander down "could ever be prosecuted for treason," unless, in Grant's words, " 'they violate their paroles.' " General Lee accepted the General-in-Chief's terms and they were upheld by the authorities in Washington.[28]

Meanwhile, on April 11, in the national capital, the President was apparently confronted with the unanimous opposition of his cabinet to his idea of using the Virginia Legislature to help end the war. That opposition, combined with the consequences resulting from the surrender of the Confederate forces under General Lee, apparently led the President to conclude, in the words of the Secretary of the Navy, that " 'he had perhaps made a mistake, and was ready to correct it if he had. . . .' " Consequently, on April 12, in an effort to "end the possibility that the Virginia Legislature would meet," the President wrote to General Weitzel in Richmond, that Judge Campbell,

> . . . assumes, as appears to me, that I have called the insurgent Legislature of Virginia together, as the rightful Legislature of the State, to settle all differences with the United States. I have done no such thing. I spoke of them not as a Legislature, but as "the gentlemen who have acted as the Legislature of Virginia in support of the rebellion." I did this on purpose to exclude the assumption that I was recognizing them as a rightful body. I dealt with them as men who have power de facto to do a specific thing, to wit, 'to withdraw the Virginia troops, and other support from resistance to the General Government,' for which in the paper handed to Judge Campbell I promised a specific equivalent, to wit, a remission to the people of the State, except in certain cases, of the confiscation of their property. I meant this and no more. Inasmuch, however, as Judge Campbell misconstrues this, and is still pressing for an armistice, contrary to the explicit statement in the paper I gave him; and particularly as Gen. Grant has since captured the Virginia troops, so that giving a consideration for their withdrawal is no longer applicable, let my letter to you, and the paper to Judge Campbell both be withdrawn or countermanded, and he be notified of it. Do not allow them

to assemble; but if any have come, allow them safe return to their homes. . . .[29]

Unfortunately, like the President's conversations with Generals Grant and Sherman, and Admiral Porter aboard the River Queen, the Lincoln-Campbell incident remains a matter of controversy.[30]

Finally, on the evening of April 11, the President delivered a carefully prepared speech focusing on the tasks of reconstruction to a large crowd gathered on the lawn of the White House. In the course of the address, Mr. Lincoln acknowledged that he had encountered opposition to his reconstruction formula. While defending his approach, the President further acknowledged that other approaches were conceivable. The President then turned to the specific case of Louisiana where he had been sharply criticized for his support for the new government of the state, established on the basis of the ten percent formula. Summarizing the key elements of the President's remarks, Allen Nevins wrote,

> . . . Lincoln made the significant statements that the new government would be better if the electorate were larger, adding that, "It is also unsatisfactory to some that the elective franchise is not given to the colored man. I would myself prefer that it were now conferred on the very intelligent, and on those who serve our cause as soldiers. . . ." But, he declared, "The question is 'Will it be wiser to take it as it is, and help to improve it; or to reject, and disperse it?'" . . . He emphasized the advances toward Reconstruction of the Union already made, which included "giving the benefit of public schools equally to black and white." Lincoln went on: "Now, if we reject, and spurn them, we do our utmost to disorganize and disperse them. We in effect say to the white men, 'You are worthless, or worse—we will neither help you, nor be helped by you.' To the blacks we say, 'This cup of liberty which these, your old masters, hold to your lips, we will dash from you, and leave you to the chances of gathering the spilled and scattered contents in some vague and undefined when, where, and how.'" If this course, discouraging and paralyzing both white and black, has "any tendency to bring Louisiana into proper practical relations with the Union, I have, so far, been unable to perceive it." By sustaining the new government the Union would encourage the hearts and strengthen the arms of the 12,000 Unionists. The Negro also would be aided. And then, "What has been said of Louisiana will apply generally to other States. And yet, so great peculiarities pertain to each State; and such important and sudden changes occur in the same State; and withal, so new and unprecedented is the whole case,

that no exclusive, and inflexible plan can safely be prescribed as to details and collaterals. . . ." While plans must be flexible, "Important principles may, and must, be inflexible. . . ."[31]

Clearly, the President was attempting to clarify the lines for the forthcoming confrontation concerning reconstruction.[32]

As these developments transpired in Virginia and in Washington, General Sherman planned the final phase of his campaign in North Carolina. Utilizing the deployment pattern which had served so well in the past, prior to Lee's surrender at Appomattox, General Sherman sought to confuse the Confederates as to the focus of his next movement: the Southern forces immediately opposing him in North Carolina under the command of General Joseph Johnston or General Lee's army in Virginia. Discussing Sherman's plan, B.H. Liddell Hart observed,

> In brief, his idea was to feign on Raleigh and actually interpose between Johnston and Lee. His left horn was to aim west towards Raleigh and then, when just short of it, swerve northwards, using the Neuse River as a flank protection. His right horn was first to aim northwards up the Weldon railroad as far as Nahunta, and then swing north-westward. The dilusion of an advance on Weldon would, however, be kept up by Kilpatrick's cavalry. The centre was to take a central path, and the three "armies" were to reunite at Warrenton, just south of the Roanoke, as a preliminary to placing the whole army north of this river. For if Johnston ventured within reach, in an attempt to fulfil his strategic mission of obstruction, Sherman was ready at any moment to cast his columns like a net around him. . . . Meantime the base was to be shifted northwards up the coast so that as soon as Sherman was across the Roanoke he could re-open his communications and draw supplies from new depots at Winton and Murfreesboro on the Chowan River. Then, if Lee had not yet quitted Richmond in an attempt to join Johnston, Sherman would turn west and pounce on Burkesville Junction, where he would have a strangling grip on Lee's remaining arteries of supply.[33]

Lee's surrender on April 9, however, significantly altered the situation confronting Sherman. Now, rather than prevent a concentration of General Lee and General Johnston's forces, Sherman's goal was to prevent General Johnston from taking his army southward. As a result, Sherman paused briefly at Raleigh "in order not to alarm Johnston into a fresh retirement," as Union cavalry under General Stoneman and General Sheridan, the latter sent south by Grant after Lee surrendered, moved upon Johnston's rear. Finally, Sherman prepared his formation for a movement southwestward, via Ashboro, through which the General hoped to assume a position across the line extending southward from Greensboro. To conceal this operation, Sherman's own cavalry was to move down the railroad from Raleigh toward Greensboro. In ordering these movements, General Sherman directed that, " 'No further destruction of railroads, mills, cotton, and produce, will be made without specific orders from an army commander, and the inhabitants will be dealt with kindly, looking to an early reconciliation.' "[34]

On April 14, General Sherman received a message from General Johnston requesting " '. . . a temporary suspension of active operations . . . to permit the civil authorities to enter into the needful arrangements to terminate the existing war.' " Sherman's concern that the Confederates might break up into guerrilla bands, as well as his recollection of his recent meeting with Mr. Lincoln at City Point, Virginia, led the General to grasp at General Johnston's offer. Earlier, immediately following General Lee's surrender at Appomattox, the Federal Chief of Staff, General Halleck, had telegraphed Sherman that, when Johnston's Confederates surrendered, it should be on the same terms which Grant had extended to Lee. In his reply to General Johnston's request, General Sherman wrote that he was authorized to arrange terms " 'between the armies' " and suggested that he was prepared " 'to abide by the same terms and conditions as were made by Generals Grant and Lee.' " Hence, the two commanders agreed to meet at a location between their respective armies on April 17. In addition, on April 14th, Sherman telegraphed Washington that he would adhere to the Appomattox formula and would not " 'complicate any points of civil policy.' " That evening, however, the entire political situation changed both dramatically and decisively. Shortly after 10:00 P.M. on Good Friday, April 14, 1865, the savior of the Union, Abraham Lincoln, was shot. He died the following morning.[35]

General Sherman received word of Mr. Lincoln's death on April 17, the day of his meeting with General Johnston. Concerned about the impact that the news of the President's death would have upon his army, the General resolved not to make this information public until after his conversation with the

Southern commander. When the two army commanders met later in the day, near Durham Station, Sherman informed his counterpart of the assassination, whereupon the Confederate commander expressed his conviction that " 'Mr. Lincoln was the best friend they had' and that the assassination was 'the worst possible calamity to the South.' '' General Sherman ''explained that he could not agree to an armistice which would permit rival governments to confer; all he could do would be to receive Johnston's surrender on the Grant-Lee terms.'' Since Confederate President Davis had only authorized an armistice in order to facilitate the opening of negotiations between the Federal and Confederate civil authorities, Sherman presented Johnston with a stark choice; surrender his army as Lee had done or the fighting would resume. General Johnston said that, while a continuation of hostilities would be unjustifiable and only lead to guerrilla war, a form of warfare which both commanders greatly feared would lead to universal disaster, the Confederate chief pointed out that, unlike Lee at Appomattox, his army was not in a militarily hopeless position. Hence, he did not feel that terms identical to those given by Grant to Lee were appropriate. Instead, General Johnston suggested that he and General Sherman formulate new terms covering the surrender of all remaining Southern armies and provide "the basis of a general peace." As B.H. Liddell Hart wrote,

> Sherman's quick brain perceived the deeper value of the proposal and seized upon the idea that at a stroke—of the pen—he might lift the danger of guerrilla warfare from the land and avoid the cost and trouble of a long military occupation. So also his broad political vision impelled him to secure the fulfilment of Lincoln's policy before the lust for vengeance had time to sweep more petty politicians off their feet. . . . Taking up Johnston's suggestion, Sherman demanded to know if he had power to control the other Confederate forces, and received the reply that, although Davis was not at hand, authority could probably be obtained from Breckenridge, the Confederate Secretary of War.[36]

As the two generals parted at sunset, they had not yet settled upon terms, but had made an intriguing beginning. Having agreed that they would meet the next day, both commanders returned to their respective armies.[37]

After returning to the Union lines, General Sherman ordered

his troops back to their encampments. Then, when the men were in their units, he issued a bulletin stating that President Lincoln had been assassinated, "exonerating the Confederate Army from complicity in the assassination and charging it to the general spirit of rebellion," As Lloyd Lewis wrote, "for hours he and his generals watched the men closely, noting that they wept, or were stunned, or stood gritting their teeth and demanding that the armistice be ended so that there might be one last savage battle." Meanwhile, General Sherman learned that, immediately prior to Lee's surrender, Mr. Lincoln had authorized the so-called Virginia Legislature to meet under the protection of the Union army. Hence, as Lloyd Lewis wrote, Sherman concluded that,

> Lincoln's actions meant that "State authorities are recognized and invited to resume their lawful functions." Such a step fitted perfectly into the picture that Lincoln had given Sherman on the River Queen.... Sherman saw that millions would be saved by allowing the Southern States, after surrender, to maintain their own civil officers and thus free the Federal Government from the expense of military occupation.[38]

This conclusion, of course, complemented Sherman's long held aversion to anarchy and his conviction that once the Southerners lay down their arms and swore allegience to the Union, both he and his army would become their " 'protectors and supporters.' "[39] Meanwhile, within the Southern lines, General Johnston met with the Confederate Secretary of War, John Breckenridge, as well as with General P.G.T. Beauregard and the Confederate Postmaster General, John Reagan, to discuss terms for the upcoming meeting with General Sherman. At the conclusion of the meeting, Mr. Reagan drafted a memorandum for Johnston's use when he met with the Union commander.[40]

When Generals Sherman and Johnston met for the second time on April 18, Breckenridge, in his capacity as a Major General in the Confederate Army and not as an official of the Confederate government, was permitted to join the two army commanders. Describing the course of this important meeting, Allen Nevins summarized,

> In the discussion of April 18, Sherman testifies that the points raised included: the question whether the States were to be dissevered; the question whether their people were to be denied representation in Congress, so that, as some Southern extremists put it, they might become

slaves to the people of the North. Understandably, but unwisely, the impulsive Sherman states that he answered "No; we desire that you shall regain your position as citizens of the United States, free and equal to us in all respects, and with representations, upon the condition of submission to the lawful authority of the United States as defined by the Constitution, the United States courts, and the authorities of the United States supported by those courts. . . . There was universal assent that slavery was dead as anything could be; that it was one of the issues of the war long since determined. . . . As to reconstruction, I told them (the Confederates) I did not know what the views of the administration were. Mr. Lincoln, up to that time, had in letters and by telegrams to me, encouraged me, by all the words that could be used in general terms, to believe in not only his willingness but his desire that I should make terms with civil authorities, governors, and even legislators, even as far back as 1863. . . ." In light of all we now know, this later statement seems extreme. There is no firm evidence that Lincoln wished Sherman to make such terms, and the idea that he did stands in opposition to all known evidence.[41]

Meanwhile, as the conference proceeded, the articulate Breckenridge, having served as Vice President of the United States during President Buchanan's Administration,

> . . . quoted laws of war, laws governing rebellions, and laws of nations . . . "in a manner so resourceful, cogent, persuasive and learned that, at one stage of the proceedings, General Sherman . . . pushed back his chair and exclaimed, 'See here, gentlemen, who is doing this surrendering anyhow? If this thing goes on, you'll have me sending an apology to Jeff Davis.' "[42]

Dismissing Mr. Reagan's memorandum of terms as " 'too general and verbose,' " General Sherman eventually wrote out his own terms. After completing his document, the General "handed the completed paper across the table saying, 'That's the best I can do.' " Sherman's terms were as follows:

> 1. The contending armies now in the field to maintain the status quo until notice is given by the commanding general of any one to its opponent, and reasonable time—say, forty-eight hours,—allowed.
> 2. The Confederate armies now in existence to be disbanded and conducted to their several State capitals, there to deposit their arms and public property in the State Arsenal; and each officer and man to execute and file an agreement to cease from acts of war, and to abide the action of the State and Federal authority. The number of arms and munitions of war to be reported to the Chief of Ordnance at Washington City, subject to the future action of the Congress of the United States, and,

in the mean time, to be used solely to maintain peace and order within the borders of the States respectively.

3. The recognition by the Executive of the United States, of the several State governments, on their officers and Legislatures taking the oaths prescribed by the Constitution of the United States, and, where conflicting State governments have resulted from the war, the legitimacy of all shall be submitted to the Supreme Court of the United States.

4. The reestablishment of all the Federal Courts in the several States with powers as defined by the Constitution of the United States and of the States respectively.

5. The people and inhabitants of all the States to be guaranteed, so far as the Executive can, their political rights and franchises, as well as their rights of person and property, as defined by the Constitution of the United States and of the States respectively.

6. The Executive authority of the Government of the United States not to disturb any of the people by reason of the late war, so long as they live in peace and quiet, abstain from acts of armed hostility, and obey the laws in existence at the place of their residence.

7. In general terms—the war to cease; a general amnesty, so far as the Executive of the United States can command, on condition of the disbandment of the Confederate armies, the distribution of the arms, and the resumption of peaceful pursuits by the officers and men hitherto composing said armies. Not being fully empowered by our respective principals to fulfill these terms, we individually and officially pledge ourselves to promptly obtain the necessary authority, and to carry out the above program.[43]

General Sherman always emphasized that he felt Breckenridge and Johnston had the power to disband all the remaining Confederate armies and that, in drafting his memorandum, he was guided by "Lincoln's message of 1864, his proclamation of amnesty, Grant's terms to Lee, the invitation to the Virginia legislature, and 'a firm belief that I had been fighting to re-establish the Constitution of the United States;' and finally, but not least, upon the universal desire to close a war which was now without means of organized resistance."[44]

Evaluating the terms embodied in General Sherman's memorandum, Allen Nevins wrote,

So many points here given vary from the known policies of Lincoln, and show such political naivete, that the whole document may easily be questioned. First of all, it is labeled both a "memorandum" and a "basis of Agreement." Both principals admitted they were not fully empowered to make such an agreement, and would have to submit it to their governments. The document thus virtually recognized the Confederate government and its President, something Lincoln had never done and no responsible officer could be expected to do now. The military commanders concerned had gone too far. Lincoln always opposed an "armistice," which is what the first provisions really implied. To send the Southern armies home with their arms appeared an open invitation to guerrilla tactics, to which Sherman and Lincoln were implacably opposed. The soldiers would await action of both State and Federal authorities and yet Sherman's plan carried a seeming recognition of the existing Confederate State governments, until their officials took the oath of allegiance. These Confederate State governments might also come into collision with Union governments already set up in several States. Parts of the agreement seemed to concede a recognition of the validity of the Confederate State governments. There could be little quarrel with the idea of re-establishing Federal courts, providing that citizens were in a state of peace. But the guarantee of political, personal and property rights could be interpreted as a re-imposition of the rights of slavery, and sometimes was, although the memorandum did not mention slavery. At this point, Sherman departed more than ever from Lincoln, who had never retreated from his determination that slavery must die. No grant of amnesty was specifically extended, but was given a broad application. Although nothing was said about Confederate debts, the agreement might have been interpreted as allowing their possible recognition as valid. In short, little was here stated that Lincoln or any Federal government could have accepted as it stood without abrogating the Administration's war aims. Although we can never know, from Lincoln's many statements and actions it seems clear that he would have done just as Johnson (Lincon's successor as President) did in rejecting this almost puerile document.[45]

By contrast, Bruce Catton and B.H. Liddell Hart felt that, had he lived, Mr. Lincoln might have accepted the terms arranged by Sherman in North Carolina. In any case, Generals Sherman and Johnston signed the draft and forwarded it to their respective governments. A few days later, Confederate President Davis approved the terms.[46]

Meanwhile, in Washington, the sad transfer of power was underway. Funeral services for Mr. Lincoln were held at the White House on April 19 and, immediately after the service, General-in-Chief Grant received word from General Sherman that he and General Johnston would meet to discuss terms on the 17th. On April 21, General Sherman's messenger arrived and gave General Grant a covering letter from Sherman, as well as the draft memorandum which both he and General Johnston had signed. In the letter, General Sherman stated,

> You will observe that it is an absolute submission of the enemy to the lawful authority of the United States, and disperses his armies absolutely; and the point to which I attach most importance is, that the dispersion and disbandment of these armies is done in such a manner as to prevent their breaking up into guerrilla bands. . . . I agreed to the mode and manner of the surrender of arms set forth, as it gives the States the means of repressing guerrillas, which we could not expect them to do if we stripped them of all arms. Both Generals Johnston and Breckenridge admitted that slavery was dead, and I could not insist on embracing it in such a paper, because it can be made with the States in detail. I know that all the men of substance in the South sincerely want peace, and I do not believe they will resort to war again during this century. . . . The question of finance is now the chief one, and every soldier and officer not needed should be got home to work. . . .[47]

In an accompanying letter to General Halleck, Sherman wrote,

> Had I pushed Johnston's army to an extremity, it would have dispersed, and done infinite mischief . . . if the President sanctions my agreement with Johnston our interest is to cease all destruction . . . influence him, if possible, not to vary the terms at all, for I have considered everything, and believe that, the Confederate armies once dispersed, we can adjust all else fairly and well.[48]

When General-in-Chief Grant read the draft, however, he immediately recognized that, unfortunately, his principal lieutenant had gone beyond his authority and concluded a "general treaty of peace, covering not only the surrender of all the Confederate armies but also the terms on which the separate Southern states would be readmitted to the Union." Within hours, he presented the Sherman-Johnston draft to the new President and the cabinet. Following discussion, the new Administration rejected the draft agreement and the new President, joined by the Secretary of War, suggested that "Sherman's action skirted the edge of treason." While the General-in-Chief heatedly defended his subordinate, he agreed with the members of the Administration that the terms would have to be renegotiated. Following the meeting, Grant prepared a formal letter to Sherman justifying the rejection, but decided to secretly go to North Carolina himself to deliver it and supervise the surrender of Johnston's army.[49] The formal letter stated,

> The basis of agreement entered into between yourself and General J.E. Johnston for the disbandment of the Southern army and the extension

of the authority of the General Government over all the territory be-
longing to it, sent for the approval of the President, is received. I read
it carefully myself before submitting it to the President and Secretary
of War and felt satisfied that it could not possibly be approved. My
reasons for these views I will give you at another time in a more extended
letter. Your agreement touches upon questions of such vital importance
that as soon as read I addressed a note to the Secretary of War notifying
him of their receipt and the importance of immediate action by the
President, and suggested in view of their importance that entire cabinet
be called together that all might give an expression of their opinions
upon the matter. The result was a disapproval by the President of the
basis laid down, a disapproval of the negotiations altogether, except for
the surrender of the army commanded by General Johnston, and directions to me to notify you of this decision. . . . Please notify General
Johnston immediately on receipt of this of the termination of the truce
and resume hostilities against his army at the earliest moment you can,
acting in good faith.[50]

Departing on the evening of the 21st, General Grant reached
Ft. Monroe on April 22, where he remained only long enough
to send the following message to General Halleck, who only two
days earlier had left Washington to take command of the Union
forces in Virginia, with headquarters in Richmond,

The truce entered into by General Sherman will be ended as soon as I
can reach Raleigh. Move Sheridan with his cavalry toward Greensbor-
ough as soon as possible. I think it will be well to send one corps of
infantry with the cavalry. The infantry need not go farther than Danville
unless they receive orders hereafter.[51]

For his part, General Halleck had picked up rumors that Confederate President Davis had fled south with a large amount of
gold. Hence, on April 23, General Halleck told General Sheridan,
" 'Pay no attention to the Sherman-Johnston truce. It has been
disapproved by the President. Try to cut off Jeff. Davis' specie.' "
Meanwhile, on April 24, the General-in-Chief quietly arrived at
Sherman's headquarters. Keeping his presence as secret as possible so as not to embarrass his friend and principal deputy,
Grant delivered his written justification for the rejection of the
Sherman-Johnston draft and summarized the discussion at the
cabinet meeting on the evening of April 21 (omitting the harsh
remarks made by the Secretary of War and the President). Grant
also delivered a letter from the Secretary of War "which said
that in any dealings with Johnston Sherman must be guided by

the order Lincoln had given to Grant during the winter—discuss no peace terms whatever but limit yourself strictly to the surrender of the army that is facing you. Sherman remarked dryly that 'it would have saved a world of trouble' if he could just have seen this earlier." General Sherman had, of course, never seen a copy of President Lincoln's March 3 directive of General Grant ordering the latter to confine his contacts with the Confederates to "purely military matters." Furthermore, Sherman would later write that the Administration had "failed also to give any hint 'of a plan of reconstruction, or any idea calculated to allay the fears of the people of the South, after the destruction of their armies and civil authorities would leave them without any government whatever.' "[52]

Even prior to the arrival of the General-in-Chief, however, General Sherman had suspected that the post Lincoln assassination climate in Washington would probably not permit ratification of his memorandum with General Johnston. On April 23, immediately prior to General Grant's arrival at his headquarters, General Sherman had written to General Johnston,

> ... I fear much the assassination of the President will give such a bias to the popular mind which, in connection with the desire of our politicians, may thwart our purpose of recognizing "the existing local governments." ... I believe this assassination of Mr. Lincoln will do the cause of the South more harm than any event of the war, both at home and abroad, and I doubt if the Confederate military authorities had any more complicity with it than I had.[53]

In addition, Sherman noted that permission for the assembly of the so-called Virginia Legislature had been withdrawn. In any case, as a result of his conversation with General Sherman, General Grant immediately wired Washington explaining Sherman's motivations. The General, often careless in his spelling, wrote,

> I reached here this morning and delivered to Gen. Sherman the reply to his negociations with Johnston. He was not surprised but rather expected this rejection. Word was immediately sent to Johnston terminating the truce and information that civil matters could not be entertained in any convention between army commanders. Gen. Sherman has been guided in his negociations with Johnston entirely by what he thought was prescedents authorized by the President. He had before him the terms given by me to Lee's army and the call of the Rebel legislature of Va., authorized by Weitzel, as he supposed with the sanction

of the President and myself. At the time of the Agreement, Sherman did not know of the withdrawal of authority for the meeting of that legislature. The moment he learned through the papers that authority for the meeting of the Va. legislature had been withdrawn he communicated the fact to Johnston as having bearing on the negociations here.[54]

As noted in the General-in-Chief's communication to the authorities in Washington, Grant directed General Sherman to give the forty-eight hours notice of the renewal of hostilities stipulated in their talks. In addition, Sherman sent Johnston a "formal demand for his surrender on the same purely military terms as Lee." The Confederate commander, even further weakened by the mass desertions from the Southern army during the truce period, wired the Confederate authorities advising acceptance. The Southern leadership, still unwilling to abandon the struggle, advised General Johnston to disperse his army and rally at a predetermined rendezvous location. The General, however, rejected this suggestion and, on April 26, on his own responsibility, surrendered his army to General Sherman on the same terms that General Grant had given to General Lee. Meanwhile, to the north, in Virginia, General Halleck was still excitedly directing his subordinates " 'to obey no orders of General Sherman, but to push forward as rapidly as possible.' " Moreover, he recommended that Union forces in the Deep South " 'take measures to intercept the rebel chiefs and their plunder.' " Halleck was still issuing these directives on April 28 when he received word that Johnston had surrendered on approved terms. Finally, the Secretary of War issued a series of war bulletins to the press which, in Sherman's words, were " 'grouped in such a way as to give the public very erroneous impressions.' " Sherman would forever resent the Secretary of War's behavior in this matter, especially as he learned more about the latter's statements concerning the Sherman-Johnston memorandum. Moreover, notwithstanding their close personal friendship which spanned decades, as a result of General Halleck's actions and directives during the final days of the war, a permanent estrangement developed between Generals Sherman and Halleck. In any case, however, with General Johnston's surrender, the war effectively concluded. Confederate President Davis and his entourage were captured and the remaining Confederate units gradually surrendered.[55] The greatest war in the history of the United States was finally over, but the trauma of reconstruction lay ahead.

CHAPTER IX

Conclusion

Throughout the American Civil War, President Abraham Lincoln attempted to establish and maintain a broad coalition of support toward the Federal war effort. Consequently, in defining the Federal war objectives, in formulating grand strategy, and, within the framework of that grand strategy, delineating the national military strategy, the President had to take into consideration the opinions of a number of articulate members of his own Administration, the Congress, the Union Army, the various state governments, and other influential citizens, including newspapermen, business leaders, and the clergy. Indirectly, the President had to take into consideration the amorphous body of public opinion which stood behind these influential leaders and popular representatives. Regionally, he had to remain sensitive to the pulse of the Northeast, the Great Lakes region, and the Ohio, Missouri, and upper Mississippi Valleys. Moreover, especially at the outset of the war, but perhaps with somewhat reduced emphasis throughout the entire conflict, Mr. Lincoln had to weigh the views of the peoples residing in the border areas of Maryland, western Virginia, eastern Tennessee, Kentucky, and Missouri. Furthermore, during the four years of the conflict, the President attempted to shape his response to the Southern rebellion in such a way as to have a positive impact upon Southern opinion. Finally, Mr. Lincoln had to take into consideration the attitudes of the European powers, particularly the British, in formulating Federal war policy.

Unfortunately for the President, none of these institutional bodies or geographic areas represented a cohesive opinion block toward the Federal war effort. For analytical purposes, at least four opinion groups cross-cut the institutional bodies and geographic regions noted above: the Radical Republicans, the Moderate Republicans, the War Democrats, and the Peace

Democrats. It should be emphasized, however, that, with respect to specific aspects of Federal war policy, these four general opinion groups often reconfigured in support or opposition to a particular course of action. Moreover, further complicating an already very clouded political environment, throughout the terrible four year war, the attitudes of many key leaders, as well as those of the public at large, evolved, often drastically. For example, within the Union Army, as the war lengthened with no end in sight, the attitudes of both the military leadership and the common soldiers evolved regarding the definition of the Federal war objectives, as well as the goals, methods, and conditions governing military operations nationally and within the various theaters of war. Finally, in formulating the Federal response to the Southern rebellion, the President had to weigh not only the attitudes of the various elements cited above, he also had to weigh his own evolving convictions. He would have to do so within an often volatile, emotionally charged political, military, social, and even personal context which, in turn, further complicated the environment in which Presidential leadership decisions were made. Perhaps the greatest asset of the Union cause during these four traumatic years was the tower of strength provided by Abraham Lincoln. More than any other single individual, he was responsible for saving the Union.

From the outset of the war, the national objectives of the United States government were total, although the scope of those objectives escalated. The conflict began as a war for total political objectives—the restoration of the Union and the total extinction of the movement supporting Southern independence. In the autumn of the second year of the war, however, under very heavy pressure from the radical wing of the Republican Party, the Administration reluctantly opted to escalate the definition of the Federal war objectives, transforming the conflict into a war for total socio-economic, as well as total political objectives. From the President's perspective, emancipation of the slaves became essential politically, militarily, internationally, and morally. This escalation in the scope of Washington's national objectives, however, did not alter the total nature of Federal war objectives. Hence, from the outset of the conflict, nothing less than total victory over the forces supporting the cause of Southern political independence was required. Compromise between the antagonists predicated upon the perpetuation of the Southern Confederacy was impossible, since a compromise along these lines would have been tantamount to a Federal defeat.

In framing Federal strategy, President Lincoln consistently recognized that it was imperative that the people of the Northern states retain their commitment to continue to make the inevitable sacrifices necessary to successfully suppress the Southern rebellion. Indeed, the Confederacy's best hope for victory was to wear the North down until it finally would acquiesce to Southern independence. From another perspective, however, Mr. Lincoln recognized that, if the struggle to restore the Union was to be ultimately successful, not only would the Southerners have to cease resistance at all levels, they would have to abandon their ambitions to achieve independence and voluntarily resume their roles as full participatory citizens within the American political system. Finally, President Lincoln, as well as others, including Generals Scott and McClellan, were, from the outset of the conflict, aware that the definition of the national objectives and the goals, methods, and conditions governing theater operations were symbiotically interconnected. They recognized that, not only would the definition of the national objectives influence the delineation of the national military strategy, the reverse was also true. The definition of the national objectives would itself be influenced by the level of wartime suffering, which, in turn, would be determined by the level of violence resulting, in part, from the implementation of the national military strategy. Indeed, the longer the war lasted, the more severe might become the level of violence. A long, harsh war would increase the probability that the definition of the national objectives would escalate. These considerations, in turn, would increase the likelihood of draconian peace terms and mutual post-war bitterness. All of this would make a post-war settlement and voluntary popular submission by the defeated side proportionately difficult. As noted earlier, in the case of the American Civil War, if the Federal government was to be truly victorious, the defeated Southerners would eventually have to willingly resume their rightful places as co-equal citizens in the Republic and be willingly accepted as co-equals by the victorious Northerners. As such, President Lincoln felt that it was imperative to suppress the Southern rebellion as quickly as possible before extremism acquired a momentum of its own which would be difficult or impossible for the President, or anyone, to control. Conversely, especially during the first year and a half of the war, the Radical Republicans wanted the war to last sufficiently long for them to pressure the Administration to escalate the national objectives to include the immediate, compulsory, uncompensated emancipation of the slaves and the destruction of the socio-economic-political power of the Southern agrarian establishment. Similarly, from the outset of the war, some military officers felt that the goals, methods, and conditions governing theater operations inherent in the national military strategy should be made more severe.

Based upon these considerations, the President argued consistently that, in formulating the national military strategy and in planning and conducting theater operations, the Union forces would have to demonstrate activity and forward progress in extinguishing the flames of the Southern rebellion. Only by demonstrating tangible progress toward that goal could the Administration retain Northern popular support for the war effort and demonstrate strength and determination to the European powers. Moreover, initially, immediate forward progress was considered to be imperative in order to strengthen pro-Union forces and undermine the secessionists throughout the Southern states. But even after the secessionists had become entrenched and the political significance of the Southern Unionists had virtually ceased to be an immediate factor in Washington's war planning, steady forward progress by the Union armies was still deemed to be essential in order to impress upon the Southerners the belief that the North was willing to make whatever sacrifices were necessary, for as long as necessary, in order to bring the war to a successful conclusion. Hence, the Federal high command repeatedly attempted to instill in the minds of such theater commanders as Generals McClellan, Buell, Rosecrans, and Thomas, among others, the political urgency to engage the enemy. Of course, some commanders, such as Generals Grant and Sherman consistently demonstrated sensitivity to the linkage between societal attitudes, foreign perceptions, and military operations. Indeed, although Mr. Lincoln seemed at times to have felt that any forward movement by the Union armies, yielding any result, was preferable to no movement at all, he was, of course, sensitive to the psychological and symbolic, as well as military, political, and economic significance of field successes, such as Antietam, Stones River, and Atlanta, and field reversals, such as the Seven Days Battles, Fredericksburg, and Chickamauga. In the final analysis, however, the President was quite aware that victory in the field was the key to final victory in war. Hence, when the Southern rebellion was young, the President felt that an early, highly visible success, whether in battle or in terms of the capture of specifically targeted locations, would abruptly terminate the insurrection. Even by mid-1863, after the forces of Southern secession had secured virtually complete control within the Southern states and had effectively displaced the Southern Unionists, after the Federal war objectives had been amended to combine total socio-economic objectives with the total political objectives originally sought, Mr. Lincoln, perhaps somewhat overoptimistically, appears to have believed that, had the extremely significant Federal victory at Vicksburg been combined with a successful exploitation of the opportunity provided by the Army of the Potomac's victory at Gettysburg to decisively destroy General Lee's army, the rebellion would have abruptly collapsed.

Early in the war, Mr. Lincoln concluded that, by applying the principle of simultaneous advances nationally and within the various theaters, the advantage of interior lines, often enjoyed by the Confederates, could be partially overcome. Consequently, throughout the war, the President urged the various theater commanders to be mutually supportive by synchronizing the timing of their operations. In advocating this, however, the President remained sensitive to the need to prioritize among the various theaters of war in allocating resources. Consequently, after the disappointing campaigns of the first eighteen months of the war in the Virginia theater, as opposed to the comparative Federal successes in the West, the President and Generals Halleck and, later, Grant relegated the Virginia theater to a secondary status compared to the West.

In many cases, the Washington leadership attempted to design aspects of its national military strategy in such a way that, if successful, they would secure more than just strictly military goals. For example, Washington's decision to focus disproportionate attention to the conquest of the trans-Mississippi portion of the Confederacy was designed not only to secure military goals; if successful, the conquest of the trans-Mississippi Confederacy would have yielded significant political, economic, and international benefits for the United States government generally, and the Lincoln Administration, particularly. Finally, while the Washington high command usually formulated national military strategy in a manner complementary to the other elements of the Federal grand strategy, occasionally one or several of the other elements of grand strategy conflicted with a particular aspect of the national military strategy. For example, the Federal naval blockade of the Southern coastline significantly complicated Washington's diplomatic strategy toward the European powers. Similarly, at the outset of the war, the President's political strategy toward the Border states, predicated, in part, upon temporary respect for Kentucky neutrality, clashed with that element of the national military strategy which called for prompt Federal occupation of the Mississippi Valley. In most cases, however, Federal military strategy was designed to coincide with and, indeed, reinforce the other elements of the Lincoln Administration's grand strategy to suppress the Southern rebellion and politically reintegrate the Union.

Based upon the experience of the Washington high command in formulating its various military strategies during the American Civil War, it is possible to construct a typology of analytically distinct, offensively oriented generic strategies.[1] The Federal experience suggests that the various national military strategies successively formulated by the national politico-military leadership represented a blend of these generic strategies. Three of these generic strategies seek to destroy or, at least, neutralize the enemy's ability to resist with concentrated armies, fleets, and/or, in the twentieth century, air forces, through the exclusive application of military power. Each of these three generic strategies, however, attempts to secure that goal differently. The "strategy of annihilation" is the first of these offensively oriented, generic military strategies. The goal of the strategy of annihilation is to directly destroy or neutralize the enemy's concentrated field forces by either of two methods: battle or maneuver. Annihilation of the enemy field forces in battle implies that, at minimum, the enemy forces will be successfully broken up as concentrated instruments of military power and, optimally, these forces will cease to be capable of performing any military function whatsoever. Alternatively, annihilation of the enemy forces by maneuver implies that the enemy would be successfully placed in an untenable position with no hope of extricating himself and, therefore, compelled to surrender. In contrast to the strategy of annihilation, the second, offensively oriented, generic military strategy to be examined, the "strategy of resource control," uses an indirect approach to neutralize the enemy concentrated field forces. The goal of the strategy of resource control is to deprive the enemy of his war-making resources and/or logistical infrastructure while, simultaneously, acquiring control over and use of these resources and assets to sustain and, optimally, enhance one's own ability to pursue the war to a successful conclusion. As such, one will grow stronger or, at least, maintain strength, while the strength of the enemy diminishes to the point where he can no longer continue to field his military forces as concentrated entities, thereby, causing them to break up into smaller bodies, without necessarily having to defeat them in battle. The limited conquest of significant portions of the enemy's territory, leading possibly to the total conquest of the enemy's entire country, is the method by which the strategy of resource control is implemented. Finally, the third offensively oriented, generic military strategy to be examined is the "strategy of resource denial." The strategy of resource denial utilizes an indirect approach to neutralize the enemy's concentrated field forces by depriving the enemy of his war-making resources or, at least, access to those resources by disrupting his logistical infrastructure, thereby weakening the enemy to the point where he can no longer sustain his field forces as concentrated bodies, again, causing them to break up. In contrast to the strategy of resource control, however, the strategy of resource denial does not involve one's own acquisition of control over the enemy's resources and assets. Several methods may be utilized individually or in concert in implementing the strategy of resource denial. The enemy may be externally isolated by means of a maritime and/or continental blockade. Raids upon the enemy territory, including twentieth century style strategic bombing raids, maritime/amphibious raids along the enemy's seacoast, and guerrilla and/or mobile ground force raids, may be used to destroy warmaking resources at their source or interdict the enemy's vital lines of communication. Finally, attrition of enemy material and manpower through costly battles or even desertion will contribute to the collapse of the enemy's ability to sustain his field armies in concentrated form. To reemphasize, however, each of three, offensively oriented, generic military strategies attempts to destroy or, at least, neutralize the enemy's ability to resist with concentrated field forces.

In addition to the influence of these three offensively oriented, generic military strategies, another generic strategy, one which might be called a military "strategy of perception control" may also be incorporated into an offensively oriented national military strategy. A military strategy of perception control attempts, through military action, to influence along desired lines, the attitudes of the enemy peoples, the international community heretofore neutral in the conflict, one's own people, and the people of any power with whom one is allied, especially those individuals occupying influential positions. More specifically, this strategy attempts to influence the attitudes of the enemy people and/or troops, especially those in positions of power, to cease resistance at all levels of conflict and terminate the war in accord with one's own national objectives. Equally important, this strategy seeks to influence the attitudes of one's own people and soldiers, again, especially the powerful members of one's own population and army, to continue to resist at whatever level of military conflict is necessary until the war has been brought to a successful conclusion. Finally, this generic strategy seeks to influence the attitudes of the peoples of foreign powers to, at minimum, refrain from actively assisting the enemy to resist and, optimally, induce these external powers to actively render whatever assistance is desired to facilitate the conclusion of the conflict on satisfactory terms. Reflecting the synergetic relationship between the various generic military strategies when several are blended in the national military strategy of a particular state, the likelihood of attaining the goals of the military strategy of perception control are often enhanced by progress toward attainment of the goals of the other three offensively oriented, generic military strategies described above. In addition, however, certain other military actions not yet reviewed may significantly contribute to the achievement of the goals of the military strategy of perception control, even though these actions only indirectly contribute to the attainment of the goals of the strategies of annihilation, resource control, and/or resource denial. These military options include: anti-population, terror raids, seizure of symbolically or psychologically significant, but otherwise insignificant locations, and highly visible, symbolic, but militarily indecisive, battlefield victories.

As noted earlier, national military strategy, in turn, is blended with other non-military strategies, such as political strategies, including the delineation of the terms of peace extended to the enemy, the diplomatic strategy, the economic strategy, the public information/media strategy, etc., to yield the overarching grand strategy. The ultimate goal of grand strategy is to mobilize and apply the national resources in such a way as to influence the enemy, one's own people, especially one's own troops, and the international community to act in such a way as to promote the attainment of one's national objectives. Hopefully, one's own people will support the war effort until the enemy is rendered incapable of sustaining concentrated resistance with his military forces. Furthermore, preferably, the enemy people and/or leadership will conclude that, with the breakup of their concentrated field forces, continued resistance would be too costly, the likelihood of final victory too slim, and the terms for peace too attractive to warrant making the continued sacrifices necessary to wage a protracted low-intensity war over a long period of time in an effort to wear the opponent down. Indeed, optimally, the enemy people, soldiers, and/or leaders will begin drawing these conclusions prior to the collapse of the enemy's concentrated field forces and that will, in itself, contribute significantly, often decisively, to the collapse of enemy resistance and the termination of hostilities. But occasionally, following the collapse of the enemy's concentrated field forces, the enemy leadership and/or people may opt to continue to resist in what then would become a protracted, low-intensity conflict. In this case, not only would the national authorities of the state on the strategic offensive be compelled to revise their national military strategy in accord with the options available for suppressing a determined people waging a protracted, low-intensity war, the national authorities may find it necessary to reevaluate their grand strategy and, possibly, even their national objectives. In extreme cases, the national authorities may conclude that depopulation of the enemy country is the only way to destroy the enemy's ability to continue resistance. Depopulation of the enemy country may be accomplished by pursuing a "strategy of extermination and/or forceable resettlement." In addition, depending upon the circumstances, the enemy resources may either be preserved for use by the victorious power or destroyed. Fortunately, the United States was spared both the horrors of a protracted, low intensity war commencing in the spring of 1865, one which would have paled the ghastly sacrifices of the four preceding years of conflict by the concentrated field armies, and the extreme measures which both sides may have felt compelled to adopt to attain their national objectives under such circumstances.

Battles during the American Civil War repeatedly illustrated the difficulties inherent in successfully annihilating a reasonably well-led, adequately equipped, concentrated, mid-nineteenth century field army. Many commanders in both blue and gray hoped to destroy the enemy field armies in a decisive battle, but, on the Confederate side, only General Robert E. Lee approached, but, even then failed to attain, that illusive goal at the Second Battle of Manassas. On the Union side, at the Battle of Nashville, General George Thomas attacked and effectively destroyed the Confederate Army of Tennessee, but that was, in large measure, due to the greatly weakened state of the Army of Tennessee and the poor leadership of its commander during the entire Nashville Campaign. On three occasions, General Ulysses S. Grant maneuvered the enemy army into an untenable position, thereby compelling it to surrender: Fort Donelson, Vicksburg, and Appomattox. In the first two campaigns, the Confederate commanders failed to effectively utilize their resources and avail themselves of alternatives. In the Appomattox Campaign, the able Confederate commander had few resources left and even fewer alternatives available, making the outcome of that Campaign virtually certain. In short, for the most part, the experience of the American Civil War dramatically emphasized the low probability of successfully annihilating the enemy's armies in battle or compelling them to surrender.[2]

At the war's outset, General Winfield Scott proposed a national military strategy which represented a blend of the generic strategies of resource denial and limited resource control, which, he hoped, would, in turn, facilitate implementation of a generic strategy of perception control. General Scott predicated his proposal upon the assumptions that there were powerful pro-Union forces throughout the South and that, given proper conditions, these Unionist elements could displace the secessionists and return the South into the American political system. Therefore, the aged General-in-Chief recommended that the Federal authorities use their military power in such a way as to strengthen Unionists throughout the South and, certainly, avoid alienating them or driving them into the arms of the secessionists, discredit the secessionist movement, attempt to create a context in which the increasingly strong Unionists could displace the increasingly unpopular secessionists, thereby terminating the insurrection, and, finally minimize post-war bitterness on both sides and maximize the prospects for the peaceful post-war political reintegration of the Union by limiting wartime damage and casualties. Specifically, General Scott's proposed national military strategy envisioned the limited use of force to attain the Administration's total political objectives. It incorporated the generic strategy of resource denial by means of a strict maritime and continental blockade. This would, hopefully, deprive the secessionists of access to foreign sources of necessary supplies, thereby forcing them to expend and, eventually, exhaust their own war-making resources. Moreover, by proposing that the Federal forces seize and permanently occupy the Mississippi Valley, General Scott also incorporated a limited version of the generic strategy of resource control. That would, of course, complement the effort to isolate the Confederacy, since it would effectively separate the Deep South and the mid-Atlantic states, which were the heart of the rebellion, from the trans-Mississippi portion of the Confederacy. Beyond that, Federal occupation of the Mississippi Valley would, implicitly, deny the secessionists access to the resources of the Valley, while, at the same time, securing Federal access to those resources for the Union war effort. Finally, General Scott hoped that, by successfully implementing those portions of his proposed national military strategy calling for enemy resource denial and limited enemy resource control, the Federal government could, with very limited force and, as a result, few casualties and little physical damage, capitalize upon the assumed political differences within the political spectrum of Southern opinion and encourage pro-Union elements within the Southern states to, themselves, take action to oust the secessionists and terminate the rebellion with a minimum resultant post-war bitterness. In addition, the symbolic significance of the Federal seizure and guaranteed Union control over the Mississippi Valley would have implicitly contributed to enhancing the morale and resolve of the peoples of the upper Mississippi, Ohio, and Missouri Valleys. But, as noted earlier, the naval blockade of the Southern coastline tended to have a negative impact upon the perceptions of the European powers.

President Lincoln accepted both the underpinning assumptions and the terms of General Scott's proposal, but the President felt that it was imperative to proceed more aggressively in the Virginia theater, rather than adopt the passive stance advocated by the General-in-Chief in the east. Hence, at minimum, to reinforce the generic military strategy of perception control by securing a symbolic field success and, optimally, to simultaneously secure the militarily significant destruction of the enemy forces in Virginia, the President directed the Union forces assembling near Washington to engage and defeat the enemy army located at Manassas, Virginia and, if successful, seize the newly established Confederate capital at Richmond. But, to reemphasize, the President's decision to order an early offensive in northern Virginia was primarily an effort to use military instruments for perception control since, like General Scott's proposal, the President's Virginia offensive was designed to discredit the secessionists, strengthen the Unionists throughout the South, and encourage the latter to use the opportunity provided by the anticipated Confederate field reversals to overthrow the secessionists and, themselves, terminate the rebellion. Simultaneously, but unlike General Scott's proposal, the Presidentially directed offensive in the east was designed to elevate the spirit of the Northerners, especially the people of the Northeast, by satisfying their desire for immediate action against the rebels in Virginia. Finally, the Manassas Campaign was designed to influence the attitudes of the European powers by dramatically demonstrating the Federal government's strength and resolve to suppress the Southern insurrection. While the First Manassas Campaign ended in a Federal disaster, it is possible that the President's national military strategy, incorporating both his ideas and the strategy proposed by General Scott which together relied upon the limited use of military force for total political objectives, might have succeeded had the Union army prevailed on that hot July day in 1861 in the battle outside the national capital. In the end, however, the Union disaster at Manassas served only to enhance the prestige and political position of the Southern secessionists throughout the South, while the power of the Southern pro-Unionists declined proportionately. Indeed, the longer the secessionist movement remained unchecked by the Federal authorities, the weaker became the Southern Unionists and the less realistic became the assumptions predicated upon Southern political dissent from the cause of Confederate independence which, in turn, underpinned Federal strategy.

For the moment, however, the President, joined by General George B. McClellan, Mr. Lincoln's second General-in-Chief, continued to predicate Federal strategy upon the assumption that the Southern Unionists constituted a powerful force and, if

Washington acted appropriately, these elements would play a decisive role in terminating the insurrection. Consequently, while retaining the resource denial, via blockade, generic component of the national military strategy heretofore pursued, President Lincoln and General McClellan added new emphasis to the resource control and perception control via military initiatives, generic components of the earlier national military strategies. Specifically, they identified a series of militarily, as well as symbolically significant targets for Union operations throughout the Southern states. The high command hoped that the capture of some or all of these specifically targeted locations, backed, in turn, by the pressure of the blockade, would make it increasingly difficult for the secessionists to continue to field their armies as concentrated bodies. More important from Washington's perspective, however, the Federal high command hoped that field successes, whether militarily significant or merely symbolic would give impetus to the perception control generic element of their national military strategy by discrediting the secessionists, strengthening the Southern Unionists before it was too late, bolstering Northern morale, and impressing the European powers. Notwithstanding the suspicion that the Confederacy lacked a limited number of militarily or symbolically vital geographic locations, the loss of which would cause irreparable damage to the cause of Southern independence,[3] President Lincoln's and General McClellan's national military strategy remained incompletely tested since Union field successes in the critical Virginia theater failed to materialize. Hence, by late 1862, the Federal high command concluded that the national military strategy pursued during the preceding year had failed to produce the anticipated results and, consequently, it would have to be reexamined.

Therefore, during the final months of 1862, President Lincoln and his third General-in-Chief, Henry W. Halleck, abandoned the, by then, anachronistic premise that there existed within the Southern states a powerful body of pro-Union loyalists capable of displacing the secessionists and accepted the fact that the secessionists had held power sufficiently long and had enjoyed sufficient military, as well as non-military success to have effectively neutralized the political power of the Southern Unionist elements and had entrenched themselves in power. Consequently, the new Federal high command escalated the resource control generic component of Federal military strategy, while, simultaneously, modifying the thrust of the perception control generic element. The high command concluded that the Federal armies would have to totally conquer the South in order to suppress the rebellion. Specifically, they hoped that, by progressively implementing a national military strategy aimed at total resource control, that, in concert with the resource denial generic strategy pursued via the naval blockade of the Southern coast, would gradually weaken the Confederates, by, not only forcing them to exhaust their available war-making resources, the seizure and permanent occupation of increasingly large portions of the South would steadily reduce the availability of those resources. If successful, the Confederate authorities would eventually become so short of war-making resources that they would be unable to sustain their armies as concentrated entities. Simultaneously, as the Federals acquired access to the resources of the South, the Union war-making strength would increase as Confederate strength decreased. In short, for the first time, the Federal high command adopted a total national military strategy in pursuit of the government's, by then, total socio-economic-political objectives. Moreover, not only would successful implementation of the resource control and maritime resource denial generic components of the national military strategy help promote the perception control generic component of the Federal military strategy by influencing the attitudes of the Southerners, the people of the North, and the Europeans along desired lines, the liberal peace terms announced by the President were designed to influence the Southern people to abandon their struggle for independence, as well as enhance the political position of the Lincoln Administration. By late 1863, however, it had become increasingly apparent that the unfavorable force-space ratio of Federal military power to Southern territory would make it virtually impossible for the Union armies to conquer the South and subdue a people who remained committed to the cause of Southern independence.[4]

Shortly after assuming control of the United States Army in early March, 1864, President Lincoln's fourth General-in-Chief, Ulysses S. Grant, again modified the national military strategy. General Grant deemphasized the resource control generic component of the Federal military strategy by ordering that, while the Southern territory which had already been seized would be held, no additional Southern territory would be permanently occupied. Instead, General Grant placed greater emphasis upon the resource denial generic component of the national military strategy. In addition to maintaining the naval blockade of the Southern coast, General Grant planned to have a portion of the Union army pin and, if possible, destroy the Confederacy's field forces, while the remainder of the Federal host raided the interior of the South and destroyed its war-making resources and logistical infrastructure. In that way, even if the concentrated Confederate field armies were not destroyed in battle, the destructive raids deep into the heart of the South would reduce and, eventually, eliminate the ability of the Confederate authorities to supply their concentrated armies, causing those forces to break up. While General Grant retained and remained very responsive to the perception control component of the national military strategy, particularly the impact of military operations upon Northern public opinion, as well as the impact of the heavy fighting and interior raids upon the attitudes of the soldiers in the Confederate armies, it was General Grant's principal lieutenant, William T. Sherman, who added another dimension to the perception control generic component of Federal military strategy. In his destructive raid across Georgia and into the Carolinas, General Sherman not only ably implemented the resource denial generic element of General Grant's national military strategy, General Sherman consciously added an anti-population approach to the perception control generic component of the national military strategy. Evaluating the impact of the anti-population aspect of General Sherman's Georgia and Carolinas raid, combined with the accompanying destruction of significant portions of the Confederacy's war-making resources and logistical infrastructure, originally envisioned by General Grant, several historians have compared General Sherman's operations to the air bombing campaigns of the Second World War and interpreted his raid as a precursor of modern air power strategy.[5] Indeed, General Sherman's operations might be seen as the negative opposite to the positive incentives of Mr. Lincoln's generous peace terms, collectively designed, in turn, to influence the attitudes of the Southern peoples, as well as the Northerners and the Europeans along desired lines.

In the early spring of 1865, following four terrible years of bloody struggle, but notwithstanding the existence of alternative military options, the concentrated field armies of the Confederacy successively surrendered and the Southern rebellion ended. Evaluating the factors accounting for the collapse of the Southern rebellion, the evidence tends to depreciate the significance of the naval blockade of the Southern coastline. There appears to be general agreement among contemporary analysts that the blockade remained ineffective throughout most of the war in severing Southern ties with the Europeans and, indeed, "never became fully effective until the actual harbors were occupied, or cut off from the interior, by the army." Moreover, while the blockade "certainly had some detrimental impact upon Confederate supply, ... clearly it did not have a decisive effect" upon the Confederate ability to continue the war.[6] Finally, as Professors Beringer, Hattaway, Jones, and Still concluded,

> If, however, the Union had succeeded early in eliminating ports captured or closed later, the blockade would have been strengthened significantly; but in view of the Confederate ability to improvise, the quantity of consumer goods brought in throughout the war, and the relative Confederate independence of imports in the latter part of the war, it seems unlikely that a more effective blockade would have broken the military stalemate or seriously affected the capabilities of the Confederate armies. Of course, a tighter blockade would have increased civilian hardships and further depressed morale and taxed the Confederacy's nationalism. But greater Union military success on other fronts would also have had a depressing effect on morale and, in addition, would have deprived the Confederacy of resources because the Union would dominate more of the South's territory. It is, therefore, difficult to hypothesize the results of more intense Union naval activity along the coasts.[7]

Similarly, the evidence fails to support the contention that the Union raids into the heartland of the South, raids which certainly destroyed a considerable portion of the Confederacy's war-making resources and logistical infrastructure, alone, created such a shortage of critical supplies as to be responsible for neutralizing the Confederacy's concentrated field armies. Indeed, notwithstanding agreement among analysts doubting the capability of the Richmond authorities to have continued to supply its field forces as concentrated entities during the coming spring, summer, and autumn campaigning seasons, the fact that the Confederate armies in the field continued to receive supplies until the last days of the war suggests that General Grant's national "military strategy influenced the outcome of the conflict, but did not determine it" and that "the Confederacy's forces dwindled and surrendered before Grant's raids could deprive them of supplies."[8]

But, even if, as a result of General Grant's national military strategy designed to destroy the war-making resources and logistical infrastructure of the South, it had become impossible for the Confederate armies to have remained in the field as concentrated entities, the Confederates could have opted to break up those armies and transform the conflict into a protracted, low-intensity guerrilla war. As Professors Beringer, Hattaway, Jones, and Still pointed out,

> ... Grant's strategy alone could not have won a war against a people sufficiently determined to maintain their independence. Grant aimed only to break up the Confederacy's main armies by severing the railroads that connected them to their supplies of food, shoes, uniforms, weapons, and ammunition. He provided no means of dealing with these armies should they disperse and thereafter continue offering organized resistance as units ranging in size from a division of several brigades down to independent companies. These units would have dominated the country, reducing Federal control to the immediate vicinity of the Union armies .... Such forces, aided by guerrilla activity, could have found some food and other supplies in the country they controlled and secured more from the invader's always vulnerable supply columns.[9]

Indeed, Generals Grant and Sherman were particularly concerned about this possibility. The evidence suggests, however, that most of the Confederacy's politico-military leaders, as well as the Southern people, themselves, were unprepared to accept the inevitable socio-economic costs which many clearly recognized were associated with such a transformation of the conflict. In other words, as concluded by Professors Beringer, Hattaway, Jones, and Still, the Confederates "did not want an independent Confederacy bad enough to continue the struggle, and they placed the welfare of their loved ones ahead of the creation of a new nation."[10]

Thus, the generic strategy of perception control through the use of military instruments component of General Grant's national military strategy, especially as it was supplement by General Sherman, may have been the decisive military factor in determining the outcome of the war. General Sherman's raids through Georgia and the Carolinas, as well as General Sheridan's campaign in the Shenandoah Valley, combined with the demoralizing impact of General Grant's campaign in Virginia, Admiral Farragut's dramatic closure of Mobile Bay, and General Thomas' decisive victory at the Battle of Nashville, depressed Southern morale, elevated Northern morale, and had a powerful positive impact upon the attitudes of the Europeans. The spectre of continued, and even intensified devastation of the South and Southern society should the Confederate independence struggle be prolonged convinced the Southern people that the cost of victory would be extremely high. Moreover, President Lincoln's reelection in November, 1864, convinced the Southerners that the Federal government would continue the struggle for at least another four years and, from that, they concluded that the chances of victory, at least in the near term, were very slim. Finally, when these considerations were juxtaposed against the eventual impact of the very attractive peace terms extended by the President to the Southern people, they concluded that the cost of defeat was much less than the cost of continuing the war. Fortunately for all Americans and, indeed, the world community, this created a context for the termination of America's terrible Civil War and the birth of a more perfect Union which would, in turn, serve as the torch of freedom and democracy during the following century and beyond.

APPENDIX

To understand the war policy of the United States government during the American Civil War or, for that matter, national security policy during any period, one must first adopt a series of working definitions. Throughout this study, the term "national objectives" refers to "those fundamental aims, goals, or purposes of a nation—as opposed to the means for seeking these ends— toward which a policy is directed and efforts and resources of the nation are applied."[1] "National policy" springs directly from national objectives, since the former represents "a broad course of action or statements of guidance adopted by the government at the national level in pursuit of national objectives."[2] "Grand strategy" is "the art and science of developing and using political, economic, psychological, and military forces as necessary during peace and war to afford the maximum support to policies in order to increase the probabilities and favorable consequences of victory and lessen the chances of defeat."[3] "National military strategy" is one component of grand strategy. National military strategy is "the art and science of employing the armed forces of a nation or alliance to secure (national) objectives by the application or threat of force."[4] As such, national military strategy performs a variety of functions. First, it establishes the goals of military operations nationally and within the theater or various theaters of war. Second, it delineates the methods to be employed in accomplishing these military-strategic goals. Third, it imposes the conditions governing the application of military force. Fourth, it prioritizes the allocation of military resources between the various theaters, as necessary. Fifth, it determines the general timing and tempo of theater operations.[5] "Theater operational planning" takes place within the framework of the national military strategy. Theater operational planning involves the actual "employment of military forces" along the general lines delineated by the national military strategy to attain the military-strategic goals assigned to that theater of war "through the design, organization, and conduct of campaigns and major operations."[6] Finally, through "tactics," unit commanders apply the combat power of their units against the enemy forces in battles or engagements.[7]

According to Carl von Clausewitz, the celebrated nineteenth century military theoretician, since war "is an act of violence meant to force the enemy to do our will," its theoretical aim would be "to overcome the enemy and disarm him." Clausewitz distinguished between "three broad objectives: the armed forces, the country, and the enemy's will."[8]

> The fighting forces must be destroyed: that is, they must be put in such a condition that they can no longer carry on the fight. Whenever we use the phrase "destruction of the enemy's forces" this alone is what we mean. The country must be occupied; otherwise the enemy could raise fresh military forces. Yet both these things may be done and the war, that is the animosity and the reciprocal effects of hostile elements, cannot be considered to have ended so long as the enemy's will has not been broken: in other words, so long as the enemy government and its allies have not been driven to ask for peace, or the population made to submit.[9]

Theoretically, "since of the three objectives named, it is the fighting forces that assure the safety of the country, the natural sequence would be to destroy them first and then subdue the country."[10]

> As a rule, destroying the enemy's forces tends to be a gradual process, as does the ensuing subjugation of the country. Normally the one reacts on the other, in that loss of territory weakens the fighting forces; but that particular sequence of events is not essential and therefore does not always take place. Before they suffer seriously, the enemy's forces may retire to remote areas, or even withdraw to other countries. In that event, of course, most or all of the country will be occupied.[11]

Moving from the theoretical to the practical, however, Clausewitz noted that:

> But the aim of disarming the enemy (the object of war in the abstract, the ultimate means of accomplishing the war's political purpose, which should incorporate all the rest) is in fact not always encountered in reality, and need not be fully achieved as a condition of peace. On no account should theory raise it to the level of a law. Many treaties have been concluded before one of the antagonists could be called powerless—even before the balance of power had been seriously altered. What is more, a review of actual cases shows a whole category of wars in

which the very idea of defeating the enemy is unreal: those in which the enemy is substantially the stronger power . . . . Inability to carry on the struggle can, in practice, be replaced by two other grounds for making peace: the first is the improbability of victory; the second is its unacceptable cost . . . . Not every war need be fought until one side collapses. When the motives and tensions of war are slight we can imagine that the very faintest prospect of defeat might be enough to cause one side to yield. If from the very start the other side feels that this is probable, it will obviously concentrate on bringing about this probability rather than take the long way round and totally defeat the enemy. Of even greater influence on the decision to make peace is the consciousness of all the effort that has already been made and of the efforts yet to come. Since war is not an act of senseless passion but is controlled by its political object, the value of this object must determine the sacrifices to be made for it in magnitude and also duration. Once the expenditure of effort exceeds the value of the political object, the object must be renounced and peace must follow. We see then that if one side cannot completely disarm the other, the desire for peace on either side will rise and fall with the probability of further successes and the amount of effort these would require.[12]

Hence, Clausewitz suggested that the choice of national military strategies by the various belligerents and their level of resolve in pursuing these national military strategies would be determined, in part, by the perceived value of the national objectives being sought. Unlimited national objectives demand nothing less than total victory and, "if we wish to gain total victory, then the destruction of his armed forces is the most appropriate action and the occupation of his territory only a consequence. To occupy land before his armies are defeated should be considered at best a necessary evil."[13] If less than total national objectives are sought, then less demanding national military strategies may be pursued. For example,

If on the other hand we do not aim at destroying the opposing army, and if we are convinced that the enemy does not seek a brutal decision, but rather fears it, then the seizure of a lightly held or undefended province is an advantage in itself; and should this advantage be enough to make the enemy fear for the final outcome, it can be considered as a short cut on the road to peace. But there is another way. It is possible to increase the likelihood of success without defeating the enemy's forces. I refer to operations that have direct political repercussions, that are designed in the first place to disrupt the opposing alliance, or to paralyze it, that gain us new allies, favorably affect the political scene, etc. If such operations are possible it is obvious that they can greatly

> improve our prospects and that they can form a much shorter route to
> the goal than the destruction of the opposing armies.[14]

From this point, Clausewitz addressed a related question, "how to influence the enemy's expenditure of effort; in other words, how to make the war more costly to him."

> The enemy's expenditure of effort consists in the wastage of his forces—
> our destruction of them; and in his loss of territory—our conquest.
> Closer study will make it obvious that both of these factors can vary
> in their significance with the variation in objectives. As a rule the dif-
> ferences will be slight, but that should not mislead us, for in practice,
> when strong motives are not present, the slightest nuances often decide
> between the different uses of force. For the moment all that matters is
> to show that, given certain conditions, different ways of reaching the
> objective are possible and that they are neither inconsistent, absurd,
> nor even mistaken. In addition, there are three other methods directly
> aimed at increasing the enemy's expenditure of effort. The first of
> these is invasion, that is the seizure of enemy territory; not with the
> object of retaining it but in order to exact financial contributions, or
> even to lay it waste. The immediate object here is neither to conquer
> the enemy country nor to destroy its army, but simply to cause general
> damage. The second method is to give priority to operations that will
> increase the enemy's suffering. It is easy to imagine two alternatives:
> one operation is far more advantageous if the purpose is to defeat the
> enemy; the other is more profitable if that cannot be done. The first
> tends to be described as the more military, the second the more politi-
> cal alternative. From the highest point of view, however, one is as mil-
> itary as the other, and neither is appropriate unless it suits the particu-
> lar conditions. The third, and far the most important method, judging
> from the frequency of its use, is to wear down the enemy. That expres-
> sion is more than a label; it describes the process precisely, and is not
> so metaphorical as it may seem at first. Wearing down the enemy in a
> conflict means using the duration of the war to bring about a gradual
> exhaustion of his physical and moral resistance.[15]

In short, in wars for limited objectives, the attacker might seize the enemy's capital, his other cities, fortresses, depots, logistical centers, politically dissident areas, agricultural regions, etc. While pursuing such a national military strategy, the attacker might find it necessary to engage the enemy field forces in battle for political reasons of prestige or to raise or sustain military and popular morale. The goal of such a national military strategy would be the capture of a sufficient number of politically, stra-tegically, economically, logistically, and/or psychologically/symbolically significant places, possibly combined with the visible defeat of the enemy's field forces, to induce the enemy to cease resistance despite the continued cohesion of his armies in the field. Indeed, given the impact of public opinion, often if a particular geographic region or battlefield victory is popularly perceived as being important to the success of the struggle, it, in fact, becomes important, irrespective of its intrinsic military value. Finally, Clausewitz noted that the enemy field armies derive strength from the territory which they defend. Thus, "giving up part of a country's land and resources during a withdrawal into the interior would ultimately weaken the defender because it would involve the forfeiture of magazines and depots as well as the production of the country." Conversely, the attacker would derive strength from the resources of the captured territory. As a result, " 'if the conquered areas are important enough, and if there are places in them vital to the areas still in enemy hands, the rot will spread, like a cancer, by itself; and if only that and nothing else happens, the conqueror may well enjoy a net advantage.' " Eventually, the enemy forces may weaken to a point where they become unable to effectively take the field.[16] Thus, Clausewitz maintained that, "in war many roads lead to success, and that they do not all involve the opponent's outright defeat. Any one of these may be used to overcome the enemy's will: the choice depends on circumstances." But, while national military strategies in pursuit of national objectives may vary, Clausewitz maintained that "fighting is the only possible means. Everything is governed by a supreme law, the decision by force of arms."[17]

> ... the violent resolution of the crisis, the wish to annihilate the enemy's forces, is the first-born son of war. If the political aims are small, the motives slight and tensions low, a prudent general may look for any way to avoid major crises and decisive actions, exploit any weaknesses in the opponent's military and political strategy, and finally reach a peaceful settlement. If his assumptions are sound and promise success we are not entitled to criticize him. But he must never forget that he is moving on devious paths where the god of war may catch him unaware. He must keep his eye on the enemy in order to be adequately prepared should he suddenly be attacked with massive force.[18]

Clausewitz recognized that the annihilation of the enemy's field army in battle was extremely difficult to accomplish and was predicated upon a series of factors. First, he maintained that the destruction of the enemy field force required both superiority in infantry and cavalry in order to defeat the enemy on the battlefield and fully exploit that success through an effective pursuit.[19] Second, Clausewitz argued that the "degree of victory" depended upon whether the enemy forces were successfully turned. Historically, turning movements could take two forms: tactical and strategic. A strategic turning movement is one which threatens something which the enemy considers vital in his far rear, usually his line of communications. In such an operation, after the attacking body pins the enemy frontally, usually by a secondary feint attack, the main body of the force on the strategic offensive moves swiftly and optimally in secret to the far rear of the enemy and takes a position astride the enemy's communications. If this operation can be successfully accomplished before the enemy can withdraw from his advanced position, the enemy would find himself in an extremely dangerous situation. Moreover,

> Such a turning movement would have a far greater chance of success if it were what may be termed a penetration, that is, an advance along a line of communications fully capable of supplying the attacking army. A penetration, which permits a long-term, essentially permanent occupation of territory, may be distinguished from a raid, which involves only transitory possession. A turning movement by a penetration offers obvious advantages over a raid, for the attacker would be able to supply himself while the defender, with his communications cut, could not . . . . On the other hand, if the attacker reaches the defender's communications by a raid, then neither of them would possess a line of communications and eventually the raiding attacker would have to leave the defender's communications. In this case the defender's situation would be determined by whether he had enough supplies on hand to afford to wait until a lack of supplies forced the attacker to leave.[20]

Assuming that the enemy chooses not to remain passively in position, he has a series of options, though none are very satisfactory. First, the enemy could attempt to smash through the pinning force to his front. Even if successful, however, the enemy would be moving even farther from his own supply base and source of reinforcements. Moreover, the main body of the attacking force, which occupied a position astride the enemy communications, would undoubtedly itself move against the enemy rear. Second, the enemy could opt to move the main body of his forces against the main body of the attacker's army positioned to the enemy's rear, astride his communications. This situation, however, would confer a significant advantage upon the main body of the force on the strategic offensive which had originally turned the enemy and now blocked his line of communications. The latter would enjoy the benefits of the tactical defensive in a position of its own choosing, against an enemy forced to assault, optimally frontally, without a line of communications or the promise of reinforcements. Third, the enemy could try to himself sever the attacker's line of communications. Even if the attacker's communications were vulnerable, however, in doing so, the enemy would probably have to split his force into three elements: a portion to watch the attacker's pinning force, another portion to protect against a rear movement by the attacker's main body, and a third portion to execute the movement against the attacker's communications. Thus, the enemy would dangerously disperse his forces and would risk destruction. Finally, depending on the availability of a lateral escape route, the enemy might be able to withdraw from his present, turned position and move roundabout to a new, more secure location.[21]

In contrast to the strategic turning movement in which the attacker strikes at the enemy's far rear, "in the tactical turning movement, two armies stand face to face and one seeks to move at least some of its forces around the opposing army to attack its flank" or immediate rear. The envelopment of the enemy force is designed "to create an opportunity for total victory by disturbing the foe and upsetting his balance and morale, thus provoking an atmosphere and situation from which a real decision could be gained." It should be noted, however, that a tactical turning movement or envelopment is distinct from a "tactical outflanking movement."[22] Discussing this in more detail, David Chandler noted,

> A "turning" movement could be executed only by a fair-sized force—at least a corps in strength—which was capable of moving into action independently of the main body. Such an attack, properly timed, could lead to the destruction of an enemy if the "turning" force was able to place itself well in the foe's rear athwart his line of retreat. An "outflanking" movement, on the other hand, was productive of less dramatic

results. It was carried out by a formation forming an integral part of the ... line, and at all times it remained linked to the main front; in no way was it a separate entity. Such an onslaught could often force an enemy to change front or partially redeploy his line, but it rarely led in itself to the major dislocation of the enemy position making possible the crushing victory ....[23]

While Clausewitz maintained that " 'the defensive form of warfare is intrinsically stronger than the offensive,' " he tended to emphasize the decisiveness of tactical turning movements and depreciated the practical significance of the strategic variety. "But he did recognize the strategic turning movement's value on the defense when the attacker's communications were long and vulnerable; he further acknowledged its hypothetical merit when he emphasized that a decisive battle demanded 'an enveloping attack or a battle with reversed fronts.' " Clausewitz's contemporary, Baron Antoine Henri Jomini maintained that the offensive was stronger strategically and at least equivalent tactically to the defensive. Hence, while Jomini "did have some faith in the frontal assault, especially if the attacker was strong enough to combine it with a tactical turning movement, ... the outcome of frontal battles relying on 'main force,' would depend, he thought, on the 'relative numerical superiority, the morale of the two armies, and other circumstances with reference to which no fixed rule can be given.' " He stressed, however, that "victories in such battles would be 'indecisive' if 'attacks were made in front' and the victor did not pursue the defeated," thereby yielding "little but attrition and the retreat of the enemy."[24] Clearly,

> Jomini preferred the strategic turning movement, the "system of modern strategy" in the "new era" created by Napoleon. He saw the opportunity for reaching the enemy's rear, where he "would have no other chance of escape than in forcing his way through your line." If Jomini had believed in the superiority of the tactical defense, he would have seen even more virtue in the strategic turning movement, for it compelled the enemy to assume the offensive to avoid being cut off from supplies and reinforcements. He disparaged the tactical turning movement, saying a general would "do better to employ strategic than tactical combinations" to seize the "enemy's communications while at the same time holding his own." He preferred the strategic because the tactical maneuver would only "dislodge" the enemy whereas the strategic would "ruin his army completely."[25]

Both Jomini and Clausewitz, however, recognized the enormous difficulty of destroying an enemy field force on the battlefield by successfully executing either a tactical or strategic turning movement and conducting an effective pursuit following the battle. Therefore, they stressed the importance of the victor's skill, as well as the morale, size, and composition of this forces. Moreover, Clausewitz noted that annihilation of the enemy field force in battle could occur only with " 'major, obvious, and exceptional mistakes on the enemy's part.' "[26]

As discussed, in wars for unlimited objectives, seizure of the enemy's territory and the destruction of his will to continue resistance would be the consequence which would follow the destruction of his field armies. Clausewitz pointed out, however, that total conquest requires an adequate force-space ratio, noting that " 'a fairly constant ratio exists between the size of a force and the area it can occupy.' " Similarly, Jomini observed that " 'a war of invasion' " is " 'very difficult if not impossible.' " Total victory would require the invading force not only to destroy the defender's field forces, in addition, the enemy's country would have to be " 'occupied and subjugated.' " Clausewitz tended to emphasize the size of the enemy territory as the principal obstacle, whereas Jomini predicted that enemy activity would prove a major obstruction to territorial conquest.[27] Concerning the latter point,

> When, in a national war, the defeated withdrew into the interior, defenders employed as a "last resort" the guerrilla warfare of a "general insurrection." In this way they could mobilize new strength, "not otherwise available" until that time. Jomini, who had fought against such a resistance in Spain, knew how formidable it could be: "The whole country is the scene of hostilities." . . . Jomini described a war in which the invader "holds scarcely any ground but that upon which he encamps; outside the limits of his camp every thing is hostile and multiplies a thousandfold the difficulties he meets at every step." The defenders enjoyed an overwhelming advantage because "each armed inhabitant knows the smallest paths and their connections; he finds everywhere a relative or a friend who aids him; the commanders also know the country, and, learning immediately the slightest movement on the part of the invader, can adopt the best measure to defeat his projects." . . . The invader would be almost helpless against the guerrillas, for "without information of their movements, and not in a condition to send out detachments to gain it, having no resource but in his bayonets, and

certain safety only in the concentration of his columns, (the invader) is like a blind man: his combinations are failures; and when, after the most carefully-concerted movements and the most rapid and fatiguing marches, he thinks he is about to accomplish his aim and deal a terrible blow, he finds no signs of the enemy but his campfires." And "while like Don Quixote, he is attacking windmills, his adversary is on his line of communications, destroys the detachments left to guard it, surprises his convoys, his depots, and carries on a war so disastrous for the invader that he must inevitably yield after a time."[28]

Conversely, Jomini considered the guerrilla warfare option to be a " 'last resort.' "[29]

Having seen such a war firsthand in Spain, he knew that the invaders retaliated with savagery and "by way of reprisals" committed "murder, pillage, and incendiarism throughout the country." These "consequences are so terrible that for the sake of humanity we ought to hope never to see it."[30]

Clausewitz also recognized the costs of a guerrilla war, observing that such a war created " 'a state of legalized anarchy that is as much a threat to the social order at home as it is to the enemy.' "[31] In the final analysis, "neither Clausewitz nor Jomini, who had more faith in the power of the offensive, had any recipe for success in waging a war aimed at the total defeat of the enemy." Therefore, in view of both Clausewitz's and Jomini's recognition of the inherent difficulties involved in destroying an enemy's field army in battle, combined with their pessimism concerning the prospects for conquering a large country, populated by a people resolute in their will to resist the invader, neither would have been optimistic concerning the Federal ability to wage a national war, decisively defeat a well-led, adequately armed Confederate army, and permanently occupy an area as large as the Confederacy without an overwhelming superiority in manpower and an iron resolve to expend the blood and treasure necessary to complete the time consuming conquest of the enemy.[32]

NOTES

CHAPTER I

1. Allen Nevins, *The War for the Union, I: The Improvised War*, 1861–1862 (New York: Charles Scribner's Sons, 1959), cited hereafter as *War, I*, 24.
2. Nevins, War, I, 29. See also Nevins, *War*, I, 27.
3. Colin R. Ballard, *The Military Genius of Abraham Lincoln* (New York: The World Publishing Co., 1952), 28, 32–37; Kenneth P. Williams, *Lincoln Finds a General*, I (New York: The Macmillan Company, 1949), cited hereafter as *Lincoln*, I, 16–59; Nevins, *War*, I, 24, 94; Allen Nevins, *The War for the Union, III: The Organized War*, 1863–1864 (New York: Charles Scribner's Sons, 1971), cited hereafter as *War*, III, 456; Richard Current, T. Harry Williams, and Frank Freidel, *American History: A Survey* (New York: Alfred A. Knopf, 1961) 380–384; Herman Hattaway and Archer Jones, *How the North Won: A Military History of the Civil War* (Urbana: University of Illinois Press, 1983), 2, 19–20, 26–27.
4. Allen Nevins, *The War for the Union, II: War Becomes Revolution* (New York, Charles Scribner's Sons, 1960), cited hereafter as *War*, II, 5–6.
5. Current, Williams, and Freidel, 392, Hattaway and Jones, 2, 84, 270, 689, 696; Williams, *Lincoln and His Generals* (New York: Alfred A. Knopf, 1952), cited hereafter as *Generals*, 28, 36–37; Warren W. Hassler, *General George B. McClellan: Shield of the Union* (Baton Rouge: Louisiana State University Press, 1957), cited hereafter as *McClellan*, 19; Nevins, *War*, I, 37, 339; Nevins, *War*, II, 5–6; Nevins, *War*, III, 1, 148, 413; K. P. Williams, *Lincoln*, I, 148–149; Bruce Catton, *The Civil War* (New York, The Fairfax Press, 1980), cited hereafter as *Civil War*, 185–186; Richard E. Beringer, Herman Hattaway, Archer Jones, and William N. Still, Jr., *Why the South Lost the Civil War* (Athens, Ga.: University of Georgia Press, 1986), 49, 53, 139; T. Harry Williams, "Military Leadership of North and South," in David Donald, Ed., *Why the North Won the Civil War* (New York: Collier Books, 1960), cited hereafter as "Leadership," 44; J.F.C. Fuller, *The Generalship of Ulysses S. Grant* (New York: Dodd, Mead and Company, 1929), cited hereafter as *Grant*, 16, 29, 366; J.F.C. Fuller, *Grant and Lee: A Study in Personality and Generalship* (Bloomington: Indiana University Press, 1957), cited hereafter as *Grant and Lee*, 31; Russell F. Weigley, *The American Way of War: A History of United States Military Strategy and Policy* (New York: Macmillan, 1973), cited hereafter as *American War*, 92, 129, 132, 133.
6. Nevins, *War*, I, 190.
7. Current, Williams, and Freidel, 392; Hattaway and Jones, 2, 84, 270, 689, 696; Catton, *Civil War*, 185–186; Beringer, Hattaway, Jones, and Still, 49, 53, 138; Weigley, *American War*, 92, 129, 132, 133; Williams, *Generals*, 36–37; Williams, "Leadership," 44; Fuller, *Grant*, 16, 29, 366; Fuller, *Grant and Lee*, 31; Nevins, *War*, I, 339; Nevins, *War*, II, 5–6; Nevins, *War*, III, 1, 148, 413; K. P. Williams, *Lincoln*, I, 148–149.

8. Nevins, *War*, I, 13, 19, 20, 29.

9. K. P. Williams, *Lincoln*, I, 17, 60–66, 72–73; Nevins, *War*, I, 77; Current, Williams, and Freidel, 384–385; Hattaway and Jones, 2, 19–20, 27.

10. K. P. Williams, *Lincoln*, I, 41; Nevins, *War*, I, 21, 44, 77, 149–151, 154; Nevins, *War*, III, 454–455.

11. C. W. Elliott, *Winfield Scott: the Soldier and the Man* (New York: Macmillan, 1937), 698; Hattaway and Jones, 35.

12. Ballard, 31–32; Elliott, 698; Hattaway and Jones, 27, 35; Russell F. Weigley, "American Strategy from its Beginnings through the First World War," in Peter Peret, Ed., *Makers of Modern Strategy* (Princeton: Princeton University Press, 1986), cited hereafter as "American Strategy," 415, 419.

13. Elliott, 722. See also Hattaway and Jones, 35.

14. Elliott, 718, 721-722; Nevins, *War*, I, 151–152; Ballard, 175; Hassler, *McClellan*, 5–6; Williams, *Generals*, 16–18; Weigley, *American War*, 93; Warren W. Hassler, *Commanders of the Army of the Potomac* (Baton Rouge: Louisiana State University Press, 1962), cited hereafter as *Potomac*, xix; Hattaway and Jones, 35; Beringer, Hattaway, Jones, and Still, 53, 251.

15. Elliot, 722–723; Ballard, 45, 175; Nevins, *War*, I, 151–152, 154; Hassler, *McClellan*, 6; Williams, *Generals*, 18; Weigley, *American War*, 129; Hattaway and Jones, 35, 134, 140, 145, 178, 185; Beringer, Hattaway, Jones, and Still, 722–723.

16. Bruce Catton, *U.S. Grant and the American Military Tradition* (Boston: Little, Brown and Company, 1954), cited hereafter as *American Tradition*, 60. See also Nevins, *War*, I, 27.

17. Lloyd Lewis, *Sherman: Fighting Prophet*, (New York: Harcourt, Brace and Company, 1932), 142. See also, B.H. Liddell Hart, *Sherman: Soldier, Realist, American* (New York: Frederick Praeger, 1958), 65.

18. Lewis, 146, 156, 161, 252, 306, 329; Liddell Hart, 62; T. Harry Williams, *McClellan, Sherman, and Grant* (New Brunswick, N.J.: Rutgers University Press, 1962), cited hereafter as *McClellan*, 64–65.

19. Lewis, 242, 252, 343; Liddell Hart, 74, 75, 97, 99, 102, 155, 228; Williams, *McClellan*, 66–67; Bruce Catton, *Grant Takes Command* (Boston: Little, Brown and Company, 1968), cited hereafter as *Grant Command*, 134.

20. Nevins, *War*, I, 153–154, 178–179; Nevins, *War*, III, 454–455; Weigley, *American War*, 133.

21. Beringer, Hattaway, Jones, and Still, 54.

22. Ballard, 6, 43, 62–63, 232, 239; Fuller, *Grant and Lee*, 31–32, 251; Nevins, *War*, III, 27, 284; Fuller, *Grant*, 31; Hattaway and Jones, 33, 88; Beringer, Hattaway, Jones, and Still, 54–55.

23. Beringer, Hattaway, Jones, and Still, 134–135.

24. Nevins, *War*, I, 285–286, 288, 372; K. P. Williams, *Lincoln*, I, 66; Fuller, *Grant and Lee*, 31; Liddell Hart, 73; Weigley, *American War*, 98–100; Hattaway and Jones, 82, 111, 130, 132–133; Beringer, Hattaway, Jones, and Still, 62, 135–139.

25. Norman Graebner, "Northern Diplomacy and European Neutrality," in David Donald, Ed., *Why the North Won the Civil War* (New York: Collier Books, 1960), 55–57, 65–66; Nevins, *War*, II, 244–245, 248, 251, 273.

26. Graebner, 57–58; Nevins, *War*, II, 258–260.
27. Graebner, 55–56, 58; Nevins, *War*, II, 244–245, 250, 258–260, 263–265, 272–273.
28. Graebner, 65.
29. Ibid, 66.
30. Graebner, 59–63, 65–66, 76; Ballard, 62–63.
31. Ballard, 7, 42, 235; Nevins, *War*, I, 77, 137, 144–146, 162; K. P. Williams, *Lincoln*, I, 63, 66, 159.
32. Nevins, *War*, I, 139–140.
33. Ibid, 140.
34. Ibid, 144.
35. Ibid, 140–144, 146, 162; Current, Williams, and Freidel, 384, 896.
36. Nevins, *War*, I, 120–129, 136, 147, 310–312, 317.
37. Ibid, 312.
38. Ibid, 129–136.
39. Ibid, 147.
40. Ibid, 179; Williams, *Generals*, 18.
41. K. P. Williams, *Lincoln*, I, 74; Fuller, *Grant and Lee*, 251; Liddell Hart, 75, 83; Nevins, *War*, I, 148, 161, 179; Weigley, *American War*, 93; Hattaway and Jones, 35; Beringer, Hattaway, Jones, and Still, 108, 134, 140, 145, 178, 185.
42. K. P. Williams, *Lincoln*, I, 74; Liddell Hart, 75, 83; Williams, *Generals*, 19–20; Nevins, *War*, I, 214; Hattaway and Jones, 35, 40; Beringer, Hattaway, Jones, and Still, 108.
43. Hassler, *Potomac*, xvi.
44. Catton, *Grant Command*, 277. See also, *Grant Command*, 296.
45. Catton, *Grant Command*, 277, 296; Williams, *Generals*, 62; Nevins, *War*, II, 43–45; Hattaway and Jones, 85–86; Beringer, Hattaway, Jones, and Still, 158–163, 238.
46. Ballard, 50–59; K. P. Williams, *Lincoln*, I, 67–104, Nevins, *War*, I, 159, 215–216; Hassler, *Potomac*, 18–19; Weigley, *American War*, 95–96; Vincent J. Esposito, *The West Point Atlas of the Civil War*, adapted from the *West Point Atlas of American Wars*, Vol. I (New York: Frederick Praeger, 1959), 18–24; Hattaway and Jones, 39–49, 86, 689, 35; Beringer, Hattaway, Jones and Still, 108–117.
47. Beringer, Hattaway, Jones, and Still, 116. See also: Hattaway and Jones, 48–49; Ballard, 58–59.
48. The Confederates, on the tactical defensive, suffered 6% casualties of their 32,000 troops versus the Federals who, on the tactical offensive, suffered a casualty rate of a little less than 10% of their 28,000 men. Beringer, Hattaway, Jones, and Still, 114, 116; Hattaway and Jones, 40, 45–48; Williams, *Generals*, 20; Weigley, *American War*, 96.
49. Liddell Hart, 98.
50. K. P. Williams, *Lincoln*, I, 104–114, 250; Ballard, 66–67, 131–132; Nevins, *War*, I, 266; Nevins, *War*, II, 44, 159–160; Hassler, *McClellan*, 8, 177, 300; Williams, *Generals*, 28, 46, 132; Weigley, *American War*, 133–134; Hattaway and Jones, 36–38, 50-52, 80; Beringer, Hattaway, Jones, and Still, 140–141;

Howard M. Hensel, *The Anatomy of Failure: Major General George B. McClellan and the Peninsular Campaign* (Montgomery: A1: Air Command and Staff College, 1985), 3, 5; Stephen Ambrose, *Halleck: Lincoln's Chief of Staff* (Baton Rouge: Louisiana State University Press, 1962), 11–12.

51. Williams, *Generals*, 90–91, 106–107; Nevins, *War*, I, 270; Ambrose, 11; Hattaway and Jones, 51–52, 94; Beringer, Hattaway, Jones, and Still, 36–38, 50–52, 80.

52. K. P. Williams, *Lincoln*, I, 118–120, 123–125; Ballard, 67; Nevins, *War*, I, 270; Williams, *Generals*, 32, 43; Hassler, *Potomac*, 248; Hattaway and Jones, 86–87; Hensel, 3, 5, 31; Beringer, Hattaway, Jones, and Still, 140–141.

53. Nevins, *War*, I, 307–308.

54. Williams, *Generals*, 34–35; Nevins, *War*, I, 309.

55. Nevins, *War*, I, 309–317, 326.

56. Nevins, *War*, I, 321–327; Bruce Catton, *Grant Moves South* (Boston: Little Brown and Company, 1960), cited hereafter as *Grant South*, 33.

57. Nevins, *War*, I, 331–340; Lewis, 183; Williams, *Generals*, 36.

58. Nevins, *War*, I, 330, 335; Catton, *Grant South*, 37, 48.

59. Nevins, *War*, II, 14.

60. Williams, *Generals*, 310, 312; Fuller, *Grant*, xi, 183; Nevins, *War*, I, 335; Nevins, *War*, II, 13; Catton, *Grant South*, 15–16, 37–39, 91–92, 296–297, 360; Catton, *Grant Command*, 8; Catton, *American Tradition*, 105–106, 108, Williams, *McClellan*, 101–103.

61. Fuller, *Grant*, 192, Catton, *American Tradition*, 106; Catton, *Grant South*, 15, 282, 322, 405–406.

62. Fuller, *Grant*, 192; Catton, *Grant South*, 26, 28–29, 39–41.

63. Catton, *Grant South*, 41–42.

64. Lewis, 184; Williams, *Generals*, 37–41; Nevins, *War*, I, 330, 381; Catton, *Grant South*, 41–43, 48, 58–60.

65. Ballard, 67–68; K. P. Williams, *Lincoln*, I, 125–126, 130–131; Williams, *Generals*, 42–44; Nevins, *War*, II, 2.

CHAPTER II

1. Nevins, *War*, I, 401, 413, 416; Nevins, *War*, II, 2, 4–8.

2. Nevins, *War*, II, 9–10.

3. Ibid, 31.

4. Ibid, 8, 9, 31–33.

5. Ibid, 114.

6. Ibid, 91–92, 114–118, 148.

7. Ibid, 92–94.

8. Ibid, 116–117, 513–514; Catton, *Grant South*, 364.

9. Nevins, *War*, II, 117.

10. Ibid, 145–146.

11. Ibid, 117–118, 137, 145–147.

12. Ibid, 147–149.

13. Hattaway and Jones, 56–57, 86, 89, 143–144; Beringer, Hattaway, Jones, and

Still, 105, 140–141. See also: Hattaway and Jones, 39–40; Beringer, Hattaway, Jones, and Still, 109–110; Weigley, *American War*, 95; Williams,
"Leadership," 54; Nevins, *War*, II, 4; Ballard, 239.

14. Nevins, *War*, II, 10.

15. Hattaway and Jones, 51–52, 56–57, 64, 89, 95, 126, 143–144, 292; Beringer,
Hattaway, Jones, and Still, 105, 121, 134, 139–140, 143, 178, 180–181, 184–
186; Weigley, *American War*, 134, 136; Hassler, *Potomac*, 31–33; Williams,
Generals, 24, 30–31, 33–35, 45, 47–49, 54–55, 64–65, 125, 187; Hassler,
McClellan, 5, 26, 40; Ambrose, 12, 18, 46, 58; Williams, *McClellan*, 26,
31–32, 104; Williams, "Leadership," 44, 46, 54; Catton, *Grant South*,
110–112, 285–286; Catton, *Grant Command*, 47; Fuller, *Grant*, 74–77;
Fuller, *Grant and Lee*, 41, 140–141; Liddell Hart, 75, 97–99, 102, 144;
Nevins, *War*, II, 4–5, 10–11, 17, 94, 96, 113, 144, 153, 288; Ballard, 114,
177–178; Nevins, *War*, I, 153.

16. Williams, *McClellan*, 27–28.

17. Weigley, *American War*, 134.

18. Williams, *Generals*, 51; Williams, *McClellan*, 23, 26–32; Williams,
"Leadership," 44–45; Nevins, *War*, I, 305; Beringer, Hattaway, Jones,
and Still, 178; Nevins, *War*, II, 401.

19. K. P. Williams, *Lincoln*, I, 123–138, 147–148; Nevins, *War*, I, 300, 385;
Williams, *McClellan*, 26; Hassler, *McClellan*, 40, 44, 48, 52–54; Williams,
Generals, 42, 52; Hattaway and Jones, 57, 144; Hensel, 4.

20. Beringer, Hattaway, Jones, and Still, 138, 186.

21. K. P. Williams, *Lincoln*, I, 481; Nevins, *War*, II, 90–91, 94; Hattaway and
Jones, 82, 110–112; Beringer, Hattaway, Jones, and Still, 135–138.

22. K. P. Williams, *Lincoln*, I, 136; Williams, *Generals*, 187; Catton, *American
Tradition*, 94; Fuller, *Grant*, 123; Nevins, *War*, II, 94–103; Weigley,
American War, 101; Hattaway and Jones, 124, 127, 142–143; Beringer,
Hattaway, Jones, and Still, 134–139, 192, 194.

23. Fuller, *Grant*, 32, Fuller, *Grant and Lee*, 33; Weigley, *American War*, 100;
Hattaway and Jones, 127; Beringer, Hattaway, Jones, and Still, 54–63, 134,
139, 185–186, 198–202.

24. Nevins, *War*, II, 15.

25. Nevins, *War*, II, 14–15; Esposito, 25; Hattaway and Jones, 58–59; Beringer,
Hattaway, Jones, and Still, 105, 117–119.

26. Nevins, *War*, II, 19–22; Catton, *Grant South*, 57; Ambrose, 15, 18; Esposito,
25; Hattaway and Jones, 58–60; Beringer, Hattaway, Jones, and Still, 121.

27. Ambrose, 6.

28. Williams, *Generals*, 47–49, 136–138; Ambrose, 9–10, 13, 18; Nevins, *War*,
II, 10–13, 151–152; Weigley, *American War*, 95, 148; Weigley, "American
Strategy," 416–417; Catton, *Grant South*, 215, 406; Hattaway and Jones 54–
56, 61–64, 136–137; Beringer, Hattaway, Jones, and Still, 117, 120–121.

29. Fuller, *Grant*, 75; Williams, *Generals*, 47–49, 54–55, 136–138; Ambrose, 12–
18; Catton, *Grant South*, 110–120; Fuller, *Grant and Lee*, 140–141; Ballard,
176–178; Esposito, 30; Hattaway and Jones, 55–56, 61; Beringer, Hattaway,
Jones, and Still, 121.

30. Fuller, *Grant*, 79; Lewis, 210; Nevins, *War*, II, 12, 17; Weigley, *American War*, 119; Weigley, "American Strategy," 429; Ambrose, 18–20, 23, 159; Catton, *Grant South*, 406; Hattaway and Jones, 64–65, 69, 71; Beringer, Hattaway, Jones, and Still, 121–122.

31. Williams, *Generals*, 48–49.

32. Ibid, 54.

33. Ibid, 58.

34. Fuller, *Grant*, 76–77; Williams, *Generals*, 48–49, 53–54, 58; Ambrose, 20–21, 23; Catton, *Grant South*, 111–120; Fuller, *Grant and Lee*, 141; Liddell Hart, 113; Nevins, *War*, II, 4, 11–13, 16–17; Ballard, 177–178; Esposito, 30; Hattaway and Jones, 61–62.

35. Fuller, *Grant*, 78–81, 193; Lewis, 210–211; Nevins, *War*, II, 1–2, 12, 17–18, 22, 23; Ballard, 178–179; Liddell Hart, 114; Fuller, *Grant and Lee*, 141–144; Catton, *American Tradition*, 72–75; Catton, *Grant South*, 121–123, 129–151; Weigley, "American Strategy," 429; Williams, *Generals*, 59–60; Ambrose, 12–34; Esposito, 25, 30; Hattaway and Jones, 62–71; Beringer, Hattaway, Jones, and Still, 122–123.

36. General Grant's total casualties were approximately 10.5% of his 28,000 man force. Due to the capitulation of most of the Confederate garrison at Fort Donelson the Confederates lost 79% of their 21,000 troops. Beringer, Hattaway, Jones, and Still, 124; Hattaway and Jones, 69–75; Williams, *Generals*, 60; Ambrose, 33–35; Catton, *Grant South*, 151–178; Fuller, *Grant*, 81–91, 193; Fuller, *Grant and Lee*, 144; Liddell Hart, 114–115; Lewis, 211, Nevins, *War*, II, 23–25; Ballard, 179.

37. Nevins, *War*, II, 26.

38. Hattaway and Jones, 88–89, 146–149, 156–158, 163, 233; Esposito, 30–31; Beringer, Hattaway, Jones, and Still, 123–125, 128–129; Weigley, "Leadership," 429; Ambrose, 34–38, 41–42; Catton, *American Tradition*, 79–80; Catton, *Grant South*, 179–202, 213–214, 282, 322; Fuller, *Grant*, 94–96; Fuller, *Grant and Lee*, 144, 147; Liddell Hart, 115–116; Nevins, *War*, II, 25–30, 65–74, 77.

39. Catton, *Grant South*, 194.

40. Fuller, *Grant*, 94–96; Liddell Hart, 116; Nevins, *War*, II, 29–30, 77; Catton, *Grant South*, 187–202, 215; Ambrose, 41–42; Weigley, "Leadership," 429; Esposito, 30–31; Hattaway and Jones, 88–89, 146–149, 156–158; Beringer, Hattaway, Jones and Still, 128–129, 154.

41. Williams, *Generals*, 70–71; Ambrose, 39; Catton, *American Tradition*, 80–81; Catton, *Grant South*, 286; Fuller, *Grant and Lee*, 145; Liddell Hart, 117; Nevins, *War*, II, 30; Ballard, 179, K. P. Williams, *Lincoln*, I, 157–159; Hattaway and Jones, 77, 148–149; Beringer, Hattaway, Jones and Still, 129–132, 188.

42. The Confederates sustained a 26.5% casualty rate of their 40,000 troops, whereas the Federals, surprised, but having the advantage of the tactical defensive the first day of the battle, sustained a casualty rate of 20.7% of their 62,700 man force. Beringer, Hattaway, Jones, and Still, 129–132, 188; Hattaway and Jones, 147–149, 163–170, 201; Esposito, 32–38; Williams,

Generals, 85, Ambrose, 41–46; Catton, *American Tradition*, 82–83; Catton, *Grant South*, 210–264; Fuller, *Grant*, 90, 94–113; Fuller, *Grant and Lee*, 145–149; Liddell Hart, 120–132; Lewis, 212–234; Nevins, *War*, II, 27, 74–87, 109–111; Ballard, 179–181.

43. Ambrose, 46–54; Catton, *Grant South*, 265–278, 304; Fuller, *Grant*, 114–115; Liddell Hart, 132–136, 141–144; Lewis, 241–242; Nevins, *War*, II, 15, 111–112, 152; Ballard, 181; Esposito, 74; Hattaway and Jones, 76, 135, 142–143, 150, 170–171, 180–181, 187, 201, 205, 421; Beringer, Hattaway, Jones, and Still, 129–134, 183, 188–189, 192, 198, 248–249, 251.

44. Williams, *Generals*, 151; Ambrose, 55–59, 63, 159; Catton, *American Tradition*, 91; Williams, "Leadership," 44; Catton, *Grant South*, 215, 265–266, 278–283; Fuller, *Grant*, 114–115; Fuller, *Grant and Lee*, 174; Liddell Hart 143–144; Nevins, *War*, II, 112, 152–154; Ballard, 181; Lewis, 241–242; Weigley, *American War*, 120, 136; Esposito, 74; Hattaway and Jones, 205–208, 214–215; Beringer, Hattaway, Jones, and Still, 133–134.

45. Williams, *Generals*, 187; Fuller, *Grant*, 123–124; Liddell Hart, 158; Nevins, *War*, II, 103–104, 112, 154; Esposito, 100; Beringer, Hattaway, Jones, and Still, 187–189.

46. Hassler, *McClellan*, 43–44, 48, 52–54, 56; Nevins, *War*, II, 34, 41–42; Ballard, 67–69; K. P. Williams, *Lincoln*, I, 130, 137–141; Williams, *Generals*, 49–51, 63–65; Williams, "Leadership," 45; Weigley, "American Strategy," 420; Hattaway and Jones, 92–96, 144–146; Hensel, 5–7; Beringer, Hattaway, Jones, and Still, 142.

47. Williams, *Generals*, 51, 63–65; Hassler, *McClellan*, 42, 44, 54, 56; Williams, *McClellan*, 32–33; Fuller, *Grant and Lee*, 150–151; Liddell Hart, 137–138; Nevins, *War*, II, 41–42; K. P. Williams, *Lincoln*, I, 141; Weigley, *American War*, 134–135; Weigley, "American Strategy", 420; Hattaway and Jones, 82–83, 87–89, 93–95, 145, 199, 233; Hensel, 6–7; Beringer, Hattaway, Jones, and Still, 142.

48. Williams, *Generals*, 63–65; Hassler, *McClellan*, 56, Nevins, *War*, II, 41–42, 401; Ballard, 114; K. P. Williams, *Lincoln*, I, 141; Hattaway and Jones, 82–83, 87–89, 93–95, 145, 199, 201, 233; Hensel, 6–7; Beringer, Hattaway, Jones, and Still, 142–143.

49. Williams, *Generals*, 65–66, 80–82; Hassler, *McClellan*, 71, 80–81, 91–92, 173; Williams, *McClellan*, 34–35; Fuller, *Grant and Lee*, 151; Nevins, *War*, II, 41–42, 45, 59; Ballard, 73, 75–76, 236; K. P. Williams, *Lincoln*, I, 139; Esposito, 39; Hattaway and Jones, 87–88, 94–95, 145–146, 174; Hensel, 7–8; Beringer, Hattaway, Jones, and Still, 145.

50. Williams, *Generals*, 66–75; Hassler, *McClellan*, 63, 71; Fuller, *Grant and Lee*, 151; Nevins, *War*, II, 42–43, 45–58, 50–56; Ballard, 70–73; K. P. Williams, *Lincoln*, I, 141–142, 152–157, 159–161; Nevins, *War*, I, 405–406; Esposito, 39–41; Hensel, 8–14; Hattaway and Jones, 98, 144–145, 155, 172–176; Beringer, Hattaway, Jones, and Still, 143–145, 147.

51. Beringer, Hattaway, Jones, and Still, 143–144. See also Hattaway and Jones, 145.

52. Williams, *Generals*, 75–84, 87–91; Hassler, *McClellan*, 75, 80, 91, 92; Fuller,

Grant and Lee, 152; Liddell Hart, 138; Nevins, *War*, II, 48–49, 56–63, 88; Ballard, 73–76, 91–96, 103, 108–109, 111–112; K. P. Williams, *Lincoln*, I, 155–156, 159–169, Esposito, 39–41; Weigley, "American Strategy," 420; Hattaway and Jones, 98, 144–145, 155, 172–176; Hensel, 8–14; Beringer, Hattaway, Jones, and Still, 143–145, 147.

53. Hassler, *McClellan*, 87.

54. Hassler, *Potomac*, 46; Williams, *Generals*, 92–96; Hassler, *McClellan*, 75, 105, 109–111, 119; Fuller, *Grant and Lee*, 152–155; Liddell Hart, 138; Nevins, *War*, II, 91, 105–108, 118–122; Ballard, 96; K. P. Williams, *Lincoln*, I, 169–171; Esposito, 41–43; Hattaway and Jones, 174, 180; Hensel, 14–16; Beringer, Hattaway, Jones, and Still, 148, 152.

55. Hassler, *McClellan*, 120.

56. The Battle of Seven Pines ended with the Confederates, on the tactical offensive suffering a 15% casualty rate (approximately 6,000), as opposed to the Federals, on the tactical defensive, sustaining a 12% casualty rate (approximately 5,000) of the number of troops engaged. Williams, *Generals*, 96–106; Hassler, *McClellan*, 105–106, 113–114, 117, 119–121, 141–142; Fuller, *Grant and Lee*, 153–156; Nevins, *War*, II, 118, 121–129; Ballard, 77–89, 96–97, 112–113; K. P. Williams, *Lincoln*, I, 171–213; Esposito, 42–43, 48–53; Hattaway and Jones, 162, 176–181, 187–189, 191–192, 335; Hensel, 16–18; Beringer, Hattaway, Jones, and Still, 148–150; Weigley, "American Strategy," 423; Hassler, *Potomac*, 46.

57. Nevins, *War*, II, 154–155.

58. Hassler, *Potomac*, 58–61; Williams, *Generals*, 107–109, 112–113, 116, 119–122, 133, 158; Hassler, *McClellan*, 134–135, 141, 149, 184; Fuller, *Grant and Lee*, 163; Nevins, *War*, II, 130–131, 133–134, 143, 150–151, 154–156; Ballard, 98, 116; Nevins, *War*, III, 29; K. P. Williams, *Lincoln*, I, 253–254; Weigley, *American War*, 137–138; Esposito, 42–43; Hensel, 18–19; Beringer, Hattaway, Jones, and Still, 163.

59. Williams, *Generals*, 122.

60. Combining the casualty rate for the Battle of Seven Pines with that of the Seven Days Battles, the Confederates, on the tactical offensive, lost approximately 30% (26,000 men), whereas the Federals, on the tactical defensive, lost about 20% (20,000 men) of the forces engaged in these battles. Beringer, Hattaway, Jones, and Still, 150–155; Hassler, *McClellan*, 137–138, 142, 149–151.

61. Liddell Hart, 139.

62. Williams, *Generals*, 114–119, 125–126, 144; Catton, *American Tradition*, 91–92; Fuller, *Grant and Lee*, 156–162, Liddell Hart, 139; Nevins, *War*, II, 131, 134–137; Ballard, 97–102; K. P. Williams, *Lincoln*, I, 217–241; Esposito, 43–47; Weigley, "American Strategy," 423; Hensel, 19–23; Hattaway and Jones, 192–201; Beringer, Hattaway, Jones, and Still, 150–154.

63. Nevins, *War*, II, 138.

CHAPTER III:

1. Williams, *Generals*, 136–140.

2. Nevins, *War*, II, 138.
3. Beringer, Hattaway, Jones, and Still, 169–170. See also: Catton, *Grant South*, 304–305; Fuller, *Grant*, 159; Liddell Hart, 153; Nevins, *War*, II, 275–277; Ballard, 181–182.
4. Hassler, *McClellan*, 189.
5. Williams, *Generals*, 134–140, 142–146, 150–151; Hassler, *McClellan*, 179, 189, 192; Ambrose, 59–69; Catton, *Grant South*, 286–287, 289; Liddell Hart, 139, 144–152; Nevins, *War*, II, 150–162, 275–277; Ballard, 114–116; K. P. Williams, *Lincoln*, I, 251–258; Esposito, 55; Hattaway and Jones, 205–217, 220, 237, 248–249, 283, 174; Hensel, 23; Beringer, Hattaway, Jones, and Still, 163, 169–170.
6. Hassler, *McClellan*, 193.
7. Williams, *Generals*, 145–146.
8. Catton, *Grant South*, 289.
9. Hassler, *Potomac*, 61; Williams, *Generals*, 147–151; Hassler, *McClellan*, 201; Ambrose, 70–71; Fuller, *Grant and Lee*, 163; Liddell Hart, 139; Nevins, *War*, II, 170; K. P. Williams, *Lincoln*, I, 258–265; Esposito, 55–56; Hattaway and Jones, 220, 222–223; Beringer, Hattaway, Jones, and Still, 163–164.
10. K. P. Williams, *Lincoln*, I, 261.
11. Hassler, *Potomac*, 64; Ambrose, 71–73; Fuller, *Grant and Lee*, 163; Nevins, *War*, II, 170–174; Ballard, 117–118; K. P. Williams, *Lincoln*, I, 265–291, 301–302, 309; Esposito, 56–57; Hattaway and Jones, 222–224; Beringer, Hattaway, Jones, and Still, 164.
12. The Confederates suffered both proportionately and absolutely fewer casualties during the campaign than did the Federals: about 9,000 casualties of the 48,000 Confederate troops compared to 16,000 to the 72,000 Federals. Beringer, Hattaway, Jones, and Still, 164–165; Esposito, 57–64; Hattaway and Jones, 224–231, 237–238; Weigley, *American War*, 108–109; Hassler, *Potomac*, 65; Williams, *Generals*, 152–159; Ambrose, 74–76; Fuller, *Grant and Lee*, 164–166; Nevins, *War*, II, 174–184; Ballard, 118–121; K. P. Williams, *Lincoln*, I, 291–358.
13. Williams, *Generals*, 159; Hassler, McClellan, 224–225, 229–230, 243, 262; Ambrose, 76–85; Nevins, *War*, II, 184–188; Ballard, 121–123; K. P. Williams, *Lincoln*, I, 359–361; Kenneth P. Williams, *Lincoln Finds a General*, II (New York: Macmillan, 1950), cited hereafter as *Lincoln*, II, 462; Esposito, 65; Hattaway and Jones, 230, 233, 241–242; Beringer, Hattaway, Jones, and Still, 167.
14. Graebner, 14.
15. Nevins, *War*, II, 248, 250–251, 263–265, 273; Graebner, 64–68.
16. Nevins, *War*, II, 267–268; Graebner, 67, 69–70; Hassler, *McClellan*, 230–232.
17. Nevins, *War*, II, 299.
18. Ibid, 272.
19. Hassler, *Potomac*, 79–80, 90; Hassler, *McClellan*, 230–232; Fuller, *Grant and Lee*, 166–167; Nevins, *War*, II, 168, 299, 300, 322, 370–372, 377; Lewis, 254–255; Catton, *Grant South*, 324; Weigley, *American War*, 110, 112; Weig-

ley, "American Strategy," 425; Hattaway and Jones, 233–234; Beringer, Hattaway, Jones, and Still, 156–158, 167–169, 173–174.

20. Fuller, *Grant and Lee*, 166; Nevins, *War*, II, 216–217; Hattaway and Jones, 232–234; Beringer, Hattaway, Jones, and Still, 158, 166.

21. Beringer, Hattaway, Jones, and Still, 166–167.

22. Even though the Confederates were on the tactical defensive, they suffered more casualties than the Federal forces: 13,700 versus 12,500. Beringer, Hattaway, Jones, and Still, 165, 167–168; Hattaway and Jones, 233, 241–244; Esposito, 65–69; Hassler, *Potomac*, 83–84; Williams, *Generals*, 165–170; Hassler, *McClellan*, 233, 235, 239–241, 255–256; Ambrose, 82–85; Fuller, *Grant and Lee*, 167–169; Nevins, *War*, II, 215–230; Ballard, 123–127; K. P. Williams, *Lincoln*, I, 361–383; K. P. Williams, *Lincoln*, II, 445–463.

23. Williams, *Generals*, 172–182; Hassler, *Potomac*, 92–93; Hassler, *McClellan*, 298, 301–302, 305, 308–309, 312–313; Ambrose, 85–87, 92; Fuller, *Grant and Lee*, 169–170; Nevins, *War*, II, 229–230, 323–334; Ballard, 127–137, 146–148; K. P. Williams, *Lincoln*, II, 463–482; Esposito, 70; Hattaway and Jones, 262, 264–267; Beringer, Hattaway, Jones, and Still, 237–238.

24. General Buell had ceased earlier efforts to repair and maintain the Memphis and Charleston Railroad and use that line to draw supplies from Memphis in favor to the two rail lines which extended south from Nashville, Tennessee to Decatur, Alabama and Chattanooga. In late July and early August, however, communications south of Nashville along the Nashville and Chattanooga, as well as north of the Tennessee capital along the Louisville and Nashville had been disrupted by Confederate cavalry raids. Esposito, 75; Beringer, Hattaway, Jones, and Still, 169.

25. Ambrose, 59, 88–89; Catton, *American Tradition*, 92; Catton, *Grant South*, 300, 306; Fuller, *Grant*, 159–160; Fuller, *Grant and Lee*, 176–177; Liddell Hart, 153; Nevins, *War*, II, 169–170, 275–283; Ballard, 182; Esposito, 75, Beringer, Hattaway, Jones, and Still, 169, 173–174; Hattaway and Jones, 217–219, 225, 231–232, 245–247.

26. Ambrose, 88–90; Catton, *Grant South*, 308; Fuller, *Grant*, 160; Fuller, *Grant and Lee*, 177; Liddell Hart, 153–154; Nevins, *War*, II, 284; Ballard, 182; Esposito, 75–76; Hattaway and Jones, 233, 249–250, 252–254; Beringer, Hattaway, Jones, and Still, 175–176.

27. Williams, *Generals*, 184.

28. Williams, *Generals*, 182–187; Ambrose, 90–92; Catton, *Grant South*, 318–319; Fuller, *Grant*, 160; Fuller, *Grant and Lee*, 177; Liddell Hart, 154; Nevins, *War*, II, 283–289; Nevins, *War*, III, 185–187; Ballard, 182–184; Esposito, 76, Hattaway and Jones, 254–255, 257–263, 289, 316–317; Beringer, Hattaway, Jones, and Still, 176.

29. At the Battle of Corinth, the Confederates, operating on the tactical offensive, sustained 4,838 casualties compared to 3,090 for the defending Federals. Beringer, Hattaway, Jones, and Still, 176; Hattaway and Jones, 245, 247, 251–252, 255–256, 262; Esposito, 101; Catton, *American Tradition*, 93, Catton, *Grant South*, 307–318; Fuller, *Grant*, 116–117; Fuller, *Grant and Lee*, 174–175; Liddell Hart, 154; Nevins, *War*, II, 280, 372–374; Ballard, 184.

30. Hassler, *Potomac*, 84, 90; Hassler, *McClellan*, 294; Catton, *Grant South*, 318; Nevins, *War*, II, 167, 169, 217–218, 289–290, 300–301, 318–322, 369; Ballard, 142; Graebner, 70–71; Hattaway and Jones, 233–234; Weigley, *American War*, 108; Beringer, Hattaway, Jones, and Still, 169, 179, 180–181.

31. Hattaway and Jones, 291, 326, 485–486, 686, 696; Beringer, Hattaway, Jones, and Still, 54–63, 105, 134, 154, 183–186, 191, 198, 201, 248, 251–252.

32. Weigley, *American War*, 92, 135; Hattaway and Jones, 291, 326, 485–486, 686, 696; Beringer, Hattaway, Jones, and Still, 132, 139–140.

33. Catton, *Civil War*, 186.

34. Catton, *Grant South*, 283.

35. Ibid, 294.

36. Lewis, 171, 187, 238–239; Liddell Hart, 90, 147; Catton, *Grant South*, 282–283, 291, 294, 317–318, 322.

37. Current, Williams, and Freidel, 392–393, Weigley, *American War*, 137–138; Catton, *Grant South*, 291–297, 356–357, 363.

CHAPTER IV

1. Nevins, *War*, II, 165.

2. Williams, *Generals*, 170; Hassler, *McClellan*, 294, 298; Lewis, 244–245; Nevins, *War*, II, 149–166, 231–237, 365; Nevins, *War*, III, 452; Ballard, 138; Current, Williams, and Freidel, 392–393; Hattaway and Jones, 34, 244, 270; Weigley, *American War*, 111.

3. Nevins, *War*, II, 232–233.

4. Ibid, 233–234.

5. Ibid, 234.

6. Williams, *Generals*, 170; Hassler, *McClellan*, 294, 298; Lewis, 244–245; Nevins, *War*, II, 166, 231–237, 365, Nevins, *War*, III, 452; Ballard, 138; Current, Williams, and Freidel, 392–393; Hattaway and Jones, 34, 244, 270; Weigley, *American War*, 111.

7. Nevins, *War*, II, 235.

8. Williams, *Generals*, 170; Ambrose, 91; Fuller, *Grant*, 33–34; Nevins, *War*, II, 231, 233–234; Hattaway and Jones, 244; Beringer, Hattaway, Jones, and Still, 169, 179–180, 184.

9. Beringer, Hattaway, Jones, and Still, 179–180.

10. Nevins, *War*, II, 269.

11. Nevins, *War*, II, 234–237, 240, 248, 250, 269–272; Nevins, *War*, III, 5, 473–513; Graebner, 65, 71–78; Ballard, 138–141, 145; Fuller, *Grant*, 35; Fuller, *Grant and Lee*, 185; Liddell Hart, 140; Current, Williams, and Freidel, 401.

12. Nevins, *War*, II, 239.

13. Ibid, 338.

14. Ibid, 235–241, 337–339, 399; Current, Williams, and Freidel, 400–401; Ballard, 139–141, 145.

15. Hattaway and Jones, 686. See also: Hattaway and Jones, 270–271, 358; Lewis, 296; Nevins, *War*, II, 512–528; Ballard, 138–139.

16. Williams, *Generals*, 215–216; Ambrose, 119; Lewis, 296, 303–304; Fuller,

Grant, 34–35; Ballard, 138–139; Catton, *Grant Command*, 16; Nevins, *War*, II, 339, 512–528; Hattaway and Jones, 270–271, 292, 357–358, 372, 485, 491, 686, 696; Beringer, Hattaway, Jones, and Still, 184.

17. Williams, *McClellan*, 101–103; Catton, *Grant South*, 15–16, 91–92, 296–297, 360; Catton, *American Tradition*, 105–106, 108; Fuller, *Grant*, 183; Catton, *Grant Command*, 8; Nevins, *War*, II, 518–519; Lewis, 303. For more on General Sherman's views concerning blacks, see: Lewis, 93, 111, 119–120, 129–130, 134, 191, 244–246, 286, 302–304, 334, 353, 369, 371, 391–394, 411, 418, 438–440, 478, 480–482, 511; Williams, *McClellan*, 63.

18. Lewis, 295.

19. Fuller, *Grant and Lee*, 260; Ambrose, 119, 159; Lewis, 295–296; Hattaway and Jones, 291, 326, 485–486, 490, 683, 686, 696, 350, 371–372, 687, 689, 695. Beringer, Hattaway, Jones, and Still, 247.

20. Williams, *Generals*, 225–226; Ambrose, 60, 108–109, 111–112, 117–118, 120–121, 160–161; Fuller, *Grant*, 45, 125; Lewis, 254–255, 269; Nevins, *War*, II, 376–377; Nevins, *War*, III, 54–55; Hattaway and Jones, 291–294, 334, 350, 371–372, 479, 485, 687, 689, 695, 375; Beringer, Hattaway, Jones, and Still, 105, 237, 244, 252.

21. Williams, *Generals*, 234; Ambrose, 144, 159, 208; Hattaway and Jones, 234–237, 248–249, 265–266, 329–337, 371–372, 685, 687, 689, 695; Beringer, Hattaway, Jones, and Still, 252.

22. Hattaway and Jones, 335–336, 348–349, 371–372.

23. Liddell Hart, 157.

24. Ambrose, 108–109, 112; Catton, *Grant South*, 325; Nevins, *War*, II, 403; Williams, *Generals*, 187–189, 193, 215; Fuller, *Grant*, 131; Hattaway and Jones, 294, 310; Beringer, Hattaway, Jones, and Still, 236–237.

25. Williams, *Generals*, 190–193; Ambrose, 109–111; Catton, *Grant South*, 324–327; Catton, *American Tradition*, 95; Nevins, *War*, II, 379; Nevins, *War*, III, 55–56.

26. Catton, *Grant South*, 323.

27. Williams, *Generals*, 193; Catton, *Grant South*, 322–323, 327.

28. Williams, *Generals*, 218; Ambrose, 112–113; Nevins, *War*, II, 378, 380; Catton, *American Tradition*, 95; Catton, *Grant South*, 228–232.

29. Catton, *Grant South*, 331–332.

30. At the Battle of Chickasaw Bluffs, the Union, on the tactical offensive, lost 1,776 men of their 25,000 man force, compared to the entrenched, defending Confederates who lost 207 men of their 13,800 man force. Beringer, Hattaway, Jones, and Still, 243.

31. Liddell Hart, 169.

32. Williams, *Generals*, 217–224; Ambrose, 112–117; Catton, *American Tradition*, 94–96; Catton, *Grant South*, 322–323, 327–346, 372–373, 430; Fuller, *Grant*, 122, 129–132, 193–194; Fuller, *Grant and Lee*, 175, 177–179; Liddell Hart, 157–166, 169; Lewis, 256–260; Nevins, *War*, II, 378–387, 401–402; Ballard, 189–190; Esposito, 102; Hattaway and Jones, 292, 300, 309–314, 370, 684; Beringer, Hattaway, Jones, and Still, 243.

33. Ambrose, 94.

34. Hassler, *Potomac*, 103.

35. At the Battle of Fredericksburg, the Union forces, on the tactical offensive, against the entrenched Confederates, lost approximately 12,500 men, compared to the defending Confederates who lost only 5,300. Esposito, 71–73; Beringer, Hattaway, Jones, and Still, 238–240; Hattaway and Jones, 303–308, 310–311, 328–329, 347–348, 350–351; Hassler, *Potomac*, 102–103; Williams, *Generals*, 194–201; Ambrose, 94–99; Fuller, *Grant and Lee*, 170–174; Liddell Hart, 140; Nevins, *War*, II, 343–350, 363–364; Ballard, 146–152; K. P. Williams, *Lincoln*, II, 482–539.

36. Williams, *Generals*, 201–206, 210–214; Ambrose, 99–102, 131; Nevins, *War*, II, 365–367; Ballard, 152–154; K. P. Williams, *Lincoln*, II, 539–552; Beringer, Hattaway, Jones, and Still, 238–240; Hattaway and Jones, 303–308, 310–311, 328–329, 347–348, 350–351.

37. Williams, *Generals*, 207.

38. At the Battle of Stones River, each side lost approximately 12,000 men: 33% of the Confederate forces and 31% of the Union forces. Esposito, 77–83; Beringer, Hattaway, Jones, and Still, 240–241; Hattaway and Jones, 305, 308–310, 314–315, 318–323, 325, 338; Williams, *Generals*, 206–208; Ambrose, 105–107; Fuller, *Grant*, 160; Fuller, *Grant and Lee*, 177; Liddell Hart, 154; Nevins, *War*, II, 374–376; Ballard, 184.

39. Beringer, Hattaway, Jones, and Still, 244.

40. Williams, *Generals*, 206–207; Ambrose, 91, 107; Lewis, 254–255; Nevins, *War*, II, 372, 377, 388–394; Nevins, *War*, III, 54–55; Beringer, Hattaway, Jones, and Still, 242–243, 245; Hattaway and Jones, 310, 324–325, 336, 415.

41. Nevins, *War*, II, 340.

42. Nevins, *War*, III, 45.

43. Williams, *Generals*, 234; Ambrose, 117–118, 120, 121, 123, 125, 127–128, 159–160; Lewis, 269; Nevins, *War*, III, 6–7; Hattaway and Jones, 343, 348, 360–361, 364–370, 375, 385, 394–396; Beringer, Hattaway, Jones, and Still, 251–252.

44. Fuller, *Grant*, 131.

45. Williams, *Generals*, 224–239; Ambrose, 117–121; Catton, *American Tradition*, 97–101; Catton, *Grant South*, 373–387, 407–429, 432–433; Fuller, *Grant*, 131–139; Fuller, *Grant and Lee*, 180–181; Liddell Hart, 166–186; Lewis, 268–273; Nevins, *War*, II, 402–405, 411–418; Ballard, 190–191, 193; Esposito, 103–104; Beringer, Hattaway, Jones, and Still, 254–255; Hattaway and Jones, 341–346, 370, 376–378, 391, 394, 401, 410, 415.

46. Catton, *Grant South*, 429–432, 436; Fuller, *Grant*, 139–140; Liddell Hart, 188; Lewis, 273–274; Esposito, 104; Beringer, Hattaway, Jones, and Still, 254–255; Hattaway and Jones, 341, 370, 377, 391, 394, 401, 410, 415.

47. Fuller, *Grant*, 143.

48. Williams, *Generals*, 229–232, 271, 274; Ambrose, 120–122, 127–128, 140; Catton, *American Tradition*, 101–105, 108, 110; Catton, *Grant South*, 433–489; Catton, *Grant Command*, 10; Fuller, *Grant*, 140–157, 194–196; Fuller, *Grant and Lee*, 182–184; Liddell Hart, 186–199; Lewis, 274–295; Nevins, *War*, II, 405, 418–425, 428; Nevins, *War*, III, 51–74; Ballard, 191; Esposito,

104–107; Beringer, Hattaway, Jones, and Still, 254–257; Hattaway and Jones, 341, 370, 377, 391–397, 401, 409–412, 415, 432–434.

49. Beringer, Hattaway, Jones, and Still, 263.

50. Catton, *American Tradition*, 107–109; Liddell Hart, 199; Nevins, *War*, III, 74–76; Lewis, 292, 301, 304; Hattaway and Jones, 415, 421–422, 435, 685; Beringer, Hattaway, Jones, and Still, 263, 265.

51. Liddell Hart, 210, Nevins, *War*, II, 408–411; Ballard, 194; Esposito, 108; Beringer, Hattaway, Jones, and Still, 241–242; Hattaway and Jones, 323–324, 256–360, 378.

52. Williams, *Generals*, 247, 250; Ambrose, 123–125; Fuller, *Grant and Lee*, 201–202; Nevins, *War*, II, 410–411; Nevins, *War*, III, 158, 189–192; Ballard, 194; Beringer, Hattaway, Jones, and Still, 252–253; Hattaway and Jones, 365, 378, 387–391, 441.

53. Williams, *Generals*, 275–276; Catton, *American Tradition*, 110–111; Fuller, *Grant*, 161; Fuller, *Grant and Lee*, 202; Liddell Hart, 210; Nevins, *War*, III, 158–159, 192; Ballard, 195; Beringer, Hattaway, Jones, and Still, 258–259; Hattaway and Jones, 402–404, 415.

54. The Confederates lost 12,700 men or 21% of their army, compared to Federal losses of 16,800 men or 15% of the Army of the Potomac at the Battle of Chancellorsville. Esposito, 84–91; Beringer, Hattaway, Jones, and Still, 253–254; Hattaway and Jones, 352, 378–384; Weigley, *American War*, 113–114; Hassler, *Potomac*, 134–137; Williams, *Generals*, 232–242; Ambrose, 132; Fuller, *Grant and Lee*, 184–192; Nevins, *War*, II, 432–452; Ballard, 154–159; K. P. Williams, *Lincoln*, II, 553–554, 560–605.

55. Beringer, Hattaway, Jones, and Still, 260.

56. Williams, *Generals*, 245–246; Fuller, *Grant and Lee*, 193–195; Nevins, *War*, III, 83–86; Ballard, 160–161; K. P. Williams, *Lincoln*, II, 612–617; Weigley, *American War*, 114–115; Esposito, 92–93; Beringer, Hattaway, Jones, and Still, 259; Hattaway and Jones, 397–398.

57. Hassler, *Potomac*, 151; Williams, *Generals*, 251–259; Ambrose, 133–135; Fuller, *Grant and Lee*, 195–197; Nevins, *War*, III, 8–91; Ballard, 161–163; K. P. Williams, *Lincoln*, II, 618–650, 661; Weigley, *American War*, 115–116; Esposito, 92; Hattaway and Jones, 398–401, 419; Beringer, Hattaway, Jones, and Still, 260–261.

58. K. P. Williams, *Lincoln*, II, 655.

59. Ibid, 660–661.

60. Ambrose, 139.

61. The Confederates lost approximately 28,000 men or 33% of their total force at the Battle of Gettysburg, compared to the Union which lost 23,000 men or 20% of its forces, Beringer, Hattaway, Jones, and Still, 261–262; Esposito, 93–99; Hattaway and Jones, 404–409; Hassler, *Potomac*, 165–167, 258–259; Williams, *Generals*, 243–247, 259–263; Ambrose, 135–139; Fuller, *Grant and Lee*, 196–201; Nevins, *War*, III, 88–112; Ballard, 163–167; K. P. Williams, *Lincoln*, II, 624, 650–729.

62. K. P. Williams, *Lincoln*, II, 753.

63. Hassler, *Potomac*, 186–189, 258–259; Williams, *Generals*, 264–271; Am-

brose, 140–144; Fuller, *Grant and Lee*, 200–201; Nevins, *War*, III, 112–116; Ballard, 167–171; K. P. Williams, *Lincoln*, II, 730–756; Esposito, 99, 117; Beringer, Hattaway, Jones, and Still, 262; Hattaway and Jones, 412–413, 415, 424–426.

64. Williams, *Generals*, 264–271; Ballard, 168–171; K. P. Williams, *Lincoln*, II, 678, 730–756; Beringer, Hattaway, Jones, and Still, 262; Hattaway and Jones, 415, 424–426.

65. Hattaway and Jones, 413–415, 424–426; Beringer, Hattaway, Jones, and Still, 262–267, 299.

CHAPTER V

1. Nevins, *War*, III, 455.
2. Ibid, 463.
3. Ibid.
4. Ibid, 76–77, 452, 454–458, 462–465; Allen Nevins, *The War for the Union, IV: The Organized War to Victory*, 1864–1865 (New York: Charles Scribner's Sons, 1971), cited hereafter as *War*, IV, 87; Lewis, 305.
5. Nevins, *War*, III, 459.
6. Ibid, 461.
7. Ibid, 154, 456–462, 466–468.
8. Ibid, 469–470.
9. Ibid, 470.
10. Ibid, 469–470, 472.
11. Ibid, 470–471; Lewis, 483; Beringer, Hattaway, Jones, and Still, 307–309, 355; Hattaway and Jones, 372, 429, 430, 485–486, 490, 686, 696.
12. Nevins, *War*, IV, 83–84.
13. Ibid, 83–86; Nevins, *War*, III, 460–461.
14. Nevins, *War*, IV, 86–87.
15. Ibid, 213.
16. Nevins, *War*, IV, 208, 212–213; Lewis, 514. See also: Current, Williams, and Freidel, 392–393; Hattaway and Jones, 34, 244, 270; Weigley, *American War*, 111; Williams, *Generals*, 170; Hassler, *McClellan*, 294, 298; Lewis, 244–245; Nevins, *War*, II, 231–237; Ballard, 138.
17. Williams, *Generals*, 285–287, 296–297; Ambrose, 144; Hattaway and Jones, 348–349, 436–437, 465–470, 694–695.
18. Williams, *Generals*, 287.
19. Williams, *Generals*, 274–275, 294; Ambrose, 145–147; Catton, *American Tradition*, 110, 117; Catton, *Grant Command*, 11–15, 100–101, 172–173; Fuller, *Grant*, 158–159; Fuller, *Grant and Lee*, 184; Nevins, *War*, IV, 2–3, 33, 144; Hattaway and Jones, 292–294, 429–432, 436, 476, 485, 519–520, 689–690; Beringer, Hattaway, Jones, and Still, 257–258.
20. Ambrose, 147, 168–170; Catton, *Grant Command*, 16, 112, 141–142; Nevins, *War*, IV, 4–6, 32–33; Lewis, 305, 312; Hattaway and Jones, 292–294, 389–390, 429–432, 436, 476, 485, 519–520, 689–690.
21. Williams, *Generals*, 276–278; Ambrose, 150–151; Fuller, *Grant and Lee*, 202; Liddell Hart, 210; Nevins, *War*, III, 159; Esposito, 109; Beringer, Hattaway, Jones, and Still, 300–301; Hattaway and Jones, 441–442, 446–448.

22. Williams, *Generals*, 278–279; Ambrose, 152; Catton, *American Tradition*, 111, Catton, *Grant Command*, 47–48; Fuller, *Grant and Lee*, 202; Liddell Hart, 210; Lewis, 305; Nevins, *War*, III, 159, 193; Ballard, 194–195; Esposito, 109–110; Beringer, Hattaway, Jones, and Still, 301–303; Hattaway and Jones, 442, 446–450.

23. At the Battle of Chickamauga, the attacking Confederates lost approximately 18,500 men, compared to about 16,000 men for the Army of the Cumberland. Esposito, 110–115; Beringer, Hattaway, Jones, and Still, 301–303; Hattaway and Jones, 442, 446–454, 456–457; Williams, *Generals*, 279–280; Ambrose, 152; Catton, *American Tradition*, 111; Fuller, *Grant*, 161; Fuller, *Grant and Lee*, 202; Liddell Hart, 210–211; Nevins, *War*, III, 193–201; Ballard, 195–196.

24. Williams, Generals, 280–289; Ambrose, 147–149, 152–154; Fuller, *Grant and Lee*, 202–203; Liddell Hart, 211; Lewis, 305–312; Nevins, *War*, III, 201–202. K. P. Williams, *Lincoln*, II, 761–767; Hattaway and Jones, 446, 469–471; Beringer, Hattaway, Jones, and Still, 303; Esposito, 115, 118.

25. Ambrose, 155–156.

26. Williams, *Generals*, 284–285, 289–290; Ambrose, 154–156; Catton, *American Tradition*, 113–116; Catton, *Grant Command*, 48–93; Fuller, *Grant*, 161–177; Fuller, *Grant and Lee*, 203–205; Liddell Hart, 211–222; Lewis, 312–328; Nevins, *War*, III, 203–211; Ballard, 197–200; Esposito, 116; Hattaway and Jones, 456–462, 473–474, 479–480; Beringer, Hattaway, Jones, and Still, 303–304.

27. Lewis, 327.

28. Nevins, *War*, III, 211.

29. Fuller, *Grant*, 211–212; K. P. Williams, *Lincoln*, II, 763.

30. Liddell Hart, 223.

31. Ibid, 159.

32. Lewis, 332–334, 336; Liddell Hart, 159, 223–224.

33. Williams, *Generals*, 285–289; Ambrose, 156–164; K. P. Williams, *Lincoln*, II, 767–774; Esposito, 118–119; Hattaway and Jones, 471–473; 476–479; Beringer, Hattaway, Jones, and Still, 304.

34. Beringer, Hattaway, Jones, and Still, 178.

35. Weigley, *American War*, 132; Beringer, Hattaway, Jones, and Still, 236, 241, 265–267, 305–307, 309–310.

36. Fuller, *Grant*, 46; Nevins, *War*, II, 69; Catton, *Grant South*, 304; Weigley, *American War*, 130–131; Beringer, Hattaway, Jones, and Still, 170–171, 183, 245–251; Hattaway and Jones, 158, 217, 250–251, 326–327, 336, 356–359, 391–392, 487–488, 490–492, 684–685.

CHAPTER VI

1. Williams, *Generals*, 297–303; Ambrose, 160–164; Catton, *American Tradition*, 116–117; Catton, *Grant South*, 321–323; Catton, *Grant Command*, 104–137; Lewis, 343–345; Nevins, *War*, IV, 6–8, 15–18; Ballard, 202, 204; Beringer, Hattaway, Jones, and Still, 309; Hattaway and Jones, 250–251, 430–

435, 474–476, 488, 491–496, 506, 509, 512–517, 548, 591, 686–688, 697–698.

2. Beringer, Hattaway, Jones, and Still, 309–314; Hattaway and Jones, 250–251, 430–435, 474–476, 488, 491–496, 506, 509, 512–517, 548, 591, 686–688, 697–698; Weigley, *American War*, 139, 142, 145–148, 151; Weigley, "American Strategy," 431–432; Catton, *American Tradition*, 117; Williams, *McClellan*, 105.

3. Catton, *Grant Command*, 93.

4. Williams, *Generals*, 274–275, 291–295; Catton, *American Tradition*, 109–110, Catton, *Grant Command*, 12–13, 93–97; Fuller, *Grant*, 158–159, 177–179, 220–221; Fuller, *Grant and Lee*, 184, 206, 208, 257; Liddell Hart, 227; Nevins, *War*, IV, 144; Beringer, Hattaway, Jones, and Still, 310–311, 315; Hattaway and Jones, 430–432, 474–476, 493–496.

5. Ibid.

6. Hassler, *Potomac*, 206; Catton, *Grant Command*, 101; Nevins, *War*, IV, 8, 33; Williams, *Generals*, 295–297; Beringer, Hattaway, Jones, and Still, 310–311, 313–314; Hattaway and Jones, 474–475, 512–514, 591, 687.

7. Williams, *Generals*, 295.

8. Williams, *Generals*, 295–297; Catton, *Grant Command*, 172–174; Beringer, Hattaway, Jones, and Still, 314–315; Hattaway and Jones, 474–475, 512–514, 516–517, 591, 687, 690.

9. Catton, *Grant Command*, 152.

10. Fuller, *Grant*, 48, 209–210, 219–243, 308–309, 321, 323; Catton, *Grant Command*, 142, 152, 167–169, 172–174; Nevins, *War*, III, 9–10; Hassler, *Potomac*, 205–206; Williams, *Generals*, 307, 337; Ambrose, 165–166; Liddell Hart, 232–234; Nevins, *War*, IV, 9, 12, 25; Ballard, 204–205; Fuller, *Grant and Lee*, 207, 208, 257; Beringer, Hattaway, Jones, and Still, 315–317; Hattaway and Jones, 517–519, 522, 524–532, 536, 591, 691; Weigley, "American Strategy," 432, 434, 435.

11. Beringer, Hattaway, Jones, and Still, 217.

12. Fuller, *Grant*, 48, 210, 213–226, 262–263; Fuller, *Grant and Lee*, 207–210; Nevins, *War*, IV, 9, 12–14, 20; Ballard, 204; Liddell Hart, 232; Lewis, 345; Hassler, *Potomac*, 206; Williams, *Generals*, 306–307, 309, 317; Catton, *Grant Command*, 138, 142–143, 148–154, 169–170, 172, 206, 248; Weigley, "American Strategy," 432–433; Williams, *Generals*, 306–307; Ambrose, 165; Catton, *American Tradition*, 124–125; Williams, *McClellan*, 107–108; Beringer, Hattaway, Jones, and Still, 315–317; Hattaway and Jones, 517–519, 522, 524–532, 536, 539, 545, 580, 591, 691.

13. Beringer, Hattaway, Jones, and Still, 321.

14. Nevins, *War*, IV, 59.

15. Nevins, *War*, III, 159–160.

16. Fuller, *Grant*, 309, 362; Nevins, *War*, III, 155–158, 172, 177–178, 453; Nevins, *War*, IV, 59.

17. Nevins, *War*, IV, 54.

18. Fuller, *Grant*, 309, 362; Nevins, *War*, IV, 58, 61–65; Catton, *Grant Command*, 160; Beringer, Hattaway, Jones, and Still, 316.

19. Fuller, *Grant*, 288–261; Hassler, *Potomac*, 212–216; Williams, *Generals*, 301–304; Ambrose, 165–167, 170; Catton, *American Tradition*, 121–122; Catton, *Grant Command*, 179–243, 246–247; Fuller, *Grant and Lee*, 213–219; Nevins, *War*, IV, 18–24, 34–36, 46–48; Ballard, 205–206; Hattaway and Jones, 545, 558, 580, 591–592; Beringer, Hattaway, Jones, and Still, 317–318.

20. Fuller, *Grant and Lee*, 218–219.

21. Fuller, *Grant*, 262–263.

22. Fuller, *Grant*, 204, 258–284; Hassler, *Potomac*, 217–218; Williams, *McClellan*, 108–109; Catton, *Grant Command*, 244–272; Fuller, *Grant and Lee*, 218–222, 229; Nevins, *War*, IV, 34, 36–44, 51; Ballard, 206–207; Hattaway and Jones, 558–559, 567, 569–572, 575–576, 579–581, 583, 587–588, 590, 592–593; Beringer, Hattaway, Jones, and Still, 318–320.

23. Fuller, *Grant and Lee*, 220.

24. Fuller, *Grant*, 258–284; Hassler, *Potomac*, 217–218; Williams, *McClellan*, 108–109; Catton, *Grant Command*, 244–272; Fuller, *Grant and Lee*, 218–222, 229; Nevins, *War*, IV, 34, 36–44, 51; Ballard, 206–207; Hattaway and Jones, 558–559, 567, 569–572, 575–576, 579–581, 583, 587–588, 590, 592–593; Beringer, Hattaway, Jones, and Still, 318–320.

25. Beringer, Hattaway, Jones, and Still, 319.

26. Hattaway and Jones, 570–571.

27. Hassler, *Potomac*, 217–219; Williams, *Generals*, 318; Williams, *McClellan*, 104; Catton, *Grant Command*, 237, 294–295; Fuller, *Grant and Lee*, 221–222; Nevins, *War*, IV, 45; Ballard, 208; Catton, *American Tradition*, 122–126; Weigley, *American War*, 132; Beringer, Hattaway, Jones, and Still, 319; Hattaway and Jones, 569–571, 588, 590, 592–593.

28. Fuller, *Grant*, 286, 290; Hassler, *Potomac*, 218, 221; Williams, *Generals*, 318–319; Catton, *Grant Command*, 248, 250–251, 274–280; Nevins, *War*, IV, 44; Hattaway and Jones, 575–576, 587–589, 592–593, 693–694; Beringer, Hattaway, Jones, and Still, 319–320.

29. Catton, *Grant Command*, 294.

30. Fuller, *Grant*, 287–299; Fuller, *Grant and Lee*, 223–230; Nevins, *War*, IV, 44–46, 48–51; Ballard, 208; Williams, *Generals*, 319–320; Catton, *Grant Command*, 280–294, 297–299; Hattaway and Jones, 576, 585–587, 589–590; Beringer, Hattaway, Jones, and Still, 319–320.

31. Hattaway and Jones, 590.

32. Fuller, *Grant*, 285–286; Fuller, *Grant and Lee*, 222; Nevins, *War*, IV, 46; Ambrose, 179; Catton, *Grant Command*, 276, 315–316; Hattaway and Jones, 568–569, 593, 603.

33. Hattaway and Jones, 569.

34. Williams, *Generals*, 325.

35. Fuller, *Grant*, 299–300.

36. Fuller, *Grant*, 299–307; Fuller, *Grant and Lee*, 229–230; Ballard, 210–212, 237–238; Hassler, *Potomac*, 224, 238; Williams, *Generals*, 324–327, 334–335; Ambrose, 173–177, 179; Catton, *Grant Command*, 295–297, 306–325; Weigley, *American War*, 126; Hattaway and Jones, 600–602, 613–614; Beringer, Hattaway, Jones, and Still, 320–321.

37. Hattaway and Jones, 681, 687, 693–694.
38. Fuller, *Grant*, 309; Fuller, *Grant and Lee*, 230–232; Liddell Hart, 234–290; Lewis, 357–408; Nevins, *War*, IV, 18, 24–28, 52–57, 148–154; Ballard, 215–217; Williams, *Generals*, 337; Ambrose, 178; Williams, *McClellan*, 67–70; Catton, *Grant Command*, 304; Hattaway and Jones, 552, 585, 594, 599, 604, 610; Beringer, Hattaway, Jones, and Still, 321–324.
39. Nevins, *War*, IV, 72–73.
40. Fuller, *Grant*, 309, 333–335; Liddell Hart, 275, 298; Lewis, 366, 394–395, 407; Nevins, *War*, IV, 58–96; Ballard, 219–220; Williams, *Generals*, 337–338; Catton, *American Tradition*, 120–121, 125–126; Catton, *Grant Command*, 295, 353–356; Weigley, *American War*, 129; Hattaway and Jones, 622–625, 688, 693–694; Current, Williams, and Freidel, 393–394.
41. Nevins, *War*, IV, 200–201.

CHAPTER VII

1. Nevins, *War*, IV, 96–98, 108; Hattaway and Jones, 620–622; Beringer, Hattaway, Jones, and Still, 187, 198.
2. Liddell Hart, 233–234.
3. Hattaway and Jones, 623.
4. Hassler, *Potomac*, 230; Ambrose, 179–180; Catton, *Grant Command*, 358–359; Fuller, *Grant*, 314–315; Fuller, *Grant and Lee*, 232; Liddell Hart, 233–234, 290–307; Lewis, 408, 414; Nevins, *War*, IV, 123, 153–154; Ballard, 217–218; Williams, *Generals*, 337; Williams, *McClellan*, 68–70; Hattaway and Jones, 622–625, 688, 693–694; Beringer, Hattaway, Jones, and Still, 324, 326.
5. Beringer, Hattaway, Jones, and Still, 327.
6. Williams, *Generals*, 327–328.
7. Nevins, *War*, IV, 105–106.
8. Hattaway and Jones, 615–619, 634; Beringer, Hattaway, Jones, and Still, 320–321, 348–349; Current, Williams, and Freidel, 394; Weigley, *American War*, 148; Weigley, "American Strategy," 433–434; Hassler, *Potomac*, 207, 230–231; Williams, *Generals*, 327–333, 336–338, 340–341; Ambrose, 177, 178; Catton, *American Tradition*, 126; Catton, *Grant Command*, 342–384; Fuller, *Grant*, 301–302, 315–320, 333–334; Fuller, *Grant and Lee*, 230, 234; Liddell Hart, 305; Lewis, 414; Nevins, *War*, IV, 97–143, 196; Ballard, 212–215, 221.
9. Ambrose, 182–184; Williams, *McClellan*, 71–77; Williams, "Leadership," 52–53; Catton, *Grant Command*, 385–391; Fuller, *Grant*, 320–327, 434–436; Fuller, *Grant and Lee*, 208, 232–233; Liddell Hart, 293, 308–330; Lewis, 424–432; Nevins, *War*, IV, 123–125, 154–158, 164–171; Ballard, 218; Weigley, *American War*, 149, 151; Weigley, "American Strategy," 434–435; Hattaway and Jones, 250–251, 488, 548, 624–625, 629–634, 637–639, 641–642, 686–688, 693–694; Beringer, Hattaway, Jones, and Still, 246–249, 325–326, 349–350.
10. Indeed, General Sherman had an extreme distrust for self-government and, as T. Harry Williams noted, "on several occasions he openly proclaimed a

315

preference for monarchy over democracy, suggesting that the 'self interest of one man' could be a 'safer criterion than the wild opinions of ignorant men.' " Similarly, particularly at the outset of the war, Sherman "doubted that a mass democracy had the fortitude to sustain a prolonged war or that a government of politicians could effectively prosecute a major military effort." Williams, *McClellan*, 52, 64.

11. Lewis, 306.
12. See note #17, Chapter IV.
13. Lewis, 308.
14. Liddell Hart, 73–74, 202–205, 232, 334, 425–427; Lewis, 306–308, 331, 397; Catton, *Grant Command*, 19–20; Ambrose, 157; Williams, *McClellan*, 52, 63–64, 73–74, 77.
15. Liddell Hart, 429.
16. Lewis, 431.
17. Williams, "Leadership," 52–53; Williams, *McClellan*, 73–74, 77; Catton, *Grant Command*, 64; Liddell Hart, 183, 232, 310, 320, 323–324, 328, 426, 429; Lewis, 269, 308, 330, 415–416, 421, 431, 442, 468, 488; Nevins, *War*, IV, 166. For Sherman's earlier views, see: Liddell Hart, 77, 80, 146–147, 150–151, 207; Lewis, 244–248, 295–298.
18. Weigley, *American War*, 148.
19. Williams, *Generals*, 338–340; Williams, "Leadership," 50; Liddell Hart, 356; Lewis, 295–296, 419, 472; Nevins, *War*, IV, 259; Ambrose, 72, 88, 92, 119, 124, 181–183, 187; Catton, *Grant South*, 401–402; Weigley, *American War*, 148–149; Hattaway and Jones, 638.
20. Catton, *Grant South*, 401–406, 462; Catton, *Grant Command*, 19–20; Lewis, 296.
21. Hassler, *Potomac*, 230; Williams, *Generals*, 338–340, 345; Ambrose, 182, 185; Williams, *McClellan*, 71; Catton, *Grant Command*, 385–391; Fuller, *Grant*, 322–327; Fuller, *Grant and Lee*, 232; Liddell Hart, 318, 321–330; Lewis, 425–426, 428, 430–432, 470–471; Nevins, *War*, IV, 125, 154, 158, 167–169; Ballard, 218; Weigley, "American Strategy," 435; Hattaway and Jones, 639–641; Beringer, Hattaway, Jones, and Still, 330.
22. Liddell Hart, 330.
23. Hattaway and Jones, 642. See also: Liddell Hart, 333; Lewis, 433–434, 442–452.
24. Hattaway and Jones, 655–656.
25. Lewis, 429, 467–470, 474, 482–483; Liddell Hart, 320, 341–346, 351–355, 359; Williams, *Generals*, 345–346; Fuller, *Grant*, 326–330; Fuller, *Grant and Lee*, 233; Nevins, *War*, IV, 160–162, 255; Hattaway and Jones, 647–649, 654–656; Beringer, Hattaway, Jones, and Still, 328–329, 331.
26. At the Battle of Franklin, the Confederates lost 6,252 men, compared to the Federal army which lost 2,326. Hattaway and Jones, 639–640, 643–647; Beringer, Hattaway, Jones, and Still, 329–330; Williams, *Generals*, 341; Ambrose, 189–192; Catton, *Grant Command*, 395; Fuller, *Grant*, 327–330; Fuller, *Grant and Lee*, 233; Liddell Hart, 347–348; Nevins, *War*, IV, 169–178; Ballard, 219.

27. Hattaway and Jones, 650.
28. Hassler, *Potomac*, 232–233; Williams, *Generals*, 341–345; Ambrose, 192–195; Catton, *Grant Command*, 395–401; Fuller, *Grant*, 330–332; Fuller, *Grant and Lee*, 233; Liddell Hart, 349–351; Lewis, 470, Nevins, *War*, IV, 178–188; Ballard, 219; Hattaway and Jones, 649–654, 656, 675, 687; Beringer, Hattaway, Jones, and Still, 330–331, 336.
29. Beringer, Hattaway, Jones, and Still, 62–63.
30. Fuller, *Grant*, 24, 33; Nevins, *War*, III, 29; Beringer, Hattaway, Jones, and Still, 54–63, 183–184, 192, 199–201, 267.
31. Beringer, Hattaway, Jones, and Still, 333–334.
32. Fuller, *Grant*, 334–335; Ambrose, 196; Nevins, *War*, III, 24–26; Lewis, 498; Nevins, *War*, II, 429; Weigley, *American War*, 132; Beringer, Hattaway, Jones, and Still, 333–334; Hattaway and Jones, 150, 432–433.
33. Beringer, Hattaway, Jones, and Still, 433–435.
34. Liddell Hart, 380–381. See also: Lewis, 435; Liddell Hart, 346.
35. Fuller, *Grant*, 326, 334–335; Fuller, *Grant and Lee*, 233; Liddell Hart, 346, 380–381; Lewis, 468, 474–475; Beringer, Hattaway, Jones, and Still, 327, 338, 351, 434, 435, 438–439.

CHAPTER VIII

1. Lincoln, *Generals*, 345–347; Ambrose, 196–197; Fuller, *Grant*, 337–338; Liddell Hart, 356–360; Lewis, 467, 471–472; Hattaway and Jones, 656–657, 660.
2. Liddell Hart, 352, 358, 360; Lewis, 472–473; Hattaway and Jones, 657.
3. Hattaway and Jones, 669.
4. Lewis, 485; Liddell Hart, 329, 358–359, 386–387; Williams, *McClellan*, 72–77; Hattaway and Jones, 657–658, 669.
5. Williams, *Generals*, 347–348; Ambrose, 197–198; Catton, *Grant Command*, 392, 401–407; Fuller, *Grant*, 32–33, 337–339, 341; Fuller, *Grant and Lee*, 236–238; Liddell Hart, 360–379; Lewis, 471, 473, 477–478, 483–515; Nevins, *War*, IV, 188–193, 256–264; Ballard, 223; Hattaway and Jones, 658–668; Beringer, Hattaway, Jones, and Still, 192–197, 331. For material focusing on the Union efforts to take Charleston by sea, see: Nevins, *War*, II, 430–432; Nevins, *War*, IV, 31–32; K. P. Williams, *Lincoln*, II, 757–758.
6. Fuller, *Grant*, 341–344; Liddell Hart, 369, 380–381; Lewis, 474–475, 499–500, 510–515; Nevins, *War*, IV, 220–253, 265–272; Hattaway and Jones, 669–670, 701; Beringer, Hattaway, Jones, and Still, 338, 340, 433, 435.
7. Nevins, *War*, IV, 301; Hassler, *Potomac*, 236; Catton, *American Tradition*, 127; Catton, *Grant Command*, 407, 426, 428; Fuller, *Grant*, 321, 338–339; Fuller, *Grant and Lee*, 232, 238; Liddell Hart, 382; Hattaway and Jones, 656, 661–663; 668–669; Beringer, Hattaway, Jones, and Still, 198, 331–332.
8. Nevins, *War*, IV, 209–210.
9. Catton, *Grant Command*, 421.
10. Ibid, 419–422.
11. Ibid, 421–422.

12. Ibid, 423.
13. Ibid, 424.
14. Ibid, 422–424; Williams, *Generals*, 350; Nevins, *War*, IV, 217–218.
15. Nevins, *War*, IV, 217–218.
16. Lewis, 522.
17. Catton, *Grant Command*, 438.
18. Ibid, 438; Lewis, 522–523, 527, 552; Liddell Hart, 385; Nevins, *War*, IV, 289–291, 323; Catton, *American Tradition*, 139.
19. Nevins, *War*, IV, 323.
20. Liddell Hart, 384.
21. Hassler, *Potomac*, 236, 240; Williams, *Generals*, 352–353; Catton, *American Tradition*, 127–129; Catton, *Grant Command*, 427–466; Fuller, *Grant*, 338, 340, 344; Fuller, *Grant and Lee*, 238–241; Liddell Hart, 381–384, 387–388; Lewis, 525–526; Nevins, *War*, IV, 264–265, 281–288, 292–318; Ballard, 224–448; Hattaway and Jones, 671–674; Beringer, Hattaway, Jones, and Still, 332.
22. Nevins, *War*, IV, 303.
23. Ibid, 303–304.
24. Catton, *Grant Command*, 454.
25. Ibid, Nevins, *War*, IV, 296–304.
26. Hassler, *Potomac*, 240; Catton, *Grant Command*, 463; Nevins, *War*, IV, 306–308. See also Footnote 21, Chapter VIII.
27. Catton, *Grant Command*, 465.
28. Ibid, 465–466; Hassler, *Potomac*, 241; Nevins, *War*, IV, 311; Catton, *American Tradition*, 129, 143–145.
29. Nevins, *War*, IV, 304–305.
30. Ibid, 304–305, 322.
31. Ibid, 320–321.
32. Ibid, 319–321, 338.
33. Liddell Hart, 386–387.
34. Ibid, 386–390; Catton, *Grant Command*, 479; Nevins, *War*, IV, 348; Lewis, 537.
35. Liddell Hart, 385, 390; Ambrose, 198–199; Nevins, *War*, IV, 326, 348.
36. Liddell Hart, 391.
37. Ibid, 391–392; Lewis, 535–536; Nevins, *War*, IV, 348–350; Beringer, Hattaway, Jones, and Still, 341–342.
38. Lewis, 538.
39. As Lloyd Lewis wrote, earlier in the war, Sherman came "to regard himself as more educator than warrior," seeking to "teach Southerners that war was terrible and peace beautiful, that rebellion meant ruin, while obedience to law meant, in the end, prosperity." Consequently, Sherman's occupation policies represented an effort to reestablish security and confidence among the population in the areas occupied by Union forces. See Lewis, 244, 297, 415, 416, 424, 474, 482–483, 558. See also: Liddell Hart, 147, 150–151, 205–207, 368, 425.
40. Lewis, 415–416, 536–538; Nevins, *War*, IV, 349.

41. Nevins, *War*, IV, 350–351.

42. Lewis, 539.

43. Ibid, 540–541.

44. Ibid, 539–541; Nevins, *War*, IV, 289, 349–353; Liddell Hart, 392–395.

45. Nevins, *War*, IV, 353–354.

46. Ibid, 349, 354; Catton, *American Tradition*, 140; Liddell Hart, 393.

47. Liddell Hart, 394.

48. Ibid.

49. Ibid; Catton, *Grant Command*, 479–483.

50. Catton, *Grant Command*, 483.

51. Ibid, 484–485.

52. Ibid, 483–486; Liddell Hart, 395–398; Nevins, *War*, IV, 354–356; Ambrose 199–200.

53. Catton, *Grant Command*, 485.

54. Ibid, 486.

55. Ibid, 485–486; Liddell Hart, 396–398; Nevins, *War*, IV, 354–356; Ambrose, 200–202.

CHAPTER IX

1. See appendix. See also: Gordon A. Craig, "Delbruck: The Military Historian," in Peter Paret (ed.), *Makers of Modern Strategy: From Machiavelli to the Nuclear Age* (Princeton, NJ: Princeton University Press, 1986), 326–353; Weigley, *American War*, passem; Beringer, Hattaway, Jones, and Still, passem; Hattaway and Jones, passem.

2. Weigley, *American War*, 135, 139, 142; Weigley, "American Strategy," 429: Beringer, Hattaway, Jones, and Still, 173, 178, 337; Hattaway and Jones, passem.

3. Weigley, *American War*, 92.

4. Ibid, 92; Beringer, Hattaway, Jones, and Still, 178, 247–250, 337, 518.

5. Fuller, *Grant,* 194, 366–367; Liddell Hart, 430; Catton, *American Tradition*, 107; Williams, *McClellan*, 47, 71–77; Weigley, *American War*, 152; Weigley, "American Strategy," 435–436; Beringer, Hattaway, Jones, and Still, 247, 314, 338.

6. Fuller, *Grant and Lee*, 259; Liddell Hart, 82; Beringer, Hattaway, Jones, and Still, 59, 63, 200–201.

7. Beringer, Hattaway, Jones, and Still, 201.

8. Weigley, *American War*, 131–132; Beringer, Hattaway, Jones, and Still, 435.

9. Beringer, Hattaway, Jones, and Still, 436.

10. Fuller, *Grant*, 336; Beringer, Hattaway, Jones, and Still, 327, 340–347, 351, 436, 439.

APPENDIX

1. Joint Chiefs of Staff, *Department of Defense Dictionary of Military and Associated Terms* (Washington: U.S. Government, 1987), 244.

2. Ibid.

3. This is the definition used by the Joint Chiefs of Staff for the term "strategy," but, for purposes of this study, it will be applied to "grand strategy." Ibid, 350–351.

4. This is the definition used by the Joint Chiefs of Staff for the term "military strategy," but, for purposes of this study, it will be applied to "national military strategy." Ibid, 232.

5. Headquarters, Department of the Army, *FM 100–5: Operations* (Washington: U.S. Government, 1986), 9–10.

6. Ibid, 10.

7. Ibid, 10–11.

8. Carl von Clausewitz, *On War* (Princeton, NJ: Princeton University Press, 1976), 90.

9. Ibid.

10. Ibid, 91.

11. Ibid.

12. Ibid, 91–92.

13. Ibid, 92–93.

14. Ibid.

15. Ibid, 93.

16. Beringer, Hattaway, Jones, and Still, 145, 150–151, 178, 185, 236, 251.

17. Clausewitz, 95–99.

18. Ibid, 99.

19. Beringer, Hattaway, Jones, and Still, 49–50, 140–141, 143, 171, 177–178, 250, 312–313; Hattaway and Jones, 47.

20. Hattaway and Jones, 82–83.

21. Beringer, Hattaway, Jones, and Still, 47, 177; Hattaway and Jones, 82–83; David G. Chandler, *The Campaigns of Napoleon* (New York, NY: MacMillan, 1966), 162–170.

22. Beringer, Hattaway, Jones, and Still, 47; Chandler, 181–182.

23. Chandler, 181–182.

24. Beringer, Hattaway, Jones, and Still, 47–48, 50, 176–177, 249, 432.

25. Ibid, 47–48.

26. Ibid, 124, 177, 250, 312–313.

27. Ibid, 50, 170–172, 177, 183, 246, 249–250, 430–432; Hattaway and Jones, 22–23.

28. Beringer, Hattaway, Jones, and Still, 339–340.

29. Ibid, 340–341.

30. Ibid, 341.

31. Ibid, 347.

32. Ibid, 51–52, 177–178, 249–250, 312–313, 430.

THE AUTHOR

Since 1986, Dr. Howard M. Hensel has served as a Professor in the Department of National Security Affairs at the Air War College. He holds a B.A. from Texas A&M University and an M.A. and Ph.D. from the University of Virginia. He has served on the faculties of the University of Virginia and the Monterey Institute of International Studies. He has also served as Adjunct Professor of National Security Affairs at the Naval Postgraduate School and has taught at the Marine Command and Staff College. Immediately prior to his appointment to the faculty of the Air War College, Dr. Hensel served for three years as Visiting Professor of National Security Affairs at the Air Command and Staff College. In addition to numerous articles in professional journals, Dr. Hensel's publications include *The Anatomy of Failure: Major General George B. McClellan and the Peninsular Campaign.* He is married and has one daughter.

DATE DUE